Schools for All: Educating Children in a Diverse Society

Schools for All: Educating Children in a Diverse Society

Lyn Miller-Lachmann

Lorraine S. Taylor, Ph.D.
State University of New York at New Paltz

Delmar Publishers
An International Thomson Publishing Company

Albany • Bonn • Boston • Cincinnati • Detroit • London • Madrid • Melbourne
Mexico City • New York • Pacific Grove • Paris • San Francisco • Singapore
Tokyo • Toronto • Washington

NOTICE TO THE READER

Cover Illustration: Alexander Piejko

Delmar Staff
Publisher: David C. Gordon
Acquisition Editor: Erin J. O'Connor
Project Editor: Colleen A. Corrice
Production Coordinator: Sandra Woods
Art and Design Coordinator: Timothy J. Conners

COPYRIGHT © 1995
By Delmar Publishers
a division of International Thomson Publishing Inc.
The ITP logo is a trademark under license

Printed in the United States of America

For more information contact:

Delmar Publishers
3 Columbia Circle
Box 15015
Albany, New York 12203-5015

International Thomson Editores
Campos Eliseos 385, Piso 7
Col Polanco
11560 Mexico D F Mexico

International Thomson Publishing Europe
Berkshire House 168-173
High Holborn
London WC1V7AA
England

International Thomson Publishing GmbH
Königswinterer Strasse 418
53227 Bonn
Germany

Thomas Nelson Australia
102 Dodds Street
South Melbourne, 3205
Victoria, Australia

International Thomson Publishing Asia
221 Henderson Road
#05-10 Henderson Building
Singapore 0315

Nelson Canada
1120 Birchmount Road
Scarborough, Ontario
Canada M1K5G4

International Thomson Publishing - Japan
Hirakawacho Kyowa Building, 3F
2-2-1 Hirakawacho
Chiyoda-ku, Tokyo 102
Japan

1 2 3 4 5 6 7 8 9 10 XXX 01 00 99 98 97 96 95 94

Library of Congress Cataloging-in-Publication Data

Miller-Lachmann, Lyn, 1956–
    Schools for all : educating children in a diverse society / Lyn
Miller-Lachmann, Lorraine S. Taylor.
        p.   cm.
    Includes bibliographical references and index.
    ISBN 0-8273-5957-8
    1. Multicultural education—United States.   2. Group work in education—United States.   3. Language experience approach in education—United States.   4. Mainstreaming in education—United States.   I. Taylor, Lorraine S.   II. Title.
LC1099.3.M55   1995
370. 19'6—dc20   94-26265
                                                                                                                      CIP

Contents

Preface xi
Dedications xiv

CHAPTER 1   *Introduction*   **1**

What is Multicultural Education?   2
Purposes and Goals of Multicultural Education   6
Issues   7
Basic Assumptions   9
Multicultural Education in the Schools   9
     Banks and Banks: Four Approaches   10
     Gibson's Five Approaches   11
     Lynch's Approach   13
     Other Approaches   14
How Can Teachers Become Culturally Sensitive?   16
The Relationship Between Culture and Education   20
An Approach to Multicultural Education   23
     Mastery Learning   24
     Whole Language   24
     Cooperative Learning   24
Parents and Families   25
Summary   25
Chapter 1 Questions   27
References   27

CHAPTER 2   *The Changing Face of America's Children*   **30**

The First Cultural Contact   30
The Indians   31
Slavery and Black Immigration   34
Nineteenth Century Immigrants   36
     English and Scots-Irish   36
     Germany   37
     Irish Catholics   38
     Immigration by Annexation   38
     Chinese   39
     Japanese   39
     The Late Nineteenth Century Immigration Boom   40
Immigration in the Twentieth Century   44
     Latin-American Immigration   44
     Asian Immigration   51

Other Immigrants   56
Internal Migration   59
The Future   61
Summary   62
Chapter 2 Questions   65
References   66

CHAPTER 3   *Children of Color in the Schools—Past and Present*   **69**

The Effects of Poverty on Educational Attainment   69
    Lowered Expectations: The "Deficit" Model and
       the "Culture of Poverty"   72
    Other Risk Factors   76
A History of Educational Inequality   79
    Overt Discrimination   79
The Arrival of Integration   81
The Civil Rights Movement and the War on Poverty   82
    Compensatory Programs   83
    Busing   83
Community Control   84
Bilingual Education   84
Persistent Problems   87
    The End of Desegregation Efforts   87
    Segregation Within Schools   88
    School Policies and Governance   95
    Segregation and School Funding: "Savage Inequalities"   95
Current Needs of Children of Color   97
    African-Americans   97
    Latinos   103
    Asian-Americans and Pacific Islanders   106
    American Indians   108
    Children in Interracial Families   109
    Cultural Diversity Among Teachers and Administrators   110
Summary   114
Chapter 3 Questions   115
References   116

CHAPTER 4   *The Current State of Multicultural Education—*
Programs and Controversies   **119**

Multicultural Efforts in Public Schools   120
    Statewide Efforts   120
    New York and California   121

        Local Efforts   124
    Multicultural Programs Serving Special Populations   134
        African-American Immersion Schools   134
        Schools Serving Other Groups   141
    Multicultural Education in Teacher Preparation Programs   145
    Summary   148
    Chapter 4 Questions   149
    References   150

CHAPTER 5   *Exceptional Children from Diverse Cultures*   **152**

    The Legal Foundation for Special Education   155
    Pre-Referral Interventions   160
    Referral Process   160
        Evaluation and Recommendation   161
        Placement   161
        IEP Planning   161
        Implementation and Program Review   163
    High Incidence Disabilities   163
        Learning Disabilities   163
        Speech and Communication Disorders   165
        Mental Retardation   170
        Emotional/Behavior Disorders   171
    Other Disabilities   174
        Hearing Impaired and Deaf   174
        Multihandicapped   177
        Orthopedic and Other Health Impaired   177
        Visually Impaired and Blind   178
        Autism and Traumatic Brain Injury   179
        Working with Parents   181
    Summary   182
    Chapter 5 Questions   184
    References   184

CHAPTER 6   *Cooperative Learning for Diverse Classrooms*   **186**

    Why Cooperative Learning?   186
    What is Cooperative Learning?   188
        Principles of Cooperative Learning   188
        Components of Cooperative Learning   188
    How Effective Is Cooperative Learning?   192
    How Do You Begin?   197
        The Role of the Teacher   197

Approaches to Cooperative Learning   199
   Prepackaged Curriculum   199
   Three Approaches   200
   Learning Together   202
Cooperative Learning in the College Classroom   207
Potential Problems   208
Two Cooperative Classrooms   208
   Mr. Smith   208
   A Morning with Miss Jones' Class   211
Summary   212
Chapter 6 Questions   213
References   214

CHAPTER 7   *Cooperative Learning Activities*   **216**

Activities to Help Students Get Acquainted   217
Team-Building and Class-Building   217
Cooperative/Collaborative Skills   221
Activities for Academic Skills   235
   Mathematics   272
   Science   272
   History/Social Studies   272
   English/Language Arts   272
Summary   273
Chapter 7 Questions   373
References   274

CHAPTER 8   *Multicultural Materials and the Whole Language Approach*   **275**

What is Whole Language?   277
Critiques and Modifications of the Whole Language Approach   280
The Promise of Whole Language in Presenting Diverse Cultures   284
   Problems of Basal Readers and Textbooks   284
   Advantages of Trade Books and Nonprint Materials   286
   The Role of Writing in Teaching about Culture   288
A Promise Unfulfilled   289
Bridging the "Cultural Gap"   293
Summary   297
Chapter 8 Questions   298
References   299

CHAPTER 9 *Selecting Multicultural Materials for the Classroom* 301

General Principles 301
 The Need for a Variety of Books 305
Specific Criteria for Selection 306
 Accuracy and Authenticity 308
 The Avoidance of Stereotyping 309
 Appropriate Language 311
 The Author's Background 312
 The Book's Perspective 314
 The Concept of Audience 317
 Integration of Cultural Information 318
 Currency of Facts and Interpretations 319
 Balance and Multidimensionality 319
 Illustrations 321
Selecting Nonprint Materials 321
Some Parting Words 326
Summary 327
Chapter 9 Questions 328
References 328

CHAPTER 10 *Strategies for Using Multicultural Materials* 330

Problems with the Current Approach 331
 Problem One: The Time of Year 331
 Problem Two: Superficial Aspects 331
 Problem Three: Reliance upon Folktales 332
Multiculturalism Across the Curriculum 333
 Science 334
 Mathematics 336
 Art and Music 336
 A Specific Example 336
Using the Community to Teach About Cultures 338
The In-Depth Teaching of a Culture Through Literature 341
 Norton's Five Phases 341
Limitations of Funding and Standardized Curriculums 344
Finding More Information 346
Summary 347
Chapter 10 Questions 348
References 348

CHAPTER 11   *The School-Home-Community Partnership*   350

Family Structure   360
Behavioral and Developmental Expectations   362
Disciplinary Styles   363
Communication Patterns   364
Linguistic Differences   367
Socioeconomic Factors   367
Parent Training   368
Biracial Children   374
Community-School Relationship   374
Summary   375
Chapter 11 Questions   377
References   377

CHAPTER 12   *Conclusion*   380

Ending Alienation in the School Environment   381
Teaching Children About Each Other's Culture   381
Avoiding Stereotyping   382
Educational Equity   383
Keep Your Hopes High   383

Author/Title Index   385
Name/Subject Index

Preface

Schools for All: Educating Children in a Diverse Society is written for pre-service and in-service teachers who will be working primarily, but not exclusively, with children in kindergarten through eighth grade. Thus, the materials and methods examined in the text are those deemed most appropriate for children of elementary and middle school age, although many of them can be adapted to preschool classes or classes on the high school level. Materials discussed as part of a whole language approach include picture books, beginning chapter books, middle grade fiction and nonfiction for the upper elementary grades, and young adult books. Many cooperative learning programs are designed with the structure of the elementary school classroom in mind, although alternatives for the more specialized classes of the middle school (and to some extent, the high school) are also included. Exercises for the middle school grades will take into account recent scholarship and approaches for these years, which have have only begun to receive attention in the educational literature. Strategies for outreach to parents will acknowledge the changing relationship between parents and children from the end of early childhood through the first years of adolescence.

Despite efforts at school integration, many classrooms in inner cities and rural areas remain exclusively comprised of African-American children. Others are exclusively Asian-American, Latino, or American Indian. In some schools, children of color from several groups make up the entire student population. In a growing number of schools, white children and children of color learn together. Finally, there remain classrooms and schools where the entire student population is white, and where teachers and administrators question the need for a multicultural approach to education.

This book is geared to teachers in all schools, including schools that are homogeneously European-American. Much of the content will focus upon the history, culture, and needs of African-American, Asian-American, Latino, and American Indian students, but some issues, such as the importance of parental involvement, cross cultures. So too does the need for all children to become aware of their own culture and how it affects the way they view the world; now they can begin to learn about and respect themselves and others. Exercises in cooperative learning will build all children's capacity to work together, and multicultural print and nonprint materials will develop each child's ability to empathize and to see the world from the perspective of someone from a different culture. Given the rapid changes in America's demographic patterns, teachers in all-white schools cannot assume that their schools will remain that way. This book will help them to respond to a changing student body and to prepare their students for life in a more diverse society. Recent conflicts between African-American and Latino youngsters and between African-American residents and Asian-American shopkeepers have highlighted the importance of building a cross-cultural awareness among children of color. Teachers need to help those students see the similarities as well as the differences among the various groups that have experienced prejudice and discrimination.

As our own society has become more diverse, so has our world become more interdependent. Economic developments, environmental challenges, and increased migration have made it imperative that our young people broaden their awareness to include the other countries and regions of the world. Although this text is not intended to teach global studies, it does discuss those areas of the world from which many of our recent immigrants have come and which many families consider to be part of their cultural heritage. Thus, materials about the history and cultures of Latin America, the Caribbean, Africa, and East and Southeast Asia are also included. Curricular approaches to the study of these areas have two aims in mind: they are designed to reinforce students' pride in their own roots and to broaden other students' awareness of the world and of the backgrounds of their fellow Americans.

The text begins with a definition of multicultural education and other terms of importance. Chapter 1 will also place multicultural education in the context the recent movement toward whole language, cooperative learning, and the involvement of parents in the process of education. Chapters 2 and 3 will provide an overview of demographic changes in the United States in general and in the schools in particular; it will also address the history of African-Americans, Asian-Americans, Latinos, and American Indians, with a special focus upon issues surrounding education. Children of interracial families will also receive attention in this chapter. Chapter 4 will discuss current multicultural education efforts, among them more inclusive curriculums, instructional approaches that stress inter-cultural understanding and conflict resolution, cultural immersion schools that focus upon special populations, and a school that uses multimedia to teach both English language skills and adaptive skills to recent immigrants from all over the world. Areas of controversy and issues for further debate are also discussed in this chapter. Chapter 5 examines cultural issues in the context of exceptional education, addressing, for instance, the disproportionate representation of children of color in special education classes and the movement toward mainstreaming exceptional children.

The next five chapters examine materials and methods for multicultural education. Chapter 6 defines cooperative learning and explores its potential for overcoming racial and cultural barriers. Chapter 7 presents specific activities, organized by grade level, that have been used successfully in classrooms and can be used by pre-service and in-service teachers in the future. Chapter 8 discusses the whole language movement and how it is particularly suited to teaching a diverse student population about the various cultures that comprise American society. Chapter 9 presents criteria for selecting print and nonprint materials, and Chapter 10 suggests ways these can be used across the curriculum. Specific readings will be offered and analyzed in depth.

Chapter 11 examines the role of the family and the community in the educational process and discusses how teachers can become more sensitive to the needs of culturally diverse parents. Parents play a crucial role in their children's educational attainment. Through interviews and discussion, this chapter explores how teachers can create a welcoming atmosphere and minimize the suspicion many culturally diverse parents feel towards the school. Ways in which the school can work in tandem with community organizations are also discussed. The book includes personal stories, interviews, case studies, and classroom profiles to provide interest and illustrate themes.

The authors would like to thank the many people who assisted in the preparation of this book. We would like to thank our editor, Erin O'Connor, who asked the impossible and occasionally even got it and Barbara Picard for many hours of typing and revisions. A number of teachers and administrators gave us access to their schools, classrooms, and curriculum materials; for this we offer our appreciation to Kenneth Holt and Josephine Hill at the Malcolm X Academy Middle School in Milwaukee, and Josephine Mosley at Dr. MLK Elementary School in Milwaukee, Carolyn Leonard at the Portland (Oregon) Public Schools, Schylbea Hopkins at Mae Jameson Academy in Detroit, and Celia Holm and Kate Todd, at the New York Public Library. We would also like to thank our colleagues for their suggestions and our families for their understanding.

In memory of A. Eugene Havens, whose students and lessons spanned the globe.

L. M-L.

For my grandparents, George and Mae Louise Wesley.

L. T.

CHAPTER 1

Introduction

The realities faced by all members of this global society mandate that we learn how to live and work together. At stake are the progress and survival of all inhabitants of the earth. Through knowledge and appreciation of our different cultures and by valuing every group's contributions to the national and international societies, we can cooperatively find solutions to the major problems that confront us. In our nation we need to prepare all children to become confident, independent, participating, and contributing members. We cannot afford the cost of failure. The purpose and goals of multicultural education directly address these aims.

In our global society children must learn to live and work together.

❖ What is Multicultural Education?

Multicultural education emerged from several major events in American history. These events began with the massive immigration of people from Eastern and Southern Europe from 1880 to 1920, which doubled the United States population (Krug, 1976). In response to the large influx of immigrants, the Nativists and Americanization movements pressured for rapid assimilation of the newcomers into the mainstream (Suzuki, 1984).

Those who adhered to Americanization believed in an American race of Anglo-Saxon superiority and the use of the public schools to Americanize the immigrants (Krug, 1976). This philosophy was expressed by Cubberley (in Krug, 1976), a highly respected educator, in a passage from his book, *Changing Conceptions of Education,*

> The Southern and Eastern Europeans are a very different type from the North Europeans who preceded them. Illiterate, docile, lacking in self-reliance, and initiative . . .
>
> Our task is to break up their groups or settlements, to assimilate and to amalgamate these people as part of our American race, and to implant in their children, so far as can be done, the Anglo-Saxon conceptions of righteousness, law and order, and popular government, and to awaken in them reverence for our democratic institutions and for those things in our national life which we as a people hold to be of abiding worth . . . (p. 7)

Public schools at that time dealt harshly with the immigrants, teaching an Anglocentric curriculum, punishing the use of native languages, and denigrating the immigrants' cultural traditions. The *melting pot* philosophy was widely accepted. That expression was first used by De Crevecoeur in 1756 when he wrote that, in America, individuals of all nations were "melted into a new race of men" (Krug, 1976). The melting pot conceptualized the immigrants' cultures as fusing with the existing American culture (Krug, 1976).

Early opponents included such people as Kallen (1956), the main author of *Cultural Pluralism* (Krug, 1976). Kallen wrote the nativist antipathy and resistance to Americanization for two generations of immigrants led to a "reappraisal of their transoceanic heritages" (Kallen, 1956, p. 96) and inspired early "cultivation and preservation of their ethnocultural pasts" (p. 97). Pluralism was defined by Kallen (1956) as equality of and respect for all cultures. He believed that American culture was strengthened through diversity.

Kallen described the intermingling and mutual respect among diverse cultures as:

> . . . an orchestration of diverse utterances of diversities—regional, local, religious . . . each developing freely and characteristically in its own enclave, and somehow so intertwined with the others as to suggest, even to symbolize, the dynamic of the whole . . . Each is a cultural reservoir whence flows its own singularity of expression to unite in the concrete intercultural total which is the culture of America. (p. 98)

Jane Addams was another early opponent of the harsh treatment of immigrants. In her work at Hull House, a settlement house in Chicago, she preached respect for immigrants, protested their treatment in "sweatshops," and worked to get factory laws passed to protect them. Jane Addams also believed that immigrants should preserve their cultural traditions while adjusting to the American mainstream (Krug, 1976).

Bronislow Malinowski (in Kitano, 1981), a resident of Poland, also advocated cultural pluralism in his writings about colonialism in South Africa. He wrote that European schools should recognize and respect African values while preparing African students to live in a European world.

Despite the effort of those strong advocates for cultural pluralism, their number remained small. The *melting pot* philosophy continued to be widely accepted until the battle over school desegregation began after the landmark decision in *Brown v. Board of Education* (1954). Increased attention to the plight of black children in America's segregated public schools focused, in part, on the cultural differences of many minority children. The school failure experienced by many of these children was, in the opinion of many educators, parents, and critics, due at least in part to cultural differences. The failure of the schools to recognize, appreciate, and

SPECIAL BOX 1–1

In another passage, Kallen's (1956) description of the "orchestration of cultures" is almost lyrical: ". . . the pursuit of happiness is the creation of cultures and the sporting union of their diversities as peers and equals; it is the endeavor after culture as each communion and each community . . . envisions its own cultural individuality and struggles to preserve, enrich, and perfect it by means of a free commerce in thoughts and things with all mankind. Cultural pluralism signalizes the harmonies of this commerce at home and abroad. It designates that orchestration of the cultures of mankind which alone can be worked and fought for with least injustice, and with least suppression or frustration of any culture, local, occupational, national or international, by any other" (p. 100).

develop instructional programs in accordance with children's cultural characteristics was seen as an important barrier to their educational progress. Poor achievement and high drop-out rates were the results.

It is important to point out that many educators, sociologists, and psychologists across the country attributed the poor achievement of African-American children to cultural disadvantages or deficits. The theory was that these children were culturally disadvantaged or deprived due to the conditions of poverty in which they lived. The lack of early reading and language readiness activities in the home and lack of exposure to such middle-class cultural activities as visits to museums, zoos, and parks and travel to well-known national sites were considered cultural deficits and used to explain failure to achieve in schools that assumed middle-class experiences in their students. Culturally biased intelligence test scores were also interpreted as showing intellectual deficits. Emphasis was on giving children the experiences needed to make up the deficits—to remediate them. There was no recognition of the value of the children's own cultural experiences. This view (widely accepted in the 1960s and early 1970s) blamed the children for their school failure rather than the schools.

Extensive evidence began to accumulate through research and teachers' experiences with minority children in other settings; alternative schools, for example, proved that these children could achieve when the curriculum was relevant and instruction was based upon their approaches to learning. In addition, many minority children who suffered poor school achievement functioned at high levels of independence outside the school. The publication, in 1970, of *The Six Hour Retarded Child* by the President's Committee on Mental Retardation also supported the fact that cultural differences played a role in the performance of many children in school.

Public schools during the 1960s continued to use a Eurocentric curriculum; a white, Anglo-Saxon Protestant cultural orientation; and textbooks portrayed only negative stereotypes of African-Americans and other minorities. Black history, as well as that of other minorities, was omitted from the history books and the use of biased, standardized tests misplaced many minority children in special classes for children with retardation and other disabilities.

The Civil Rights movement that began in the 1960s and increased in momentum with the passage of the Civil Rights Act in 1964 had a major impact on the increasing acceptance of cultural pluralism. As African-Americans struggled for equal opportunities in employment, education, housing, and political power, they also became more culturally conscious and expressed it in slogans such as *Black is Beautiful* and *Black Power*. The movement also raised the consciousness of other minorities who were inspired to demand recognition and respect for their cultural differences, traditions, and rights as American citizens. Women, persons with disabilities, persons of different sexual orientation, and other groups that suffered discrimination began to organize. The women's movement and gay movement have continued to grow and to increase the public attention to the needs of these groups.

Many white ethnic groups, primarily from Southern and Eastern Europe, also began to pressure for courses in ethnic studies. This was partly due to white backlash against the increased national attention to the needs of African-Americans. Black studies, special compensatory programs, financial aid, Head Start, and other anti-poverty programs were initially designed to redress the severe discrimination faced by the African-American population. The *Black is Beautiful* and *Black Power* slogans also encouraged the expression of similar attitudes among various white groups.

In response to the pressure by white ethnic groups, many school districts and universities developed courses and programs in ethnic studies which became very popular during the 1970s. In fact, some writers have described the '70s as the "decade of the ethnics," (Novak, 1972). As cultural pluralism became more widely accepted, federal support for the development of these new programs came through the Bilingual Education Act of 1968 and the Ethnic Heritage Studies Law of 1972. By 1973, at least thirteen states had laws that mandated ethnic studies in the curriculum and twenty-five others had policy statements on ethnic studies (Gibson, 1976). According to Gibson, multicultural education programs rapidly expanded at that time. In addition, such legal victories as *Lau v. Nichols* (1974), resulted in the provision of special language programs for children who speak little or no English.

During the 1960s and 1970s, multicultural education emphasized raising achievement levels of minority students and improving human relations in the schools in order to ensure successful integration. Advocates

SPECIAL BOX 1–2 *An African-American Teacher in the '60s, '70s*

During the 1960s and early '70s I was a public school teacher in one of our largest cities. Schools were severely segregated and despite the momentous *Brown* decision, all of our students and teachers were black. However, the administrators were white. Housing segregation reinforced the segregated schools since children went to their neighborhood school and teachers preferred to work as close as possible to their homes. Furthermore, vacancies were most plentiful in the most troubled schools and those were usually in the poor, black communities. It was possible to request a transfer to schools outside our segregated communities; however, the procedure protected the status quo since the black teacher had to be observed and approved by the white principal of the requested school. School integration existed only in temporary circumstances where a neighborhood was changing from white to black.

Despite the fact that all of the children in our school were black, we were required to teach the K–12 curriculum designed for all public schools. It was particularly difficult to motivate the older students in the areas of social studies since none of our instructional materials included African-Americans. Concerned teachers searched constantly for relevant materials such as *Ebony* magazine and local black newspapers, which included important information about the contributions of African-Americans in our society.

The over-age eighth-grade students were primarily males who needed role models and heroes—and motivation to remain in school. I will never forget the boredom on the faces of those students when we discussed the Golden Age of Greece and Rome or the early American settlers and the Pilgrims. Multicultural education represents a movement to reform school systems such as that in which I taught.

worked to make schools more responsive to the needs of minority students and the curriculum more inclusive of their cultures and contributions to our nation. Many programs focused on adding cultural information on minorities to the standard curriculum, primarily in the area of social studies. Alternative school models were also developed to decrease drop-out rates and to raise achievement levels through more relevant curriculum and instructional approaches. Many teacher education programs added new requirements in order to prepare teachers to work with culturally and linguistically diverse students.

❖ Purposes and Goals of Multicultural Education

The ultimate purpose of multicultural education is to create a more just society through major reforms of education; to make it more inclusive and representative of the diverse group in our nation; and to make it more effective, equal, and equitable for the culturally and linguistically diverse children in our society. Major themes of multicultural education are: (1) a balanced view of history; (2) matching instruction with learning styles; (3) equal opportunities for all children to learn; (4) promoting multicultural ideals throughout the educational system; and (5) promoting intergroup respect, positive relations, and student self-esteem (Gottfredson, Murray, Nettles, & McHugh, 1992).

Some important goals include: (1) changes in the total school environment to create a climate that promotes the appreciation of diversity and the contributions of many groups to this nation's progress; (2) changes in the curriculum and instructional materials to make them more inclusive and relevant; (3) the use of instructional approaches that address the unique characteristics and needs of all students; (4) changes in the values that schools promote; and (5) greater diversity among the teachers and administrators who provide education for our children.

❖ Issues

Some of these goals have evoked great controversy across the nation. Opposition to changes in the curriculum has been expressed by many who hold the view that the traditional curriculum is good for all students and it will be thrown out of the schools if multicultural education is adopted. A recent effort in New York illustrates the controversy about curriculum reform. The former chancellor of public schools had ordered the adoption of a new *Rainbow Curriculum* that includes and promotes positive acceptance of all groups in the society. The inclusion of homosexuals in this first-grade curriculum, with a family structure that might include "two mommies or two daddies," resulted in the refusal of some schools to adopt the new curriculum and a serious confrontation between the chancellor and several local school boards (*New York Times*, Dec., 1992).

A recent survey by the New York State United Teachers found that 75 percent of New Yorkers thought that teaching the common heritage shared by all Americans is a very important goal of public education; only 45 percent considered it very important to teach history from the perspective of different racial/ethnic groups. A majority of the respondents disagreed that students would do better if courses focused on their own racial and ethnic histories (New York State United Teachers Education Opinion Survey, 1991).

Opponents of multicultural education also fear the loss of unity in the country as a result of the emphasis on differences. The melting pot philosophy in which immigrants gave up their unique cultural differences to become an American, to be assimilated in the mainstream, is the preferred aim for public education among this group.

Gibson (1976) has pointed out other problems: the lack of sufficient evidence that multicultural education will increase academic success; the confusion of idealogy and theory; and the expectation, in some models, that the goals can be attained within a traditional education system.

Other important issues involve community reactions to multicultural education and the focus and content of programs. In Pittsburgh, for example, some white parents viewed the program as unbalanced and overemphasizing black culture (Gottfredson, Murray, Nettles, & McHugh, 1992). The need to present a balanced program may be a distinct challenge to the schools, and the attitudes of the community will play a crucial role in the success of a multicultural education program. In a recent survey, New York State residents expressed that it is the primary responsibility of the family, rather than the schools, to teach children social responsibility and pride in their racial and ethnic backgrounds (New York State United Teachers Education Opinion Survey, 1991). In addition, the decision must be made whether to design the program for culturally diverse students or about diverse cultures. However, this issue is really moot since most authorities agree that both groups must be included if the program is to succeed in attainment of its goals and objectives.

In view of the reality that our public schools are attended by increasing numbers of minority children who come from many different cultural and linguistic backgrounds, it is obvious that changes must occur in our educational system despite the fears and controversey. The challenge that we face is to respect and maintain our own unique cultures and, at the same time, respect the rights and cultural traditions of others. We must also assure the participation of all Americans in the mainstream culture, to realize the motto, *E Pluribus Unum.* All children are entitled to educational equality and equity in our public schools.

Children come from many different cultural and linguistic backgrounds.

❖ Basic Assumptions

Certain basic assumptions are inherent in multicultural education. First, all children can learn and achieve in school to a high level of competence. Second, in a society that includes many diverse groups, we must learn to live and work in harmony if we hope to continue national and international progress in the coming century. Third, schools are major agents of change in the nation. Through multicultural education, children can acquire new skills, attitudes, and understanding that will promote cooperation, collaboration, tolerance, and appreciation of our differences and those of people around the world. Finally, the educators who teach our children and administer our schools should be representative of the diverse cultures that comprise this society.

❖ Multicultural Education in the Schools

Current definitions of multicultural education vary in perspective. Banks and Banks (1989) define it in terms of concept, process, and a reform movement. In their definition, the concept is that of equal educational opportunities for all children. The process refers to the ongoing educational process involved in meeting the goals of multicultural education, and the reform movement involves changing the educational system so that it serves the needs of all children for quality education (Banks & Banks, 1989).

Definitions that use an educational perspective are particularly useful for teachers. For example, the National Council for Accreditation of Teacher Education states that:

Multicultural education is a process through which individuals develop ways of perceiving, evaluating, and behaving within cultural systems different from their own. (Gibson, 1984)

Suzuki's (1984) definition is also useful because it defines the term educationally as: "multidisciplinary educational program that provides multiple learning environments that match [instruction to] the academic, social [and linguistic] needs of the students" (p. 70). These definitions direct teachers to attend to the unique individual characteristics of learners in the classroom and to help students learn to communicate and interact with children from different cultural backgrounds. The definitions also underscore the influence of culture on a child's learning and the importance of teachers' knowledge in this area.

Banks and Banks: Four Approaches

Several authors have categorized the approaches to developing programs in multidisciplinary education (Table 1–1). Banks and Banks (1993) describe four approaches to multicultural education, based upon levels of integration. The lowest levels use additive approaches while the upper levels begin to transform and integrate the curriculum with multicultural content.

Level One, the contributions level, adds ethnic heroes, holidays, and cultural events to the traditional curriculum. Banks and Banks point out that this approach allows teachers to recognize minorities' contributions quickly; this sometimes satisfies the political demands of a community for representative heroes and cultural contributions in the school's curriculum. However, this approach is very limited in scope, does not provide students with comprehensive understanding of the social and political contexts in which the heroes lived and worked and the significance of their contributions, and fails to reform the curriculum.

Level Two, also an additive approach, makes additions to the curriculum of content, themes, concepts; however, the curriculum remains unchanged. The teacher includes multicultural content into the curriculum such as a relevant piece of African-American literature or a unit on the twentieth century novel. As Banks and Banks (1993) note, the multicultural content is usually viewed from a mainstream perspective.

The transformation approach, Level Three, involves changes in the curriculum and "enables students to view concepts, issues, themes, problems from several ethnic perspectives . . . " (Banks & Banks, 1993, p. 203). Thus, in studying United States history, music, art, and, science, the influence of diverse groups who have participated in and shaped the American culture and society must be taught. Banks and Banks refer to this as "multiple acculturation" (p. 204).

Level Four, the social action approach, encompasses the elements of the transformation level with additional components. The aim of this instruction is to develop students' decision-making skills and abilities for social criticism and social change. In this approach, students acquire the knowledge, values, and skills needed to become participating members of the society who will help to realize democratic ideals (Banks & Banks, 1993).

Gibson's Five Approaches

Earlier, Gibson (1976) found five approaches to programs in the 1970s based upon different purposes, goals, and assumptions (Table 1–1). The first approach was described as "education of the culturally different." The major purpose of this type of program was to equalize educational opportunity for culturally different students, with the assumption that culturally different children have unique learning needs. In this approach, it was assumed that the difference between the mainstream culture, which is dominant in public schools, and the child's culture caused learning difficulties for the child. The focus of this type of program is limited to the culturally different children and it ignores the majority population. The approach is therefore inadequate in meeting the goals and purposes of multicultural education.

The second approach was categorized as "education about cultural differences of cultural understanding." The purpose of this approach was to teach students the meaning of culture, help them to understand and accept others' rights to be different, and teach them to value cultural differences. Underlying assumptions included the belief that schools should provide cultural enrichment for all students, that multicultural education can provide cultural enrichment and foster understanding and acceptance of cultural differences, and that these programs can decrease racism and prejudice and increase social justice (Gibson, 1976, p. 9).

This program is broader in scope and addresses affective as well as cognitive goals. However, the entire system is not included and that will make if difficult to attain the goal of multicultural education. Teachers and other school staff need in-service training in order to successfully implement the program. The parents and community must also be involved.

Gibson labeled the third approach, "education for cultural pluralism." The goal and purpose was to "preserve and extend cultural pluralism in American society" (Gibson, 1976, p. 11). Basic assumptions included the belief that maintenance of cultural diversity is important to the survival of diverse groups; that schools should aim to preserve and expand cultural pluralism through multicultural education; and that these programs will alleviate racism and oppression in the society, promote academic achievement, and increase the power of minority groups (Gibson, 1976).

The fourth approach, "bicultural education," aimed to produce learners who could function in two different cultures and has been often used in conjunction with bilingual education programs. The purpose and

TABLE 1-1 Multicultural education curriculum approaches and models

Author	Approaches	Strengths	Limitations
Banks (1993)	1. Contributions	Recognition of minority contributions and heroes; adds ethnic heroes, holidays, and cultural events to traditional curriculum.	Lacks true curriculum reform; traditional, mainstream perspective maintained.
	2. Additive approach	Adds content, themes, and concepts to the traditional curriculum.	Lacks curriculum reform; mainstream perspective retained.
	3. Transformation	Changes in curriculum are made; several perspectives on events; concepts are available to students.	Curriculum does not prepare students for social action.
	4. Social action	Curriculum reform and student preparation for social action, criticism, and change.	Limitations are removed. Students prepared for promoting change.
Lynch (1989)	1. Additive approach	Thematic material added to the curriculum.	Primarily for minority children; no attempt to change curriculum; lacks focus on global multicultural education.
	2. Folkloric multicultural education	Customs, festivals, dress of minority groups added to mainstream curriculum.	Emphasis on the exotic and differences; limited to aims for multicultural education. Lack of emphasis on development of skills and positive attitudes; science, math (more prestigious) areas of curriculum remain unaffected.
	3. Permeative phase	Entire curriculum infused with multicultural education; "commitment to cultural diversity," appropriate content, methods, materials included.	Over-emphasis on differences; specific teaching and learning strategies lacking; systematic evaluation lacking.
	4. Anti-racist phase	Student and teacher training in racism and fascism awareness; largely a "political movement."	Too narrowly focused.
	5. Collaborative approach	Focus on teaching/learning approaches to improve inter-ethnic relations; use of cooperative learning groups.	Prejudice reduction is not a specific aim.

TABLE 1–1 continued

Author	Approaches	Strengths	Limitations
	6. Prejudice reduction approach; a composite approach	Combines the best of all previous approaches/models.	Limitations are eliminated.
Gibson (1976)	1. Education of the culturally different	Recognition of cultural differences as possible source of school learning problems; addresses learning needs of culturally different children.	Not comprehensive; does not include the entire school system; lacks staff training, parent, and community involvement; focus on culturally different.
	2. Education about cultural differences	All students are taught the meaning of culture, to value cultural differences and respect others' right to be different.	Does not include the entire school system; omits the staff training, parent and community involvement.
	3. Education for cultural pluralism	Additional aims include extention of cultural pluralism in the society; promotes academic achievement for minorities. Most comprehensive approach.	
	4. Bicultural education	Recognition of children's need and preparation to function in two different cultures.	Limited to bicultural students; majority group children, parents, community, and school staff neglected.
	5. Anthropological perspective		Not an educational approach.

goals of this approach were similar to others and also rejected assimilation and acculturation. This is another limited view of multicultural education. The broad segments of the majority children, parents and community, and school staff have been neglected. Gibson's fifth approach used an anthropological perspective, focused on learning about other cultures from many sources and in many different natural settings, and was not school-based.

Lynch's Approach

Lynch (1989) has also classified programs, but in terms of the curricular responses to increasing diversity in educational systems around the world, (Table 1–1). Lynch, like Banks and Banks and Gibson, classified the earlier approach used by many schools during the '70s as an additive approach to curricular reform. This type of program adds thematic subject areas to the present curriculum such as a unit on Native American Medicine or African-American Explorers, and was designed to raise the low self-image and achievements of minority children (Lynch, 1989). He describes this curriculum model as often viewed by the majority as being of low status and primarily designed for minority groups. The additive approach does not attempt to change the curriculum for all children and fails to meet the criteria for "global multicultural education" advocated by Lynch (1989).

Lynch described a second phase in curriculum reform as knowledge of the customs, dress, and festivals of some or many minority groups introduced into the mainstream curriculum with the emphasis on difference or the exotic aspects of minority cultures. This model also fails to meet the broad aims of multicultural education. In this approach there is a "lack of emphasis on skills and attitude development and failure to reform more 'prestigious' areas of the curriculum" (Lynch, 1989, p. 36).

The permeative phase, a later phase of curriculum reform aimed at infusing the entire curriculum with a "commitment to cultural diversity" (Lynch, 1989, p. 37), includes appropriate content, instructional materials, and methods. However, this model also has certain weaknesses such as continued overemphasis on difference, lack of systematic evaluation, and lack of specific teaching/learning strategies. The next phase is labeled the anti-racist phase, which developed in the mid-1980s. Lynch points out that this was a largely political movement in which proponents pressed for major changes in schooling as a means of fighting the racism viewed by some as endemic in market economies. In this model, white racism was condemned and teachers and students trained "out of their prejudice" in racism awareness training sessions.

In the sixth phase described by Lynch (1989), programs have been developed that take the best of all the previous models to produce a composite approach that he labeled "prejudice reduction."

Other Approaches

Another curricular response to cultural diversity has been based upon collaboration among different disciplines led by social psychologists in the United States, Canada, and Israel. This movement focused on teaching/learning approaches that could improve interethnic relations, particularly by the use of various types of cooperative group work (Lynch, 1989).

An example of this model is the program, *A Call for Cooperative Pluralism: From Me to We* (Nakagawa, 1990). This program focuses on all people as opposed to specific groups and emphasizes "people skills." While many programs have an ethnic studies approach to learning about cultural differences and focus on African-Americans, Asian-Americans, Latinos and Native Americans, the cooperative pluralism program takes a holistic view. It emphasizes learning to view issues from a variety of perspectives. For example, in a lesson about justice, examples would be given from the perspective of various groups. Program goals are self-identity, diversity, ideals, interdependence, and interpersonal relationships. The program is designed as a complement to traditional multicultural education approaches and blends cooperative learning and democratic education principles with traditional content (Nakagawa, 1991).

Many states have produced resource guides for teachers such as a unit of study on "Africa revisited," which gives students an opportunity to read African folktales and portray them through puppetry, role playing, and creative writing (New York City Board of Education, 1992); and units on "Mexican celebrations." Efforts to integrate content are such examples as a multicultural perspective on United States and New York State history, in which units of instruction integrate the histories, perspectives, and contributions "of all people, women, African-Americans, American Indians, and ethnic minorities" (New York City Board of Education, 1990), and *Children of the Rainbow: First Grade*, a manual for first-grade teachers that provides suggestions and teaching materials that reflect the multicultural composition of New York City's public schools (New York City Board of Education, 1991).

The Pittsburgh multicultural education program at Prospect Middle School (Gottfredson, Murray, Nettles, & McHugh, 1992) is a good example of a comprehensive program. The Prospect School plan aims to demonstrate that schools can be reformed to integrate children of different ethnic backgrounds. Activities are designed to reach, involve, and utilize parents and community resources and build community ownership of pluralistic education in the school. Instructional arrangements are identified that will increase learning, improve race relations, limit conflict, and enhance self-esteem in children. Curriculum modification, training of school personnel to create a positive environment, and improved treatment of students and evaluation of the program are included in the program goals.

The program includes activities that will restructure the delivery of instruction such as elimination of tracking, accommodating diverse learning styles, and developing appropriate co-curricular activities. Activities that will improve human relations in school and community include conflict resolution, parent and community involvement, and cooperative learning. Enhancement of the school curriculum is achieved through infusing multicultural content into existing courses and developing new courses and co-curricular activities based on the aims of multicultural education. This comprehensive program addresses every

FIGURE 1–1 Pittsburgh Multicultural Education Program

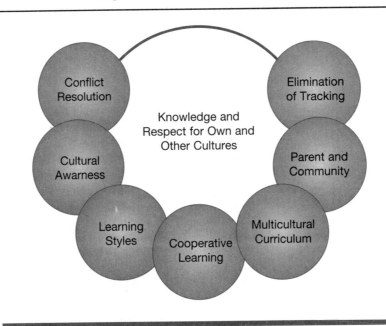

SOURCE: Gottsfredson, T., Murray, W., Nettles, N. & McHugh, R. (1992). Reproduced with permission of the principal, Prospect Middle School, Pittsburgh, PA.

aspect of school life and will also reach into the community. Activities are included that will foster positive relations among students, for staff development, and for curricular modification. The program is graphically presented, (Figure 1–1).

❖ How Can Teachers Become Culturally Sensitive?

Studies have shown that teachers will need preservice or in-service training in multicultural education in order to acquire the skills and understanding to teach culturally diverse children (Ladson-Billings, 1991; Demetrulias, 1990; Moultry, 1990; Thompson & Meeks, 1990). Research has also shown that *one-shot courses* and workshops are insufficient (Hafner & Green, 1992). In a survey conducted among student teachers in Ohio, 30 percent to 40 percent showed a lack of empathy with minority problems involving institutional racism. The student teachers also lacked knowledge about implicit causes of human behavior and expressed no confidence in education and politics as sources for changing people's beliefs and behavior regarding the values of cultural pluralism (Moultry, 1990).

SPECIAL BOX 1–4   *A Beginning Teacher Learns*

When I taught social studies at Eastern District High School in Brooklyn, NY, from 1981 to 1983, it was 75 percent Latino, 25 percent black, and 100 percent poor. My first year there I discovered that we had classes for a full week after the final exams were graded and the final grades turned in. Keeping the students in class and motivated to learn was a challenge under those circumstances.

In the winter of 1982, the trial of Jack Henry Abbott took place. Abbott, a convicted murderer who had spent most of his life behind bars, had been released on probation after the publication of his eloquently written book about prison life, *In the Belly of the Beast*. Five weeks after his release, he stabbed a waiter to death outside an East Village restaurant.

I chose to present the trial to my tenth-grade social studies class, through articles published in *The New York Times* and elsewhere. Abbott's defense centered on his misunderstanding of the waiter, Richard Adan, and his intentions. Abbott wanted to use the restroom; the restaurant did not have one inside. Adan asked Abbott to step outside, as he had often done with male patrons with similar needs. When Adan led Abbott to a secluded location behind the dumpster, Abbott quickly pulled a knife and stabbed Adan once in the heart.

My inner-city, mostly Puerto Rican, students understood the issue right away. For them, as well as for Abbott, a request to "step outside" signified an invitation to fight. The location was a perfect one for a fight; there would be no witnesses.

One of the daily *Times* accounts contained a description of the knife Abbott used to kill Adan. After reading the article, seven of my twelve students—girls as well as boys—pulled out their concealed knives to compare them to the murder weapon.

Abbott was white, my students predominantly Latino and black. What they shared was a life of poverty. From the story, my students learned two things. The first was a magnitude of the distance between two cultures, a distance that created a miscommunication so great as to cost one man his life and the other his only hope of freedom. The other was that poverty and violence crossed ethnic and racial lines; they are not innate characteristics of Puerto Ricans, African-Americans, or anyone else. I did not feel frightened when my students pulled out their knives; rather, I knew that my lesson had made a connection. By finding the common ground in our experiences and communicating openly, in an environment in which all feel safe, we can bridge the differences of class, race, and culture.

My second year at Eastern District, I shared a classroom with the bilingual social studies teacher, a Puerto Rican man who had grown up in the South Bronx and had taught seventh grade in a rural school in Puerto Rico before returning to teach in New York City. He had chosen a career in teaching because a teacher with the ASPIRA program, an outreach program for Latino students at risk, had convinced him to go back to school after four years of truancy and drug use. He said no student could put anything over on him; he had done it already. Students treated him with respect because he understood them, their heritage, and the countries from which they came, and he knew how tough it was to be an adolescent in the inner city, caught between two cultures.

Very active in political and cultural activities, this outstanding teacher introduced my husband and me to Latin-American music and literature. With him we attended concerts and shopped at Spanish bookstores and record stores. I decided to take courses to recharge my Spanish, which I had let slip since my junior year in high school. Even after we left New York City for Wisconsin in the summer of 1983, I organized Latin-American music concerts and stayed involved in the same political issues of which I had first become aware from my colleague.

For those of us who are teaching in culturally diverse situations, it is important to realize we are not only teachers, we are also students. Textbooks can tell us only so much. After that, we must be ready to learn from our colleagues, from the parents, and from the children themselves.

Another study involving fifty elementary teachers examined the familiarity of teachers with multiethnic literature. The majority was unfamiliar with all of the various titles listed under Asian-American, Jewish-American, African-American, Native American and Latino literature (Thompson & Meeks, 1990). Studies have also found evidence of stereotyped perceptions and expectations of minorities among teachers (Demetrulias, 1990).

Teacher training programs in multicultural education have identified important goals and competencies. Examples of goals for teachers include: to recognize the differences between home and school cultures and the potential conflicts and opportunities they may create for children; to be able to incorporate in the instructional environment activities and materials related to the native cultures of the students; and to recognize the potential bias in existing tests of intelligence, language, and concept development and other areas for linguistically and culturally diverse children (Holmes, 1976). Competencies include the ability to provide instruction using such methods and strategies as mastery learning, cooperative learning, and diverse instructional styles (Gottfredson, Murray, Nettles, & McHugh, 1992). Teachers also need knowledge and understanding of cultural and linguistic diversity as they relate to the academic and social learning and behavior of children in the classroom.

Culture has been defined from many perspectives. It refers to the shared set of values, attitudes, lifestyles, customs, and personality types among a group of people (Mindel & Haberstern, 1982). Culture includes all of the systems, techniques, and standards that make up a group's way of life (Abrahams, 1972). It also refers to a group's way of perceiving, judging, and organizing ideas, events, and situations met in daily life (Shade, 1989), and cultures differ in their approaches to learning and exchanging knowledge (Leacock, 1973). Leacock has described an American Indian student who refused to present her paper orally in class. The student explained that the American Indian style of discourse was followed in her family where the purpose of discourse was aimed toward reaching consensus rather than winning an argument. This placed the teacher's expectations in conflict with the student's cultural values.

Styles of behavior in adult/children interactions may differ among cultures. A familiar example is found among Puerto Rican and American Indian children who may not make eye contact with a teacher who is scolding them. While many teachers may think that this behavior is sullen or rude, it expresses respect or acquiescence in those cultures.

FIGURE 1–2 Cultural Identity of an American

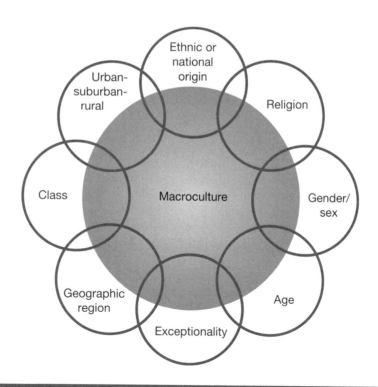

SOURCE: Gollnick, G. and Chinn, P. (1990). Multicultural education in a pluralistic society, Third Ed. New York: Macmillan. Used with permission.

Cultures may also differ in the general styles of interpersonal relations and related attitudes that their members share.

Language is one of the most important components of culture. In a discussion of the determinants of educational achievement among Latinos, Bean and Tienda (1987) noted that language is the most crucial factor. Latinos speak the second most prevalent language in this country and it is maintained at a high rate; thus, proficiency in both English and Spanish is needed. Bean and Tienda also stress the need for understanding the cultural conflict experienced by Latinos as they are forced to become bicultural with respect to learning processes, communication styles, and general human relations (Bean & Tienda, 1987).

It is important to point out that we all share the mainstream American culture. Some refer to this as the *macroculture* and the smaller more diverse subcultures are *microcultures* to which we individually belong (Banks & Banks, 1989). Acculturation is the process of learning the values, behaviors, communication styles, dress, customs, and beliefs of the macroculture. It is the process of becoming Americanized. Immigrants to this country differ in their routes of entry and have different rates and patterns of acculturation. Acculturation is important in understanding cultural differences (Figure 1–2).

❖ The Relationship Between Culture and Education

Cultural anthropologists have made significant contributions to our understanding of the relevance of culture for education. Cultural anthropologists study the similarities and differences among cultures (Kitano, 1981). From their perspective, a specific culture includes the system of beliefs, thoughts, and behaviors that are learned and shared by members of a specific group. These characteristics are expressed through the customs, arts, language, social institutions, and material goods of the culture (Kitano, 1981). Anthropologists offer insight in the areas of curriculum, teacher training, analysis of educational processes, and factors that affect school achievement (Spindler, 1973, cited in F.A.J. Ianni & E. Storey). They have supported the concept of cultural pluralism, the equality of cultures, and a child's right to maintain that culture (La Belle, 1976, cited in J.I. Roberts & S.K. Akin Sanya). According to LaBelle, language and culture are interdependent and schools must help children maintain their primary language while assisting them to acquire the second language and cultural study in the curriculum from K–12. LaBelle also supported the recognition of different learning styles and curriculum modification when needed. Finally, he noted the importance of the child's culture in planning educational programs and the primary goal of "preparing minority students for life in the mainstream in a culturally sensitive manner."

It is evident from the nature of culture that it can exert powerful influence on a child's attitudes and approaches to learning, verbal skills and communication patterns, academic achievement, interpersonal interactions, and responses to disciplinary methods and authority figures in the classroom. Although research on learning styles has not supported the notion that different racial/ethnic groups learn in specific ways, it helps a teacher to know that culturally determined, general approaches to learning and problem-solving do exist and may suggest certain instructional methods for the teacher.

Knowledge of the cultural patterns for interpersonal relationships and interactions may help to explain a child's social interactions with peers and teachers in the school environment. For example, a child's affective expression may be influenced by culture. Some children will be more reserved and others more gregarious, and this may be related to cultural differences in affective expression.

Parents from different cultures may use different criteria to measure the independence, competence, and interpersonal skills of their children (Taylor-Gibbs & Nahme-Huang, 1989). Parents may also differ in their attitudes toward independence and may place differential emphasis on early training for independence and later encouragement of independence in adolescents (Taylor-Gibbs & Nahme-Huang, 1989). Cultures also differ in the value of particular characteristics and abilities and these become important sources of self-esteem for children (Taylor-Gibbs & Nahme-Huang, 1989). A child's criteria for self-evaluation will be influenced by these values.

In addition, cultures differ in their attitude toward achievement and socialization practices. Children learn to manage their aggression and sexual impulses according to cultural practices. The strategies used to teach children how to cope with anxiety differ among various cultures. Some families may reinforce acting out behaviors as a defense against anxiety. Other families will teach children to use internal responses (Taylor-Gibbs & Nahme-Huang, 1989).

In an extensive discussion on assessing minority students, Taylor-Gibbs and Nahme-Huang (1989) point out important aspects of a child's cultural background and can assist in diagnosing problems and selecting appropriate interventions. Although they viewed this list in terms of psychological interventions, educators can also benefit from its use when seeking solutions to children's problems at school. These include:

- attitudes;
- norms;
- child-rearing practices;
- language;
- immigration history;
- belief systems;

- acculturation;
- socioeconomic effect on lifestyle;
- community experiences;
- opportunities; and
- aspirations. (Taylor-Gibbs & Nahme-Huang, 1989)

Research has provided a great deal of educationally relevant information about some of the minority cultures. However, it is always important to remember that these findings are very general and any individual child or family will be uniquely different and may share few or none of these general characteristics. For example, studies show some evidence that Japanese-American children have a lower self-concept than Caucasian-American peers; this finding is associated with the ethnic difference or physical appearance of Japanese-American children (Nagata, 1989). These children may need assistance at school in building a more positive self-concept. Another study found that Japanese-American parents may avoid praising their children at home. This is important to consider when a behavioral approach is used at school and the teacher wishes to extend it to the home setting. It could be important to discuss this with the parents and present the benefits of positive reinforcement for the child (Nagata, 1989). Teachers also need to be aware of the stereotype that all Japanese-American students are above average in math and sciences. A Japanese-American student who is failing math should not be viewed any more seriously than a Caucasian-American student failing the same subject (Nagata, 1989). In the area of language, some researchers have found that language is not an important factor for Japanese-Americans because most currently speak English (Nagata, 1989).

In contrast, language differences may be very important for American Indian children since many tribal languages are different from English in both vocabulary and structure (LaFromboise & Graff-Low, 1989). Another important finding is that many American Indian families may not pressure a child to perform and this may cause conflict for these children and families when faced with the emphasis placed on individual achievement and success in our schools. The cultural emphasis is on cooperation. Studies also show that when American Indian students have problems, the entire community owns the problem and its members may be valuable resources to the school (LaFromboise & Graff-Low, 1989).

Several of the educationally relevant findings on African-American culture are in the areas of language, interpersonal relations, and major cultural values. Language is an important aspect of culture for African-American students since some of them speak both Black English and standard English. Teachers need to become familiar with Black English and appreciate its cultural value to the student. It will be important to help students understand the need to be proficient in both languages rather than to devalue their home language. Teachers should ask for information about Black English vocabulary or structure when needed. However, it is also important to remember that communication patterns will vary among children according to acculturation and socioeconomic status.

School personnel can benefit from knowledge and understanding of culturally related preferences in interpersonal interactions. Many African-American families are likely to judge a person's competence more on the basis of interpersonal skill and warmth than on formal competence and credentials (Taylor-Gibbs & Nahme-Huang, 1989).

Teachers can make a critical difference for children through knowledge and understanding of cultural differences. Since studies show that teachers may hold stereotyped perceptions of minority children (Demetrulias, 1990), recognition of your biases is an important first step in becoming culturally sensitive. Secondly, understanding the influence of culture on children's learning and behavior will help teachers to diagnose problems in the classroom. Finally, knowledge of other cultures will foster the teacher's ability to see things from other perspectives. As the number of culturally and linguistically diverse children increases in our schools, it becomes increasingly urgent for teachers to become culturally sensitive and competent. Take time to learn about the different cultures and languages in your school. Visit community programs and activities and talk with community representatives. Ask questions about the cultures represented. If your school and community lack diversity, visit schools in other districts and communities where the population is more diverse.

❖ An Approach to Multicultural Education

The most effective approach to multicultural education, in our view, is its integration in a broader educational framework. We believe that multicultural education is most effective when it is an integral part of all that is taught in our schools, both the explicit and implicit curriculum, and that the entire system should reflect its goals and purposes. The curriculum should reflect all of the diverse cultural and linguistic groups in our society; it should not be limited to only those groups in a particular school. In many schools the population may be entirely Caucasian—or largely homogenous. These schools need multicultural education integrated into the curriculum in the same manner as schools with more diverse populations. All children need to develop appreciation and respect for the diversity in our society and the need to combat intolerance for differences in gender, socioeconomic class, religion, race, ethnicity, language, sexual orientation, and abilities. Furthermore, we believe that there are several approaches to instructional organization and delivery that are particularly appropriate for the integration of multicultural education in the school and accomplishment of its goals. These are mastery learning, whole language, and cooperative learning.

Mastery Learning

Mastery learning is an instructional approach and philosophy developed by Benjamin Bloom (1976) at the University of Chicago. It represents the belief that all students can learn to a high level of achievement when instruction is developed to assure that goal. Formative evaluation is used to measure the ongoing progress of students and to modify or extend instruction as needed. Each student learns at a different pace and reaches instructional objectives of a lesson before moving on. The responsibility of the teacher is to provide the resources needed by students to accomplish the instructional goals and objectives.

Whole Language

Whole language is a philosophy and a theory about the way that children learn language. The philosophy has been summarized by Strickland (1991) in the following terms: " . . . language is best learned in authentic, meaningful situations, ones in which language is not separated into parts" (p. 3). When the whole language approach is used, reading, writing, listening, and speaking are integrated.

Characteristics of a whole language classroom have been described in the literature. Some of these include: the children's immersion in a wide variety of language experiences, many demonstrations of written and oral language, practice time for reading and writing for real purposes, and teacher feedback, redirection, and encouragement (Pike & Maras, 1991).

There are many benefits for children in a whole language classroom. These include the child-centered classroom and curriculum; curriculum that is developed according to the abilities, interests, and needs of the students; and the encouragement of children to choose meaningful learning experiences, to think both creatively and critically and to use their strengths.

Cooperative Learning

Cooperative learning is an approach to teaching that structures lessons to promote group interaction and social skills with the ultimate goal of academic achievement. Johnson, Johnson, and Holubec (1990) have defined it as the instructional use of small groups so that students work together to maximize their learning. In contrast to traditional, competitive learning activities, cooperative learning helps students of different abilities and backgrounds to learn to appreciate their differences. Studies show positive gains for many different types of students. Both academic and social/emotional goals are accomplished. The essential components are positive interdependence, face-to-face promotive interaction, individual accountability, interpersonal and small group skills, and group processing.

In contrast to competitive learning, all students are valued participants in a cooperative learning task. In classrooms of diverse students, where the goal is appreciation and the valuing of diversity, this approach is a valuable tool. The emphasis on interdependence relates to a major goal of multicultural education.

These instructional approaches will be described in greater detail in Chapters 6 and 7, where many examples of their application will be given.

❖ Parents and Families

Another important aspect of multicultural education is the involvement of parents and families. The importance of parental participation in children's education has been well established as an essential component of effective school programs (Allen, 1978; Imber, Imber, & Rothstein, 1979; Mangione & Honig, 1987; Sharma, 1988). However, the traditional approaches used to engage white, middle-class parents may not meet the need of parents from other cultural and linguistic groups. Although these parents will value education highly and want the best possible education for their children, cultural, linguistic, and socioeconomic factors may present difficulties in establishing school-family partnerships (Prewitt-Diaz, Trotter, & Rivera, 1989).

Cultural differences may exist in family structure, level of acculturation, developmental and behavioral expectations for children, child-rearing practices, communication patterns, and other important areas. Parents may need interpreters, provisions for transportation, training in educational assistance to children at home, support groups, meetings in the community as opposed to at the school, and understanding of their culturally based styles of interpersonal relationships by the school personnel. Minority parents will need to be empowered so they can fully participate in educational decision-making for their children. Parent and family participation in the school will be extensively discussed in Chapter 11.

❖ Summary

Multicultural education has evolved in the gradual shift of a society based upon the melting pot view to that of cultural pluralism. Several major events have influenced the change. The *Brown* decision, which brought about school desegregation, and the Civil Rights movement had major impact on the development of racial and ethnic group pride and identify in African-Americans. The movement led to consciousness raising and awareness in other groups as well—women, gays, people with disabilities, and those who routinely spoke a language other than, or in addition to, English. As cultural pluralism became more widely accepted, bilingual education, ethnic studies, the women's movement and the gay movement increased in recognition and respect.

Schools have responded to desegregation; various movements through curriculum modification and some changes have also occurred in teacher education programs. Efforts to reform the curriculum and improve the preparation of teachers to function in classrooms of increasing diversity continue at the present time.

Many definitions and goals for multicultural education have been developed by various authors. We believe in a broad definition and the total integration of multicultural education throughout the school curriculum. The goal of multicultural education is to promote a more just society in which diversity is affirmed and valued. Multicultural goals and ideals can be realized throughout our educational system through recognition of diverse learning styles and family values, traditions, communication patterns, and child-rearing practices. Promoting intergroup respect and positive relations among the students in our school population is an important part of this.

Although some goals have stirred great controversy, multiculturalism is widely accepted in many states. Many school districts have developed successful, comprehensive programs in which student achievement has improved, intergroup relations are more positive, and community and family involvement have increased. As diverse cultural and linguistic groups have become more involved in their positive identity and preservation of their cultures and languages, the names of these groups have become an important aspect of empowerment. We have researched the most acceptable names at this time and this text will refer to major groups as African-American, or Latino, Asian-American and American Indian.

Approaches to multicultural education range from narrowly focused perspectives to very broad ones. In narrowly focused programs, simple additions of holidays, ethnic heroes, foods, and special events might be added to the curriculum. An example of a broad comprehensive approach, in which the entire curriculum is integrated, is when staff training is provided, community involvement and support are present, and tracking is eliminated.

Teachers will need to become more culturally sensitive and prepared to implement multicultural education through in-service or preservice training. Studies have demonstrated the need for this training. Knowledge and understanding of diverse cultures and languages in our society will allow teachers to plan and implement more effective instruction. This will ensure the educational achievement of all students. In addition, that knowledge can facilitate positive relations among diverse students and effective partnership with parents and families.

Parents play an important role in their children's education.

❖ CHAPTER 1 Questions

1. What is the basis of the fear that multiculturalism will be divisive?

2. What is the primary flaw in the cultural deficit theory to explain poor educational achievement among disadvantaged children?

3. Why is the recognition and understanding of cultural differences important to educators?

4. Discuss the important aspects of language and culture that may influence educational outcomes for a student.

5. In considering various approaches to multicultural education, explain why the more limited models are criticized.

6. The Civil Rights movement has inspired and motivated several major movements in our society. Briefly discuss these movements and their effect on the schools.

❖ References

Abrahams, R. D. (1972). *Language and cultural diversity in American education*. Englewood Cliffs, NJ: Prentice Hall.

Allen, K. E. (1978). The teacher therapist: Teaching parents to help their children through systematic contingency management. *Journal of Special Education Technology, 2*, 47–55.

Banks, J., & Banks, C. A. (Eds.). (1989). *Multicultural education: Issues and perspectives.* Boston: Allyn and Bacon.

Banks , J., & Banks, C. A. (Eds.). (1993). *Multicultural education: Issues and perspectives* (2nd ed.). Boston: Allyn and Bacon.

Bean, P., & Tienda, M. (1978). *The Hispanic population of the United States.* New York: Russell Sage Foundation.

Bloom, B. (1976). *Human characteristics and school learning.* New York: McGraw Hill.

Demetrulias, D.M. (1990). Ethnic surnames. *Education Research Quarterly, 14*(3), 2–6.

Gibson, M. (1976). Anthropological perspectives on multicultural education. *Anthropology and Education Quarterly,* VII(4).

Gottstredson, I., Murray, W., Nettles, N., & McHugh, R. (1992). *Meeting the challenges of multicultural education: A report from the evaluation of Pittsburgh Prospect Multicultural Education Center for Research on Effective Schooling for Disadvantaged Students.* Report No. 27. March, 1992. Baltimore: Johns Hopkins University.

Hafner, A., & Green, J. S. (1992). *Multicultural education and diversity: Providing information to teachers.* Paper presented at the annual meeting of the American Association of Colleges for Teacher Education (AACTE) San Antonio, TX. (ERIC Document Reproduction Service No. ED 342 762).

Holmes, E. A. (1976). *Toward a competency-based license for multicultural education.* Paper presented at the Conference on Multicultural Education. Washington, DC, Social and Behavioral Sciences, Inc.

Imber, S. C., Imber, R. B., & Rothstein, C. (1979). Modifying independent work habits: An effective teacher-parent communication program. *Exceptional Children, 46,* 218–221.

Johnson, D. W., Johnson, R. T., & Holubec, E. J. (1990). *Circles of learning: Cooperation in the classroom* (3rd ed.). Edina, MN: Interaction Book Co.

Kallen, H. M. (1956) *Cultural pluralism and the American idea: An essay in social philosophy.* Philadelphia: University of Pennsylvania Press.

Kitano, M. (1981). *A re-examination of educational issues.* Presentation in the College of Education Dialogue Series, Las Cruces, New Mexico, Feb., 1981. (ERIC Document Reproduction Service No. ED 205 409).

Krug, M. (1976). *The melting of the ethnics: Education of the immigrants 1880–1914.* Bloomington, IN: Phi Delta Kappa Educational Foundation.

LaBelle, T. J. (1976). An anthropological framework for studying education. In J. I. Roberts & S. K. Akinsanya (Eds.), *Educational patterns and cultural configurations.* New York: David McKay Co.

Ladson-Billings, G. (1991). Beyond multicultural illiteracy. *Journal of Negro Education, 60*(2), 147–157.

LaFromboise, T. D., & Graff-Low, K. (1989). American Indian children and adolescents. In J. Taylor Gibbs & L. Nahme-Huang (Eds.), *Children of color: Psychological interventions with minority youth.* San Francisco: Jossey-Bass.

Lally, J. R., Mangione, P., & Honig, A. (1987). *The Syracuse University family development research program: Long range impact of early intervention with low-income children and their families.* San Francisco: Center for Child and Family Studies, Far West Laboratory for Educational Research and Development.

Leacock, E. (1973). The concept of culture and its significance for school counselors. In F.A.J. Ianni & E. Storey (Eds.), *Cultural relevance and educational issues.* Boston: Little Brown & Co.

Lynch, J. (1989). *Multicultural education in a global society.* London: Palmer Press.

Mindel, C. H., & Haberstein, R. W. (Eds.). (1981). *Ethnic families in America: Patterns and variations* (2nd ed.). New York: Elsevier.

Moultry, M. (1990). *Multicultural education among seniors in the College of Education at Ohio State University.* Paper presented at the annual meeting of the American Educational Research Association, New Orleans, LA, April 6–8.

Nakagawa, M. (1991). *A call for cooperative pluralism: From me to we.* Olympia, WA: Office of the State Superintendent of Public Instruction.

Nagata, D. K. (1989). Japanese American children and adolescents. In J. Taylor Gibbs & L. Nahme-Huang (Eds.), *Children of color: Psychological interventions with minority youth.* San Francisco: Jossey-Bass.

New York City Public Schools (1990). *United States and New York State history, Grade 7: A multicultural perspective.* Brooklyn: New York City Board of Education.

New York City Public Schools (1991). *Children of the rainbow: First grade.* Brooklyn: New York City Board of Education.

New York City Public Schools (1992). *Promoting harmony: A compilation of sample lessons.* Brooklyn: New York City Board of Education.

New York State United Teachers (1991). *Public attitudes on the debate over multicultural education in New York State.* Education Opinion Survey, 1991.

New York Times, Dec. 1, 1992. School board in Queens shuns Fernandez meeting, p. B3.

New York Times, Dec. 17, 1993. Navajos weigh return to old name: Diné, p. A26.

Novak, M. (1972). *The rise of the unmeltables.* New York: Macmillan.

Pike, K., & Maras, L. (1991). Whole language and special education: One teacher's journey. *The Forum, 17*(3), 5–7.

Pipkin, R., & Yates, D. (1992). Multicultural education: A middle school's approach to preparing tomorrow's leaders. *ERS—Spectrum, 10*(4), 37–40.

President's Committee on Mental Retardation Report, 1970.

Prewitt-Diaz, J. O., Trotter, R., & Rivera, V. (1989). *The effects of migration on children: An ethnographic study.* State College, PA: Centro de Estudios Sobre la Migracion.

Shade, B. (1989). *Culture, style and educational process.* Springfield, IL: Charles E. Thomas.

Sharma, V. (1988). *A traditional services model for preschool children preparing to enter kindergarten involving parents, teachers and public schools.* Miami, FL: Nova University.

Smith, D. D., & Luckasson, R. (1992). *Introduction to special education: Teaching in an age of challenge.* Boston: Allyn and Bacon.

Spindler, G.D. (1973). Anthropology and education: An overview. In F.A.J. Ianni & E. Storey (Eds.), *Cultural relevance and educational issues.* Boston: Little Brown & Co.

Strickland, K. T. (1991). Toward a new philosophy of language learning. *English Leadership Quarterly, 13*(1), 2–4.

Suzuki, B. (1984). *Socioeconomic pluralism: Its meaning for the future and education.* San Diego, CA: San Diego State University, National Origin Desegregation Assistance Center. (ERIC Document Reproduction Service No. ED 272 587).

Taylor-Gibbs, J., & Nahme-Huang, L. (1989). *Children of color: Psychological interventions with minority youth.* San Francisco: Jossey-Bass.

Thompson, D., & Meeks, J. W. (199). *Assessing teachers' knowledge of multiethnic literature.* Paper presented at the annual meeting, American Reading Forum, Sarasota, FL: December 12–15.

CHAPTER 2

The Changing Face of America's Children

The First Cultural Contact

Even before the arrival of the first European settlers almost four hundred years ago, contact between cultures has been part of American life. Both wars and alliances between Indian Nations had taken place since antiquity. The elementary school curriculum features the holiday of Thanksgiving and emphasizes the positive elements of cultural contact; in fact, the Indian peoples who shared their knowledge of agriculture helped the early settlers to survive.

However, the contact between cultures in the Americas has also meant discrimination, subjugation, and, in the case of the Indian Nations, genocide. As European settlers gained a foothold in their new land, they sought to enslave the Indians. This occurred principally in the West Indies and in the colonies of Spanish America, and it soon failed, as the Indians' greater knowledge of the terrain enabled them to escape. Others died in captivity from diseases, brought by the Europeans, to which they had no resistance.

What evolved in the present-day United States was the system of indentured servitude, by which a new immigrant would work for a certain number of years without pay in exchange for passage to this country. Many Europeans came under this arrangement (including a large number of debtors, for whom a trip to America was the best alternative to debtor's prison), as did a small number of people taken forcibly from Africa. By the end of the seventeenth century, though, the system of slavery evolved, and most of the Africans who were captured from their homelands in Sub-Saharan West Africa and brought to the new continent no longer obtained their freedom (Takaki, 1993).

The rapid increase in European immigration that resulted from the system of indentured servitude, as well as the importation of slaves from Africa, meant that the Indians were no longer necessary to the settlers' success in agriculture. Furthermore, the increase in population led settlers to covet the Indians' lands. The Indians were unfamiliar with the concept of private property, as all their lands were held communally, by the tribe. Conflict ensued when the European arrivals began to claim those lands as their own.

By the end of the seventeenth century, three cultural groups were established in the Americas—the Indians who had inhabited the lands for centuries, the Europeans who first arrived approximately a century after Columbus' initial voyages, and the Africans who were brought by the Europeans as slaves. In the area that would become the United States, the system of slavery existed primarily in the South, where a plantation economy required large amounts of labor. In the north, where small farms were the norm, slavery never gained much of a foothold and was prohibited in most northern states by the time the Constitution was ratified.

❖ The Indians

Although previous historians had believed that only 500,000 to 1.5 million Indians inhabited the present-day United States, scholars today estimate the Indian population at the time of the Europeans' arrival at approximately ten million (Thornton, 1987). (The lower estimate did not take into account the diseases that decimated the Indian population even before the first wave of settlers arrived in a given area, nor did it use systematic techniques to count the members of each Nation. Low estimates also had a political purpose; if the lands were seen as "uninhabited," the settlers could justify their claims upon them.) The Indians lived in hundreds of Nations in Alaska, in the continental United States and Canada; each Nation had its own means of subsistence, language, culture, and form of self-governance. Elsewhere in the Americas—in the present-day West Indies, Mexico, Central America, and South America—other Indian Nations lived, and the majority of Latinos in the United States are, at least in part, of Indian heritage. Some Nations were quite large. Others formed loose federations or consisted of breakaway groups from a larger group. While some larger Nations formed highly organized and hierarchically governed societies (the most notable being the Aztecs in Mexico and the Incas in Peru), most North American Indian Nations were smaller, more close-knit bands that engaged in hunting and subsistence agriculture, governed themselves democratically, and emphasized harmony among themselves and with nature.

From the initial contact with Europeans, the Indian population declined until the middle of the twentieth century, when it began to increase dramatically (Thornton, 1987). Historical statistics, particularly in the nineteenth century, do not accurately reflect the magnitude of this decline. However, this was because of the political pressures to undercount, the changing definitions of Indian citizenship status (not granted United States citizenship until 1924, Indians may not have even been considered United States residents for the purposes of the Census unless they dwelled on federally-administered reservation lands in Oklahoma and elsewhere), and the Census takers' limited contact with Indian settlements (Thornton, 1987). For instance, in 1860, the Indian population in the United States was reported at 44,021. A decade later, in 1870, that population had dropped to 25,731. However, between 1880 and 1890, the Indian population jumped from 66,407 to 248,253, a result not of the rapid increase in the Indian population during the decade, but of the resettlement of so many Indian peoples upon reservations (U.S. Census-A, 1870-1890). The devastating effects of the resettlement can be seen in the following ten-year Census, for the Indian population in 1900 dropped to 237,196 (U.S. Census-A, 1900). Another, slightly sharper, drop occurred between 1910 and 1920 (U.S. Census-A, 1910–1920) (Figure 2–1.)

According to the 1990 Census, about two million Indians live in the United States today (U.S. Census-A, 1990). Most of the growth in the Indian population has been in the past fifteen years, in part due to a high birth rate and in part due to individuals of mixed heritage claiming their Indian roots (Johnson, 1991). The decline in the Indian population had a number of causes. In the first place, the Europeans brought diseases, such as influenza, smallpox, and measles, to which the Indians were not accustomed and had no resistance. In some cases, European-Americans actively encouraged the spread of these diseases, as when United States military

FIGURE 2–1 American Indian Population, 1860-1990

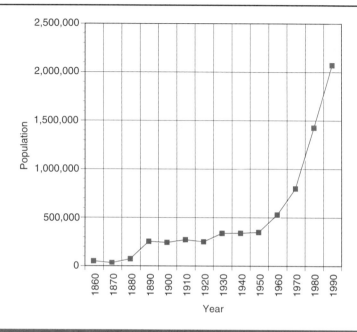

SOURCE: U.S. Census, 1860–1990.

officials in the nineteenth century gave smallpox-infected blankets to the Indians. While relatively few Indians were killed outright in battles with United States military forces or murdered in settler or Army rampages, the steady encroachment of settlers upon ancestral lands took their toll. The Indian Removal Act of 1830 led to the forced relocation of virtually all the Indian Nations residing east of the Mississippi River. Many died on their way to reservations in the West; it is now estimated that more than eight thousand Cherokee alone died during the *Trail of Tears*. (Thornton, 1991). Malnutrition and disease claimed even more Indians as they struggled to create new lives on bleak, uninhabitable western reservations.

As Indians came into contact with European settlers, intermarriage further decreased their population. Many of the earliest European settlers, single white men, took Indian wives. While this was far more common in Latin America, where the first arrivals were generally soldiers rather than settlers with families, North American explorers, traders, and farmers also married Indians and raised their children in a white society. In some cases, Indians married African-Americans—escaped slaves or free persons—and became part of African-American communities. The reverse also occurred when escaped slaves joined Indian communities or formed their own Nations, such as the Black Seminoles (Katz, 1986). After their relocation to reservations, many Indian children were sent to boarding schools, where they were restricted from seeing their families and indoctrinated in the values of white society. Others were adopted by white families. With their traditional bonds weakened and their backgrounds disparaged, many married non-Indians and gave up their Indian identity altogether. In fact, much of the growth in the Indian population since 1970 can be attributed to their descendants who have traced their roots and claimed their Indian heritage (Johnson, 1991).

❖ Slavery and Black Immigration

While American Indians were the only group to experience actual genocide—that is, their destruction because of their race and culture—African-Americans experienced a subjugation that has persisted in various forms since their arrival three hundred years ago. In contrast to the Indians, the black population in America has increased steadily through birth and immigration, but until after the Civil War, with the arrival of blacks from the West Indies, no black who came to America did so voluntarily.

Although slavery has existed since ancient times, the form of chattel slavery that predominated in the Americas was a relatively new development. Earlier, slaves were members of conquered groups, to be released after a fixed period of time or when the balance of power changed. In the Americas, however, slaves were seen as personal property like farm animals, and their descendants also became the property of their owner. Part of an emerging market economy, slaves were bought and sold, divided up with the rest of an estate, or auctioned off to pay an owner's debts, with families often broken up and *sold down the river* (i.e., further south).

Those who supported slavery advanced a number of theories in justification of the institution, many of which persist, in one form or another, today. Africa was portrayed as a backward, *dark* continent, and information about West Africa's history, culture, language, and social and economic development was suppressed. This led slaveowners and supporters of the institution to believe that the men, women, and children they brought over in chains, on overcrowded, miserable slave ships, were leaving a barbaric life for a better existence in the *new world*. Supporters of slavery also promoted racial theories of intelligence that placed white, European-descended people at the top and held that Africa's descendents had little more intelligence than the farm animals who shared their economic status as chattel. Blacks, it was argued, could never learn to read and write. However, at the same time, it was also a crime to teach a black slave to read and write. While the treatment of slaves on individual plantations varied greatly, apologists for slavery argued that all slaves enjoyed benefits denied to free men and women—guaranteed shelter and food, steady employment, *cradle-to-grave* security, and the benevolent guidance of the white master. As a result, the argument went, the slaves were happy, and few rebelled (Takaki, 1993). While nineteenth century abolitionists documented the cruel realities, only recently has the evidence of widespread slave resistance and rebellion been explored and integrated into the school curriculum as well (Katz, 1990).

For a variety of economic reasons, most notably the cultivation of cotton, slavery took hold mainly in the South (Takaki, 1993). By the time the Constitution was ratified, most northern states had prohibited the institution, and the Constitution only allowed the importation of slaves until 1808. Thus, most of the blacks who came to the present-day United States ended up in the South, and none arrived from Africa after 1808. After that time, the growth in the black population was due to natural increases rather than immigration. Children of mixed race, usually the offspring of slave women who had been violated by their masters, were classified as black and spent their lives in slavery.

Not all African-Americans, however, were slaves. In the years before Emancipation, ten to fifteen percent had already obtained their freedom (U.S. Census-A, 1860). They faced many occupational restrictions and were denied the right to vote, but many became educated and prospered in business and the professions (Takaki, 1993). A number of these free blacks or their descendents gained their freedom as indentured servants or when the northern states abolished slavery. In fact, approximately 7 percent of all blacks lived in the North and North Central states before the Civil War, a percentage that increased slowly from 1870 until 1940, when it rose dramatically (U.S. Census-A, 1860–1940), (Figure 2–2). In the South, blacks became freedmen when their owners voluntarily granted them their freedom, a process known as *manumission,* or when they or others purchased their freedom. Even so, free blacks in the South lived in fear that they could be forced back into slavery; the Fugitive Slave Act, passed in 1850, imperiled even northern blacks, some of whom migrated to Canada to avoid accusations that they had escaped Southern plantations.

Early on, African-Americans established a major presence. At the time of the first United States Census in 1790, 757,208 African-Americans lived in the United States, constituting 19.3 percent of the total population. In 1790, more than 90 percent lived in the South (Census-A, 1790). The percentage of African-Americans held steady (at 19 percent for the next two decades), but the end of the slave trade, coupled with an increase in immigration from Europe, lowered the percentage of African-Americans after 1810 (U.S. Census-A, 1800-1930). In 1820, African-Americans made up 18.4 percent of the total United States population (U.S. Census-A, 1820). This percentage dropped steadily for more than a century. In 1930, the percentage of African-Americans reached its lowest point, with that group constituting 9.7 percent of the country's total pop-

FIGURE 2-2 Percentage of African-Americans Living Outside the South, 1790–1900

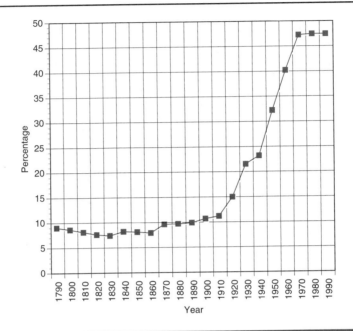

SOURCE: U.S. Census, 1790–1990.

ulation (U.S. Census-A, 1930). The closing of European immigration in the mid-1920s and a somewhat higher birth rate ultimately led to an increase in African-Americans' share of the population, which now stands at 12.1 percent (U.S. Census-A, 1990) (Figure 2–3). According to Census projections from the mid-1980s, African-Americans would have had an even larger share were it not for the dramatic increase in the 1980s of immigration from Asia and Latin America (U.S. Census-A, 1980–1990).

❖ Nineteenth Century Immigrants

English and Scots-Irish

The first European immigrants came from a variety of lands, but the largest groups were English and Scots-Irish. Dutch settlers colonized New Amsterdam, and most remained after the British captured the colony and renamed it New York. Fleeing religious persecution, French Huguenots settled in Maryland and elsewhere. Also fleeing religious per-

FIGURE 2–3 African-American Population, 1790–1990, Total and as Percentage of U.S. Population

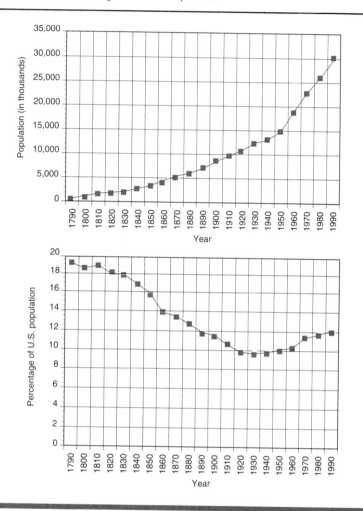

SOURCE: U.S. Census, 1790–1990.

secution were Sephardic, or Mediterranean, Jews, who established communities in New York; Newport, Rhode Island; Philadelphia; and Charleston, South Carolina.

Germany

After 1800, immigrants began to arrive from Germany. Like the English and Scots-Irish, the first wave of German immigrants sought plentiful land and other economic opportunities. German Jews, in particular, wanted to live and work without the restrictions imposed upon them in Europe. After the failure of the 1848 Revolution, politically liberal Germans—Jews and non-Jews—gave up on the old country and moved to the United States, where democracy had already been established. Many of these new German immigrants became active in the movement to abolish slavery. Whatever their occupations and interests, the German immigrants tended to settle in close-knit communities in the South and Midwest, where they preserved their language and culture through separate schools (Bergquist, 1992).

Irish Catholics

While Ireland had contributed many immigrants to the new nation, the initial arrivals were Scots-Irish—Protestants of Scottish heritage who lived in the northern part of Ireland. Famine in the 1840s brought a new kind of immigrant—poor and Catholic. More than one million Irish died of starvation between 1845 and 1855 as a result of the *potato famine*; another 1.5 million emigrated to the United States during this period. All in all, some 5.5 million Irish arrived between 1815 and 1920 (Takaki, 1993). The Irish faced widespread hostility and discrimination in housing and employment. Nonetheless, they remained in the new country, knowing that a return to Ireland meant likely starvation. Despite continued anti-Catholic and anti-Irish sentiment, Irish-Americans eventually achieved success in mainstream society.

Immigration by Annexation

During the first half of the nineteenth century, additional ethnic groups joined the population, not through voluntary immigration, but through the passage of territory to the jurisdiction of the United States. Besides various Indian Nations, French-speaking people in Louisiana and Spanish speakers in Florida and the Southwest became part of the population. The Louisiana Cajuns were allowed to retain many aspects of their language, culture, and system of governance; for example, even today, Louisiana's laws are based upon Napoleonic Code rather than English Common Law. However, the Latino residents of Mexico, who became part of the United States through the 1845 annexation of Texas and the 1848 Treaty of Guadalupe Hidalgo, which concluded the Mexican War, suffered an especially cruel fate. Most had their property confiscated, and virtually all of their local political power passed to Anglo-Americans (Takaki, 1993). Despite falling into poverty and wage labor, the original Latino residents of New Mexico, Arizona, Colorado, and California have retained much of their language, culture, and community, and they have sought to distinguish their culture and history from that of later immigrants from Mexico.

Chinese

When the 1849 California Gold Rush brought a flood of easterners seeking their fortunes, they were joined for the first time by immigrants from Asia—Chinese who had heard about *Gold Mountain* and were being recruited to work in the minefields and in building the railroads. A large number of Chinese men crossed the Pacific Ocean, hoping to make their fortunes and return (Takaki, 1993). Many perished. Only a few became wealthy enough to bring their wives and families to the United States. Discrimination against the laborers culminated in the Chinese Exclusion Act of 1882, which, in addition to barring new arrivals, hastened the departure of many of those already here. Immigration from China virtually ceased after that time; only after World War II did the numbers of Chinese-Americans born in China and Taiwan come close to matching those in the period between 1854 and 1882 (Lai, 1980). However, the Chinese families that did put down roots formed very visible communities in several American cities, most notably San Francisco, where Chinatown became a preserve for Chinese language and culture and a first stop for successive waves of twentieth century immigrants (Takaki, 1993).

Japanese

During the late nineteenth and early twentieth century, another Asian group, the Japanese, became part of the American mosaic. Some came directly to California as tenant farmers and farm workers; others moved to Hawaii and joined the United States population when Hawaii became a territory of the United States in 1898. The Japanese prospered in their new land, with many buying farms of their own, establishing small businesses, or entering the professions. Their integration into American society seemed complete—until the outbreak of the Second World War. Then, tens of thousands of Japanese-American families on the West Coast (though not in Hawaii) were interned and their property confiscated. This event traumatized the more than 100,000 Americans of Japanese descent who were interned; although most started over and succeeded in building new lives, their experiences have only begun to emerge in the literature and in discussions of reparations. (In 1988, a reparations bill finally became law, offering each surviving internee a sum of $20,000.) The end of World War II and the closing of the camps led many Japanese to migrate to other parts of the United States; the majority who stayed in California came into contact with the increasing number of Americans of all backgrounds who were migrating to the West. At the same time, legal restrictions against intermarriage eased, leaving many young, upwardly mobile Japanese to choose Caucasian mates. Today, Japanese-Americans have an unusually high rate of intermarriage and offspring who are biracial and bicultural (Kitano, 1980).

The Late Nineteenth Century Immigration Boom

The end of the Civil War and the settling of the West brought immigrants from Scandinavia who were accustomed to cold climates and long, dark winters. They established farming communities on the fertile soil of Wisconsin and Minnesota. Like the Germans in the same areas, they tried to maintain their customs, but they also mingled with and married those in other European immigrant groups (Christianson, 1992).

From 1880 to 1924, the majority of immigrants came to the United States from Eastern and Southern Europe. They came for a variety of reasons, principally economic, but also religious and political. Most of the late nineteenth century immigrants, particularly those from Italy and Poland, were Catholic, and this rekindled the anti-Catholic fervor that emerged at the time of the Irish immigration. Other immigrants included Russian and Eastern European Jews who fled religious persecution; these more observant Jews settled in large cities and forced the prosperous, liberal, and relatively secular German and Sephardic Jewish communities to adjust to the newcomers. The Eastern European immigration more than doubled the size of the United State's Jewish population, and, at the beginning, established Jewish businessmen often employed the newcomers in crowded, dangerous, and underpaid sweatshop labor at the same time as many of the more progressive Jewish leaders lobbied for their better treatment (Shapiro, 1979). With the frontier and most of its land gone, the immigrants from Southern and Eastern Europe crowded into the cities and worked as wage laborers in a variety of new industries. In some cases, particular ethnic groups dominated in an industry, such as Jews in textiles and Poles in meat packing and other food processing (Figures 2-4 and 2-5).

The massive migration from Southern and Eastern Europe had a major impact upon the American population as a whole, as the ten-year increase went from nine million between 1870 and 1880 to an average of thirteen million for every decade between 1880 and 1920 (U.S. Census-A, 1870-1920). The official goal, as reflected in the public schools and other government institutions, was the assimilation of the immigrants. Political leaders argued that the United States was a melting pot, where immigrants and members of ethnic groups would give up their separate language, customs, and culture in favor of a mainstream American culture. Nineteenth century immigrants did assimilate to a certain degree, learning English, changing their surnames in some cases, moving up the economic ladder, and gaining political power. Most, however, remained in ethnic enclaves through the middle of the twentieth century; many continue to live near family and friends in ethnic neighborhoods—Italian neighborhoods in Brooklyn or Polish neighborhoods in Chicago, for instance—even today. Furthermore, certain groups, such as the Germans and Japanese, maintained schools in their native language, and religious Jews established a separate system of education. Public libraries offered

FIGURE 2–4 Percentage of Foreign-Born Population in U.S. from Selected Countries, 1870 and 1920

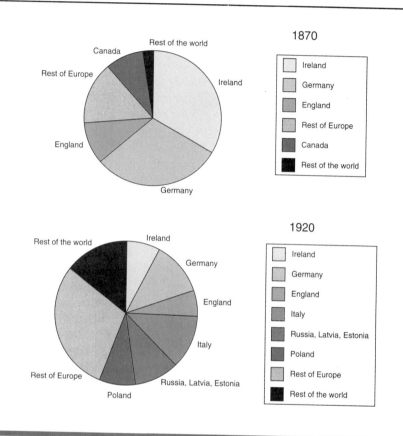

SOURCE: U.S. Census, 1870, 1920.

courses in English and adult education, but librarians learned early on that they would only be able to attract immigrants if they offered native-language materials and respected, through their attitudes and acquisitions, their patrons' original culture (Wendell, 1911; Solis-Cohen, 1927).

Though the melting pot ideology dominated, perhaps more in theory than in actuality, it became clear that a total emphasis upon assimilation had its drawbacks. When schools and other social institutions forced young immigrants to give up their past, it devalued that past and the immigrants' self-esteem. Because they learned the new language more quickly, children gained a position of power over their parents, and the devaluation of the parents' heritage further damaged traditional relations

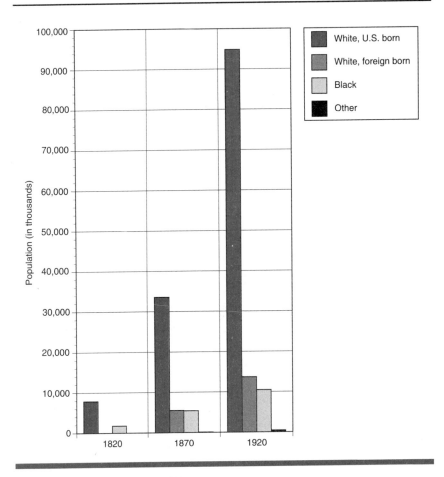

FIGURE 2–5 U.S. Population, by Race and National Origin, 1820, 1870, 1920

SOURCE: U.S. Census, 1820, 1870, 1920.

between parents and children. Schools were often major culprits, championing the children and ignoring the parents, thereby increasing conflicts between parents and children and removing much of the influence parents had in ensuring their children's success in school. This was most pronounced among ethnic groups that did not maintain separate schools, that had less rigid religious and social norms, and in which the parents themselves had received very little education in their country of origin. Under the pressures of assimilation, traditional social controls were weakened, with an increase in gangs, crime, and other pathologies among immigrant youth. Other young immigrants became alienated from a school system that treated them as lesser Americans unless they conformed and achieved according to mainstream definitions of success. The drop-out rate among immigrant children was high; many left to work alongside their parents in factories or on farms (Olneck & Lazerson, 1980).

Despite the melting pot ideology, other groups were not given a chance to *melt*. Separated by their skin color and a 150-year legacy of slavery, African-Americans remained separate and, in the definitions of the mainstream culture, inferior. Prohibited from learning to read and write under slavery, African-Americans hungered for the chance to learn after Emancipation, but the complex web of restrictions and regulations in the South after the Civil War (restrictions later known as "Jim Crow") denied the newly-freed slaves their educational and occupational opportunities. Despite the promise of emancipation, black skin continued to be a badge of caste, associated now with poverty rather than with slavery; again laws and attitudes combined to deny black Americans their full place in society.

Other Americans, particularly the Indians and the original Hispanic residents of the Southwest, continued to be treated as vanquished peoples rather than as full citizens. Like African-Americans, though to a lesser degree, they were marked by skin color. Both groups continued to experience legal restrictions well into the twentieth century. American Indians were victimized by capricious treatment at the hands of federal authorities as reservations were established, moved, terminated, and reinstated. The Mexican settlers who became Americans involuntarily in the 1840s were often forced into farm labor; in the twentieth century, migrant work programs attracted additional agricultural laborers—both documented and undocumented—from Mexico, many of whom were sent back at the end of the growing season. Little effort was made to educate the children of the farm workers, who toiled alongside their parents, and long-standing residents of the United States lived in peril of deportation along with their temporary co-workers. Legal barriers, similar to Jim Crow, existed for Mexican-Americans in Texas and elsewhere (Gann & Duignan, 1986). Thus, for the enslaved and the vanquished—African-Americans, American Indians, and the initial Mexican-Americans—the norm in the nineteenth and early twentieth centuries was subjugation rather than assimilation. At the same time, segregation and discrimination allowed each of these groups to retain more aspects of their original culture than did many of the European immigrants, simply because, for racial and political reasons, they could not melt.

The mostly European immigration of the nineteenth century came to an end in the mid-1920s, when isolationist, anti-Jewish, and anti-Catholic sentiment resulted in a series of laws restricting immigration. Quotas were established, with the numbers reduced for those from *undesirable countries*. The definition of "undesirable" has changed greatly since the mid-1920s, depending in large part upon the demand from certain countries (by definition, a country which a large number of people wanting to leave was considered undesirable) and, in large part, from attitudes surrounding race and social class. During the 1930s and 1940s, quotas restricting the immigration of Jews from Central and Eastern Europe led to countless deaths in the Holocaust. Today, immigration laws waive quotas if a potential immigrant has a *well-founded fear of persecution* in his or her home country, but such laws to aid political and religious refugees have not been interpreted consistently, and have thus been a source of controversy. In any case, the attempt to restrict immigration, beginning with the Chinese Exclusion Act of 1882 and continuing through the 1920s and up to the present, itself underscores the failure of the melting pot model.

❖ Immigration in the Twentieth Century

Latin-American Immigration

Mexico. As the doors of the United States closed to European immigrants in the 1920s, a new wave of immigration began along the country's southern border. After the Treaty of Guadalupe-Hidalgo in 1848, Mexicans crossed back and forth to reunite with families and to find work (Gann & Duignan, 1986). According to the 1910 Census, only 221,915 United States residents were born in Mexico; another 162,959 were born in the United States of Mexican parentage (U.S. Census-A, 1910). During the 1910s and 1920s, immigration increased significantly, the result of revolution and political instability in Mexico as well as the

Immigration has brought increased diversity to urban schools.

availability of agricultural jobs in the southwestern United States (Takaki, 1993). The border remained relatively open throughout the 1920s despite the formation of the Border Patrol in 1924. Both single men and entire families crossed in search of work on farms and in urban factories (Gann & Duignan, 1986).

In 1930, the population of Mexican-born Americans reached a peak, as 498,900 immigrants in the previous ten years raised the total to 641,462 (U.S. Census-A, 1920-1930). The Great Depression, the influx of dispossessed American farmers into migrant labor, and increased enforcement of immigration laws reduced the number of Mexican-born residents counted in the 1940 Census to 374,433 (Kerr, 1992; U.S. Census-A, 1940). Not until 1960 did the Mexican-born population exceed 1930 levels (Kerr, 1992; U.S. Census-A, 1950-1960). However, the 1970s and 1980s saw renewed heavy immigration from Mexico. Between 1971 and 1980, 637,200 Mexicans came to the United States according to the Immigration and Naturalization Service, and between 1981 and 1990 the number of immigrants rose to 1,653,300 (Immigration and Naturalization Service, 1970–1990).

A steadier and more dramatic increase has been reported in the American-born population of Mexican heritage—that is, second, third, fourth, and fifth generation Mexican-Americans. Until 1920, that number was smaller than the Mexican-born population (U.S. Census-A, 1820–1920). By 1960, it had exceeded 1.5 million (U.S. Census-A, 1960). Today, there are approximately 13.5 million Americans of Mexican heritage, both Mexican- and American-born (U.S. Census-A, 1990).

While it is clear that the Mexican-American population has grown enormously through immigration and natural increase, Census figures, especially before 1980, have been less than reliable (Bean & Tienda, 1987). Much of the undercounting was due to the nature of the immigration, specifically, the large number of immigrants from Mexico who came without documentation. Although the immigrants' United States-born children automatically became United States citizens, fear of deportation led many Mexican immigrants and their families to avoid Census takers as well as any other governmental agency. In fact, attempts to deport undocumented workers alternately peaked and declined at various times during the first half of the century (Gann & Duignan, 1986; Takaki, 1993). In the 1930s and early 1940s, deportations averaged twelve thousand per year (Gann & Duignan, 1986). That number increased steadily into the 1950s; in 1954, more than one million Mexican immigrants were deported (Gann & Duignan, 1986). To underscore the degree of undercounting in the Census, the number of Mexican immigrants deported in 1954 was more than twice the number of Mexican immigrants reported in the United States in 1950 (Gann & Duignan, 1986; U.S. Census-A, 1950). Conversely, the 1986 Immigration Reform and Control Act, which offered amnesty and a path to citizenship for undocumented immigrants arriving before 1982, led many Mexican immigrants to declare themselves and their families for the first time.

The issue of *illegal immigration*, especially in the context of immigrants from Mexico and elsewhere in Latin America, has been a source of controversy. The terminology itself is highly charged, as many have questioned the laws and procedures that have been used to exclude immigrants from Latin America (Bean & Tienda, 1987). Furthermore, the specter of illegality has been used to discriminate against and stereotype all Mexican-Americans (and other Latinos), including those whose families have lived in the United States for many generations (Shorris, 1992). Although laws and court decisions have guaranteed certain rights to all immigrants regardless of their legal status, such as the right to attend public schools and to take advantage of those schools' free lunch programs, fear, ignorance, and prejudice surrounding the issue of illegal immigration have combined to prevent immigrants from taking full advantage of those rights (Suarez-Orozco, 1989).

Deportations aside, Mexican immigrants have had a high rate of emigration—leaving the United States for Mexico—as well as immigration. In this respect, they have differed from earlier immigrants from Europe, Africa, or Asia, who could not return easily, or at all. Although assimilation has taken place with successive generations, Mexican-Americans' ties to their country of origin have remained stronger. Frequent crossings, both to visit and to live, have led many analysts to speak of a "porous frontier" (Gann & Duignan, 1986, p. 127). This has also helped Mexican-Americans to retain more of their language and culture at the same time as it has created unique strains between generations. Whereas European immigrant children often rejected their parents' culture in the process of assimilation, children of Mexican immigrants tend to develop for themselves a bicultural identity. Ambivalence and conflict are natural components of this process, especially during the adolescent years.

In the early twentieth century, most Americans of Mexican heritage lived in rural areas of Texas, New Mexico, Arizona, and California. Texas and California attracted migrant agricultural workers, some of whom then took jobs elsewhere in the Midwest and West. Small urban barrios emerged in Los Angeles, Chicago, Houston, and other cities. This process of urbanization accelerated after 1950. Although Mexican-Americans have the lowest rate of urbanization among Latinos, three-quarters of United States residents of Mexican heritage lived in urban areas by 1960, most of them in the Southwest. Today, approximately 80 percent of Mexican-Americans live in metropolitan areas (Bean & Tienda, 1987).

Puerto Rico. Behind Mexican-Americans, the second highest percentage of Latinos in the United States are of Puerto Rican heritage (Figure 2–6). Puerto Ricans in the United States are not immigrants, but rather internal migrants. They became part of the United States when Spain ceded the island of Puerto Rico at the end of the Spanish-American War and were

---

FIGURE 2–6 National/Ethic Origins of Latinos, 1990

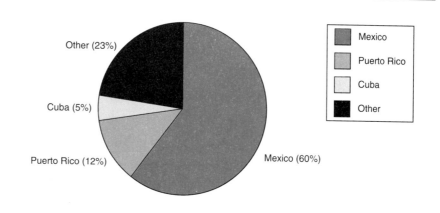

Other (23%)

Cuba (5%)

Puerto Rico (12%)

Mexico (60%)

Legend:
- Mexico
- Puerto Rico
- Cuba
- Other

SOURCE: U.S. Census, 1990.

granted citizenship in 1917. Puerto Ricans enjoy all the rights of United States citizens, including the right to vote and full access to government programs and benefits. Despite their legal status, few Puerto Ricans came to the mainland until the mid-1940s, when cheap air fares from the island to New York City became available and industries in the Northeast offered employment (Fitzpatrick, 1980). This migration has increased steadily; the 1990 Census reported 2,728,000 Puerto Ricans living on the mainland, most of whom are concentrated in New York City and other cities in the Northeast (U.S. Census-A, 1990). A substantial number of Puerto Ricans live in Chicago, Washington, D.C., and Miami as well.

Like immigrants from Mexico, internal migrants from Puerto Rico retain close ties to their land of origin. Air travel allows frequent visits, and many Puerto Ricans return to the island to retire. In some cases, parents in the United States send troubled children to relatives on the island, hoping that a slower pace and more rural lifestyle will salvage their youngsters. As a result of urban concentration and ties to the island, migrants from Puerto Rico continue to speak Spanish, even as their children and grandchildren learn English and forget their native language. Nevertheless, second and third generation mainland residents have adapted a bicultural identity to their own personal experiences (Fitzpatrick, 1980). A complicating factor in this process is race, for slavery existed in Puerto Rico, Cuba, and the other islands of the West Indies. Many of the islands' residents are black or of mixed race (including Indian), and while there is relatively little racial prejudice in Puerto Rico, black Puerto Ricans on the mainland have faced problems not experienced by their lighter-skinned counterparts (Fitzpatrick, 1980).

Cuba. Cuban-Americans comprise the third largest Latino group. Like Puerto Rico, Cuba became a United States territory in 1898 at the end of the Spanish-American War, but the island gained its independence in 1936. Until 1960, fewer than 100,000 Cubans lived in the United States, although relations between the island nation and its neighbor to the north remained close (U.S. Census-A, 1960). All this changed in 1959, when revolutionaries led by Fidel Castro overthrew the Batista dictatorship. Between 1959 and 1962, over 155,000 Cubans came to the United States; most were well-to-do professionals, businesspeople, and government officials (Perez, 1980). Because of American hostility to the revolutionary government, the new arrivals received refugee status. This facilitated their integration into American society, though few first generation immigrants achieved the status they had enjoyed in Cuba. Despite the suspension of air travel to Cuba between 1962 and 1965, more that thirty-thousand Cubans arrived in those years, mostly through third countries (Perez, 1980). A United States-sponsored airlift between 1965 and 1972 brought in an additional 257,000 Cubans (Perez, 1980). Most of those arriving between 1962 and 1972 were a notch below their predecessors in terms of class background; they included skilled workers, shopkeepers, and middle-class professionals who had become disillusioned with Castro's rule (Perez, 1980; Gann & Duignan, 1986). Then, in 1980, the Mariel boatlift brought in more than 125,000 Cubans; among them were political prisoners, common criminals expelled by Castro, and the urban and rural poor. In contrast to previous immigrants, most of whom considered themselves white, a greater proportion of these Cubans were black (Shorris, 1992). Despite the improved race relations in Cuba under Castro and despite black Cubans' fears of discrimination in the United States, persistent economic hardship and the oppressiveness of Castro's increasingly closed regime drove many black Cubans to seek asylum in the United States.

The first wave of Cuban immigrants, those who arrived before 1972, settled primarily in Miami, though some migrated as far north as New Jersey. They formed political committees and prepared themselves for Castro's imminent downfall and their return. Although they could not go back and forth like their Mexican-American and Puerto Rican counterparts, Cuban Americans retained their language and culture along with their hopes for returning to their homeland. In this sense, the first generation of pre-1972 immigrants fit the description of an exile population (Perez, 1980). Their children and grandchildren, however, do not maintain the same ties to Cuba, nor do they share their elders' political passions (Perez, 1980). Many have assimilated fully into American society, while others maintain some aspects of their Cuban heritage. Though some were incarcerated in remote detention camps for months, the 1980 immigrants mainly settled in already-established Cuban communities. There, racial and class divisions have combined with the problems common to all new immigrants—language barriers, unfamiliarity with mainstream culture, and lack of appropriate job skills—to limit their economic success as well as their integration into American society (Gann & Duignan, 1986). The 1980 Mariel refugees also had to contend with negative images associated with the small number of criminals whom Castro sent to the United States along with the more than 100,000 individuals and families who sought to escape increasing poverty and political repression on the island.

Dominican Republic. Although relatively small in numbers, Dominican-Americans are a highly concentrated and visible population in New York City and in smaller cities in the Northeast. The first Dominicans came to the United States in the 1940s and 1950s; most were upper middle-class intellectuals who opposed the Trujillo dictatorship. Political instability in the 1960s brought more immigrants, but the major influx has been in the 1980s, the result of economic hardship. Dominican immigration has followed the pattern of chain migration, in which family members and fellow townspeople follow an earlier immigrant to the new community (Hendricks, 1980). In New York City, individual apartment buildings can be inhabited by residents of a single village in the Dominican Republic. Relatively recent immigrants, Dominicans have remained in their close-knit communities and have integrated little into the mainstream. Racially (and in many aspects, culturally) similar to Puerto Ricans, they are often mistaken for Puerto Ricans (Hendricks, 1980). According to the 1990 Census, approximately 250,000 Dominicans live in the United States (U.S. Census-A, 1990). Taking into account undocumented immigrants, independent observers estimate the number at more than double the official figure. More than 400,000 Dominicans are said to be living in New York City alone (Rimer, 1991).

Central and South America. Throughout the century, small numbers of Central and South Americans have made their way to the United States, many in search of employment opportunities, others seeking refuge from violence or political oppression at home. Each country has had its own pattern of migration. Those from Argentina, Bolivia, Chile, and Peru have tended to locate in California, while Venezuelans and Uruguayans have settled in Miami (Bean & Tienda, 1987). Still, immigrants from those countries, as well as from the rest of Central and South America, are more widely dispersed than other Latino groups. On the whole, Central and South Americans are more diverse in terms of education, background, occupation, and income. Many are highly-educated professionals (Orlov & Ueda, 1980).

In the 1980s, the United States experienced a dramatic and controversial immigration from Guatemala, El Salvador, and Nicaragua. Political violence in each of those countries propelled an undetermined number of refugees northward, via Mexico. Estimates range from a total of 200,000 to more than one million, most of whom were undocumented and faced deportation if caught (Shorris, 1992; Zolberg, Suhrike, & Asuayo, 1987). They came at a time when the United States sought to tighten immigration restrictions; although the Refugee Act of 1980 offered asylum to those with

a well-founded fear of persecution, the law has been applied inconsistently (Shorris, 1992). United States authorities have claimed that the immigrants left their homelands because of economic hardship rather than political persecution. The immigrants and their advocates, many of whom are
affiliated with churches, have pointed out that, in countries where tens of
thousands had already been murdered by *death squads*, deportation meant
certain death (Ferris, 1987). Nicaraguan refugees, fleeing a leftist government, have received better treatment than Salvadorans and Guatemalans,
whose right-wing governments rely upon United States support. Even so,
more than half of the Nicaraguan refugees who have applied have been
denied asylum (Zolberg, Suhrik, & Asuayo, 1987). All segments of society,
from wealthy businessmen and professionals to landless peasants, have
been represented. Among the immigrants are Mayan Indians, people of
European descent, and those of mixed European and Indian heritage, who
comprise the majority of Central Americans (Shorris, 1992). Almost all of
the Central American immigrants have settled in cities throughout the
United States, with particular concentrations in Miami (Nicaraguans),
Washington, D.C. (Salvadorans), Chicago (Salvadorans), New York City,
Houston, Los Angeles, and San Francisco (all groups). However, some of
the immigrants, Guatemalan Indians in particular, have become migrant
farm workers (Ashabranner, 1985).

SPECIAL BOX 2–1

Latinos in the U.S. today are a very diverse group. There is no one single
Latino culture, but a mosaic of cultures that reflect the origin and experiences
of each individual. Some of the issues that distinguish and divide Latinos are
as follows:

- national origin: including whether or not the individual was born in the
  U.S.
- generational status: whether the individual is first, second, third, fourth,
  or fifth generation, and the degree of acculturation experienced with
  each generation.
- race: Most Mexicans and Central and South Americans are *mestizo*, of
  mixed European and Indian heritage. Latinos from the Caribbean
  (Puerto Ricans, Cubans, and Dominicans), where slavery existed for
  more than two centuries, may be of African, Indian, European, or
  mixed heritage. In most Latin-American countries, light skin is seen as
  more desirable; however, racial prejudice in Puerto Rico and post-rev-
  olutionary Cuba is considered less strong than in the United States.
- reason for arrival: for specific job opportunities, to escape severe economic hardship, or to flee political violence and oppression.

■ legal status: Puerto Ricans are automatically United States citizens, as are all U.S.-born children of immigrants. Immigrants married to U.S. citizens are entitled to permanent residence, and legal residence is granted to all immigrants who have specific jobs that cannot be filled by United States citizens. Due to the political situation in their countries, Cubans and many Nicaraguans have been granted permanent residence. In addition, the 1986 Immigration Reform and Control Act provides amnesty, legal residence *(a green card),* and a path to citizenship for all immigrants arriving before 1982. However, many immigrants from Latin America remain in the U.S. illegally and live in fear of deportation.

■ ties to country of origin: whether there is extensive travel back and forth, whether the immigrants are in exile, but hold out hopes of returning one day, or whether immigrants are unable, or unwilling, to return.

■ amount of time in the United States.

■ political alliances and agendas: Cuban immigrants have been active in anti-Communist causes and in promoting United States opposition to Castro's regime. Mexican-Americans have been instrumental in the formation of the United Farm Workers and other unions to protect workers in industries in which they have concentrated. Efforts to reform immigration laws have been made in the context of the recent flood of refugees from Central America.

■ socioeconomic status and levels of education in the country of origin.

■ socioeconomic status and levels of education in the United States.

■ rural or urban background of the immigrants.

■ residence patterns in the United States: whether the group has settled in rural or urban areas and whether urban life represents a transition for the immigrants and their families; also where immigrants have chosen to live and the extent of concentration in ethnic communities.

■ occupational patterns in the United States: whether the immigrants are able to pursue the same occupations and achieve the same socioeconomic status in the United States (rare among upper- and middle-class immigrants, with the exception of professionals pursuing specific job opportunities), the degree of concentration in certain occupations (such as migrant farm work), and whether the children pursue occupations similar to those of their parents in the United States.

Asian Immigration

Asia has been a second major source of immigrants to the United States in the twentieth century. Prior to 1947, relatively few Chinese—on average, about two thousand per year—were admitted; most of these were wives and children of men already in the United States (Lai, 1980). Japanese immigrants continued to arrive until the 1924 Immigrant Exclusion Act.

A revision in immigration laws precipitated the most recent immigration from Asia. The Immigration Act of 1965 relaxed national quotas and permitted family members and skilled workers to enter irrespective of the quotas (Figure 2–7).

The Philippines. Immigrants from the Philippines have been the largest beneficiaries of the new policy. Like Cuba and Puerto Rico, the Philippines became part of the United States after 1898. Although it too received its independence in the 1930s, the United States established an

FIGURE 2–7 American Immigration, 1980–1990

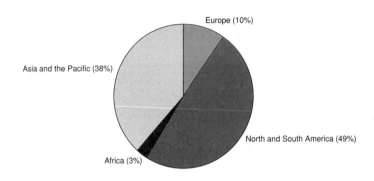

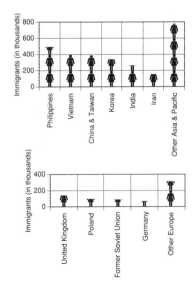

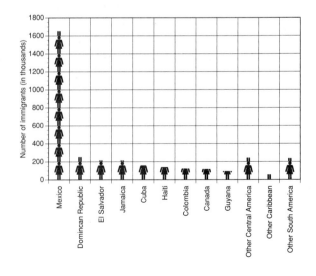

SOURCE: U.S. Census, 1990.

educational system, instituted English as an official language, and constructed military bases. After World War II, many Filipina women married United States servicemen; when they came to the United States, they brought their extended families (Chan, 1991). An oversupply of highly-trained professionals, technicians, and skilled workers has led millions of Filipinos to emigrate throughout the world in search of work (Chan, 1991). Approximately one million have come to the United States, where they have tended toward the health-care professions (Chan, 1991). Today, a nursing shortage in the United States continues to attract many Filipinos, who are leaving behind not only a shortage of good jobs in their own country, but also continuing political unrest related to the fall of dictator Ferdinand Marcos (Chan, 1991).

Filipino immigrants have enjoyed many advantages not shared by other immigrant groups. Though many speak Tagalog or other island languages as their first language, they are fluent in English and have had contact with American culture before their arrival. Because of the extensive cultural contact, Filipinos have had very little trouble assimilating into American society. Most are educated in a trade or profession and arrive with specific employment opportunities. While not wealthy, the majority of Filipino immigrants and their children are at least middle-class or lower middle-class. Because of their skills and ability to go where the jobs are, Filipinos are dispersed throughout the United States, though California has attracted the largest number (Chan, 1991). Most Filipinos live in metropolitan areas, in suburbs as well as cities. Like the Japanese, they have a relatively high rate of intermarriage (Chan, 1991; Lee, 1991). At the same time, Filipino immigrants often send money home to relatives, and, despite high air fares, visit when possible.

Korea. Frustrated by employment opportunities in their own country, 646,600 Koreans have come to the United States between 1961 and 1990 (U.S. Census-A, 1960–1990). The close ties between Korea and the United States since the end of World War II and the Korean War have made the United States an attractive magnet for those seeking a better life. Many of the first migrants were, in fact, Protestants educated in American missionary schools (Kim, 1980). Well educated and with strong religious beliefs and family and community bonds, the Koreans have concentrated in cities such as Los Angeles or New York, where many have succeeded in small businesses (Lee, 1991). By forming mutual credit associations and pooling their resources, first generation Korean-Americans have bypassed banks in forming their businesses (Chira, 1990). While some of the businesses have failed, the Korean immigrants have demonstrated their willingness to work long hours as a family unit to attain success.

Despite their economic gains, Korean immigrants have assimilated little. Their close-knit communities and overwhelming presence in inner-city businesses have made them the targets of hostility from other minority groups. Long hours of hard work make it difficult for the newcomers to learn English well (Chira, 1990). Many of the burdens of assimilation have been borne by the children of the immigrants, who must reconcile their parents' culture and beliefs with new opportunities and realities. Many immigrants have encouraged their children to enter highly skilled and lucrative professions, but often the educational and job opportunities take second generation Korean-Americans far from home and community (Lee, 1991).

China, Hong Kong, and Taiwan. Chinese from mainland China, Hong Kong, and Taiwan are another highly visible group of Asian immigrants. With Chinese communities that have existed for almost a century, family reunification has been an important motive for immigration. More recently, the Communist Revolution in 1949, and the overcrowding and economic hardship in Taiwan and Hong Kong, where many anti-Communist residents of China fled, and the prospect of Hong Kong's merger with China have brought 800,000 Chinese to the United States between 1947 and 1990 (U.S. Census-A, 1940–1990). Recent immigrants join the estimated 1,645,000 second, third, fourth, and fifth generation Chinese-Americans (U.S. Census-A, 1990). Despite the stereotype of Chinese-Americans as small businesspeople and scientists, they work in a wide variety of occupations and inhabit all socioeconomic levels. Like the Jewish immigrants of the late nineteenth century, many recent Chinese arrivals work in crowded, underpaid, and often illegal textile factories owned by earlier groups of immigrants (Reid, 1986). Chinese- Americans have concentrated in cities, principally San Francisco and New York, but later generations are as likely to reside in suburbs and to be dispersed throughout the country. The assimilation of later generations adds another level of diversity to an immigrant population whose pre-arrival backgrounds and experiences may vary greatly.

Asian Indians. One of the fastest-growing Asian-American groups in the 1980s was Asian Indians. Between 1961 and 1980, 208,000 Asian Indians arrived in the United States; the 1980s saw 262,000 new immigrants (U.S. Census-A, 1960–1990). Though India's ties have been closer to Great Britain than to the United States, a common language has facilitated the immigration process. Most of the Asian Indians who have come to the United States are urban and college educated; they have taken jobs in universities, hospitals, and corporations (Jensen, 1980). Initially, most of the immigrants congregated in the New York metropolitan area, but many have dispersed to other cities and suburbs (Jensen, 1980). Most of the immigrants are Hindu or Sikh, but assimilation has taken its toll on religious life and particularly upon marriage customs. Second generation Asian Indians have insisted upon choosing their own partners, and intermarriage is a source of conflict within families and communities (Jensen, 1980).

Pacific Islanders. Since the 1970s, a relatively small but highly concentrated migration of Pacific Islanders—particularly from American Samoa and Guam—has affected urban communities in California, Hawaii,

Oregon, and Washington State (Shore, 1980). This migration was precipitated by poor economic conditions and followed the chain migration pattern. Like Puerto Ricans, the migrants are United States citizens; however, a lack of knowledge about the background and culture of Pacific Islanders has led to mislabeling and stereotypes. At the same time, the Pacific Islanders have had a difficult time adapting to urban life. In contrast to the immigrants from East and South Asia, they are a rural people, with strong ties to extended family and traditional villages (Shore, 1980). Many of the problems faced by Pacific Islanders parallel those faced by American Indians who leave the reservation for life in the city.

Southeast Asia. Since 1975, the single fastest-growing group of Asian-American immigrants has been refugees from war-torn Southeast Asia. More than 870,000 people from Vietnam, Cambodia, and Laos have entered the United States between 1975 and 1990 (U.S. Census-A, 1970–1990). Though virtually all have escaped war and brutal political violence and have received refugee status in the United States, the similarities end there. When South Vietnam fell in 1975, approximately 130,000 entered via processing stations in Guam and the Philippines (Wright, 1980). Many of the first refugees were well-placed government officials, members of the military, and their families. They were disproportionately urban, Catholic, and educated, though only one-fifth had attended university (Wright, 1980) Their previous contact with Americans and American culture facilitated their adaptation, but many had difficulty adjusting to decreased job opportunities and a lower standard of living, as well as Americans' ambivalence to the war.

A second wave of immigrants came from refugee camps in Thailand and elsewhere. Among these refugees were additional Vietnamese, Cambodians, and Laotian ethnics, such as the Hmong (Nahme-Huang, 1989; Chan, 1991). Having witnessed unspeakable acts of political violence, endured tremendous hardship en route, and spent years in limbo in refugee camps in Thailand and elsewhere, these immigrants suffered varying degrees of trauma that have impeded their adjustment to American society. Most had minimal contact with American culture before their arrival. Language barriers and differences in religious beliefs and cultural practices have led to serious misunderstandings (Nahme-Huang, 1989). Some Cambodians and Vietnamese were highly educated professionals who have experienced downward mobility; others, such as the Hmong, were rural people with little education and few job skills. Some of the immigrants were unaccompanied minors, mostly teenage boys, who were placed with foster families (Nahme-Huang, 1989; Ashabranner & Ashabranner, 1987). In the late 1980s, negotiations between the United States and Vietnam led to the arrival of several thousand Amerasian teenagers—wartime children of Vietnamese mothers and American fathers—who had generally grown up in poor, rural areas, where they had received little education and were shunned by their

Vietnamese peers (Nahme-Huang, 1989). Because many refugees still remain in camps in Southeast Asia and because of better relations between the governments of the United States and Vietnam, Southeast Asians will continue to migrate to the United States in coming years to be reunited with families already here.

As refugees, the Southeast Asian immigrants received minimal government benefits until they found jobs. Children and teenagers entered the public schools, where they have learned English and come into contact with the diverse cultures in the neighborhoods in which they lived. While some 40 percent settled in California, others were sent to rural areas, towns, and cities throughout the country. Texas, Minnesota, Wisconsin, Oregon, and Pennsylvania are some of the states with concentrations of Southeast Asian refugees (Chan, 1991). In some cases, the refugees were greeted with hostility by the surrounding community, which interpreted the benefits as favoritism. Lingering hatreds associated with the Vietnam War and with the *secret war* in Laos involving the Hmong have contributed to ignorance and suspicion of the new arrivals. In other cases, refugees have moved to be with others who share their religion, culture, and experiences. There is some evidence that both white and minority youth have singled out Southeast Asian children and teenagers for persecution, thus perpetuating the traumas they and their elders have experienced (Nahme-Huang, 1989)

Other Immigrants

In the 1980s immigrants came to the United States from a variety of other places—Eastern Europe, Ireland, Africa, the Middle East, and elsewhere. Another significant migration came from the English- and French-speaking Caribbean. Since the late nineteenth century, a small number of black Americans came from Jamaica, Barbados, Trinidad and Tobago, Grenada, St. Lucia, St. Kitts, and other English-speaking islands in the West Indies. This immigration has increased in the last few decades. Between 1961 and 1990, about 600,000 new United States residents arrived from the English-speaking Caribbean (U.S. Census-A. 1960–1990). African-Americans from the West Indies have experienced a different history from those in the United States. While slavery occurred in the West Indies, the slaves gained their freedom earlier and, in the absence of Jim Crow laws and other restrictions, many more had the opportunity to own land and receive an education. Despite economic and political problems in Jamaica, Grenada, and other countries, many of the immigrants are well-educated, middle-class people who have come to the United States for greater economic opportunities (Ueda, 1980). A number of today's African-American business and political leaders trace their heritage to the West Indies (Ueda, 1980). Other West Indian immigrants, however, have experienced poverty and inadequate schooling in

SPECIAL BOX 2–2

The principal stereotype of Asian-Americans is that of the *model minority*." Asian-American children, it is believed, are always punctual, bright, hard-working, obedient, and especially good in math and science. Asian-American adults achieve success in scientific and technical fields or in business. The model minority thesis posits that Asian-American families are always strong, organized in a strict age-based hierarchy, and rarely in need of psychological or social services. This stereotype, though a positive one, ignores the differences among individual Asian-Americans, their families, and their communities; it also implicitly condemns anyone who does not conform. The following are some issues that will help us look beyond the stereotype of the model minority to understand the reality of each Asian-American:

- individual variations in temperament, interests, and ability.
- background in the country of origin: which country (including any third countries in which the immigrant may have lived), how much education was available to the immigrant, the immigrant's social class, and whether the immigrant's previous experience was urban or rural. Some immigrants endured a great deal of dislocation, violence, and trauma before their arrival in the U.S.
- reasons for immigration: for specific professional opportunities, for non-specific opportunities, such as the possibility of one day starting a business, for economic survival, or to escape political violence.
- time that the individual family has spent in the United States: Many children of Chinese and Japanese heritage are now fifth generation Americans while others are arriving daily.
- generational issues surrounding acculturation: Many Asian cultures emphasize respect for one's elders. This pattern comes under challenge in the United States through the peer group, mass culture, and in the schools. Children who must act as their parents' interpreters also gain a measure of power. Among assimilated Asian-Americans, the issue of intermarriage has become significant and, in many cultures, divisive. In any case, second, third, fourth, and fifth generation Asian-Americans must develop an identity that balances two cultures.
- residence patterns in the United States: whether in a self-contained Asian-American community, in predominantly white areas, or in neighborhoods with other people of color.

their countries of origin, and their Creole-influenced English has been a barrier rather than an asset in their new home (Sontag, 1992).

Although Haiti gained its independence from France after a slave revolt in 1803, the country has suffered greatly in recent years. For decades, Haitians chafed under the brutal and corrupt dictatorship of the Duvalier family. "Baby Doc" Duvalier's fall in 1989 led to instability and violence as his supporters fought reform. In addition, overcrowding and few resources have given the island nation the lowest per capita standard of living in the Western Hemisphere. It is estimated that more than one million Haitians have fled, with hundreds of thousands of those coming to the United States, mostly in rickety boats (Dreyfuss, 1993). The United States has rarely offered asylum. Many Haitians have been deported; untold others live invisible lives as illegal aliens in inner cities all over the country. Miami and New York are believed to have the largest Haitian populations (Dreyfuss, 1993). Predominantly Creole-speaking (though middle-class Haitians also speak French), the Haitian immigrants come from all levels of society. Some have university educations; others are barely literate. Immigrants from Haiti have encountered hostility among virtually all segments of American society. Haitian-American leaders have charged that the new immigrants receive worse treatment because they are black. On the other hand, African-Americans have at times objected to the newcomers, fearing competition for ever-scarcer jobs and resources (Portes & Stepick, 1993).

Like all immigrants to the United States, the most recent immigrants are disproportionately young. The median age of Mexican-Americans, Puerto Ricans, and Southeast Asian refugees is twenty-five years; for the population as a whole it is thirty-three (Bean & Tienda, 1987; Chan, 1991). Several factors may account for a relatively young immigrant population. One is the tendency for single young men to emigrate; in the case of some Southeast Asians and Central Americans, this has included unaccompanied minors (Ashabranner & Ashabranner, 1987). Families with young children tend to migrate, seeking educational opportunities and a better life for their children (Takaki, 1993). Finally, the birth rate for many immigrant groups is substantially higher than the national average, especially for those with rural origins. Poverty also tends to raise the birth rate, both in the country of origin and in the United States. As an example of the latter two factors—poverty and rural origins—the mostly urban, middle-class Cuban immigrants have a birth rate far lower than poor and rural immigrants from Mexico and elsewhere in Latin America (Bean & Tienda, 1987).

In the previous century, many immigrant children did not attend or complete school. Child labor was widespread, and jobs existed for those with little education. Today, all children, including those without legal documents, are required in most states to attend school until the age of sixteen, and education had become much more important in determining a young person's future employment opportunities. As a result, children of color, and immigrant children in particular, are disproportionately represented among America's schoolchildren. While African-Americans comprised 12.1 percent of the United States population in 1990, they comprised 15 percent of the nation's school-age population (U.S. Census-A, 1990). Latinos comprised 9 percent of the total population and 11.9 percent of the school-age population (U.S. Census-A, 1990). Asian-Americans, 2.9 percent of the total population, were 3.3 percent of the school-age population, and American Indians comprised 1.1 percent of the school-age population despite being only 0.8 percent of the total population (U.S. Census-A, 1990).

❖ Internal Migration

The migration of African-Americans from the South to the cities of the Northeast, Midwest, and Far West has been one of the greatest population shifts in the history of the United States. In 1900, as in all the years since 1790, more than 90 percent of all African-Americans lived in the South, with most of those in the rural South (U.S. Census-A, 1790–1940). Between 1900 and 1940, the migration north was gradual. African-American communities, segregated by race but integrated in terms of social class, developed in New York, Philadelphia, Chicago, Detroit, Cleveland, and other cities of the Northeast and Midwest. The migration accelerated after 1940, when wartime industries expanded, creating new employment opportunities (Takaki, 1993).

For African-Americans in the rural South, migration north had its allure. Despite the promise of Reconstruction, life after slavery continued to be insecure and harsh. The white power structure soon reasserted itself as former slaves found themselves working the same lands, but now as sharecroppers, and eternally in debt. Although parents sought for their children the education they were denied on the plantation, few schools existed, and children were often forced to work in the fields alongside their parents (Takaki, 1993). Even when African-American children could attend school, those schools started after the harvest was finished and ended before planting began. The curriculum provided an inferior education, suitable, school officials argued, for the students' probable station in life. The 1896 Supreme Court decision *Plessy v. Ferguson* legalized the segregation of schools and other facilities based upon race. Jim Crow laws in the South placed a number of other restrictions upon African-Americans and denied them the equal protection of the law. Fear and, injustice ruled the lives of most African-Americans in the South and, when opportunities arose, that fear urged them northward (Takaki, 1993).

By 1980, only 53 percent of African-Americans remained in the South, a number that held steady in the next decade (U.S. Census-A, 1980–1990). For a variety of reasons, the urban North began to lose its attraction. The *Brown v. Board of Education* (1954) decision and the Civil Rights movement of the 1960s ended legalized segregation in the South. The political and economic situation of African-Americans in the South improved as educational and job opportunities opened up (Bodovitz, 1991). Educated African-Americans flocked to southern cities such as Atlanta, where they took professional and managerial jobs in a revitalized, more tolerant *New South*. Cases of overt violence and discrimination decreased, and a new generation of African-American political leaders emerged.

As conditions in the South improved for African-Americans, conditions in the large cities of the north worsened. The slow shutdown of industries in the *Rust Belt* deprived less well-educated factory workers of their livelihoods. Workers of all races and ethnic groups suffered, but the impact upon class-integrated and self-reliant African-American communities was devastating. With the least seniority, African-American workers were the first to lose their jobs. Many women were forced onto the public assistance rolls because their husbands could no longer support them and their families (Takaki, 1993; Wilson, 1987).

At the same time, other city dwellers, principally members of other immigrant groups, began to move to the suburbs. The rise in construction after World War II, coupled with the *Baby Boom*, led many young families out of the city into homogeneous planned communities. Many of those communities specifically excluded African-Americans; others did so in more subtle ways. Cities lost their tax base and much of their diversity (Massey & Denton, 1993). Ironically, inner city schools across the Northeast, Midwest, and West Coast became as segregated and underfunded as those in the South before the 1954 *Brown v. Board of Education* decision (Kozol, 1991). With the flood of immigrants to America's cities, diversity has once again increased, but all city dwellers—whites, African-Americans, Puerto Ricans, and recent immigrants—face the same problems: an eroded tax base, a decline in city services, and a high proportion of residents in need of services.

Since 1980, many African-Americans have themselves abandoned the inner cities, not for a return to the South, but for the same type of class-segregated suburbs favored by their white counterparts. Whereas middle-class African-Americans formerly lived in Harlem, Chicago's South Side, and other urban neighborhoods along with their less well-off brethren, today's business leaders and professionals live either alongside white suburbanites of similar status or in suburbs that are predominantly African-American (Bodovitz, 1991). Various communities in Prince Georges County, Maryland are examples of the latter trend, as prosperous African-Americans seek neighborhoods free of racial tension and school districts ready to welcome their children with a more inclusive curriculum (Dent, 1992). Lower middle-class and working-class African-Americans, Latinos, and Asian-Americans have also moved to the suburbs in search of personal safety, better schools, and job opportunities in corporations and service industries that are located in the suburbs. In many cases, individual suburban communities have become quite segregated by race and ethnicity (Massey & Denton, 1993). Moving to a suburban community with others of the same heritage has become one step in the assimilation process for many immigrant groups. Today, one can find suburban towns that are almost exclusively Filipino-American, Cuban-American, Mexican-American, or Puerto Rican. Other immigrants and their descendents have dispersed to suburbs throughout the country as they become acculturated and economically secure.

In the past century, the United States has become a much more mobile nation in general. Air travel has made it possible for Puerto Ricans to move to the mainland, for Americans on the mainland to move from one region to another, and for newcomers to arrive from distant lands. Today, even the most isolated, homogeneous locale can experience the influx of any racial or immigrant group for any reason. For instance, dozens of Guatemalan Maya Indian refugees came to a predominantly white Florida town because its name was Indiantown and the refugees thought they would be welcome there (for the most part, they were.) (Ashabranner, 1985). During the 1980s, the United States government resettled thousands of Cambodian and Hmong refugees in rural areas of Wisconsin, Minnesota, Oregon, and other states. An upstate New York suburb, which a local columnist nicknamed "Velveetaland" for its bland homogeniety, has become home in the 1990s to a number of Pakistani immigrant families, the result of chain migration. Those who come through chain migration may work in a single industry (examples include farm workers, cannery workers, and fishermen) or in a variety of fields, including professional occupations.

❖ The Future

Using current rates of immigration and natural increase, scholars have estimated that the population of the United States will become increasingly diverse in the next century. The United States Census recently projected that between 1990 and 2025 the white population will grow 25 percent (Cortes, 1991). Because the African-American population is on average younger than the white population, its rate of increase for the same period is projected to be 67 percent (Cortes, 1991). The Asian-American and American Indian population is projected to grow 79 percent, and the Latino population is projected to increase 187 percent (Cortes, 1991). With its population almost tripling in the next forty years, Latinos will comprise 24 percent of the United States population, according to the Census (Cortes, 1991). African-Americans will comprise 15 percent of the total, and Asian-Americans 12 percent (Cortes, 1991). Including a small but growing percentage of American Indians, almost 50 percent of the nation will be composed of people of color (Cortes, 1991).

A complicating factor in this equation, however, is that of intermarriage. Several immigrant groups, most prominently Japanese-Americans, have high rates of intermarriage in subsequent generations. In the future, increasing numbers of Americans may trace their roots to more than one

SPECIAL BOX 2–3

In recent years, many Asian children, predominantly those of Korean heritage, have been adopted by middle-class Caucasian families. Estimates are that forty thousand children have come to the United States in this way. A smaller number of adoptees have come from Latin America. Some of the children have been adopted at birth, but a larger number have come from foster homes or orphanages in their country of origin, placed there while the paperwork was processed. Other children were given up for adoption in their preschool years because of economic hardship or neglect. These children are part of interracial families in which they may or may not be taught their heritage. In general, they are more assimilated than the children of immigrants from Asia, but they will have unanswered questions about who they are and from where they came.

group. Today's Census does not provide for residents to indicate a mixed heritage, but that is certain to change. Intermarriage also poses new issues for offspring seeking to forge their identity as children and teenagers.

Finally, the growing diversity of America's population is certain to have a major impact on the schools of the future. As stated earlier, immigrant groups, African-Americans and American Indians, have a younger population than the national average, with more children of school age and below. Thus, a larger share from each of those groups is likely to be in the schools; by 2025, a majority of the nation's elementary and secondary students will be children of color. Many of these youngsters will be concentrated in urban areas, in homogeneous suburbs, or in isolated rural areas. Others, though, will inhabit racially and ethnically integrated suburbs or towns and small cities that are integrated by class as well as by race and ethnicity. Those who teach in the schools of tomorrow will inevitably encounter children of color, and their teaching success will depend in large part upon their understanding of a broad array of histories, personal experiences, beliefs, cultural practices, languages, and needs.

❖ Summary

As the seventeenth century ended, established cultural groups in America included American Indians, the first inhabitants of the land, Europeans who first came during the sixteenth century, and Africans brought here as slaves.

The American Indian population has fluctuated dramatically in numbers due to sloppy Census methods, politically inspired low counts, diseases that periodically decimated the population (and which, at times, were intentional), changing definitions of Indian citizenship, intermarriage, increased numbers of persons claiming Indian heritage, and a high birth rate. The present population is estimated at two million, and approximately 50 percent of the American Indians continue to live on reservations.

African-Americans first came to America involuntarily as slaves and their population was centered in the South. African-Americans now live in all types of communities throughout the country. However, many reside in tightly segregated living conditions, often mired in poverty. The population has continued to increase through high birth rates and recent immigration of West Indians and Africans.

The history of African-Americans has suffered distortions and omissions. The justification of slavery required this distortion of facts and put forth a portrait of Africa, from which the slaves came, as being backward and primitive. Also, acts of resistance to slavery and the recognition of many individual accomplishments and contributions to the society have been omitted from history books until recently. Slaves were portrayed as subhuman in order to prevent of assuage the guilt of slave owners and those who supported them. Although slaves were considered subhuman, and therefore unteachable, it was, at the same time, a crime to teach a slave to read or write. European-Americans lived with this discrepancy as with many other conflicting aspects of slavery.

There are two important things to remember about slavery and African-Americans: there was slavery in the North at one time, but to a much smaller degree than in the South—where it flourished; and ten to fifteen percent of former slaves had been freed *before* Emancipation. The majority of the African-American population (90 percent) remained in the South until the 1940s, when massive migration to northern cities began. Separate but equal characterized the lives of black people in the South and they remained without rights to vote, to live where they chose, attend good schools, obtain decent jobs, enjoy equal justice in the courts, or live free of fear of violence until the *Brown* decision of 1954 desegregated the schools and the Civil Rights movement finally brought basic human rights.

African-Americans, about 12 percent of the population, have remained the major group of color in the United States throughout the three hundred years of their presence here. However, the Latino population is rapidly overtaking that position. It has been predicted that by 2025 Latinos will be the largest group of color.

Other immigrant groups included in the United States population first came in the nineteenth century. The English and Scots-Irish, Dutch, Germans, and Irish have contributed to the population. Other groups have become part of the United States mosaic through United States accessation of territories. This includes various Indian nations, French speakers in Louisiana, and Spanish-speaking residents of Florida and the Southwest. Latino residents of New Mexico, Arizona, Colorado, and California continue to maintain much of their language and culture.

Asian immigrants first came during the 1849 California Gold Rush to make their fortune and bring their families to the United States or return to their home country. However, the Chinese Exclusion Act of 1882 prevented the immigration of any new arrivals and motivated others to leave. Some Chinese families established communities in San Francisco and several other American cities.

The Japanese entered America in the late nineteenth and early twentieth centuries as tenant farmers and farm workers in California and Hawaii. Many prospered until the Second World War resulted in the detention of thousands of Japanese on the West Coast. They have finally received reparations for their suffering. Many have migrated to other parts of the United States and intermarried at a high rate with Caucasian- Americans.

Other immigrant groups include those from Scandinavia, who settled in Minnesota and Wisconsin at the end of the Civil War, and Eastern and Southern Europeans, who came for economic, political, and religious reasons. In addition, Russian and Eastern European Jews fleeing persecution settled in large cities where many established businesses.

According to the melting pot belief, all of these immigrant groups would melt into an American. There are many reports of the personal experiences suffered by immigrants who had to forget their culture and language in order to become an American. Furthermore, African-Americans in particular have never had the opportunity to melt. American Indians and Latino-Americans have also experienced prejudice and discrimination in their efforts to participate fully in the American mainstream.

Twentieth century immigration has differed from that of earlier periods. Increased numbers of Mexicans have steadily crossed the United States border, both legally and illegally. Between 1981 and 1990, the number reached 1,653,300. Current debates are focused on the means for improved border patrol to reduce the number of illegal entries.

The Puerto Rican population differs from Mexican-Americans in that Puerto Ricans, who are United States citizens, migrate primarily internally, back and forth between the mainland United States and Puerto Rico. Spanish is maintained at a high rate among this population, possibly due to their frequent migration to the Spanish-speaking environment.

Cuban Americans in the United States only became the third largest Latino group since 1960, when Fidel Castro took charge in Cuba. The first immigrants were well-to-do professionals and government officials and were followed by workers, shopkeepers, and middle-class professionals. In 1980, the Mariel boatlift brought additional immigrants, including not only the poor, but political prisoners and common criminals. Cuban immigrants, treated as refugees, settled primarily in Miami, retaining their language and culture since they hoped to return to Cuba upon Castro's defeat.

Smaller groups from the Caribbean and Central and South America include immigrants from the Dominican Republic, Argentina, Bolivia, Chile, Peru, Venezuela, Guatemala, El Salvador, and Nicaragua.

Asia has also provided a major source of immigrants to the United States in the twentieth century. Due to the Immigration Act of 1965, which relaxed national quotas, immigrants from the Philippines, Korea, the Chinese mainland, and Asian Indians have come in increasing numbers. California, Hawaii, Oregon, and Washington State have received a small number of Pacific Islanders who have fled conditions of poverty in their countries.

However, the fastest-growing population of Asian-Americans includes refugees from Vietnam, Cambodia, and Laos escaping the conditions of war and political violence. These immigrants face cultural and language barriers more intense than other groups. Amerasian children, for example, shunned by their Vietnamese peers, have also encountered prejudice as they enter United States schools and communities.

Other immigrants to the United States from French- and English-speaking Caribbean countries have also increased in recent decades. Like the Central American immigrants of the 1980s, Haitians seeking asylum in the United States continue to press the United States government for changes in the policy that considers them economic rather than political refugees.

At the present rates of immigration among all of these groups, estimates are that the diversity of the United States population will continue to increase in the next century when the nonwhite population of the United States will comprise almost 50 percent of the total. The need for multicultural education in our schools is both obvious and urgent.

❖ CHAPTER 2 Questions

1. What is the major difference between the presence of African-Americans and other immigrant groups in our society?

2. What are the important factors that have influenced the condition of American Indians in the United States?

3. Describe the effects of distorting and omitting the history of African-Americans and other groups of color on the education of white American students in our schools.

4. Compare the immigration experience of Europeans with that of Latinos in the United States.

5. In what important respects has immigration in the twentieth century differed from earlier periods of immigration?

6. What distinguishes Puerto Ricans and Mexicans from other groups of immigrants to our country?

7. What do you expect as long-term effects of current immigration patterns? What are the implications for public schools?

❖ References

Ashabranner, B. (1985). *Children of the Maya: A Guatemalan Indian odyssey*. New York: Dodd, Mead.

Ashabranner, B., & Ashabranner, M. (1987). *Into a strange land: Unaccompanied refugee youth in America*. New York: Putnam.

Bean, F. D., & Tienda, M. (1987). *The Hispanic population of the United States*. New York: Russell Sage Foundation.

Bergquist, J. M. (1992). German-Americans. In J. D. Buenker & L. A. Ratner (Eds.), *Multiculturalism in the United States: A comparative guide to acculturation and ethnicity*. Westport, CT: Greenwood Press.

Bodovitz, K. (1991). Black America. *American Diversity: American Demographics Desk Reference Series, 1* (July 1991), 8–13.

Chan, S. (1991). *Asian Americans: An interpretive history*. Boston: Twayne Publishers.

Chira, S. (1990, May 22). New York's clamor intrudes on Koreans' insularity. *The New York Times*, p. B1.

Christianson, J. R. (1992). Scandinavian-Americans. In J. D. Buenker & L. A. Ratner (Eds.), *Multiculturalism in the United States: A comparative guide to acculturation and ethnicity*. Westport, CT: Greenwood Press.

Cortes, C. E. (1991). Pluribus and unum: The quest for community amid diversity. *Change, 25* (September/October 1991), 9–13.

Dent, D.J. (1992, June 14). The new black suburbs. *The New York Times Magazine*, 18–25.

Dreyfuss, J. (1993, May 23). The invisible immigrants. *The New York Times Magazine*. 20–21, 80–84.

Ferris, E. (1987). *The Central American refugees*. New York: Praeger.

Fitzpatrick, J. F. (1980). Puerto Ricans. In S. Thernstrom (Ed.), *Harvard encyclopedia of American ethnic groups*. Cambridge, MA: Harvard University Press.

Gann, L. H., & Duignan, P. J. (1986). *The Hispanics in the United States: A history*. Boulder, CO: Westview Press.

Gibbs, J. T. (1989). Biracial adolescents. In J. T. Gibbs, L. Nahme-Huang, & Associates (Eds.), *Children of color: Psychological interventions with minority youth*. San Francisco: Jossey-Bass.

Hendricks, G. (1980). Dominicans. In S. Thernstrom (Ed.), *Harvard encyclopedia of american ethnic groups*. Cambridge, MA: Harvard University Press.

Jensen, J. M. (1980). East Indians. In S. Thernstrom (Ed.), *Harvard encyclopedia of American ethnic groups*. Cambridge, MA: Harvard University Press.

Johnson, D. (1991, March 5). Census finds many claiming new identity: Indian. *The New York Times*, p. A1.

Katz, W. L. (1986). *Black Indians: A hidden heritage*. New York: Atheneum.

Katz, W. L. (1990). *Breaking the chains: African American slave resistance*. New York: Atheneum.

Kerr, L. A. N. (1992). Mexican-Americans. In J. D. Buenker & L. A. Ratner (Eds.), *Multiculturalism in the United States: A comparative guide to American ethnicity*. Westport, CT: Greenwood Press.

Kim, H. (1980). Koreans. In S. Thernstrom (Ed.), *Harvard encyclopedia of American ethnic groups*. Cambridge, MA: Harvard University Press.

Kitano, H. H. L. (1980). Japanese. In S. Thernstrom (Ed.), *Harvard encyclopedia of American ethnic groups*. Cambridge, MA: Harvard University Press.

Kozol, J. (1991). *Savage inequalities*. New York: Crown.

LaFromboise, T. D., & Low, K. G. (1989). American Indian children and adolescents. In J. T. Gibbs, L. Nahme-Huang, & Associates (Eds.), *Children of color: Psychological interventions with minority youth*. San Francisco: Jossey-Bass.

Lai, H. M. (1980). Chinese. In S. Thernstrom (Ed.), *Harvard encyclopedia of American ethnic groups*. Cambridge, MA: Harvard University Press.

Lee, J. F. J. (1991). *Asian American experiences in the United States: Oral histories of first to fourth generation Americans from China, the Philippines, Japan, India, the Pacific Islands, Vietnam and Cambodia*. Jefferson, NC: McFarland.

Massey, D. S., & Denton, N. A. (1993). *American apartheid: Segregation and the making of the underclass*. Cambridge, MA: Harvard University Press.

Nahme-Huang, L. N. (1989). Southeast Asian refugee children and adolescents. In J. T. Gibbs, L. Nahme-Huang, & Associates (Eds.), *Children of color: Psychological interventions with minority youth*. San Francisco: Jossey-Bass.

Olneck, M. & Lazerson, M. (1980). Education. In S. Thernstrom (Ed.), *Harvard encyclopedia of American ethnic groups*. Cambridge, MA: Harvard University Press.

Orlov, A., & Ueda, R. (1980). Central and South Americans. In S. Thernstrom (Ed.), *Harvard encyclopedia of American ethnic groups*. Cambridge, MA: Harvard University Press.

Perez, L. (1980). Cubans. In S. Thernstrom (Ed.), *Harvard encyclopedia of American ethnic groups*. Cambridge, MA: Harvard University Press.

Portes, A., & Stepick, A. (1993). *City on the edge: The transformation of Miami*. Berkeley: University of California Press.

Reid, A. (1986. October 5). New Asian immigrants, new garment center. *The New York Times*, p. A1.

Rimer, S. (1991, September 16). Between two worlds: Dominicans in New York. *The New York Times*, p. A1.

Shapiro, E. (1979). German and Russian Jews in America. *Midstream*, *25*(4) (April 1979), 42–51.

Shore, B. (1980). Pacific Islanders. In S. Thernstrom (Ed.), *Harvard encyclopedia of American ethnic groups*. Cambridge, MA: Harvard University Press.

Solis-Cohen, L. M. (1927). Library work in the Brooklyn ghetto. In L. M. Janzow (Ed.), *The library without walls*. New York: H. W. Wilson.

Sontag, D. (1992, November 28, 1992). Caribbean pupils' English seems barrier, not bridge. *The New York Times*, p. A1.

Suarez-Orozco, M. M. (1989). *Central American refugees and U.S. high schools: A psychosocial study of motivation and achievement*. Stanford, CA: Stanford University Press.

Takaki, R. (1993). *A different mirror: A history of multicultural America*. Boston: Little, Brown and Co.

Thornton, R. (1987). *American Indian holocaust and survival: A population history since 1492*. Norman, OK: University of Oklahoma Press.

Thornton, R. (1991). The demography of the trail of tears period: A new estimate of Cherokee population losses. In W. L. Anderson (Ed.), *Cherokee removal: Before and after*. Athens, GA: University of Georgia Press.

U.S. Census (1790–1990). *Census of the population of the United States.* Washington, DC: Bureau of the Census.

Ueda, R. (1980). West Indians. In S. Thernstrom (Ed.), *Harvard encyclopedia of American ethnic groups.* Cambridge, MA: Harvard University Press.

Wendel, F. C. H. (1911). The stranger within our gates: What can the library do for him? *Public Libraries, 16*(1911), 91.

Wilson, W. J. (1987). *The truly disadvantaged.* Chicago: University of Chicago Press.

Wright, M. B. (1980). Indochinese. In S. Thernstrom (Ed.), *Harvard encyclopedia of American ethnic groups.* Cambridge, MA: Harvard University Press.

Zolberg, A.R., Suhrike, A., & Asuayo, S. (1987). *Escape from violence: Conflict and the refugee crisis in the developing world.* New York: Oxford University Press.

CHAPTER 3

Children of Color in the Schools—Past and Present

The Effects of Poverty on Educational Attainment

The United States has always been perceived as a land of opportunity. Immigrants arriving penniless, or poor children born in rural shacks or urban slums, could attain prosperity through hard work, perseverance, and not a little luck. After the formation of public schools in the middle of the nineteenth century, education became one road to upward mobility. Poor youngsters who obtained high school diplomas could find clerical and technical work; others attended college and entered professions. For many children of immigrants and the poor, teaching was the profession that lifted them out of poverty and guaranteed even greater opportunities for their children.

Yet in earlier years, education was not crucial for economic success. Wealthy businessmen and even Presidents were sometimes barely literate. A skilled trade often proved more lucrative than a profession requiring years of schooling. Until recently, unskilled auto workers enjoyed job security, health insurance, pensions, and wages that exceeded those of teachers.

In the past several decades, however, economic changes have made education a far more critical determinant of later success. The high-paying unskilled jobs that sustained the less well-educated in earlier years have in large part disappeared overseas, where wages for unskilled workers are lower. Other factory jobs have become obsolete due to technological innovations. Our economy has shifted from a manufacturing base to a service-oriented one, in which knowledge, information, and innovation have become the highest-priced commodities. The service jobs available to those without much education are predominantly minimum wage, with little job security and few benefits.

In the 1980s the gap between the wealthiest Americans and the poorest widened substantially (Congressional Budget Office, 1992). A variety of factors accounted for this, but a major one was the elimination of high-paying unskilled jobs in the manufacturing sector and their replacement with lower-paying ones in the service sector. At the same time, people from all sides of the political spectrum lamented the general decline in school achievement. Nothing short of America's competitiveness was at stake, for other countries, particularly those of Europe and the Pacific Rim, had challenged the United States' economic and technological supremacy.

Although the long-term decline in reading, writing, mathematics, and critical thinking skills is purported to be at all levels of ability and income and among all racial groups, nowhere is this trend more alarming than among the children of the poor and children of color. For a country with a history of class mobility, both upward and downward, lower educational attainment among poor children threatens to widen and solidify class differences in American society. If the least educated are children of color, race and ethnicity become increasingly associated with lower socioeconomic status. There is little avenue of upward mobility for the *knowledge-poor*, those who are not highly educated and prepared to compete in an information and service oriented economy.

Today, both poor children and children of color are overrepresented among the lower achievers and those who drop out before completing high school. A common stereotype posits that poor children are primarily black, Latino, and American Indian (Asian-Americans, the model minority, are rarely poor in this scheme), and that virtually all black, Latino, and American Indian children are poor. However, poor children, children of color, and low-achieving children are not one and the same. Furthermore, according to the stereotype, blacks, Latinos, and American Indians do badly in school because of their race and ethnicity, as opposed to their higher representation in the ranks of the poor. And by the same token, poor children are *expected* to do less well than their better-off peers. The reality is far more complex.

In 1990, almost 20 percent of American children under eighteen lived below the poverty line (U.S. Census-A, 1990). This percentage has remained constant since the 1981–82 recession, at which time it rose to an eighteen-year high (Figure 3–1). According to the Census, 15 percent of white children, 44 percent of black children, and 37.7 percent of Latino children live in poverty (U.S. Census-A, 1990). (Since Latinos may be of any race, some of those youngsters may be counted as white or black as well.) In 1988, almost 18 percent of Asian-Americans and Pacific Islander eighth-graders lived in poverty, while 40 percent of American Indian children in the eighth grade were poor (U.S. Dept. of Education-A, 1990). Without minimizing the shameful nature of these statistics, those who work with children of color should also note that more than half of all black, Latino, and American Indian youngsters do not live in poverty. In addition, while half of the children in poverty are black and Latino, the other half are predominantly white (Figure 3–1).

FIGURE 3–1 Percentage of Children under 18 Living in Poverty, 1990

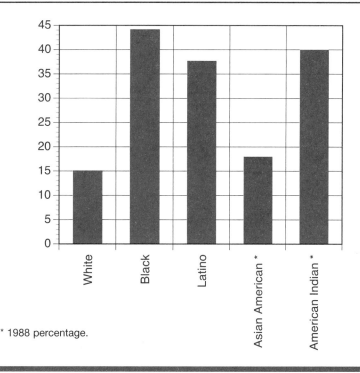

* 1988 percentage.

SOURCE: U.S. Department of Education, National Center for Education Statistics, National Educational Longitudinal Study of 1988, base year survey: A Profile of the American Eighth Grader.

Growing up in poverty is considered to be one of the main risk factors for low achievement and dropping out of school. Several recent studies have shown that poor children of all races and ethnic groups score lower on standardized tests than more advantaged students (Natriello, McDill, & Pallas, 1990). They are almost twice as likely to repeat a grade and more than twice as likely to drop out before finishing high school (Natriello, McDill, & Pallas, 1990).

Lowered Expectations: The "Deficit" Model and the "Culture of Poverty"

A multitude of factors may account for the school problems of poor children. Even before the children are born, their mothers are less likely to receive pre-natal care; as a result, a larger (though still small) percentage of these children suffer learning and other disabilities that impede their school success. They are more likely to spend their early years in crowded, substandard housing with few books and toys to provide intellectual stimulation. They may never travel outside their immediate area and have less access to recreational facilities. Without proper diet and medical attention, they may miss school due to illness, a major cause of being retained in grade. Illnesses such as recurrent, untreated ear infections may also inhibit their ability to learn unless early intervention occurs. Their health may be undermined as well by toxic substances at home (such as lead paint and lead pipes) and in their neighborhoods; often the least expensive neighborhoods are those near toxic waste dumps and polluting factories. Frequent moves and bouts of homelessness (which increased significantly during the 1980s) are a source of disruption, especially if the child is also forced to change schools.

Many of these causes, related to an individual child's development and upbringing, have been combined into a *deficit* or *cultural deprivation* theory of poverty. Those who take this to extreme, ignoring the vast differences in personal relationships, experiences, and motivations, are likely to assume that poor children cannot learn, that their fate has been sealed from birth. Children who begin life with inadequate family resources *do* face obstacles and problems not confronted by their more advantaged peers, but blaming their families and assuming at the outset that the children will fail may play an even more significant role in bringing about that failure. Whatever the damage caused by few material resources, poor health care, inadequate nutrition, and toxic substances, far more children are damaged by mainstream society's *lowered expectations* and *lack of concern*.

Added to a family's inadequate resources are those tied to the community. Poor communities, whether they be isolated rural villages, mobile home parks on the edges of suburban towns, or urban ghettoes, are by their very nature separated from more prosperous, mainstream communities. Abandoned farms and factories point to the disappearance of local employment opportunities; new jobs are often located in suburbs far from mass transportation routes. Many of these communities, especially poor black ones, have become increasingly isolated as better-off members move to the suburbs, leaving those remaining without a variety of support structures, including churches, retail stores, and job contacts. Young people are left without the positive example of their more successful neighbors (Wilson, 1987). Language differences may further isolate a poor community, especially one with a large immigrant population. When young members of the community leave to shop or to attend school, they often face the prejudice of those around them, further damaging their self-esteem.

In writing about poor communities, many have raised the notion of a *culture of poverty*. Poor people do not achieve in school or in mainstream society, it is argued, because they, as a community, have adopted the values of a different culture, one at complete odds with the mainstream. Joblessness, living for pleasure in the present rather than success in the future, "making it" on the streets or in criminal gangs, teenage pregnancy, and births out of wedlock are hallmarks of this culture, which exists irrespective of race, ethnicity, or geographic location. (In fact, Oscar Lewis, who first named this phenomenon, did much of his research in the slums of Mexico, as well as among Puerto Ricans in New York.) By definition, a culture of poverty has its own autonomous set of traits, traits which exist regardless of economic and social conditions and prevent the upward mobility of those that subscribe to it (Wilson, 1987). Like the deficit or cultural deprivation theories, the culture of poverty theory has had the effect of blaming the victims and dismissing any possibility of group success. Little attention in this model is given to individual differences in ability and motivation; for the proponents of the culture of poverty thesis, the community plays a negative, and all-important, role. Sociologists such as William Julius Wilson also argue that what is seen as a full-blown culture is actually a response to broader economic changes that include the chronic lack of jobs (leading to idleness and employment by criminal syndicates), the social isolation and collapse of basic institutions in poor communities as more successful members move out, and the unavailability of employed men who can conceivably marry and support a family (leading to teenage pregnancy and out-of-wedlock births) (Wilson, 1987).

Finally, much of the responsibility for lower achievement among poor children of all racial and ethnic groups lies, directly or indirectly, with the schools themselves. The system of funding schools through local property taxes creates great inequities, as suburban districts with high property values can raise significantly more money for schools than poor urban, suburban, or rural districts. For instance, in Camden, New Jersey, the 1988-89 per pupil expenditure was $3,538, while in Princeton, New Jersey, the per pupil expenditure was $7,725 (Kozol, 1991). New York City spent $5,585 per pupil in 1988–89, while the Long Island suburb of

Manhasset spent $11,372 (Kozol, 1991). For poor districts, funding inequities translate into larger classes; fewer enrichment classes; insufficient and outdated textbooks, library books, and materials for the classroom; fewer computers and media resources; inadequate laboratories; and unsafe, crumbling buildings. All of these impact upon the learning ability of the students (Kozol, 1991).

Poor children, in both class-integrated and class-segregated schools, suffer as well from lowered expectations on the part of teachers and other school staff. Perhaps responding consciously or unconsciously to the cultural deprivation or culture of poverty model, teachers may assume that children at the bottom of the socioeconomic scale will end up at the bottom of the class, and they may not make the effort to challenge and motivate their students. In one middle-class suburban district in upstate New York, controversy erupted when the school board proposed redistributing the children from a large mobile home park—children who had become concentrated in one elementary school—evenly among all the elementary schools. Most of those involved in the debate assumed that the children from that area would do less well than the other students in the district; some parents, teachers, and administrators in the receiving schools expressed fear that the children would strain the schools' resources and "drag the scores down." Such lowered expectations frequently reinforce themselves. Children often internalize what those in authority believe of them. Others will tune out unchallenging, boring classes or become disruptive. Still others will be denied assistance for problems that could be easily overcome, such as visual or hearing impairments or dyslexia, because they are already believed to be achieving at their best.

Another school factor that impedes the progress of many poor children is *negative school climate*. This term refers to the sum total of qualities that make up the school environment. A school that is physically unsafe, that suffers vandalism and violence against teachers and students, and that features constant disruptions, interrupting class time, is a difficult place in which to learn. According to a 1988 United States Department of Education survey of eighth-grade students and teachers across the country, a significantly larger percentage of high-poverty schools were identified as having problems (U.S. Dept. of Education-A, 1990). While students in high poverty schools identified their schools as having problems of weapons possession, vandalism, fights among students, and physical and verbal attacks against teachers approximately 50 percent more often than students in low poverty schools, the teachers in these schools identified these problems two to six times as often as their colleagues in low poverty schools (U.S. Dept. of Education-A, 1990). When the same survey was broken down by race and ethnicity, poverty remained the variable that created the most significant differences (U.S. Dept. of Education-A, 1990) (Table 3–1).

Despite these obvious problems, it is all too easy for teachers, who by the nature of their occupations are middle class, to overemphasize the

TABLE 3–1 School Climate

Problem	Total	Race/ethnicity					School poverty[1] status	
		White	Black	Latino[2]	Asian Pacific Is.	American Indian	High poverty	Low poverty
		Eighth-grade students						
Possession of weapons	11.3	9.7	16.8	13.7	14.3	15.3	15.4	10.6
Vandalism of school property	14.5	12.8	19.6	17.6	20.0	19.4	20.0	13.6
Physical conflicts among students	16.6	14.8	25.6	17.8	17.2	22.3	22.6	15.6
Physical abuse of teachers	7.9	7.0	9.6	10.4	11.3	9.6	9.9	7.6
Verbal abuse of teachers	11.5	10.9	14.1	13.0	11.3	13.0	13.7	11.1
		Eighth-grade students						
Possession of weapons	1.4	1.4	1.6	0	0	7.3	4.3	0.9
Vandalism of school property	4.9	4.6	8.5	7.3	2.5	9.5	10.0	4.3
Physical conflicts among students	7.0	6.8	12.2	1.8	0	7.3	18.9	4.4
Physical abuse of teachers	1.7	1.6	1.9	0	0	7.3	6.3	0.7
Verbal abuse of teachers	10.1	10.0	10.6	9.7	6.9	20.9	21.4	7.6

[1] High poverty schools, in this indicator are defined as schools in which 50% or more of the students receive a free or reduced price lunch. In low poverty schools, less than 50% receive a free or reduced price lunch.

[2] Latinos may be of any race.

SOURCE: U.S. Department of Education, National Center for Education Statistics. National Education Longitudinal Survey, base year survey. 1988 (student responses): Schools and Staffing Survey, base year survey. 1987–1988 (teacher responses).

effects of poverty on school achievement. While perhaps a quarter of children in the United States have experienced poverty, this does not mean they have been poor all their lives. The recent recession has caused widespread unemployment and underemployment; even those who are comfortably middle class can lose a job and fall into poverty at any time. Divorce is often a cause of sudden poverty; studies show that after a divorce, the standard of living of women and children falls, while that of men rises (Wallerstein & Blakeslee, 1989). Finally, the startling success rates at a number of schools with a high percentage of low-income students—schools where students perform better than their middle-class counterparts elsewhere in the district—points to several issues. Despite their limited resources, poor parents want their children to succeed in school and to have a better life. The children themselves, who share the same abilities, talents, and interests as their middle-class counterparts, can succeed when success is *expected* of them (and often even when it is not). Often, children in poverty grow up with greater independence, self-reliance, devotion to work, and responsibility than middle-class children who have not had to struggle for their basic needs and whose material desires have always (or nearly always) been satisfied.

Finally, many schools that serve poor children are capable of treating them and their parents with respect and of meeting their educational needs. A long-term study of a group of elementary schools in Pittsburgh found that three schools which served the poorest children in the city produced test scores among the city's highest (Sizemore, 1985). The researcher, Barbara Sizemore, attributed the schools' successes to a combination of the following factors: the principals' leadership, a strong working relationship between administration and faculty, close monitoring of student achievement, a highly organized school environment, a highly organized curriculum, an expanded school day, with opportunities for in-school and after-school tutoring, high expectations for students, strict discipline, a working relationship with parents and others in the community based upon the value of high achievement, and a willingness to circumvent the central bureaucracy when necessary (Sizemore, 1985).

Other Risk Factors

While poverty is seen as one of the major risk factors for poor school performance, it is not the only factor. The United States Department of Education has identified six risk factors that, in certain combinations, significantly raise a student's chance of low achievement and dropping out of school. The risk factors are:

▌ poverty;
▌ a single-parent family;
▌ children who are left home alone more than three hours per day;
▌ parents (and especially mothers) who have no high school diploma;
▌ siblings who have dropped out of high school; and
▌ limited English proficiency (U.S. Dept. of Education, 1992),
    (Table 3–2).

Natriello, McDill, and Pallas (1990) have explored in depth the reasons many (though not all, and in most cases, not even a majority) children with multiple risk factors perform less well in school. Parents who experienced school problems and did not complete high school tend to be less involved in and less positive about their children's schooling, a problem many schools across the country are trying to change. (For example, at DuSable High School in Chicago, parents of enrolled students are being allowed to enroll themselves in the regular school program in order to obtain their high school diplomas, often decades after they dropped out.) When the parent is a single mother, the effects of her negative experiences with school may be magnified. In addition, the mother is generally the main contact person between home and school and the person who spends the most time with the child, thereby accounting for the greater importance of her school achievement.

In defining limited English proficiency, two factors are taken into account—whether the child and the family use a language other than English as their primary means of communication and whether the youngster is able to understand, read, and communicate in English well enough to learn in an English-only classroom (Natriello, McDill, & Pallas, 1990). Like parents who did not complete high school, parents with limited English proficiency tend to be less involved in the school. They often have trouble communicating with school personnel and assisting children with their assignments (Natriello, McDill, & Pallas, 1990). Many schools have made little effort to accommodate non-English speaking

TABLE 3–2 Student Characteristics

Percentage of eighth-graders with various risk factors by race/ethnicity: 1988

Race/ ethnicity	Risk factors						Percentage with factors[1]			
	Parent is single	Parents have no high school diploma	Limited English proficiency	Income less than $15,000	Sibling has dropped out of school	Home alone more than 3 hours per day	Zero	One	Two	Three or More
Total	22.3	10.5	2.3	21.3	10.0	13.6	53.4	25.6	13.7	7.3
White	17.7	6.2	0.8	14.1	8.8	12.0	61.5	24.2	10.1	4.2
Black	46.5	15.8	1.6	47.0	13.0	19.5	27.9	28.5	26.2	17.4
Latinos[2]	23.4	33.4	8.8	37.5	16.0	16.3	30.5	30.8	22.5	16.2
Asian/Pacific Islander	14.2	8.8	7.1	17.8	6.1	15.9	57.9	26.9	10.1	6.2
American Indian	31.1	13.4	8.6	40.1	15.1	18.6	31.4	32.3	22.2	14.1

[1] Individuals who did not respond to any one of the six risk factors were excluded. Complete data were available for 92% of the sample.

[2] Hispanics may be of any race.

SOURCE: U.S. Department of Education, National Center for Education Statistics, National Education Longitudinal Study of 1988, base year survey: *A Profile of the American Eighth Grader*, 1990.

parents. In order to utilize the parents' skills and potential contributions to the school and to enlist their cooperation in boosting their children's performance, schools must offer a welcoming environment and personnel who can communicate with the parents in their first language. Youngsters with limited English proficiency are also likely to be the children of immigrants or immigrants themselves, with all the social and psychological dislocations that the immigration process creates. Thus, school must look upon immigration as a resource for the educational process in addition to providing support services for immigrants and their families. (One very effective school that has been enriched by the presence of its immigrant student body is the International High School in New York City, which is described in more detail in Chapter 4.)

Children of color are more likely to experience some of the above factors indicating educational risk. In addition to their overrepresentation among those living in poverty, described earlier, some are more likely to be living in single-parent families, and the single-parent families are more likely to be poor for longer periods of time. This is especially true of African-American youngsters (U.S. Census-A, 1990). A 1988 Department of Education survey of eighth-graders showed that Latino and American Indian children were slightly more likely than average to live in single-parent households as well (U.S. Dept. of Education, 1992). For Latino children, the most prevalent risk categories were parents without high school diplomas, siblings who had dropped out of school, and limited English proficiency (U.S. Dept. of Education, 1992). Limited English proficiency was also a problem for almost one-tenth of American Indian, Asian-American, and Pacific Islander eighth-graders as well (U.S. Dept. of Education, 1992). Well over half of all African-American, Latino, and American Indian youngsters had at least one risk factor (U.S. Dept. of Education, 1992). The Department of Education considered a combination of two or more risk factors to be "particularly detrimental to success in school," (p. 74) and, according to the 1988 survey, 43.6 percent of African-American eighth graders, 38.7 percent of Latino eighth-graders, 16.2 percent of Asian-American eighth-graders, and 36.3 percent of American Indian eighth-graders had two or more risk factors (U.S. Dept. of Education, 1992).

As just discussed, there are a number of reasons why children of poverty are at heightened risk for school failure. Some of those reasons involve school funding, organization, climate, and the expectations maintained for poor children. These problems, and more, have been encountered by children of color. For such children, who are disproportionately at risk, fewer resources and lowered expectations will create in today's knowledge-based economy a caste system in which racial and ethnic characteristics will be associated with an ever more permanent poverty. In a democratic society and in a competitive global economy in which not even one person, let alone entire communities, can go to waste, this hardening of class, ethnic, and racial lines cannot happen. In the next section, we will discuss ways in which school systems have denied access to children of color or perpetuated inequities over the past two centuries, and programs in the past four decades that have sought to address these inequalities.

❖ A History of Educational Inequality

Overt Discrimination

As Chapter 2 pointed out, slaves in the South, where 90 percent of all African-Americans lived until the twentieth century, were forbidden to read and write. When emancipation came in 1865 few schools existed, and these closed their doors to the newly-freed slaves. Nonetheless, African-American parents sought an education for the children, so that their children would have the opportunities that had been denied to them. In some cases African-Americans started their own schools, an approach endorsed and directly aided by noted leaders such as Booker T. Washington and W. E. B. DuBois. Desire for an education for their children was one of the principal reasons for the African-Americans' great migration northward after 1900 (Takaki, 1993). This value placed upon education has persisted in African-American families and communities up to the present.

The 1896 Supreme Court decision *Plessy v. Ferguson* upheld separate but equal facilities that were, in practice, rarely equal. Segregated black schools in the South received a fraction of the funding of white schools. Buildings and textbooks were old and falling apart. Most of the textbooks presented African-Americans as slaves, with no treatment of slave resistance (except to show how the rebels were put "in their place") or of the contributions made by African-Americans to American society. In addition to learning a curriculum that reinforced white supremacy, black students were only allowed to attend school for part of the year; the rest of the time they were expected to work alongside their sharecropper parents in the fields. Black schools were often inconveniently located, with bus service denied the youngsters. Often black students passed a white-only school and school busses carrying white students while they had to walk to their school many miles away. Because of segregation, black schools were almost entirely staffed by black teachers. Though many of those teachers did not have as much formal education as their white counterparts, they were dedicated to helping their students gain self-esteem and succeed. Most sought to circumvent the state-mandated curriculum. Personal experiences and family stories became a way of recovering the truth about African-American culture, history, and accomplishments.

During the late nineteenth and early twentieth centuries, other groups were denied access to education as well. Chinese immigrants

African-American families have traditionally placed a high value upon education.

were barred from a number of public facilities, including the schools. The children of Mexican-American migrant workers in the rural Southwest often found no schools to attend. Those without legal status kept their children away from the schools, fearing that school officials would turn them over to immigration authorities. Even when Mexican-American children attended school, they found the environment a hostile one. Few teachers knew Spanish, and many looked down upon their students. In districts in Texas and elsewhere, the use of a language other than English on school grounds was cause for severe corporal punishment. If language barriers prevented Mexican-American, Chinese-American, or Japanese-American children from learning in English, they were considered to be mentally retarded and unable to learn, even if they were fully literate in their native language.

The process was even more traumatic for American Indian children, many of whom were sent by government authorities to schools off the reservation, where they were given new non-Indian names, prohibited from speaking their traditional languages, and forced to give up the culture of their birth. In order to bring about their assimilation into white society, the young Indians in off-reservation boarding schools were denied regular access to their families and community. This process began when the youngsters turned six; even at graduation twelve years later, school officials discouraged their return to the reservation.

When immigrant children attended school in the late nineteenth and early twentieth centuries, their placement tended to be inconsistent. Some were placed in the grade corresponding to their age, even if they could not understand English or had not attended school in their country of origin. Many of these children quickly failed. Other children were placed in lower grades, but this placement often carried a stigma and led to social problems. The problem was especially troublesome if the child had attended school in the country of origin and may have even been ahead of American children in some areas.

Before the reform efforts of the 1960s and 1970s, school officials regularly *steered* African-American, Latino, Asian-American, and American Indian children into manual occupations, regardless of the abilities of the individual child. Malcolm X's experience, in a junior high school in Michigan in the 1940s, was typical (Malcolm X, 1964):

> Mr. Ostrowski [Malcolm's English teacher]...half smiled and said, "Malcolm, one of life's first needs is for us to be realistic. Don't misunderstand me, now. We all here like you, you know that. But you've got to be realistic about being a nigger. A lawyer—that's no realistic goal for a nigger. You need to think about something you *can* be. You're good with your hands—making things. Everybody admires your carpentry shop work. Why don't you plan on carpentry?..."
>
> ...I realized whatever I wasn't, I *was* smarter than nearly all those white kids. But apparently I was still not intelligent enough, in their eyes, to become whatever I wanted to be.
>
> It was then that I began to change—inside. (pp. 36–37)

This process was especially hurtful to children of color who worked hard and took school seriously, because their, and their parents', faith in education did not lead to a better life. While many African-Americans, Latinos, Asian-Americans, and American Indians continued to struggle and eventually succeeded in breaking into professions that had been exclusively white, discrimination in school and society dashed the hopes of all but the most determined and fortunate.

❖ The Arrival of Integration

The 1954 *Brown v. Board of Education* decision brought about monumental changes in American schools. No longer were separate but equal facilities sufficient, for, as the Supreme Court argued, separate was inherently unequal. Gradually, the schools of the South began to integrate and, as expected, the white establishment resisted this integration. Racist mobs harassed African-American schoolchildren as they rode the buses or walked through white areas. Invariably, African-Americans bore the brunt of integration. Children were bused out of their neighborhoods to predominantly white schools; white children were almost never bused in. When they arrived, administration, staff, and students rarely welcomed them or their parents, whose participation in school affairs was actively discouraged. Neighborhood schools lost some of their best and most motivated students, who took advantage of the new opportunities. Minimal integration justified the continued underfunding of predominantly black schools. Moreover, many of the caring and courageous African-American teachers lost their jobs after integration. Some were dismissed after segregated black schools closed; others could not meet new rules for teacher certification.

After integration, many white families left the public schools to avoid contact with children of diverse cultures. Those who could afford them chose private schools or moved to suburbs with restrictive deeds. In some cases, clusters of all-white schools within a larger school district broke off to form a separate district in order to avoid integration. Federal courts continued to hear cases involving desegregation and mandatory busing of children both within and between districts. During the Civil Rights movement of the 1960s, school desegregation became a battleground not only in the South but also in northern cities such as Boston and Chicago.

Despite the protests and the angry confrontations at the school doors, and despite the integration process that occurred *with all deliberate speed*, the South became the region of the country with the most highly-integrated schools (Celis, 1993). In many southern communities today—rural, urban, and suburban—white and black children attend schools together and sit side-by-side in the classroom. In the 1960s a government commission headed by sociologist James Coleman observed the benefits of integration—better race relations and higher achievement on the part of Black students (U.S. Department of Health, Education, & Welfare, 1966). Much of the greater success of black students at previously all-white schools stemmed simply from their presence; for the first time most of them were at schools with adequate funding, facilities, and materials. In fact, during and after the reforms of the 1960s, much of the conflict over integration and educational equity shifted from the South to the north.

❖ The Civil Rights Movement and the War on Poverty

The activism of the 1960s sparked a variety of efforts at school reform, some of which were directed to poor children in general and some of which were directed to specific racial and ethnic groups. Few could deny, however, that, in spite of the Civil Rights movement, tremendous inequalities existed, as well as tremendous segregation. Furthermore, as Jonathan Kozol, Herbert Kohl, and others documented in their moving testimonials of teaching in the segregated inner city schools of the urban Northeast in the 1960s, insensitive white teachers undermined the self-esteem of black students as effectively as any white supremacist in the South (Kozol, 1967; Kohl, 1967). Himself fired for giving his fourth-grade students a poem by Langston Hughes, Kozol observed that a curriculum that failed to include the heroes or the daily realities of poor black children would forever alienate those children from the educational system (Kozol, 1967).

Compensatory Programs

The war on poverty led to a number of compensatory education programs directed to poor Americans in general, regardless of race, ethnicity, or place of residence. The most famous of these was Head Start, which offered classes for preschool children in their year before kindergarten. Head Start also initiated programs for mothers, focusing on parenting, nutrition, health care, and school readiness. Although evaluative studies of Head Start were often plagued by flawed methodology and ideological bias, the best studies showed the program to be effective, particularly for a child's early school career (Natriello, McDill, & Pallas, 1990). The tendency for Head Start's benefits to fade out by the middle elementary grades fueled calls for the Follow Through program and the Title I/Chapter I compensatory education programs. A variety of elementary and secondary programs received federal funding to aid children of poverty, and some of those programs were more effective than others. Unfortunately, the money received from the federal government even at the height of funding levels for compensatory education programs was insufficient to make up for the vast difference in local funding between rich and poor districts (Kozol, 1991). Except for the patchwork of compensatory programs, many of which only reached a small number of eligible students for less than an hour a day, most poor students languished in large, overcrowded classes where there was little hope of receiving individual attention for their needs (Kozol, 1967, 1991).

Busing

While the 1960s war on poverty generated compensatory education programs, court-ordered desegregation, mostly by means of busing, was an outgrowth of the civil rights struggle that had taken place for more than a decade. Opposition to desegregation spread quickly from the South to the north, and the courts found racially-segregated neighborhoods and the schools to be in violation of the letter and spirit of the *Brown v. Board of Education* decision. Rapid migration of African-Americans from the rural South to the urban north had created large segregated areas, or ghettoes, that included middle class as well as poor families. The schools that served the ghettoes were generally inferior, as white-controlled school boards diverted resources to their side of town (Kozol, 1967, 1991).

Some districts initiated voluntary desegregation plans to prevent a federal desegregation order. In many of those voluntary plans, a limited number of places at white schools were made available to African-American children. Yet many parents objected to their children riding buses for two or more hours each day; usually, it was black children who did most of the riding. Inflexible bus schedules often prevented participation in extracurricular activities, reinforcing the status of bused children as outsiders. In other districts, a school in a predominantly black neighborhood was refurbished and turned into a magnet school, with a special program designed to attract white students. Many of the *magnet schools* were quite successful in promoting diversity and improving educational opportunities for all students. Still, they came under fire for draining off the best and the brightest, leaving the remaining ghetto schools just as segregated, underfunded, and inferior, but with an even more troubled student body. Financially strapped urban districts that carried out voluntary desegregation plans often found themselves without money to keep the buses and the magnet-school programs going. Court-ordered programs sparked tremendous hostility, dividing white communities as well as contributing to racial strife. Boston became a symbol of northern opposition to integration in the early 1970s, as school board member Louise Day Hicks led mobs to attack the buses carrying black children to formerly all-white schools.

Community Control

During the late 1960s, the idea of Black Nationalism gained importance, and integration lost some of its support among the African-American leadership. Though not necessarily foes of school integration, Black Nationalists believed that questions of school governance and curriculum deserved greater attention, and that blacks should move to take control of their own schools rather than depend upon the courts and the United States Justice Department to allow them into white schools. The struggle over community control in New York City in 1968 exemplified the new priorities. In that year, an experimental program allowed three predominantly minority districts to select their own school boards. The board elected in the Ocean Hill-Brownsville neighborhood of Brooklyn quickly moved to hire teachers that represented more fairly the racial and ethnic backgrounds of the students. The community board also asserted the right to change the curriculum to reflect the students' history, culture, and special needs. Advocates of decentralization faced off against the teachers' union, which resisted the potential firing of white teachers and their replacement by teachers of color with less seniority (Berube & Gittell, 1969). Although the community board did not get to keep the right to hire teachers and change the curriculum, the idea of community control gained support nationwide as a means of empowering neighborhoods and giving people of color a voice in their schools.

❖ Bilingual Education

African-Americans were not the only beneficiaries of the Civil Rights movement. In the fields and *barrios* of the Southwest, a new generation of Latino leaders was emerging. Under pressure, school districts opened their doors to and began to accommodate the special needs of migrant children. Federally funded programs offered summer classes in regions that saw few Latino children during the regular school year. Citizens, legal residents, and the undocumented all benefited from increased access to regular school and compensatory education programs.

In the case of Latino and Asian-American students, however, the most debated reform of the 1960s and 1970s was bilingual education. Under the melting pot model of the previous decades, non-English-speaking students were left to sink or swim in regular classrooms. The Bilingual Education Act, initially passed by Congress in 1968, provided financial assistance to local education agencies for the purpose of developing and maintaining new and innovative programs to meet the needs of limited English-proficient students. At first directed to students whose first language was Spanish, the law was reauthorized and expanded to include other languages; the reauthorization also reaffirmed the goal of desegregation as it applied to Latino and Asian-American students. In addition, the 1974 Supreme Court case *Lau v. Nichols* asserted that school districts had to provide special language programs, whether "English as a second language (ESL)" classes or bilingual education programs, for students who spoke little or no English.

The emergence of bilingual education coincided not only with the upsurge in minority activism but also with an enormous increase in immigration from Latin America and Asia. There was no national bilingual program; rather, new immigrants who lacked English proficiency were placed in a variety of settings. One model offered English as a second language in self-contained classrooms until the students learned enough English to keep up in regular classes. A second model, and perhaps the best known one, was the bilingual transition program. Here, the students received instruction in English as a second language and, at the same time, they kept up with their academic subjects in their native language. A variation of this transition program offered some classes (often math and science) in English and others in the native language until the students learned sufficient English to end instruction in their native language. A third model was the bilingual maintenance program, which allowed students to maintain proficiency in their native language at the same time as they learned English. This type of program was most favored by those who intended to return to their country of origin. Finally, the total immersion model followed the traditional pattern of teaching all subjects in English immediately with no special instruction in the native language. Sometimes, but not always, those students received classes in English as a second language to help them along (Smith & Luckasson, 1992). Immigrant parents who supported the total immersion model were generally ones who had no intention of returning to their land of origin. In New York City, for example, Russian and Chinese parents have been the strongest supporters of total immersion for their children (Berger, 1993).

Studies of bilingual education have cited many benefits. Students with limited English proficiency who were fluent in another language could progress in their academic subjects, and in many schools, the bilingual students boasted the highest achievement and motivation. Immigrant children adjusting to a new land avoided a source of loneliness, confusion, and humiliation as they took classes with those who shared their experiences and feelings. Bilingual classes preserved the children's native language and culture, a significant advantage if the children would be returning to their native country or if, as in the case of American Indian children, they lived in two worlds. Beyond the actual content of the classes, bilingual programs acknowledged the value of diverse cultures and languages in American society as well as the need for children with limited English proficiency to feel comfortable and succeed in school.

Bilingual education has also presented educators with special challenges. One is finding qualified teachers who are proficient in both the children's native language and in English. When a large number of Haitian children arrived in New York, the district advertised for "Bilingual-French" teachers, not realizing that Haitians speak a Creole language that bears little resemblance to the French taught in colleges or spoken in Paris. In the cases of less commonly spoken languages, no qualified bilingual teachers could be found, so the children were placed in intensive ESL classes or in English-only classrooms. Sometimes bilingual or ESL teachers lack proficiency in English and therefore can not help children develop an adequate understanding of their new language. Schools often lack textbooks and other materials to teach academic subjects in languages other than English. Another challenge involves older children who speak another language at home but who, because of a lack of educational opportunities in their country of origin, can neither read nor write. School officials question whether those children should be taught basic literacy skills in their native language or in English. In any case, children who do not attend school before immigration are years behind in all their subjects and need assistance beyond instruction in their native language.

Finally, there was no agreement on the amount of time that must be devoted to instruction in a child's native language or when to move a child from the separate bilingual class to the all-English classroom. Some experts in the field estimated that it required five to seven years of second language learning for limited-English proficient students to perform complex academic tasks in the second language. Students first developed face-to-face communication skills in English and were then at risk for being moved too soon to all-English instruction (Cummings, 1981). Others argued that children who remained in bilingual classes for that length of time failed to learn English properly and became isolated from their monolingual peers (Berger, 1993).

Some school districts resisted bilingual education for ideological reasons. Critics argued that immigrant children should be taught primarily in English, the mainstream language, when they are young and can learn languages quickly. Opponents of bilingual education resented the expense, and considered native-language instruction a waste of the student's time and a recipe for failure in an English-speaking society. Even though schools were mandated to provide bilingual programs, lack of support for those programs in many school districts undermined their effectiveness and guaranteed that limited-English proficient parents would have little control over the placement and education of their children.

❖ Persistent Problems

The End of Desegregation Efforts

Compensatory education, integration, community control, and bilingual education were all reforms of the 1960s and 1970s that attempted to make schools more responsive to poor children and children of color. Ronald Reagan's election to the Presidency in 1980, however, led to a curtailment of reforms and of federal funding for education in general. Compensatory education programs were among the first victims, as Head Start and other programs lost most of their funds. A smaller number of children were served; at the same time, more American children joined the ranks of the poor.

The Reagan Administration also put the brakes on busing and other forms of school desegregation. The Justice Department prosecuted few desegregation cases, and many of the districts that had enacted voluntary or mandatory integration plans now sharply curtailed them. In some cases, the primary motive was financial; the federal government had stopped funding busing programs and had cut back its contributions to school districts in general. In districts where significant conflict had accompanied integration, white leaders seized upon the federal government's new recalcitrance in civil rights matters to flout earlier desegregation orders. In a sample of ten states, only three—Georgia, Louisiana, and Virginia—increased their percentage of blacks enrolled in white schools from 1980 to 1988. Two other southern states—Florida and Alabama—grew more segregated. Of the northern states, Connecticut, Massachusetts, Michigan, and New Jersey, became more segregated, as did California (Judson, 1993).

By the 1980s, many whites had voted with their feet, moving to suburbs to escape integrated schools. To an increasing extent, desegregation was no longer an issue within school districts but rather between them. Yet in the 1974 case *Milliken v. Bradley*, the Supreme Court ruled that busing could not be mandated as a means of desegregation between districts. With the departure of whites of all income levels, inner cities increasingly became home to black and immigrant families. While segregated urban neighborhoods had existed in northern cities since the nineteenth century, the term *hypersegregation* emerged to describe the inner cities of the late twentieth century (Massey & Denton, 1989).

To determine whether a metropolitan area—a city and its surrounding suburbs and satellite cities—is hypersegregated, social scientists examine five dimensions. They are:

1. the extent to which each neighborhood's racial distribution mirrors the metropolitan area as a whole;
2. the existence of places where people of different races can come into contact with each other;
3. the extent to which individual minority neighborhoods are adjacent to each other, creating ghettoes that extend for many miles in every direction;
4. the concentration of minority-group members in the inner city; and
5. the population density of minority areas (Massey & Denton, 1989).

Hypersegregated cities are seen as particularly detrimental to the prospects of those who live there because of the residents' extreme isolation from mainstream society (Massey & Denton, 1989). African-American children living in hypersegregated metropolitan areas attend schools that have a nearly or totally 100 percent African-American student body—as segregated as those in the South before 1954. Furthermore, their teacher may be the only white person the children in these areas will come into contact with on a day-to-day basis. In 1989, ten United States metropolitan areas were determined to be hypersegregated. Chicago led the list, followed by Detroit, Cleveland, Milwaukee, Newark, Gary, Indiana, Philadelphia, Los Angeles, Baltimore, and St. Louis (Wilkerson, 1989; Massey & Denton, 1989, 1993).

Hypersegregation and the curtailment of school desegregation programs in the 1970s and 1980s are only two factors leading to an increase in segregation. A study by the Harvard [University] Project on School Desegregation, released in 1993, showed immigration patterns, such as chain migration and higher immigrant and minority birth rates to be contributing factors as well. The result was a level of segregation in the 1991-92 school year that was higher than any other year since 1968 (Celis, 1993). In total, 66 percent of African-American students attended schools where the majority of students were African-American or Latino, and 74.3 percent of Latino students attended schools with a predominately African-American and Latino student body (Celis, 1993). The study did not indicate how many of the schools in question had mixed student bodies, but noted this as an increasing trend (Celis, 1993).

Segregation Within Schools

Resegregation. Whereas hypersegregation is used to describe neighborhoods and schools that are almost totally comprised of one minority group, usually African-Americans, the term *resegregation* refers to segregation of children by race or ethnicity within a desegregated school (Eyler, Cook, & Ward, 1983). In fact, busing and other methods of desegregation are no guarantee that children of color will actually attend class alongside white children.

Resegregation occurs through the practice of sorting or tracking children into homogeneous ability groups for instruction. Schools are often insensitive to cultural differences when grouping students according to levels of ability (Eyler, Cook, & Ward, 1983). Resegregation is frequently a problem in magnet schools, where access to special programs may be denied to children of color in order to reserve enough places for whites who may be attracted to the school. In a 1991 report before the United States Senate Committee of Labor and Human Resources, Lawrence H. Thompson, on behalf of the General Accounting Office, described extensive within-school discrimination and inadequate enforcement of the equal access provisions of Title VI (Thompson, 1991). In more than 50 percent of the nation's school districts, minority students were disproportionately represented in low-track, non-college-bound, and special education classes (Thompson, 1991). In addition, about 10 percent, or seventeen hundred, of the nation's middle schools were grouping students by ability, with disproportionate numbers of minority students in the lower tracks (Thompson, 1991). Ability grouping was being used in all academic subjects in these schools, without consideration for individual variation or potential. Students remained with the same group all day without opportunities to interact with and learn with students from higher tracks and other ethnic and racial groups. A 1988 Department of Education study of eighth-graders showed a similar, but even more widespread problem, with only about 15 percent of students in mixed ability classes (Mansnerus, 1992). Asian-American students were four to five times as likely as American Indian students to be in the top track (Mansnerus, 1992). African-American students were two-and-a-half times as likely as their white counterparts to be in the lowest track (Mansnerus, 1992). Children in the wealthiest socioeconomic quarter were three times as likely as children in the poorest to be in the top track, but only one-third as likely to be in the bottom track (Mansnerus, 1992).

Resegregation and ability grouping often go hand-in-hand with unequal resources, with those in the top tracks receiving more than those at the bottom. While special education classes are smaller than regular education classes, those in the bottom tracks of the regular education classes tend to receive the least of all. Special programs in magnet schools, with their disproportionately white student body, offer extra resources and experienced teachers, who compete for the privilege of teaching these classes.

Bilingual programs, special education, and programs for the talented and gifted contribute to resegregation in integrated schools. By congregating children from one or two ethnic and racial groups in each of these programs, school administrators prevent children from diverse backgrounds from coming into contact with each other. Although the administrator's goal is not necessarily separation but rather the meeting of each child's educational needs, insensitivity to the child and the child's culture often results in unintended resegregation. A lack of awareness of culturally-based strengths and abilities may prevent many children from gaining enrichment in talented and gifted programs. Other children of color may be inappropriately placed in special education programs for learning or behavioral problems out of ignorance or prejudice (Holliday, 1987). Finally, children may spend too much time in, or be inappropriately placed in, bilingual programs with no opportunity to meet and converse with English-speaking children (Berger, 1993).

Bilingual Programs. While bilingual programs have helped countless youngsters adjust to a new, English-speaking society, students who participate in bilingual programs are also at risk for remaining in segregated school situations. The lack of agreement over how many hours a day, or how many years, a student should spend in bilingual classes is a major issue. Some students may remain in separate classes for the majority of their day, without sufficient contact with their monolingual peers. They may spend years in these classes, making little progress toward coping in English-only classes. According to a report to the New York City school board, twenty-five thousand students had been in separate bilingual programs for four or more years, and sixty-two hundred of those students had been in the programs for six years or more (Berger, 1993). Inadequate, inaccurate, and subjective testing procedures may lead to the placement in bilingual classes of children who do not belong there, but who may only have a foreign surname. In New York, one Latina child who barely spoke Spanish was placed in bilingual classes because her mother had just brought her from Puerto Rico after a ten-month visit. Another Latina child, fluent in English but shy with the strangers who tested her, was placed in bilingual classes even though her mother was third generation American, her Ecuadoran-born father had lived in the United States for eighteen years, and she had lived her entire life in Queens, where she spoke only English (Berger, 1993).

Special Education Classes. Although improved testing procedures for children with limited English proficiency has reduced their presence in special education classes for the mentally retarded or learning disabled, children of color are still disproportionately represented in these classes, as well as in classes for the emotionally disturbed. Especially overrepresented are male children, African-Americans, and those whose parents have not attended college (U.S. Dept. of Education, 1989) (Table 3–3). African-Americans are twice as likely to be placed in special education classes (U.S. Dept. of Education, 1989). The use of inappropriate assessment instruments and procedures, assumptions based on socioeconomic status, and linguistic and

TABLE 3–3 Student Participation in Various Curricula

Percentage of students in special education classes and disability concentration ratio, by individual and family characteristics at the secondary level: 1985-1986

Characteristic	Percentage of 1987 secondary students in special education classes	Percent of 1980 sophomores	Disability concentration ratio*
Sex			
Male	68.5	49.7	1.4
Female	31.5	50.3	0.6
Race/ethnicity			
White	65.0	70.0	0.9
Black	24.2	12.2	2.0
Latino	8.1	12.6	0.6
Other	2.7	5.2	0.5
Educational attainment of household head			
Less than high school graduate	41.0	31.1	1.3
High school graduate	36.0	27.8	1.3
Some college/2-year degree	14.0	20.9	0.7
College graduate or more	8.9	13.6	0.7

SOURCE: U.S. Department of Education, Office of Special Education and Rehabilitative Services, National Longitudinal Transition Study, *Youth with Disabilities During Transition: An Overview of Descriptive Findings from the National Longitudinal Transition Study,* May, 1989: Annual Report to Congress on the Implementation of the Handicapped Act, various years.

cultural differences have led to misdiagnosis, misclassification, and errors in the placement of these students (Prasse & Reschly, 1986).

Despite extensive litigation and legislation, overrepresentation of African-American and Latino students in special education continues, and segregation and isolation of these students occurs in classes where they are present in disproportionate numbers. In one community school district in New York City, a predominantly white elementary school was integrated by bringing in African-American and Latino children classified as mentally retarded from outside the neighborhood. Although the African-American and Latino children shared the building with their white and Asian-American peers, the two groups rarely saw each other (Kozol, 1991). Little attention was given to the impression made by the presence of impaired African-American and Latino children upon the white children and how it would reinforce the white children's stereotypes of their fellow New Yorkers.

Talented and Gifted Classes. Talented and gifted classes, in which African-American and Latino students are seriously underrepresented, are another source of resegregation and discrimination within schools. Children in talented and gifted programs receive resources unavailable to other children. Often the classes are taught by experts in a particular field, and the youngsters benefit from individual attention and work in small groups. Talented and gifted students enjoy greater access to laboratories, libraries, and computers. White children are almost twice as likely to be placed in talented and gifted classes as children of color (Kitano, 1991). Since teacher nominations and intelligence tests are the principal means by which talented and gifted students are identified, students with diverse cultural backgrounds or limited English proficiency are frequently excluded (Frasier, 1991). Culturally biased intelligence tests prevent many children of color from being identified as talented and gifted at the same time, as they misidentify too many as mentally retarded. Also problematic is the teacher nomination process because of stereotypes and assumptions that African-American, Latino, and American Indian children are unmotivated and poorly prepared for advanced work. Few teachers currently have the training to identify gifted children of color, whose behavior in class may differ from the behavior of talented and gifted white students (Frasier, 1991). In fact, gifted African-American males may be considered disruptive and placed in special education classes for the emotionally disturbed, while gifted Latino and American Indian children may value cooperation and community to the extent that they do not speak out in class, thereby allowing their gifts to go unnoticed. Language difficulties may prevent the placement of Latino, Asian-American, and American Indian students. In any case, the absence of children of color in classes for the talented and gifted is another source of resegregation in integrated schools and another way in which the schools reinforce white children's sense of superiority while depriving children of color of resources, enrichment, and encouragement.

Steering. Along with tracking, placements in special education, and exclusion from talented and gifted programs, children of color continue to be steered into stereotypical careers. Despite individual differences in ability and interests, Asian-American children tend to be guided into math, science, and engineering (Lee, 1991; National Education Association-C, 1987). Teachers and counselors often assume that such students have limited English proficiency, but that they are otherwise hard-working, motivated, and able—in short, best suited for technical fields where English proficiency is less important. In trying to meet these expectations, many Asian-American youngsters experience tremendous pressure and guilt, particularly if they are not good in math and science or if their interests lie elsewhere (Lee, 1991). Furthermore, Asian-American students might not receive the kind of well-rounded education that will allow them to achieve in their chosen profession. Statistics have shown a wage gap between Asian-American and white engineers, with stereotypes persisting into adulthood and blocking the career paths of many Asian-Americans (Barringer, 1992).

SPECIAL BOX 3–1

The steering of children of color into low-status jobs still continues in high schools across the country. In *Savage Inequalities*, Jonathan Kozol recounts an interview he had with a group of inner city high school students in Camden, New Jersey. He describes a Cambodian student who escaped war in her country only to experience disillusionment in the office of her guidance counselor:

Chilly, which is the nickname of a young Cambodian girl, speaks up for the first time: "I'll give you an example. I went to my counselor. He said, 'What do you want?' I said, 'I want to be a lawyer. I don't know what courses to take.' He told me, 'No, you cannot be a lawyer.' I said, 'Why?' He said, 'Your English isn't good.' 'I'm seventeen. I've been here in America four years. I want to be a lawyer.' He said, 'No. You cannot be a lawyer. Look for something else. Look for an easier job.'" (p. 155)..."You know, I have problems with my self-esteem. I wasn't born here. Every day I think, 'Maybe he's right. Do something else.' But what I'm thinking is that fifteen minutes isn't very long for somebody to counsel you about a choice that will determine your whole life. He throws this book at me: 'Choose something else!'" (p. 156)

Although generally not as overt as when Malcolm X was a child, steering continues to dampen the hopes of African-American, Latino, and American Indian children. Such steering also comes in the form of placements in special education classes and in the bottom track of regular education classes. Whereas the top tracks in elementary and middle school feed into the honors and college-bound programs in high school, those in the bottom track receive basic skills and vocational training through such courses as business or consumer math, shop, and word processing. Years ago, training in blue-collar careers might have led to secure and well-paying, if not prestigious, powerful, or intellectually-fulfilling, employment. Today, many vocational programs are outdated, preparing youngsters for jobs that no longer exist in the United States. Other options still lead to work, but only in low-paid clerical and service areas, where benefits are few and job security nonexistent. For those assigned to the bottom tracks—students who are disproportionately African-American, Latino, American Indian, and from poverty homes—a number of factors make it difficult to get into the college-bound track and eventually into college. These factors include the low expectations teachers have of bottom-track students and assignments consistent with those expectations, peer pressure, loss of instructional time to discipline problems, lack of preparatory coursework, and lack of access to college counselors (Kozol, 1991). As a result, African-American, Latino, and American Indian children are not

SPECIAL BOX 3–2

In having her options narrowed by tracking, Chantal's experience was typical. Part Mexican-American and part American Indian, she had attended Head Start and done well in mixed-ability classes in elementary school, although frequent moves at the end of her elementary years had hurt her school performance. In the seventh grade, she moved with her family to a small town in Idaho. She and her siblings were the only Mexican-Americans or American Indians in the school, and they were among the poorest students. Her mother, who had completed the eighth grade, ran a one-person cleaning service. Her stepfather, a timber mill worker who had a tenth-grade education, had been disabled in a mill accident.

Upon her arrival, Chantal was placed in low-track classes, she earned mostly Bs and Cs with minimal effort. She continued in low-track classes in eighth and ninth grade even though her standardized test scores placed her above the fiftieth percentile in math and in the top quarter in reading. In high school, she took two years of mathematics—basic algebra and business math. She took one general science course and English and social studies courses that, at most, required two-page papers. By graduation, she had written no research papers. Her electives were home economics and service, which consisted of internships as a school library clerk and an office assistant. Her grade point average was 2.7.

After graduation, Chantal moved East to work as a nanny in order to earn money for college. However, she soon learned that she lacked the basic courses for college, including geometry and a second year of science. She would have to take several remedial courses, at her own expense, if she wanted to enter a degree-granting program, even at a two-year college. Moreover, she had never spoken to a college counselor, so she did not know she would have to take the SAT or the ACT to be admitted to most four-year colleges. She signed up for the tests the following year and took them with virtually no preparation.

Despite these obstacles, Chantal achieved a respectable score on the ACT. She also attempted an expository writing course as a special student at a local four-year college. She found the work difficult, especially the assignment to write an eight-page research paper, but she enjoyed the challenge. The professor was impressed with her effort and commitment, but shocked at her lack of preparation for college work. She earned, in her professor's words, "a solid B." One wonders how she would have done had she been placed in mixed-ability college-bound classes and given access to a guidance counselor who recognized her abilities.

as much openly discouraged from pursuing managerial, professional, and technical careers (although this does still occur) as placed in ability-grouped classes that often preclude their pursuing these careers.

School Policies and Governance

In addition to hypersegregation, resegregation, and their related problems, the issues of staffing, governance, curriculum content, and community control remain at the forefront. New York City's conflicts over decentralization and community control have recurred in one form or another as minority parents and community leaders have demanded greater involvement in the schools. In some cases, the conflict has centered on the right to dismiss incompetent or culturally insensitive teachers and administrators. White teachers and administrators may not be the only ones at issue. In one high school in New York City, a white social studies teacher's insensitive remarks in class prompted a walkout and calls for his removal, but African-American parents and community leaders also demanded the ouster of the Puerto Rican principal, whom they believed favored the Latino students. The reverse happened in Houston, where Mexican-American students protested what they felt to be favoritism toward African-American students on the part of an African-American principal. Students and parents of color have objected to the unequal allocation of resources within districts, as when students at a predominantly Mexican-American high school in Chicago walked out to protest the lack of books in the library. Demands for a more inclusive or multicultural curriculum have sparked opposition from those who believe that the inclusion of more diverse topics and authors will undermine academic standards and Western scholarly tradition. At times, white administrators, teachers, parents, and students have charged *racism in reverse* and claimed that perspectives highly critical of the mainstream have actually increased racial and ethnic divisions. Similarly, attempts to meet the needs of particular ethnic and cultural groups, such as American Indians and African-American males, have been criticized by those both within and outside the group as fostering segregation. Conflicts within the wider society—between African-Americans and Jewish-Americans and between African-Americans and Korean-Americans, for instance—have carried over into the schools, dividing staff and students and turning various attempts to create a multicultural curriculum into a community-wide battleground. Finally, entrenched bureaucracies, time constraints, and lack of funds have stymied attempts to rewrite the curriculum and to broaden the selection of classroom materials. As Chapter 4 will discuss in more detail, past and present efforts to reorganize schools and to create *curriculums of inclusion* have run into the same controversies that divide American society as a whole.

Segregation and School Funding: "Savage Inequalities"

Ultimately, one cannot examine persistent problems in the schools without exploring the enormous disparities in funding and resources that place most children of color at a significant disadvantage. As discussed earlier in this chapter, the system of funding schools through local property taxes denies resources to children in poor communities, with very little of the difference made up through federal compensatory education programs or state equalization funds. In fact, a ruling by the New Jersey Supreme Court in the 1980s struck down that state's formula for equalization aid to schools, arguing that it had actually provided more money to wealthy districts (Kozol, 1991). Special grants (requiring extra staff to apply for the grants) and support for talented and gifted programs are two means by which federal and state money has benefitted wealthy, predominantly white districts. The fact that African-Americans and immigrants tend to live in inner cities or in satellite cities with a limited tax base—areas that in many cases are considered hypersegregated—means the minority poor suffer the most from funding disparities. This was the argument made in 1968 by the plaintiffs in the landmark case *San Antonio Independent School District v. Rodriguez*. Demetrio Rodriguez and his fellow plaintiffs argued that the predominantly Mexican-American residents of the Edgewood district (San Antonio and its suburbs were divided into six separate districts) paid a higher tax rate than the predominantly white, upper middle-class residents of the Alamo Heights district, but could spend less than half as much to educate each pupil. This translated into lower-paid teachers, larger classes, less support staff, dilapidated and overcrowded buildings, and fewer books and other instructional materials. In 1974, the Supreme Court ruled against Rodriguez, with the majority on the Court asserting that the Edgewood district's schools provided a minimal education and the Constitution only guaranteed a minimal standard necessary for exerting one's political rights, not "absolute equality" (Kozol, 1991). The Court's decision served to legitimize unequal funding that was based on local property taxes. Even though the highest courts in various states (including Texas) have demanded some effort at equalization, the disparities between rich and poor districts remain in all regions of the country. As Jonathan Kozol pointed out in his now-classic *Savage Inequalities*, those who could afford it the least have been hurt the most—children with limited English proficiency, children whose own parents have suffered the effects of inadequate educations, and poor minority children who see in their crumbling buildings and underpaid teachers the low esteem in which they are held by mainstream society (Kozol, 1991).

Many other analysts besides Kozol have argued that children of color have special needs and that the effective education of these children requires more money, not less. As the statistics show, African-American, Latino, and American Indian children have lagged behind their white counterparts in a number of key areas, though the disparities are not uniform within and among groups. For instance, drop-out rates among African-Americans are significantly lower than those for Latinos or American Indians, and they have improved markedly over the past decade (U.S. Dept. of Education, 1992). Latinos and Asian-Americans are diverse groups, with children of some nationalities experiencing greater school success than children of others. Culturally determined behaviors, learning styles, linguistic backgrounds, and individual, family, and community factors all play a role in determining the educational needs of each child. Some of those needs can be discussed in terms of a group as a whole, but there will also be great individual variations. And while increased funding will help in meeting those needs, it is not the only, or even necessarily the most important, factor. Greater diversity within schools and within classes, increased awareness of and sensitivity to each child's cultural heritage, a more inclusive curriculum, school staffs that more closely reflect the backgrounds of the students, and a more open, accessible, and democratic leadership structure contribute as well to the educational success of children of color. In the next section, the specific needs of African-American, Latino, Asian-American, and American Indian children will be examined in more detail.

❖ Current Needs of Children of Color

African-Americans

At present, African-Americans are the largest minority group and the largest group of children of color in the schools. Historically, African-Americans have suffered the most from segregation and discrimination in the schools, and recent research shows the problems of hypersegregation and social isolation to be most severe for African-American communities as a whole (Massey & Denton, 1989). However, the value placed upon education in African-African culture has remained strong in spite of the obstacles. In key measures of educational achievement, African-Americans have lagged behind, but an overwhelming majority complete high school despite multiple risk factors.

Between 1971 and 1990, African-American youngsters have improved their proficiency in reading and mathematics as compared to their white peers, significantly narrowing the gap between the two groups (National Assessment of Educational Progress, 1991). However, their writing proficiency scores did not improve between 1984, when the writing proficiency test was first instituted, and 1990 (National Assessment of Educational Progress, 1991). Among eighth-graders, the scores actually fell (which they did for white students as well) and among eleventh-graders, the scores peaked in 1988, only to fall back to their 1984 levels (National Assessment of Educational Progress, 1991) (Tables 3–4, 3–5, and 3–6.)

Grade delay rates for African-American children are quite discouraging. Although students are generally retained in order to give them a chance to catch up and to meet grade-level expectations, over-age students are more likely to experience social problems and dissatisfaction with school. They are more likely to drop out than their peers who also read at a lower level, but have not been retained (Hess, 1986). More than one out of four African-American children have been retained in kindergarten, first, or second grade. Further along, the chances for retention increase, to the point that almost half of all African-American males have been retained at least once by eighth grade (U.S. Census-B, 1989) (Table 3–7).

In spite of lower scores and high rates of grade retention, school persistence has increased among African-American students. In 1972, 90.5 percent of all African-American tenth-graders enrolled the following year (U.S. Census-B, 1972). By 1990, that percentage had increased to 95 percent, less than two percentage points below the rate for white students (U.S. Census-B, 1990). Obviously, that rate does not take into account students

TABLE 3–4 Trends in the Reading Proficiency of 9-, 13-, and 17-year-olds

Average reading proficiency (scale score), by age and race/ethnicity: 1971-1990

Year	Age 9				Age 13				Age 17			
	All races	White	Black	Latino	All races	White	Black	Latino	All races	White	Black	Latino
1971	208	214	[1]170	—	255	261	[1]222	—	[1]285	[1]291	[1]239	—
1975	210	217	[2]181	183	256	262	[1]226	233	[1]286	293	[1]241	252
1980	[1,2]215	[2]221	[2]189	190	259	[2]264	[1,2]233	237	286	293	[1]243	[1]261
1984	211	[2]218	[2]186	187	257	263	[2]236	240	289	[2]295	[2]264	[2]268
1988	212	218	[2]189	194	258	261	[2]243	240	[2]290	295	[2]274	[2]271
1990	209	217	[2]182	189	257	262	[2]242	238	[2]290	[2]297	[2]267	[2]275

Average reading proficiency (scale score), by age and sex: 1971-1990

Year	Age 9		Age 13		Age 17	
	Male	Female	Male	Female	Male	Female
1971	201	214	250	261	279	291
1975	204	216	250	262	280	[1]291
1980	[1,2]210	[1,2]220	[2]254	263	282	[1]289
1984	[2]208	214	253	262	[2]284	294
1988	[2]208	216	252	263	[2]286	294
1990	204	215	251	263	284	297

— Not available
[1] Statistically significant difference from 1990.
[2] Statistically significant difference from 1971 for all except Latinos. Statistically significant difference from 1975 for Latinos.
NOTE: Reading Proficiency Scale has a range from 0 to 500
Level 150: Simple discrete reading tasks
Level 200: Partial skills and understanding
Level 250: Interrelate ideas, and make generalizations
Level 300: Understands relatively complicated information
Level 350: Learns from specialized reading materials

SOURCE: National Assessment of Educational Progress, *Trends in Academic Progress: Achievement of American Students in Science, 1969-70 to 1990, Mathematics, 1973 to 1990, Reading, 1971 to 1990, and Writing, 1984 to 1990*, 1991.

TABLE 3–5 Trends in the Mathematics Proficiency of 9-, 13-, and 17-year-olds

Average mathematics proficiency, by age and race/ethnicity: 1973-1990 (scale score)

Year	Age 9				Age 13				Age 17			
	All races	White	Black	Latino	All races	White	Black	Latino	All races	White	Black	Latino
1973	[1]219	[1]225	[1]190	[1]202	[1]266	274	[1]228	[1]239	304	310	[1]270	277
1978	[1]219	[1]224	[1]192	[1]203	[1]264	[1]272	[1]230	[1]238	[1]300	[2]306	[1]268	276
1982	[1]219	[1]224	[1]195	[1]204	269	274	[1,2]240	[2]252	[1,2]299	[1,2]304	[1]272	277
1986	[1]222	[1]227	[2]202	205	269	274	[2]249	[2]254	302	308	[1,2]279	283
1990	[2]230	[1]235	[2]208	[2]214	[2]270	276	[2]249	[2]255	305	310	289	284

Average mathematics proficiency, by age and sex: 1973-1990 (scale score)

Year	Age 9		Age 13		Age 17	
	Male	Female	Male	Female	Male	Female
1973	[1]218	[1]220	[1]265	267	309	301
1978	[1]217	[1]220	[1]264	[1]265	[2]304	[1]297
1982	[1]217	[1]221	269	268	[2]302	[1,2]296
1986	[1,2]222	[1]222	[2]270	268	305	299
1990	[2]229	[2]230	[2]271	270	306	303

[1] Statistically significant difference from 1990.
[2] Statistically significant difference from 1973.
NOTE: Mathematics Proficiency Scale
Level 150: Performs simple addition and subtraction
Level 200: Uses basic operations to solve problems
Level 250: Uses intermediate level mathematics skills to solve two-step complex problems
Level 300: Understands measurement and geometry and solves more complex problems
Level 350: Understands and applies more advanced mathematical concepts

SOURCE: National Assessment of Educational Progress, *Trends in Academic Progress: Achievement of American Students in Science, 1969-70 to 1990, Mathematics, 1973 to 1990, Reading, 1971 to 1990, and Writing, 1984 to 1990*, 1991.

who have already dropped out, students who are enrolled year after year but do not attend classes, and students who will subsequently drop out. According to Census figures in 1990, 77.6 percent of all nineteen- and twenty-year-old African-Americans had completed high school, an improvement of almost ten percentage points over the 1973 figures (U.S. Census-B, 1974-1990). While 25.8 percent of African Americans had dropped out by that age in 1973, only 15.6 percent had dropped out in 1990 (U.S. Census-B, 1974–1990). Among whites, the percentage of nineteen- and twenty-year-old dropouts was 10.4, a figure that had remained relatively unchanged since 1973 (U.S. Census-B, 1974–1990). In 1990, 6.8 percent of African-American nineteen- and twenty-year-olds were still enrolled in high school (U.S. Census-B, 1990), (Figure 3–2). The percentage of African-American high school graduates twenty-five to twenty-nine years old who have completed one or more years of college increased from 24.6 percent

TABLE 3–6 Trends in the Writing Proficiency in Grades 4, 8, and 11

| | **Average writing proficiency, by age and race/ethnicity: 1984-1990 (scale score)** | | | | | | | | | | | |
| | Grade 4 | | | | Grade 8 | | | | Grade 11 | | | |
Year	All races	White	Black	Latino	All races	White	Black	Latino	All races	White	Black	Latino
1984	179	186	154	163	*206	*210	190	191	212	218	195	188
1988	186	193	154	169	*203	*207	190	188	214	219	200	199
1990	183	191	155	168	198	202	182	189	212	217	194	198

| | **Trends in average writing proficiency, by sex: 1984-1990** | | | | | |
| | Grade 4 | | Grade 8 | | Grade 11 | |
Year	Male	Female	Male	Female	Male	Female
1984	176	*184	*199	214	201	223
1988	176	195	193	*213	204	223
1990	174	193	187	208	200	224

* Statistically significant difference from 1990.
NOTE: Average NAEP writing assessment scores were produced using the Average Response Method (ARM). The ARM provides an estimate of average writing achievement for each respondent as if he or she took 11 of the 12 writing tasks given, and as if NAEP had computed average achievement across that set of tasks.

NOTE: Writing Proficiency Chart
Level 100: **Unsatisfactory**—Failed to reflect a basic understanding of the task
Level 200: **Minimal**—Recognized the elements needed to complete the task, but were not managed well enough to insure the intended purpose
Level 300: **Adequate**—Included features critical to accomplishing the purpose of the task and were likely to have the intended effect
Level 400: **Elaborated**—Reflected a higher level of coherence and elaboration; beyond adequate

SOURCE: National Assessment of Educational Progress, *Trends in Academic Progress: Achievement of American Students in Science, 1969-70 to 1990, Mathematics, 1973 to 1990, Reading, 1971 to 1990, and Writing, 1984 to 1990,* 1991.

in 1971 to 42.5 percent in 1991 (U.S. Census-B, 1971–1991). As a group, African-Americans have demonstrated remarkable school persistence despite multiple risk factors, low achievement scores, and high grade retention rates.

African-Americans' collective success in completing high school obscures two very serious problem areas. One is the continued existence of segregated schools where drop-out rates may approach 50 percent or more (Hess, 1986). These schools may be considered "dumping grounds" for alienated, low-achieving students as underfunded districts practice a kind of "educational triage" (Hess, 1986).

The operative policy of educational triage has created aggregates of students in which dropping out can no longer be spoken of as a marginal activity. In these schools, in fact, dropping out is the norm. Similarly...

non-performance in class is the behavioral norm, and often the rule articulated informally by student leaders. (p. 50)

The second problem is that of the "endangered" African-American male. Grade retention rates and drop-out rates for African-American males are far higher than those for African-American females, and as many scholars and journalists have pointed out, there are more young African-American males in prison than there are in college (Steele, 1990). Low employment rates—a consequence of low educational attainment, discrimination, economic changes, and other factors—have contributed to the shortage of marriageable partners, cited by sociologist William Julius Wilson as a principal cause of teenage pregnancy and out-of-wed-lock births (Wilson 1987). Researchers have found that African-American boys experience lower self-esteem in school and higher self-esteem with their peers than their white counterparts. In fact, they often see their "social assets" as compensation for their "academic liabilities" (Hare & Castenell, 1987). Home factors may play a role, as some evidence points

TABLE 3–7 Percentage of seventh-grade students who are 13 years old or older: October 1972–91

October	Total	Family Income			Sex		Race/ethnicity		
		Low	Middle	High	Male	Female	White	Black	Latino
1972	24.2	39.3	25.9	14.3	29.3	19.1	21.5	34.2	39.3
1973	23.8	41.5	24.6	15.1	27.6	19.7	21.2	35.6	34.2
1974	23.4	—	—	—	28.8	17.7	20.2	32.8	37.7
1975	22.5	37.4	23.6	14.4	27.0	18.0	20.3	31.8	28.8
1976	21.8	39.5	21.8	15.4	25.7	17.7	20.1	25.9	34.9
1977	22.0	39.0	24.2	11.1	26.2	17.4	19.6	27.8	38.0
1978	21.8	39.8	22.0	14.1	25.8	17.5	18.5	32.1	37.1
1979	22.2	40.3	21.8	15.1	25.9	18.4	19.1	34.4	—
1980	24.3	40.2	24.9	16.8	28.7	19.5	21.7	30.3	36.1
1981	23.6	39.8	23.4	15.6	26.2	21.0	20.0	34.1	37.1
1982	26.1	46.8	25.3	16.6	30.5	21.4	22.4	38.3	38.3
1983	29.1	43.0	30.4	17.6	35.4	22.0	25.4	36.0	44.8
1984	29.7	49.7	28.6	19.0	33.8	25.2	25.5	40.6	43.0
1985	27.5	44.6	26.0	19.6	32.3	22.5	23.9	38.8	34.5
1986	29.6	47.3	30.0	18.1	34.1	24.9	24.4	43.5	44.8
1987	29.7	46.2	29.5	19.3	35.7	23.3	26.7	36.2	40.5
1988	30.2	52.9	28.7	18.3	36.3	23.7	25.8	42.6	43.6
1989	31.7	48.4	31.3	22.5	36.3	26.7	28.0	42.3	39.1
1990	32.7	50.3	33.4	20.3	38.2	26.8	28.0	45.9	43.7
1991	29.7	47.9	29.9	17.9	33.6	25.8	25.5	40.7	40.0

—Not available.
NOTE: Low income is defined as the bottom 20% of all family incomes; high income is defined as the top 20% of all family incomes; and middle income is defined as the 60% of family incomes between high and low income.

SOURCE: U.S. Department of Commerce, Bureau of the Census, October current Population Survey.

FIGURE 3–2 High School Drop-out Rates for 19- to 20-year-olds from Selected Groups, 1973—1990

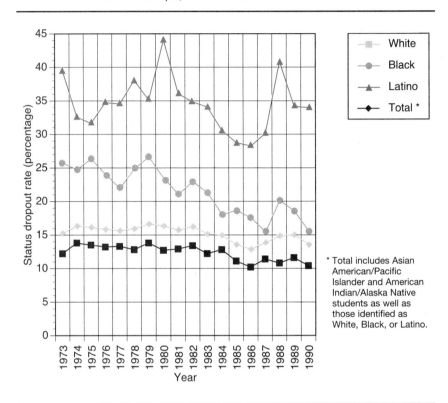

* Total includes Asian American/Pacific Islander and American Indian/Alaska Native students as well as those identified as White, Black, or Latino.

SOURCE: U.S. Census, October current Population Survey, 1973–1990.

to lower expectations for boys and different patterns of child-rearing, especially in mother-only homes (Hare and Castenell, 1987). However, the school itself plays a major role. Boys in general tend to have more conflicts with their predominantly female teachers in the early grades; these conflicts are magnified when racial, class, and cultural differences are brought into the equation. The brightest and most assertive boys are also the most likely to be identified as discipline problems. For African-American boys, constant run-ins with teachers are likely to lead to harsh and demeaning criticism, lower grades, fewer efforts to help with problems, and punitive placements in special education and bottom-track classes:

> Existing evidence concerning race and sex differences in the quality of the school experience suggests that the lower attainment, greater negative attitudes, and higher attrition rates of black boys may, in part, be due to the unique problem that they present to the schools. Put simply, black

males are probably the most feared, least likely to be identified with, and [the] least likely to be effectively taught group. If this is true, then the responsibility for their lower attainment should be shifted from them, their families, and peers, to the alien, indifferent if not hostile, climate of the schools. Furthermore, their reportedly more negative attitude toward school should be seen, not as the cause of their low attainment, but as a consequence of their mistreatment. (Hare & Castenell, 1987, p. 211)

In identifying the educational needs of African-American youngsters, the problem of segregated, dumping ground schools and the unique situation of the African-American male are paramount. Also crucial is the need to provide equitable treatment for African-American students in integrated schools—including the hiring of African-American teachers and administrators—so that those students are not resegregated or treated as outsiders. More flexible teaching styles are important to accommodate the varied learning styles of African-American students. In 1987, the National Education Association made a variety of other recommendations, including multicultural curriculum content and educational materials "that represent blacks accurately and adequately and that can help perpetuate positive self-concepts," (p. 8) higher standards for achievement and the support and encouragement to attain those standards, early childhood education programs, and increased funding for teachers and educational materials. (National Education Association-A, 1987)

Latinos

Latinos are the second largest group of children of color in the schools, and many analysts believe that they may overtake African-Americans sometime in the next century. Immigration has brought increasing numbers of Mexican-American students and students from the Caribbean and Central and South America to this country. Latino students are a diverse group, not only in terms of national origin, but also in terms of socioeconomic status. Furthermore, the families of many Latino students have lived in the United States for generations, while others may have just arrived. Finally, Latinos, classified as Hispanic in the Census, may be of any race. Black Latinos, most of whom hail from Puerto Rico, Cuba, or the Dominican Republic, have experienced patterns of segregation and discrimination similar to those of African-Americans.

In contrast to their African-American peers, Latino students tend to drop out more frequently than their risk factors would indicate. Although their achievement scores in reading, mathematics, and writing are the same or slightly higher than those of African-Americans, Latinos are almost twice as likely to drop out before completing high school. Limited English proficiency and parents who did not complete high school are two risk factors that may increase this likelihood. In previous decades, many Mexican-American and other Latino youngsters worked in fields and factories instead of attending school. Even today, Latino youngsters are, in general, more likely to work and to work longer hours in high school than their white or African-American peers, and when they leave school early, they are more likely to have jobs (National Education Association-D, 1987).

Between 1973 and 1991, the Census data show an increase in the percentage of all Latinos completing high school, from 54.7 percent in 1973 to 59.7 percent in 1990 (U.S. Census-B, 1974-1990). In 1990, 34 percent of nineteen- and twenty-year-old Latinos had dropped out of school, with 6.3 percent still enrolled (U.S. Census-B, 1990). Among twenty-five to twenty-nine-year-old high school graduates, 40.2 percent had completed one or more years of college (U.S. Census-B, 1990). Unfortunately, the data do not separate the Latino population by national origin or duration of time in the United States. However, a study by Bean and Tienda (1987) provides separate data on drop-out rates for Mexican-Americans, Puerto Ricans, Cuban-Americans, and others using 1980 figures. That study showed native-born Mexican-Americans with a drop-out rate of 30.4 percent, and a rate of 59.4 percent for their foreign-born peers (Bean & Tienda, 1987). Puerto Ricans born on the mainland dropped out at a rate of 31.9 percent; their island-born peers' rate was 47 percent (Bean & Tienda, 1987). Native-born Cuban-Americans had a drop-out rate of 11.4 percent, equivalent to the rate for white teenagers; their Cuban-born counterparts had a 16.1 percent drop-out rate (Bean & Tienda, 1987).

Grade delay is a significant problem among Latino students and is a factor contributing to students' later dropping out. Foreign-born Latinos of all nationalities were at least twice as likely as their United States-born peers of the same nationality to be over-age (Bean & Tienda, 1987). In some cases, children are held back because of a lack of education in their country of origin, but in spite of bilingual education programs, limited English proficiency continues to be a principal factor for both foreign-born and United States-born Latinos. Approximately one-third of Latino students have repeated at least one grade by the time they are thirteen (U.S. Census-B, 1989).

In assessing the educational needs of Latino students, language is perhaps the most significant issue. While many Latino youngsters speak little or no Spanish, others are recent immigrants who speak only Spanish. Some of them may not read or write Spanish, however, because of lack of access to schools in their country of origin. Many immigrants and first or second generation Americans wish to retain their language and their ties to their country of origin; these wishes should be respected by school personnel and taken into account when designing an educational program. At the same time, school officials must recognize that English proficiency is crucial to upward mobility in the United States and that permanent placement in a bilingual or Spanish-only program may condemn Latino children to low-wage employment, while isolating them from their English-speaking peers. There is no reason why children cannot be fluent in two languages or achieve in all their subjects while maintaining a bilingual, bicultural identity. Thus, high expectations should be maintained for Latino students, and resources and support—in both English and Spanish—should be available to allow those students to achieve their maximum potential. A number of books and other educational resources in Spanish exist for those involved in bilingual programs.

Another special need of Latino students revolves around the low educational attainment of many of their parents. Since grade retention, bottom-track placements, and dropping out are related to the parents' low achievement, schools must address the lack of educational opportunities—both in their country of origin and in the United States—that have handicapped the parents of Latino students. Many of the parents are not in a position to assist their children with schoolwork or school problems because of language barriers and their own lack of experience (or negative experience) with the schools. Thus, schools should reach out to Latino parents, making sure that the school staff can communicate with the parents in Spanish. Schools should also offer workshops and classes for Latino parents so they can resume their educations and learn more about what is going on in their children's classes.

As is the case with African-American students, Latino students often attend segregated high schools where low achievement and dropping out are the norm. Often, Latinos and African-Americans attend these dumping ground schools together. A policy that addresses the problem of educational triage in poor, inner-city schools will go a long way toward boosting Latino students' achievement rates and levels of satisfaction with school. The National Education Association has also pointed out the need to recruit more bilingual teachers and Latino teachers and to build links with community organizations as well as with parents (National Education Association-D, 1987). Testing procedures must be improved so that students will not be placed inappropriately in bilingual classes and will not be denied access to talented and gifted or other enrichment programs because of their ethnicity, cultural heritage, socioeconomic background, or language (National Education Association-D, 1987). Curriculum changes must be instituted so that bilingual and English-only classes follow the same curriculum. This way, when bilingual students make the transition to English-only classes, they will not discover that they have been given a "dumbed down" program and are missing two to three years worth of work (National Education Association-D, 1987). Textbooks and other materials should offer positive images of the various Latino cultural heritages, and material on Latin America and Latinos in the United States should be part of the curriculum for everyone (National Education Association-D, 1987).

Observers have pointed out that Latino students often lack confidence in their abilities, and this lack of self-confidence affects their school performance. Attitudes toward Latino students need to change. Stereotypes of Spanish speakers as slow learners, expectations that

Latinos will drop out (which often leads to overcrowded classes with the expectation that many will soon leave), a failure to respect the parents and to recognize the high aspirations they have for their children, and a lack of sensitivity to learning styles that may be culturally related must give way to a more enlightened, culturally sensitive approach (National Education Association-D, 1987). Teachers must believe in the intelligence of Latino students and challenge them. They must respect the names of Latino children by pronouncing them correctly and work to end Latino students' isolation from schoolmates of different national, ethnic, and racial groups (Garza Flores, 1991, 1992).

Asian-Americans and Pacific Islanders

Although Asian-Americans comprise the third largest minority group, within this group are some of the fastest-growing nationalities in the United States. Filipino-Americans, Asian Indians, and Southeast Asians have exceeded all others in their rate of increase due to immigration. Like Latinos, Asian-Americans and Pacific Islanders encompass a number of national groups and vary in terms of the amount of time they have spent in the United States. Very few Japanese-Americans have arrived recently, and some Chinese-American youngsters are fourth and fifth generation Americans. These youngsters speak English at home, as do most Asian Indians. Recent immigrants from the Philippines and the Pacific Islands may have grown up with English as an official language, but they may speak other languages at home. Most immigrants and first generation Americans from elsewhere in Asia do not speak English at home, though their levels of English proficiency vary. In contrast to their Latino peers, few Asian-American children and their families expect to return to their country of origin, so the motivation to maintain their native language is lower. Though many Asian-American children take bilingual classes, a smaller percentage do, and those children stay in the bilingual program for less time than their Latino counterparts (Berger, 1993).

As a group, Asian-American children are comparable to white children in terms of school achievement, promotion to modal grade level, and high school graduation rates. However, there are some differences among nationalities. Because of lack of educational opportunities in their country of origin and the many years they spent in limbo in refugee camps, many Vietnamese (especially Amerasians), Hmong, and Cambodian youngsters have been placed in classes below modal grade level. Those arriving as teenagers are especially likely to graduate high school at age twenty or older. While these youngsters may experience social isolation in school, their peers who have been placed according to chronological age rather than academic development may suffer great stress as they attempt to catch up. High school drop-out rates among Pacific Islanders are higher than for Asian-Americans as a whole; though the sampling is small, their drop-out rates approach those for American

Indians (with whom they share many cultural characteristics) and Latinos. Often "lost" because of their small numbers, immigrant youngsters from the traditional rural villages of American Samoa and Guam may have difficulties with a school curriculum and approach that is ignorant of and alien to their culture (*New York Times*, 1992).

In assessing the needs of Asian-American students as a whole, particular attention must be given to addressing the stereotype of Asian-Americans as a model minority. As demonstrated by the problems experienced by Southeast Asian and Pacific Islander youth, Asian-Americans come with a variety of backgrounds and experiences, some of which have led to a difficult school adjustment. Individual differences and learning styles often run counter to the stereotype. Asian-American children who dislike science and math but who enjoy the humanities may experience subtle or overt discouragement on the part of school authorities (Lee, 1991). Youngsters who have been taught to respect teachers and other authority figures may not seek help when they need it and may not question expressions of prejudice or inappropriate and discriminatory placements. Those who have psychological problems because of wartime trauma, family pressures, or any other reason may be ignored, as may those who become involved in drugs, gangs, and other social pathologies that afflict youngsters of all races, ethnic groups, and social classes (Nahme-Huang, 1989).

The model minority stereotype has also contributed to attacks against Asian-American students by their peers. In poor, inner city districts, Asian-American students may be accused of taking a disproportionate share of scarce resources and of enjoying more favorable treatment on the part of teachers and administrators (Nahme-Huang, 1989). The belief that Asian-American children are goody-goodies who will not fight back makes them vulnerable to attacks by bullies and bigots of all ethnic groups. In some schools, especially those that have many diverse groups in attendance, teachers have shown favoritism to Asian-American students, creating conflict between them and their non-Asian peers. Other teachers have expressed the same kind of resentment toward Asian-American children as the youngsters have endured from their peers.

Language is another area where Asian-American children have special problems and needs. Language barriers often deter the full involvement of parents, unless the school values parental involvement and the staff can communicate with the parents in their native language (National Education Association-C, 1987). A lack of language-trained psychologists prevents students with emotional problems from receiving services. The testing and education of bilingual, ESL, and special education students may be inadequate because of a lack of personnel (National Education Association-C, 1987). In fact, the great differences between Asian languages and English, including differences in the alphabet, call for more, not less, ESL and English instruction. Language problems may deter Asian-Americans from seeking careers in teaching, thus depriving Asian-American children of role models (National Education Association-C, 1987).

Other needs identified by the NEA include a greater sensitivity to the way Asian-Americans are presented in textbooks and other educational materials. Materials should be free from stereotypes and should present a more honest and multidimensional portrait of the Asian experience in North America (National Education Association-C, 1987). Racial incidents should not be covered up, whether in the curriculum (as in the case of the exploitation of Chinese railroad workers or the internment of the Japanese in World War II, for instance) or in the school (National Education Association-C, 1987). Cultural values, such as the emphasis upon discipline, the importance of family, and respect for authority, should be taken into account when dealing with Asian-American students and managing culturally diverse classes (National Education Association-C, 1987). Finally, teachers should recognize the ethnic diversity among Asian-Americans. Teachers should not try to guess at a child's nationality, but rather they should inform themselves of the history, language, and culture of each. The nations of East, South, and Southeast Asia do not share a common language, as do most of the nations of Latin America, and nations such as Japan and Korea, Japan and China, and Cambodia and Vietnam have experienced recent hostilities.

American Indians

American Indians are the smallest single group of children of color, and they are divided by nation and region. The category of American Indians includes Alaska Natives and some Hawaiians. Indians may live on reservations or they may live in cities and towns in the Midwest, Southwest, and West. Indian reservations are among the poorest communities in the country. Most are in isolated rural areas known for their harsh climate. Poverty, alcoholism, and despair characterize the lives of many on the reservation, but reservations are also places where traditional cultures, languages, and religions flourish, providing a source of community and strength. For Indian youngsters living off the reservation, poverty and isolation from cultural roots have created difficulties in school and at home (LaFrombiose & Low, 1989). While some Indians have assimilated and given up their cultural identity, others who are of mixed race have reasserted their Indian heritage. These latter two groups may be indistinguishable in terms of circumstances and school performance from their white, African-American, Latino, or Asian-American peers.

Among those who live on reservations or consider themselves to be full-blooded American Indians, the statistics on school achievement are discouraging. The drop-out rate among American Indians is 35.5 percent by tenth grade, and their risk factors are similar to those for African-Americans and Latinos (Campbell, 1992).

Foremost among the problems faced by American Indian youngsters and those of mixed heritage is that of identity. After centuries of attempts to destroy Indian cultures, including the confinement of Indian children to boarding schools to force their assimilation, most Indian parents and children approach government-run schools with fear and distrust. Indian values of community and cooperation often run counter to the schools' emphasis upon competition and individual achievement. Successful schools must use teaching methods that build upon collective values and the personal learning styles of Indian students (Swisher & Deyhle, 1992). The schools must reach out to parents and community leaders, giving them a voice in the operation of the school; only in this way will the past mistakes of government-run schools be overcome. Recognizing that many youngsters speak traditional languages as well as English and that many children and parents wish to retain their traditional languages, the schools should teach those languages along with English and English as a second language (National Education Association-B, 1987; Reyhner, 1992b). School staffs should be prepared to communicate with Indian parents in the local language. Whether they live on or off the reservation, American Indian youngsters live in two worlds. Schools must acknowledge the potential conflict and promote a positive self-image by means of a multicultural curriculum. Outdated textbooks and other materials with stereotyped views of Indians must be replaced by materials that are presented from the perspective of Indians themselves (Reyhner, 1992a). In recent years, there has been an increase in locally-generated and small-press materials by and about American Indians. Those who work with American Indian children and teenagers must utilize those materials in the place of materials now being used that tell the Indians' story from the perspective of the white mainstream (National Education Association-B, 1987).

Children in Interracial Families

There are few estimates of the number of children of mixed heritage or living in interracial homes. The numbers range from six-hundred thousand to five million (Gibbs, 1989). These children may be the product of mixed marriages of parents, grandparents, or great-grandparents. They may be any combination of ethnic groups, including African-American and American Indian, Black Amerasian, or Asian and Latino (many Asians migrated to Latin America before coming to the United States), or African-American and white. They may define themselves in various ways, with siblings adopting different identities. For example, the part Mexican-American, part American Indian, and part white teenager described earlier in this chapter was the oldest of three siblings. She considered herself to be white, although she was aware of the discrimination she had experienced because of her mixed heritage. Her younger sister, who had experienced even more discrimination and suffered from learning disabilities as well, considered herself to be American Indian. She attended cultural events on the reservation, and most of her friends were Indians who lived on the reservation. The girls' younger brother, who was heavily involved in sports and had been placed in the college-bound mathematics program, took pride in his Mexican-American heritage and insisted upon learning Spanish even though no one spoke Spanish at home.

Other children in interracial families are adoptees. Transracial adoptions involving African-American, Asian, and Latin-American children and white families have increased during the 1980s. Opposition by African-American social workers and the governments of various Asian and Latin-American governments has curtailed some transracial adoptions. Like children of mixed heritage, those of interracial and international adoptions must struggle to develop a personal identity, with the parents often playing a major role in reinforcing or denying the heritage of the birth parents. Identity conflicts may be heightened by strained relations between children and parents during the adolescent years, with the adoption experience itself becoming a major source of conflict. A study of younger African-American children adopted by middle-class white families showed higher achievement among these children than among both white children and African-American children adopted by middle-class African-American parents. However, the study did not examine social adjustment or academic performance in adolescence and young adulthood (Moore, 1987).

Children in interracial families have many of the same needs as the children of color whose heritages they share. A fully multicultural curriculum can provide positive images for all dimensions of an interracial child's background. Because children of mixed heritage may be particularly sensitive to criticism of whites in America, care must be taken in presenting a more truthful version of history so that the children do not feel "caught in the middle." An interracial youngster whose identity is not yet secure, may feel uncomfortable in culturally mixed groups (Gibbs, 1989). Finally, teachers must be aware of stereotypes and expectations that may be magnified in combination with each other, as well as the unique pressures that children in interracial families may experience (Gibbs, 1989).

Cultural Diversity Among Teachers and Administrators

Rapport between children of color and their teachers plays a crucial role in determining the quality of a child's educational experience. Research points to teacher attitudes and personality clashes between teachers and students as a principal reason for the low achievement of African-American students. Many teachers expect African-American children to perform poorly and thus maintain low expectations for those students. African-American students are often "socialized to assume a posture of persistence, assertiveness, and problem-solving"—attitudes that clash with teachers' expectations that students will be submissive and take direction from above. A common student response in these situations is a kind of "learned helplessness," reflecting no effort to perform in school (Holliday, 1987). Other students respond by becoming discipline prob-

There is a need for more teachers and administrators from culturally diverse backgrounds.

lems, contributing to teachers' fear, dislike, prejudice, and anger. While patterns of misunderstanding and stereotyping have been studied extensively in the case of African-American students and their mostly white teachers, similar patterns can be found for Latino, Asian-American, and American Indian schoolchildren. They exist when teachers have little in common with their students and know little about the students' culture.

Diversifying the pool of teachers is one way of improving the situation. Teachers who share the students' ethnic and cultural backgrounds can serve as role models. They are also more likely to understand the experiences, attitudes, learning styles, and values of their students, although class differences and differences in national origin must be taken into account. For instance, black teachers of West Indian origin often have difficulty relating to black students, especially disadvantaged ones, from the United States. In integrated schools, a more diverse faculty can instill a sense of pride and belonging in students of color while teaching white students how to live and work together in a multicultural society. Finally, teachers of color can more effectively present a multicultural curriculum in which they have greater background. A teacher who has shared African-American songs, folktales, and stories with her own family as a child is in a special position when presenting them to students. A teacher from the same cultural background is a valuable resource when reading works written in dialect or with phrases in other languages.

Unfortunately, segregation and a shortage of teachers of color still exist in America's schools. Before 1954, most of the teachers in all-black southern schools were black, but many of them lost their jobs with the tightening of certification requirements. Increasingly, African-American students were taught by white teachers who understood little of their culture. As black ghettoes expanded in northern cities, white teachers remained as their white students departed. Most resented teaching their new students but were unable to leave. Newly-trained African-American teachers, however, were almost invariably assigned to the most troubled and segregated schools. While most tried to reach out to their students, they also questioned policies that sent new white teachers to relatively peaceful, well-funded schools while they ended up at poorly-funded, dumping ground schools. Some left the profession; others, lacking seniority, were the first laid off when school districts suffered funding cutbacks. In the 1987–88 school year, 88 percent of the public school teachers in the United States were white, 70 percent were female, and 49 percent were under forty years of age (U.S. Dept. of Education-B, 1990). Though African-Americans were approximately 15 percent of the student population, only 8.2 percent of teachers were black (U.S. Dept. of Education-B, 1990).

Other groups are represented among teachers in even smaller numbers. This is an especially serious issue because of the critical need for teachers for those whose native language is not English. Lack of qualified teachers has led to problems with many bilingual programs; many programs are forced to hire native-language speakers who barely know English or teachers from outside the group who are only partially fluent in the students' native language. In 1987–88, only 2.9 percent of the nation's teachers were of Latino heritage even though Latinos were almost 12 percent of the school-age population (U.S. Dept. of Education-B, 1990). Asian-Americans and Pacific Islanders made up 1 percent of the teaching force and approximately 3 percent of the student population, while American Indians, 1.1 percent of the school-age population, comprised 0.9 percent of the teachers (U.S. Dept. of Education-B, 1990) (Table 3–8).

Also in short supply are administrators of color. Besides providing role models for culturally diverse students and positive, nonstereotyped images for all students, administrators set the tone for the entire school. Administrators who are sensitive to the needs of students of color can create environments in which the students are not tracked, segregated, or otherwise given second-class status. Administrators set and maintain expectations for the entire school, and they can support and reinforce teachers who have high expectations for their students of color. Administrators are better placed to eliminate the "institutional racism" that stymies the efforts of even the most well-meaning teachers (Holliday, 1987). Finally, school and district administrators of color can take a leadership role in developing and instituting a multicultural curriculum. In 1987-88, however, 89 percent of all school and district administrators were white, with 75 percent men (U.S. Dept. of Education-C, 1990). African-American administrators comprised 8.6 percent of the total, with Latinos 3.2 percent (U.S. Dept. of Education-C, 1990). Asian-

TABLE 3–8 Selected Characteristics of Teachers and School Administrators: School Year 1987—1988

Characteristics	Teachers				Administrators			
	Public school	Percent of total	Private school	Percent of total	Public school	Percent of total	Private school	Percent of total
Total	2,323,204	100.0	307,131	100.0	77,890	100.0	25,401	100.0
Sex								
Male	681,161	29.3	66,785	21.7	58,585	75.2	12.131	47.8
Female	1,631,168	70.2	239,975	78.1	19,118	24.5	13,243	52.1
Not reported	10,875	0.5	370	0.1	—	—	—	—
Race/ethnicity								
American Indian, Alaskan Native	24,670	1.1	2,827	0.9	821	1.1	—	—
Asian or Pacific Islander	21,307	0.9	3,987	1.3	434	0.6	—	—
Black	190,018	8.2	7,165	2.3	6,696	8.6	771	3.0
White	2,050,400	88.3	288,432	93.9	69,048	88.6	24,056	94.7
Not reported	36,810	1.6	4,719	1.5	890	1.1	—	—
Ethnic origin*								
Latino	67,084	2.9	8,569	2.8	2,483	3.2	629	2.5
Non-Latino	2,207,746	95.0	292,566	95.3	73,245	94.0	24,167	95.1
Not reported	48,374	2.1	5,995	2.0	2,162	2.8	604	2.4
Age								
Under 40	1,124,105	48.4	170,130	55.4	14.430	18.5	7,608	30.0
40 to 49	752,301	32.4	83,021	27.0	34,163	43.9	9,849	38.8
50 or more	416,857	17.9	49,378	16.1	28,827	37.0	7,682	30.2
Not reported	29,941	1.3	4,601	1.5	469	0.6	—	—

— Too few sample cases for a reliable estimate.
* Latinos and non-Latinos may be of any race.
NOTE: Details may not add to totals due to rounding or missing values in cells with too few sample cases, or item nonresponse. Cell entries may be underestimates due to item nonresponse.

SOURCE: U.S. Department of Education, National Center for Education Statistics, Schools and Staffing Survey, *Selected Characteristics of Public and Private School Administrators (Principals): 1987–88, 1990; Characteristics of Public and Private School Teachers, 1987–88, 1990.*

Americans and Pacific Islanders were 0.6 percent and American Indians 1.1 percent (U.S. Dept. of Education-C, 1990).

We need a more culturally and linguistically diverse population of teachers and administrators to serve our school-age population. This change may decrease student-teacher conflict, provide role models, and improve educational attainment for all children. We also need to make sure that our schools are governed in a way that represents all segments of the community so the needs of students and their parents—regardless of race, ethnicity, or socioeconomic status—are treated with respect. Chapter 4 will examine some communities as they are today and how they are implementing successful programs for multicultural education.

❖ Summary

Education has been a primary route for upward mobility for immigrants to the United States. As well-paid unskilled jobs disappear and service-oriented jobs increase, education is crucial to survival in this society. Yet children of color, many among the most recent immigrants, have shown dismal rates of progress in our schools. A primary factor is the poverty in which many of the children must live. School achievement has been closely associated with socioeconomic class, and poor children are almost twice as likely to repeat a grade and drop out of school.

Although poverty is a major factor in the lowered achievement, other conditions are also important. Limited health care and poor diet contribute to learning problems and the lack of community resources also has negative impact on the overall education of the children. Inferior schools, where there is a lack of instructional materials and educational technology, lowered teacher expectations for students, and a climate of disorder and violence impede students' progress in learning also play a major role. In addition, many children of color face other risk factors identified by the United States Department of Education as placing children at risk for school failure: single-parent households, educational level of the mother, a sibling who has dropped out of school, and limited English proficiency. Single-parent families are prevalent among 51 percent of African-American children; 33 percent of Latino children have parents without high school diplomas. Limited English proficiency is also a factor for many Latino students.

The history of certain groups in our country also shows institutionalized efforts to limit their educational advancement. For example, in the time of slavery it was forbidden to teach slaves to read and write. After slavery separate but unequal schools ensured inferior education until 1954. Many African-American students still continue to attend inferior schools in inner city communities where property taxes are inadequate to fund quality educational programs. Chinese immigrants in the late 19th and early twentieth centuries were barred from the schools. Mexican-American migrant workers in the Southwest faced lack of schools and language barriers. American Indian children were sent to boarding schools and were forced to give up their language and culture.

In 1954, the *Brown* decision had a major impact on the public schools. While some improvement occurred, the turmoil caused by white resistance across the country and the hostility faced by many children turned many schools into a battleground where no one could learn. At present, many communities continue to seek ways to integrate their students and have developed various models in this effort. Magnet schools and city-wide residential plans for students are some examples.

The Civil Rights movement also focused, in part, on improving education and community control. Head Start programs and compensatory programs such as Title 1 are some of the results of the movement. Community groups have fought for the hiring of more teachers of color and for a multicultural curricula.

At the same time, Latino students were the beneficiaries of bilingual education programs established to address their needs. The Bilingual Education Act of 1968 required the schools to develop programs to aid students who were assessed as limited English proficient. This act resulted in several models of programs that recognized the necessity to teach these students in their primary language while they acquired sufficient English proficiency to use English for academic instruction. These programs have made a significant improvement in the education of many students whose primary language is not English. However, bilingual education has provoked intense conflict in communities where it became the focus of school budget cuts, curriculum reform, or new immigrant groups entering a school system.

Despite efforts to improve education for children of color through desegregation, compensatory education, community control of the schools, and bilingual education, housing patterns, resistance to school reform, emphasis on basic skills, and national standards and funding inequities have contributed to the maintenance of inferior schools for many children of color.

Among the most pressing needs of children of color are:

1. a decrease in the number who are below modal grade level, which places them at risk for dropping out;
2. careful evaluation of bilingual education programs;
3. parent education programs;
4. greater sensitivity to the portrayal of Asian-Americans and other groups in educational materials and textbooks to insure multidimensional portrayals;
5. open discussions of discrimination against Asians;
6. improved achievement among American Indian students and a reduction in their school drop-out rate;
7. instructional materials and methods that more closely match the culture and learning styles of American Indian students;
8. a comprehensive multicultural education program throughout our educational system; and
9. increased recruitment of teachers and administrators from culturally diverse groups.

❖ CHAPTER 3 Questions

1. What is the relationship between poverty and educational attainment for children of color?
2. Discuss the flaws in the cultural deficit and culture of poverty theories used to explain low achievement among children in poverty.

3. Provide an explanation for the continuation of school desegregation in the United States after *Brown v. Board of Education*.

4. School funding through property taxes has resulted in inequities in the education of children who live in poor versus affluent communities. Should this system be abolished? Provide your rationale.

5. What are some of the ways in which schools can be held accountable for the equal and equitable education of all children?

6. What are some specific changes needed in the schools to ensure educational achievement for children of color?

❖ References

Barringer, F. (1992, September 20). A census disparity for Asians in U.S. *The New York Times*, p. A1.

Bean, F. D., & Tienda, M. (1987). *The hispanic population of the United States*. New York: Russell Sage Foundation.

Berger, J. (1993, January 4). School programs assailed as bilingual bureaucracy. *The New York Times*, p. A1, B4.

Berube, M. R., & Gittell, M. (Ed.). (1969). *Confrontation at Ocean Hill-Brownsville: The New York school strikes of 1968*. New York: Praeger.

Campbell, B. N. (1992). Foreword. In J. Reyhner (Ed.), *Teaching American Indian students*. Norman, OK: University of Oklahoma Press.

Celis, W., 3rd (1993, December 14). Study finds rising concentration of black and Hispanic students. *The New York Times*, p. A1.

Congressional Budget Office (1992). *Measuring the distribution of income gains*. Washington, DC: Congressional Budget Office.

Cummings, J. (1981). The Role of Primary Language Development in Promoting Educational Success for Language Minority Students. In California State Dept. of Education (Ed.), *Schooling and language minority students* (pp. 3–49). Los Angeles: Evaluation, Dissemination and Assessment Center, California State University, Los Angeles.

Eyler, J., Cook, V.J., & Ward, L.E. (1983). Resegragation: Segregation within desegragated schools. In C.H. Rossell and W.D. Harvey (Eds.), *The consequences of school desegragation* (pp. 126–162) Philadelphia: Temple University Press.

Frasier, M. M. (1991). Disadvantaged and culturally diverse gifted students. *Journal for the Education of the Gifted, 14*(3), 234–245.

Garza Flores, H. (1991–92). Please do bother them. *Educational Leadership* (December 1991/January 1992), 58–59.

Gibbs, J. T. (1989). Biracial adolescents. In J. T. Gibbs, L. Nahme-Huang & Associates (Eds.), *Children of color: Psychological interventions with minority youth*. San Francisco: Jossey-Bass.

Hare, B. R., & Castenell, L. A., Jr. (1987). No place to run, no place to hide: Comparative status and future prospects of black boys. In M. B. Spencer, G. K. Brookings & W. Allen (Eds.), *Beginnings: The social and affective development of black children*. NJ: Lawrence Erlbaum Associates.

Helping Samoan Students Beat Odds. (1992, July 29). *The New York Times*, p.B7.

Hess, G. A., Jr. (1986). Educational triage in an urban school setting. *Metropolitan Education, 1*, 39–52.

Holliday, B. G. (1987). Towards a model of teacher-child transactional processes affecting black children's academic achievement. In M. B. Spencer, G. K. Brookings, & W. Allen (Eds.), *Beginnings: The social and affective development of black children.* NJ: Lawrence Erlbaum Associate.

Judson, G. (1993, January 10). Pattern of increasing scholastic segregation. *The New York Times*, p. B6.

Kitano, M. M. (1991). A multicultural educational perspective in serving the culturally diverse gifted. *Journal for the Education of the Gifted, 15*(1), 4–19.

Kozol, J. (1967). *Death at an early age.* Boston: Houghton-Mifflin.

Kozol, J. (1991). *Savage inequalities.* New York: Crown.

LaFromboise, T. D., & Low, K. G. (1989). American Indian children and adolescents. In J. T. Gibbs, L. Nahme-Huang & Associates (Eds.), *Children of color: Psychological interventions with minority youth.* San Francisco: Jossey-Bass.

Lee, J. F. J. (1991). *Asian American experiences in the United States: Oral histories of first to fourth generation Americans from China, the Philippines, Japan, India, the Pacific Islands, Vietnam and Cambodia.* Jefferson, NC: McFarland.

Malcolm X, w. Alex Haley. (1964). *The autobiography of Malcolm X.* New York: Ballantine.

Mansnerus, L. (1992, November 1). Should tracking be derailed? *The New York Times Education Life*, 14–16.

Massey, D. S., & Denton, N. A. (1989). Hypersegregation in U.S. metropolitan areas: Black and Hispanic segregation along five dimensions. *Demography, 26*(3) (August 1989), 373–391.

Massey, D. S., & Denton, N. A. (1993). *American apartheid: Segregation and the making of the underclass.* Cambridge, MA: Harvard University Press.

Moore, E. G. J. (1987). Ethnicity as a variable in child development. In M. B. Spencer, G. K. Brookings, & W. Allen (Eds.), *Beginnings: The social and affective development of black children.* NJ: Lawrence Erlbaum Associates.

Nahme-Huang, L. N. (1989). Southeast Asian refugee children and adolescents. In J. T. Gibbs, L. Nahme-Huang & Associates (Eds.), *Children of color: Psychological interventions with minority youth.* San Francisco: Jossey-Bass.

National Assessment of Educational Progress (1991). *Trends in academic progress: Achievement of American students in science, 1969–70 to 1990, mathematics, 1973 to 1990, reading, 1971 to 1990, writing, 1984 to 1990.* Washington, DC: U.S. Dept. of Education.

National Education Association (1987a). American Indian/Alaska Native concerns. In . . . *And justice for all: The NEA executive committee study group reports on ethnic minority concerns.* Washington, DC: National Education Association Publishers.

National Education Association (1987b). Asian and Pacific Islander concerns. In . . . *And justice for all: The NEA executive committee study group reports on ethnic minority concerns.* Washington, DC: National Education Association Publishers.

National Education Association (1987c). Black concerns. In . . . *And justice for all: The NEA executive committee study group reports on ethnic minority concerns.* Washington, DC: National Education Association Publishers.

National Education Association (1987d). Hispanic Concerns. In . . . *And justice for all: The NEA executive committee study group reports on ethnic minority concerns.* Washington, DC: National Education Association Publishers.

Natriello, G., McDill, E. L., & Pallas, A. M. (1990). *Schooling disadvantaged children: Racing against catastrophe.* New York: Teachers College Press.

Prasse, D., & Reschly, D.J. (1986). A case of segregation testing or program efficacy? *Exceptional Children, 52*(4), 333–348.

Reyhner, J. (1992a). Adapting curriculum to culture. In J. Reyhner (Ed.), *Teaching American Indian students*. (pp. 96–103). Norman, OK: University of Oklahoma Press.

Reyhner, J. (1992b). Bilingual education. In J. Reyhner (Ed.), *Teaching American Indian students*. (pp. 59–77). Norman, OK: University of Oklahoma Press.

Sizemore, B. A. (1988). The Madison Elementary School: A turnaround case. *Journal of Negro Education, 57*(3), 243–266.

Smith, D.D., & Luckasson, R. (1992). *Introduction to special education: Teaching in an age of challenge*. Boston: Allyn and Bacon.

Steele, S. (1990). *The content of our character: A new vision of race in America*. New York: St. Martin's Press.

Swisher, K., & Deyhle, D. (1992). Adapting instruction to culture. In J. Reyhner (Ed.), *Teaching American Indian students*. (pp. 81–95). Norman, OK: University of Oklahoma Press.

Takaki, R. (1993). *A different mirror: A history of multicultural America*. Boston: Little, Brown and Co.

Thompson, L.H. (1991). *Within-school discrimination: Inadequate title VI enforcement by education's office for civil rights*. Washington, DC: General Accounting Office.

U.S. Census (1790–1990). *Census of the population of the United States*. Washington, DC: Bureau of the Census.

U.S. Census (1990). October current population survey. Washington, DC: Bureau of the Census.

U.S. Department of Education (1992). *The condition of education/1992*. Washington, DC: U.S. Department of Education.

U.S. Department of Education, National Center for Education Statistics, School and Staffing Survey (1990). *Characteristics of public and private school teachers, 1987–88*. Washington, DC: U.S. Dept. of Education.

U.S. Department of Education, National Center for Education Statistics, National Educational Longitudinal Study of 1988, base year survey (1990). *A profile of the American eighth grader*. Washington, DC: U.S. Department of Education.

U.S. Department of Education, National Center for Education Statistics, School and Staffing Survey (1990). *Selected characteristics of public and private school administrators, 1987–88*. Washington, DC: U.S. Dept. of Education.

U.S. Department of Education, Office of Special Education and Rehabilitative Services, National Longitudinal Transitional Study (1989). *Youth with disabilities during transition: An overview of descriptive findings from the national longitudinal transition study, May, 1989*. Washington, DC: U.S. Dept. of Education.

U.S. Dept. of Health, Education, and Welfare (1966). *Equality of educational opportunity*. Washington, DC: U.S. Dept. of Health, Education, and Welfare.

Wallerstein, J. S., & Blakeslee, S. (1989). *Secondchances: Men, women and children a decade after divorce*. New York: Ticknor and Fields.

Wilkerson, I. (1989, August 5). Study finds segregation in cities worse than scientists imagined. *The New York Times*, p. 16.

Wilson, W. J. (1987). *The truly disadvantaged*. Chicago: University of Chicago Press.

The Current State of Multicultural Education— Programs and Controversies

The first major efforts toward multicultural education occurred in the 1960s and 1970s, with school desegregation, the Civil Rights movement, and *Black Pride*, which spawned similar campaigns by American Indian, Latino, and other groups. From the activism of the 1960s and 1970s came bilingual education and the incorporation of materials in the curriculum that presented the perspective of groups other than mainstream white middle-class Americans. By the end of the 1970s, however, the tide had turned, and cultural diversity was no longer a priority in many schools. With the election of Ronald Reagan in 1980, many federal education programs lost their funding. Even writers and illustrators of color felt the impact, as their publishers lost the crucial school market for their books, and they found it harder to get their later manuscripts published (Myers, 1985).

The 1983 publication of *A Nation at Risk* represented another blow for multicultural education inasmuch as it called for a *back to basics* approach emphasizing a standard set of skills for all students (National Commission on Excellence in Education, 1983). The report led to a *climate of account-ability* in which teachers' performances were measured by their students' standardized test scores (Willinsky, 1990). As a result, many teachers elim-inated enrichment activities and began to *teach to the test*, that is, to tests that have themselves been criticized for cultural bias (Hilliard, 1990). Other teachers sought refuge in standard curricular materials already approved by their supervisors. As Willinsky (1990) observed,

> This climate of accountability has taken its toll on the nature of teaching and the work of the classroom. As increased pressure has been placed on school districts for performance, the teaching profession has suffered a loss of autonomy to packaged kits and programmed learning materials which have shifted teachers into the position of managers or technicians. (p. 18)

Renewed efforts to create a more inclusive curriculum in response to the increasing cultural diversity of our schools and our nation have taken place within this climate of accountability. In fact, some have used the evidence of disproportionately high drop-out rates and low achievement among chil-dren of color to argue for a different approach, one that is more, not less, sen-sitive to their cultural backgrounds (Holt, 1991–1992). Nevertheless, the ten-sion between the need to cover *the basics* and the need to meet the needs of all children in a changing society, as well as the question of who defines the basics and how they are taught, lie at the heart of many of the controversies surrounding current multicultural education efforts. Many of those involved on both sides of the debate raise the question of *pluribus* (diversity) versus *unum* (unity). Some argue that by teaching about diverse cultures we are losing our sense of ourselves as a unified nation (Schlesinger, 1992; Ravitch, 1991–1992). Others advocate teaching all children about the coun-try's diverse ethnic heritage so that they can work together in its inevitably multicultural future (Cortes, 1991). Still others call for special programs to meet the needs of specific groups—most notably African-Americans and American Indians—whose cultural traditions have been most forcibly sup-pressed in the past (Harris, 1992; Reyhner & Eder, 1992).

❖ Multicultural Efforts in Public Schools

Statewide Efforts

After a period of stagnation and even decline, the number of states and individual school districts with multicultural education programs began to increase in the late 1980s (Mitchell, 1987; Stevenson & Gonzalez, 1992). In 1987, Bruce Mitchell reported that twenty-four states and the District of Columbia had some sort of official multicultural program for the public schools (Mitchell, 1987). However, the existence of a state program did not mean all the public schools in the state (or any of the schools, for that matter) consistently included lessons about culturally diverse groups in the curriculum. Most of the states that reported multicultural programs had hired a statewide coordinator for multicultural education. Some required courses in multicultural education for teacher certification, but that requirement existed as well in a few states without multicultural programs. Most of the twenty-four states with multicultural programs screened textbooks and the curriculum as a whole for overt racist and sexist content; the District of Columbia did not. Many states without multicultural programs also screened textbooks and the curriculum. Finally, in 1987, only twenty-two states allocated any funding whatsoever to multicultural education; that funding exceeded $1 million in only nine of the states—Alaska, Arizona, Connecticut, New Jersey, New York, Ohio, Utah, Washington, and Wisconsin (Mitchell, 1987). Representatives of states without multicultural education programs cited the state's lack of cultural diversity and "a lack of understanding of the need for multicultural education" as reasons (Mitchell, 1987, p. 11).

New York and California

In 1987, however, two of the nation's largest states—New York and California—announced major new initiatives in multicultural education. Leaders of both states responded to the cultural diversity in their states and the fact that, at least in California, "minorities" were fast becoming the majority in the public schools (Cortes, 1991). The first changes in both states occurred in the high school history curriculum (Schlesinger, 1992). In New York, for instance, the three-semester Global Studies class in grades nine and ten had previously focused almost exclusively upon the history of Mesopotamia, Greece, Rome, and Europe. After the revision, the course was divided into seven segments—the Middle East, Latin America, South Asia, East Asia, Africa, Western Europe, and Eastern Europe—with cultural as well as historical information included. The high school United States history curriculum was also made more inclusive, with additional information on the Iroquois influence upon the Articles of Confederation and the Constitution, and more coverage of the African-American experience. California's revision of the history curriculum focused mainly upon the selection of new textbooks that eliminated cultural biases and presented information about previously ignored or misrepresented groups (King, 1992; Schlesinger, 1992).

New York. After revising the high school social studies curriculum, the New York State effort continued, with the appointment in 1987 of a task force, "Minorities: Equity and Excellence," to study revisions of the entire K–12 curriculum (Sobol, 1990). The report issued in July 1989 contained strong language that expressed minority task force members' concerns about the existing curriculum and their sense of urgency about the need for change. (Sobol, 1990). As a result of the report, State Education Commissioner Thomas Sobol called for a curriculum of inclusion that would provide all public school students in New York State, in grades K–12, with an "understanding of American history and culture, of the history and culture of the diverse groups which comprise American society today, and of the history and culture of other people throughout the world" (Sobol, 1990, p. 29).

The implementation of a statewide curriculum of inclusion in New York has been hampered by a variety of factors. As Sobol himself has pointed out, "New York State syllabi are not mandated. Their use in the classroom depends on their wide availability and on teachers' and administrators' perception of their worth" (Sobol, 1990, p. 29). That is to say, teachers and administrators have had to be *convinced* of the need for such a curriculum. Although Sobol called for a curriculum available to and appropriate for all children, teachers and administrators in less culturally diverse areas have not always acknowledged the need for a multicultural approach, and for that reason, multicultural units have been implemented inconsistently. Teachers often have a great deal of leeway. One of this book's co-authors, for instance, was contacted by the principal of an upstate New York elementary school to advise an individual second-grade teacher who had expressed an interest in adding multicultural content to her lessons. The acceptance of New York's curriculum of inclusion has also been hampered by the flood of negative publicity the report and recommendations have received in the press. Many of the critics responded to the task force's strong language and to certain task force members who subsequently generated controversy with anti-Semitic or otherwise extremist statements (Sobol, 1990; Schlesinger, 1992). Commissioner Sobol later convened a new task force, which toned down the language, but Schlesinger and other influential intellectuals continued to object to the new curriculum's emphasis upon what they considered to be ethnic separatism (Schlesinger, 1992).

California. California's efforts were not without controversy as well. Unlike New York and most other states, California purchases virtually all textbooks on a statewide level. (Texas is another large state with a statewide textbook adoption policy.) In the late 1980s, the State Board of Education in California appointed an advisory body to develop the *History/Social Science Framework* for recommending textbooks in those disciplines that offered a more culturally diverse perspective and more information about culturally diverse groups in the United States and around the world (King, 1992). For two years, participants in the *Framework* reviewed textbooks and found all of them deficient in at least one area (King, 1992). Nonetheless, the educators felt the schools could not operate without textbooks, so they approved what they believed to be "the best of a bad lot" (Kohl, 1991, p. 39).

California's textbook adoption unleashed controversy from all sides. The mainstream media and many African-American educators hailed the effort as a significant, though perhaps imperfect, step in the right direction. The same intellectuals who criticized New York State's curriculum of inclusion decried the process of the *Framework*, which they felt allowed every particularistic group to make its demands in lieu of scholarly integrity, but they generally applauded the result (Schlesinger, 1992). On the other side, many supporters of multicultural education, including some members of the *Framework* committee, condemned the state's choices. Committee member Joyce Elaine King expressed objections to history textbooks that described African rulers as willing, even enthusiastic, participants in the slave trade, pointing out the fundamental responsibility of Europeans for slavery in the Americas (King, 1992). (This issue has been the subject of intense historical controversy for decades, along with the related issue of the extent to which negative aspects of history should be toned down for students at each level.) Other objections included the way in which the textbooks presented the slaves themselves, who, for the most part, did not appear as individuals but as members of a group, without a pre-slavery culture and without the personal feelings and thoughts that one would describe as their humanity (Kohl, 1991). Despite the objections of the *Framework* committee, the textbook publishers mounted a publicity campaign to have their books adopted, a campaign reinforced by the mainstream media (King, 1992). Even so, five school districts in California, including Oakland, Hayward, and San Jose, refused to buy the books that had been approved by the state committee. The city school districts of Los Angeles, San Francisco, and Berkeley eventually bought the books, but only on condition that the publisher provided supplemental materials to meet the objections of King, other advisory committee members, and minority community leaders in those cities (King, 1992).

The Bottom Line. Despite the controversies and the problems of implementation, state efforts like those in New York and California have had some positive benefits. Virtually all the parties in the California "textbook wars" (with the exception of diehard conservatives, who objected to any change from the traditional curriculum) acknowledged that the new textbooks were an improvement over their predecessors (King, 1992). As the largest state and one that adopts textbooks statewide, California exerts enormous power over the publishers of textbooks, who must conform to any new standard or lose millions of dollars in potential sales. The improvement in textbooks crosses disciplines; in basal readers published since the late 1980s, for instance, one can find children of color in typical middle-class settings. History and social studies textbooks contain more information about culturally diverse individuals and groups, and they also explore the darker side of American history, including slavery, Jim Crow, and the betrayal and extermination of the Indians. State-sponsored efforts have also encouraged school districts to consider the use of other materials besides textbooks and basal readers. The California textbook reevaluation, in fact, occurred at the same time as the California Reading Initiative, which advocated the use of trade books in language arts classrooms and allocated funding for the purchase of those books (Cullinan, 1989). Although the California Reading Initiative did not specifically mention multicultural books, teachers were able to choose books based upon their own interests and the perceived needs of their students.

The statewide push for multicultural education has led as well to the inclusion of coursework in cultural diversity for those training to be teachers. In some colleges and universities, ethnic studies courses or courses in multicultural awareness are part of broader requirements for graduation; in others, the courses are specific to the major in education. States are also sponsoring in-service training for those already in the profession. Finally, support on the state level has encouraged local school boards and superintendents who are forging ahead with their own programs for multicultural education.

Local Efforts

With respect to multicultural education, the greatest vitality today appears to be at the local level. In the absence of state programs and standards, local school districts have initiated a number of programs and have adapted programs developed elsewhere to the needs of their students. In 1991, the National Association of State Boards of Education released a study that showed statewide efforts to be narrow, flawed, and poorly implemented, while the programs of local school districts "have been more aggressive and comprehensive in their efforts to implement multicultural education programs and respond to diverse student needs" (Stevenson & Gonzalez, 1992, p. 358). Stevenson and Gonzalez surveyed thirty of the country's largest school districts in 1991 and found that twenty of the thirty districts—suburban as well as urban districts—had implemented a multicultural curriculum. Of the remaining ten districts, eight responded to the survey and two did not. These eight districts—seven urban and one suburban—did not have a multicultural curriculum. Four of the urban districts planned to implement one in the near future; three urban districts had no plans for a multicultural curriculum; the suburban district declined to give information on future plans (Stevenson & Gonzalez, 1992).

Of the districts with a multicultural curriculum, three-quarters had implemented it since 1985. Most of the curricula were broadly multicultural, with some including gender and sexual orientation as well. Four urban districts (three of which had a student population that was more than 60 percent African-American) described a focus that was primarily African-centered (Stevenson & Gonzalez, 1992). Stevenson and Gonzalez also found that all but one of the districts that had embraced multiculturalism incorporated multicultural materials and programs into existing curricula in language arts, social studies, and mathematics. Among the variety of materials used were textbooks with multicultural content, stories, written narratives, and specially prepared essays and curriculum units. With respect to instructional methods, "cooperative learning was the dominant instructional mode used by the sampled districts to deliver multicultural curricula" (p. 361). Other methods included team teaching, student-directed learning, and peer instruction Finally, they found that all but one of the districts with multicultural education programs conducted extensive in-service training for teachers and administrators (Stevenson & Gonzalez, 1992).

For the most part, school boards and superintendents enjoyed widespread community support for their programs, though most reported at least some opposition. Nonetheless, the cultural diversity of the communities in question, written school board policies, court desegregation orders, state mandates, and the involvement and support of parent and community groups such as the PTA, the NAACP, and the Urban League contributed to the ultimate acceptance of the changes. Officials acknowledged the need to involve all parties at all stages of planning and implementation in order to minimize opposition. Stevenson and Gonzalez (1992) say:

> The school officials surveyed . . . were also asked to offer any special problem-solving or problem-avoiding advice to districts planning to establish and implement multicultural curricula and programs. Generally, they indicated that multicultural education must be broad, must incorporate many ethnic groups and all genders, and must be needs-based. They further cautioned that ethnically representative community involvement and input reflecting the spectrum of thought on multiculturalism must be secured prior to implementation. The respondents also stressed that a clear vision of the goals, objectives, and expected outcomes of multicultural education must be developed to provide focus for curricular development and program implementation. They agreed that all school system personnel—custodians, aides, teachers, and administrators alike—must be of one accord in awareness about and understanding of their role and contribution to cultural diversity. To that end, in-service training on cultural diversity was deemed important for all school system personnel, not just teachers. (p. 365)

The principal weakness that most school officials identified with their program was the lack of measures to evaluate its success. Some used subjective criteria; others examined the performance of culturally diverse students on standardized tests. The researchers acknowledged the inadequacy of existing measures and expressed fears that, without solid proof of their effectiveness, multicultural programs will remain vulnerable (Stevenson & Gonzalez, 1992).

Columbus, Ohio. Columbus, Ohio, is a typical large urban school district that in 1989 began the implementation of a multicultural education program. In 1991, the district served sixty-four thousand students in ninety-two elementary schools, twenty-six middle schools, and seventeen high schools. The student population in 1991 was 49.5 percent European-American, 47.5 percent African-American, 2.5 percent Asian-American, and 0.5 percent Latino or American Indian. A large percentage of the European-American students were Appalachian, and 52.4 percent of the students were low-income (Miranda et al., 1992). Of the 4,591 teachers and administrators, 22 percent were members of minority groups; 48 percent of the 1,914 noncertified staff members were minorities (Miranda et al., 1992).

The Columbus district's multicultural education program focused upon staff development and in that aspect lay its strength (Miranda et al., 1992). The district appointed a Staff Development/Multicultural Education Department, with a four-year budget of $450,000, to coordinate programs with teachers and noncertified staff with the ultimate goal of implementing a multicultural curriculum and improving interaction with the various groups of students who attended the Columbus schools (Miranda et al., 1992):

> The Staff Development/Multicultural Education (SD/MCE) Department was responsible for (a) increasing educators' [sic] knowledge of other cultures, (b) helping educators infuse perspectives of different cultures into the curriculum, (c) providing educators with professional development about instructional methodologies to enhance each student's success in the classroom, and (d) assisting each school with the development of a three-year plan for MCE. (p. 3)

To these ends, according to Miranda et al., the district assigned six administrators to work with the staffs of each school; they were responsible for informing the staff about the district's commitment *to*, definition *of*, and goals and expectations *for* multicultural education. The administrators also organized training sessions in alternative teaching strategies, such as cooperative learning. The district initiated three in-service multicultural education courses and offered graduate credit to the participants. The courses—the first on the history of African-Americans, Appalachians, Asian-Americans, American Indians, and Latinos, the second on teaching strategies and curricula, and the third a practicum with demonstration lessons—were quite successful. In the first year, two hundred educators applied to take the courses, but only seventy-five could be accommodated. Finally, the district appointed an advisory committee to oversee the staff development and the overall implementation of the multicultural education plan. That committee included teachers, administrators, community members, and multicultural education specialists from local universities. The district was able to utilize the expertise of professors from Ohio State University and other local institutions of higher learning. At the time of the report, the program had only been in existence for one year, too soon for a thorough evaluation. The authors pointed out both the need to evaluate once new methods, lesson plans, and units were in widespread use and the importance of making a commitment for at least five to seven years for a multicultural education program to have its full impact (Miranda et al., 1992).

Portland, Oregon. While the Columbus effort focused on staff training and development, with an exploration of alternative teaching strategies, the school district in Portland, Oregon, began with a revision of the curriculum itself. Portland has the largest school district in the Pacific Northwest, with fifty-six thousand students in ninety-two schools. The student population, as of October 1993, is 70.1 percent European-American, 15.3 percent African-American, 8.3 percent Asian-American, 4.2 percent Latino, and 2.1 percent Native American. Within the category of Asian-American is a large number of students of Pacific Islander origin. Beginning in the mid-1980s, the Portland district's implementation of multicultural education was considered the first of its kind in the country, and it became the model for many efforts that followed (O'Neil, 1991–92). Led by former (now retired) Superintendent Matthew Prophet, school officials acknowledged that both teachers and students had very little awareness of perspectives beyond the dominant one, and in order to teach a more inclusive curriculum, they would need to know about the contributions of people of color in all subject areas, not just language arts and social studies (O'Neil, 1991–92). The district commissioned educational psychologist Asa Hilliard III to produce a textbook of *baseline essays* focusing on the experiences and contributions of Africans and African-Americans in the disciplines of history and social studies, science and technology, mathematics, language arts, art, and music.

The first edition of *African-American Baseline Essays* was published in 1987, with a revised edition released in 1990, and an additional revision in 1992. At the foundation of the essays was the belief that, in the words of Superintendent Prophet, "early civilization evolved in Africa, and . . . Africa is the cradle of civilization. Egypt was and still is a significant African civilization. People of African descent have a history that precedes slavery and civil rights. The culture of African people was not destroyed by slavery" (O'Neil, 1991-92, p. 24). School officials planned to follow up the African essays with similar sets of essays focusing on Hispanic groups, Asians and Asian-Americans, Pacific Islanders, American Indians, and European-Americans (O'Neil, 1991-92), though budgetary problems have slowed the production of the other essays. Again, in the words of Superintendent Prophet (O'Neil, 1991–92):

> Another overriding principle is that each of the six geocultural groups has made significant contributions. No geocultural group is innately inferior or superior to another. People, wherever they are, are interdependent and need one another. We're attempting to build in all of our kids, whatever their ethnicity or cultural identity, an awareness of their

culture and ethnic heritage. We're trying to have them develop an understanding and respect and appreciation for the history, culture, and contributions of all groups of people, trying to eliminate personal and national ethnocentrism so that one understands that a specific culture is neither intrinsically inferior or superior to another. We're trying also to give some general suggestions that we think teachers should integrate into what they do that will bring about greater understanding and appreciation of cultural diversity. (p. 24)

Along with the baseline essays, the Portland district produced lesson plans for a revised K–5 curriculum that highlighted the contributions of Africans and African-Americans, a curriculum that would eventually highlight other previously ignored groups as well, once the baseline essays on those groups were completed (O'Neil, 1991-92). Because of that curriculum, Prophet noted a greater implementation of multicultural education in the elementary grades in his district and a stronger focus upon content related to African-Americans than to other groups (O'Neil, 1991-92).

Since their publication, the *African-American Baseline Essays* have attracted a great deal of attention. A number of other school districts adopted them as the guiding principles for their own curriculum revisions. Among the school districts to embrace the baseline essays include Atlanta, Baltimore, Detroit, and Indianapolis (Martel, 1991–92; Browder, 1992). They also became the key source for revised curriculums at African immersion schools in Detroit, Milwaukee, Pittsburgh, Washington, D.C., and elsewhere (Schlesinger, 1992).

The first Portland Baseline Essays emphasize the need to present the history and culture of Africans and African-Americans.

Much of the attention to the essays, however, was in the form of criticism. Scholars and teachers called into question their accuracy and the credentials of those who produced them. A Washington, D.C., high school social studies teacher, Erich Martel, evaluated the essays in 1991 and described major inaccuracies, as well as assertions that were, at best, debatable. Most of the problems surrounded the history of ancient Africa, the argument that Egypt was a Black-African country (at least until it was invaded by Arabs), and Africa's influence upon ancient Greece (Martel, 1991–92). Martel questioned the facts and interpretations in the Science and Technology essay as well as the credentials of the essay's author, Hunter Havelin Adams III. His findings for the other essays were somewhat more positive (Martel, 1991–92):

> With minor exceptions, the Math essay contains very usable information. While the Language Arts and Music essays' coverage of ancient Egypt is compromised by inaccuracies, their surveys of African-American literature and music appear sound. However, educators may want to consult specialists in African and African-American music and literature on the accuracy of particular claims before using them. (p. 22)

Martel's criticisms of some of the baseline essays have been seized upon by conservative critics of multicultural education, who have used allegations of inaccuracies and uncredentialed scholars to condemn the entire project (Browder, 1992). Critics have also attacked Superintendent Prophet's statement, in an interview responding to Martel's points, that "the content of the essays is of less importance than the overriding principle of respecting all geocultural groups" (O'Neil, 1992, p. 25; Browder, 1992). Critics charge that curriculum revisions should be based upon established—rather than nontraditional or revisionist—scholarship, and that truth should not be sacrificed to a political or moral agenda (Schlesinger, 1992). In fact, the African origins of civilization and Africa's connection to Egyptian civilization continue to be hotly debated, and an emerging body of scholarship from Africa itself promises to alter the balance even further. As evidence of a major shift in scholarly interpretation, more and more Africa experts are beginning to treat Egypt as an African country, at least in terms of its culture and early history. At the same time, the Portland Public Schools have continued to revise the *African-American Baseline Essays*, in part in response to legitimate criticism and in part as a result of increased scholarly production from and about Africa. Because new evidence and interpretations constantly emerge with respect to events and ways of life in ancient times, teachers and administrators must keep informed and continually question both the established versions and the newer revisionist ones.

The *African-American Baseline Essays* have attracted the greatest amount of criticism and controversy. Less attention has been given to the essays on other groups, which were completed in the early 1990s.

SPECIAL BOX 4–1 *Afrocentric Perspectives*

From the moment the European powers began to use Africa as a source for slave labor, the history of the continent was told from the perspective of Europeans. A stereotype emerged of Africa as the "dark continent"—mysterious, dangerous, and savage. Europeans used such portrayals to justify the cruelty of the slave trade and, centuries later, the abuses of colonialism. In many European-written histories, the people of Africa were portrayed in similar terms to the wild animals, with whom they were often identified. Illustrations often exaggerated and distorted racial features, making Africans look exotic, frightening, or ridiculous. Few books distinguished between regions and individual ethnic groups; often they treated the entire continent as if it were one country. Histories used terminology imposed by European invaders—words such as "tribe," "hut," and "savage"—to demean Africans. As a whole, the books made African people appear inferior, uncivilized, less human. A paternalistic attitude pervaded these books: The "civilization of Africa" was the "white man's burden."

As the people of Africa began to struggle for independence from their colonial masters, African historians and social scientists emerged to tell the continent's story from their own perspective rather than that of the Europeans. One of the first was Frantz Fanon, an Algerian sociologist whose study of the destructive effects of colonial rule, *The Wretched of the Earth* (1963), has had a major influence upon how social scientists ever since have viewed the so-called Third World. In the late 1960s the Senegalese scholar Cheikh Anta Diop described the African origins of civilizations and offered evidence pointing to a "Negro" Egypt in *African Origin of Civilization: Myth or Reality?* (1974). British and other European scholars immediately attacked his work, but it has had profound influence upon the works of other African and African-American scholars, who have assembled an impressive body of evidence to support their claims. These scholars' works have been termed "Afrocentric" (or "Africentric") because they present African points of view and achievements and highlight the contributions of African people to the development of human civilization.

Those who attack the works of Diop, Chancellor Williams, Molefi Kete Asante, and others as myth and pseudo-science often ignore (or even embrace) the long history of pseudo-science and outright racism in Europeans' works about Africa. Until very recently, European scholars were advancing theories regarding Africans' skull size and genetic predisposition to low intelligence. Accounts of African cultural developments, African resistance to the slave trade, and the destructive effects of colonialism upon African culture and society—most of which have been written by Africans themselves—are essential to understanding the continent's past and present. Contrary to the assertions of some of their critics, African writers have not shied away from describing the continent's problems either, and many, like Kenya's Ngugi wa Thiong'o, Nigeria's Wole Soyinka or South Africa's Stephen Biko, have paid the price of imprisonment or death. Their voices and their perspectives deserve the respect that has too long been denied them.

Historian Arthur Schlesinger, Jr., an outspoken critic of the African essays and of the Afrocentric curriculum in general, has attributed the increased controversy to past racism and its effects upon African-Americans (Schlesinger, 1992):

> Like other excluded groups before them, black Americans invoke supposed past glories to compensate for real past and present injustices. Because their exclusion has been more tragic and terrible than that of white immigrants, their quest for self-affirmation is more intense and passionate. In seeking to impose Afrocentric curricula on public schools, for example, they go further than their white predecessors . . . (p. 71)

Racism and racial division has intensified the conflict, as many traditional scholars have refused to see any merit in the works of their Afrocentric counterparts and, in fact, resist any changes to the way African and African-American history and culture has been taught (or not taught) over the years. Extremists on both sides have commanded media attention with inflammatory rhetoric that fans racial tensions and prevents a measured search for the truth. Yet Portland's baseline essays examine the histories of five other groups besides African-Americans. Few of those essays, which also highlight the contributions of previously ignored or (as in the case of American Indians) forcibly suppressed groups, have been questioned. Taken together, they incorporate new perspectives into the curriculum; these perspectives are those of members of the group itself and, in that sense, are valuable as historical documents. One may find within them completing on the origins of civilization and other issues, as a number of groups—not only Africans and Europeans—have located in their own regions the birth of civilized life.

Shoreham-Wading River. Though not as highly publicized or as controversial as the Portland baseline essays, the Human Rights Education Program implemented in the Shoreham-Wading River School District on Long Island, New York, represents a major contribution to multicultural education as well. The Shoreham-Wading River district is a typical middle-class suburban district, with very little cultural diversity among either students or staff (Adams, Pardo, & Schniedewind, 1991–92). Nonetheless, school officials acknowledged in the late 1980s that their students needed an appreciation not only of their own culture, but also of all the other cultural groups that make up the nation and the world (Adams, Pardo, & Schniedewind, 1991–92). For these school leaders, multicultural education is for all children equally, not just those from minority groups.

The Shoreham-Wading River district's conception of multicultural education is broad, encompassing race, ethnicity, national origin, social class, religion, physical ability/disability, gender, and sexual orientation (Adams, Pardo, & Schniedewind, 1991–92). By identifying multicultural education with human rights education, school officials express certain objectives and goals, including the encouragement of greater tolerance and understanding and the building of cooperative behaviors and peace-making skills. The program relies heavily on the theoretical approach of James Banks, who has described human rights education for all children as a necessary element for preparing those children to live in a culturally diverse democratic nation in an increasingly interdependent world (Banks, 1991; Adams, Pardo, & Schniedewind, 1991–92). The impetus for the program came from teachers and administrators, including the super-intendent, David Jackson, who reaffirmed his support when he discovered racist, anti-Semitic, and anti-gay graffiti in the high school in 1990. Under the leadership of the middle school assistant principal, the Human Rights Curriculum Committee, which was comprised mostly of teachers, developed the program over a period of years and enlisted the coopera-tion of district personnel. A consultant with the State University of New York system, Nancy Schniedewind worked with the district to develop in-service courses and strategies for instruction and curriculum planning (Adams, Pardo, & Schniedewind, 1991-92).

Shoreham-Wading River's Human Rights Education Program takes place at all levels, from elementary school to high school, and involves changes in instructional strategies as well as in the curriculum. The emphasis is upon helping children to see events from a variety of per-spectives outside of their own personal and cultural one. To that end, children read fiction and personal narratives from a number of cultural groups in the past and present, including American Indians throughout their history, African-Americans in the contemporary United States, Jews during the Holocaust, and immigrants to the United States in the late nineteenth century. Children are also asked to write narratives and sto-ries from the perspective of other groups. In many cases, they realize what they are learning is not covered in mainstream textbooks, and what they write may be a means of filling in the "missing pages" (Adams, Pardo, & Schneidewind, (1991–92).

> When students find information on our multicultural heritage that is not available in the books, they are taught to explain it as "missing pages." The ongoing discovery of missing pages continues to heighten students' critical awareness of whose culture is represented most consistently in texts, books, magazines, and the media. (p. 41)

Equally important, according to district officials, is the "process," that is, the "focus on providing alternative patterns for student interaction" (Adams, Pardo, & Schniedewind, 1991–92, p. 37). Cooperative learning lies at the foundation of the process; it "necessitates that students work together toward common goals" so that "they come to value each others' unique experiences and contributions" (Adams, Pardo, & Schniedewind, 1991–92, p. 38). Through extensive in-service training, teachers have learned how to incorporate cooperative learning and other cooperative

SPECIAL BOX 4–2 *The Fate of the Rainbow Curriculum*

The controversy surrounding New York City's *Children of the Rainbow* curriculum illustrates what can happen when educators and the community fail to work together to develop and implement a multicultural education program. Shortly after taking office in 1990, the chancellor of the New York City Public Schools, Joseph Fernandez, began working with teachers and district administrators to develop a broad multicultural curriculum. Such a curriculum was desperately needed. New York City is the home of the nation's largest school district, with close to one million students. African-American and Latino students make up the majority of the student population, but immigrants from more than fifty countries also attend New York City Public Schools.

Along with lessons about diverse racial and ethnic groups, the Rainbow Curriculum, as it was known, touched upon gender issues, people with disabilities, and gay and lesbian families. A first-grade lesson discussed children with gay parents and recommended a well-reviewed picture book on the subject, *Heather Has Two Mommies*. A first draft of the curriculum was released in the fall of 1992, and controversy erupted instantly. One of the thirty-two Community School Boards (which have administered the elementary and middle schools in each Community School District ever since the 1968 battle over decentralization), the one in District 24 in Queens, refused to use the lesson or the book. Board members (all of whom were white in a district in which the student population in the public schools is 47 percent Latino and only 20 percent white) condemned the entire curriculum. In this mostly Catholic district, the board members had the support of many of the parents, including Latino parents, who objected to the school's presentation of homosexuality in the first grade. Yet many of those involved in the dispute did not live in the district, did not have school-age children, or did not send their children to the public schools. (Many of the district's parents—white parents in particular—send their children to parochial schools.)

Fernandez responded to the District 24 Board's objections by suspending the entire Board, a move he was allowed according to the agreement following the decentralization battle. He argued that the Board did not represent the students in the district. In many ways, he was correct. Very few people turn out for Community School Board elections; the average turnout has been estimated at 7 percent of eligible voters. The low turnout has allowed many districts to return school board members who are not representative of the population as a whole and who might have the support of highly organized and well-funded groups, including the teachers' union and conservative religious groups. Turnout among minority groups in New York City is consistently lower than among whites. Nonetheless, Fernandez's suspension of the District 24 Board was an extreme step that cost him the support of many influential New Yorkers.

Fernandez alienated those who held power over him in other ways too. His memoir, *Tales Out of School*, published in the spring of 1993, contained frank criticisms of several members of the central Board of Education, including a Latina member from the Bronx. Having lost the support of several central Board members who might otherwise have approved of his innovative approach to education, Fernandez left the district in June 1993 when the central Board voted narrowly not to renew his contract. The lesson on gay parents—admittedly a small part of the Rainbow Curriculum—was dropped. The rest of the Rainbow Curriculum remained in limbo as a result of Fernandez's departure, along with many other innovations, including a leadership high school for Latino students. The 1993 Community School Board elections received a great deal of media attention, along with the attention of the religious right and their opponents, but turnout was not much higher. Most incumbents won reelection, though an Asian-American woman gained a seat on the Board of District 24 and has since raised the issue of multicultural education before her fellow Board members. Many have pointed out that culturally diverse parents and community members need to participate more in Community School Board elections and meetings if a curriculum sensitive to their needs is to be developed and implemented.

educational practices in their classroom. Teachers and students also learn strategies for conflict management so that whenever cultural conflicts emerge, as they inevitably will when people of different backgrounds live and work together, they can be resolved in a way that contributes to mutual respect and understanding (Adams, Pardo, & Schniedewind, 1991–92). Some examples of cooperative learning and conflict management techniques include a peer mediation program in the middle school to resolve conflicts between students, and an interage cooperative research project involving second-graders and fourth-graders for the Martin Luther King Jr. celebration (Adams, Pardo, & Schniedewind, 1991–92).

❖ Multicultural Programs Serving Special Populations

African-American Immersion Schools

Segregated schools have long been a fact of life for many African-American schoolchildren. After the Civil War, African-American children attended separate schools in both the South and the North; legal segregation was upheld in the 1896 *Plessy v. Ferguson* Supreme Court decision. In contrast to the separate but equal ruling, the segregated black schools were clearly unequal, with lower-paid teachers, larger classes, run-down buildings, and fewer and older textbooks, all of which portrayed black people as inferior (Harris, 1992). Segregation persisted in large urban districts even after the 1954 *Brown v. Board* Supreme Court decision declared it illegal. De facto segregation resulted from *white flight*, restrictive covenants in white neighborhoods, and the concentration of poor African-American families in hypersegregated urban ghettoes. As Jonathan Kozol pointed out in *Savage Inequalities*, these schools have remained unequal due to funding disparities between inner cities and the wealthier suburbs that surround them (Kozol, 1991).

Because of the value African-American families have historically placed upon education, many African-American children have persisted in school and achieved despite the schools' limited resources. Nonetheless, African-American educators express alarm at the *achievement gap* between black and white students, an achievement gap which is often attributed, in Felix Boateng's words, to "the continuous deculturalization of the African-American child and the neglect of African-American cultural values in the curriculum" (Boateng, 1990, p. 78). Educators cite other statistics as evidence of urban school systems' inhospitability to their African-American pupils. A study by K. C. Holt (1991–92) brought out several important facts: In Milwaukee, where 27.6 percent of the students are African-American males, 50 percent of the students suspended in the 1989–90 school year were African-American males; between 1978 and 1985, African-Americans comprised 94.4 percent of all students expelled from the Milwaukee schools; the average grade for that city's African-American high school students in 1986–87 was "D," and only 19% had an average grade of "C" or higher (Holt, 1991-92). Considered by Massey and Denton to be one of the United States' most hypersegregated cities, Milwaukee is third among urban school districts in suspending more blacks than whites from school (Massey & Denton, 1989; Holt, 1991–92).

Acknowledging both the reality of school segregation in hypersegregated cities and the failure of those urban schools to meet the needs of their African-American students, many black educators have called upon urban public school districts to establish *African-American Immersion Schools* that approach curriculum and instruction from an Afrocentric perspective. Some educators wanted to restrict these schools to African-American males only, arguing, as Hare and Castenell have done, that this group of students is the most often identified for behavior problems, the least understood, and the worst served by the existing system (Hare & Castenell, 1987). As envisioned by some of their proponents, these all-male schools would have had a predominantly African-American male professional staff to provide role models for children who did not have day-to-day contact with a male parent or guardian. In reality, the teaching staff is integrated. Districts gave existing teachers the right to remain or to transfer to other schools, and many white teachers who supported multicultural education chose to stay in order to contribute to the development of these schools. Threats of a lawsuit led the schools to admit girls and students of other racial and ethnic backgrounds, but the student body of the African-American Immersion Schools remains almost exclusively African-American and, in the case of Detroit's Malcolm X Academy, predominantly male as well (*New York Times*, 1992).

The best known of the African-American Immersion Schools are the Malcolm X Academy, a Detroit elementary school, and Dr. Martin Luther King Jr. Elementary School (formerly Victor Berger Elementary School) and the Malcolm X Academy Middle School in Milwaukee. These schools opened their doors in the 1990–91 school year and since then have inspired similar efforts in Baltimore, Portland, Philadelphia, Pittsburgh, Washington, D.C., and New York City, among others.

Fundamental to the African-American Immersion Schools is the principle that black students can achieve (1) if curricular materials and instructional techniques affirm their culture and heritage, and (2) if high expectations for their behavior and achievement are maintained. To the first end, the curriculum incorporates information about Africa and African-Americans in all subject areas. This information is not added on as an afterthought to the textbook or compartmentalized into holidays and Black History Month, but is an integral part of the course of study. First-graders at King Elementary School, for example, learn to count in English and in Kiswahili, the dominant language in East Africa. The pipe-

Dr. Martin Luther King Jr. Elementary School in Milwaukee seeks to provide African-American students a sense of their heritage.

cleaner spiders they make in art are used to illustrate stories about Anansi, the clever spider of West African folklore (Scherer, 1991–92). The schools have embraced the approach to African and African-American history and culture that lies at the heart of Portland's *African-American Baseline Essays*. For their own background and for use in the classroom, teachers select narratives and interpretations authored by Africans and African-Americans themselves (Harris, 1992). While structured phonics and basal reading text offer skills-based instruction at the elementary and middle school level, students also read African folklore, biographies about black achievers, and historical and contemporary fiction by black authors. Beyond boosting the self-esteem of African-American students and giving them a sense of pride in their heritage, the African-centered, or Afrocentric, curriculum openly challenges the dominant perspective that for centuries has ridiculed, misrepresented, or ignored people of African descent (Harris, 1992).

Instructional methods as well as curriculum materials are designed to reaffirm the students' heritage at the African-American Immersion Schools. Scherer (1991–92) found that teachers and administrators acknowledge the wide variation in learning styles and endorse approaches that accommodate each one; no student is to be left behind. Also, there is an emphasis upon hands-on approaches and active learning. For instance, one third-grade class at King Elementary School writes to pen pals in Africa, and all the students at the school learn to memorize, recite poetry, and tell stories in the tradition of the West African *griots* (Scherer, 1991-92). In the rural African tradition, the entire village functions as extended family and school for the children; the staff at King Elementary School has translated that into contemporary reality by creating a "school family" made up of several classes in different grades (Harris, 1992; Scherer, 1991–92). Children in each school family take part in peer tutoring and cooperative projects, with "family meetings" held every two weeks (Scherer, 1991–92).

The second component of the African-American Immersion Schools consists of high expectations for staff and students. The staff combines strict discipline with a warm, caring atmosphere. Students are required to wear uniforms based upon what is standard attire in the business world (*New York Times*, 1992). The Malcolm X Academy students in Detroit recite a daily pledge: "We at the Malcolm X Academy will strive for excellence in our quest to be the best. We'll rise above every challenge with our heads held high. We'll always keep the faith when others say die. March on till victory is ours: Amandla!" (*New York Times*, 1992). A second-grade class motto at King Elementary School goes,

I know I am.

I know I can.

I know I will.

If it's to be,

It's up to me (Scherer, 1991–92, p. 19).

In enforcing disciplinary rules and insisting upon hard work and achievement, the schools have enlisted the support of parents and the broader community. The Malcolm X Academy in Detroit is a public *school of choice*, to which parents apply and students are chosen by lottery (*New York Times*, 1992). When the Malcolm X Academy was relocated to an all-white neighborhood in 1992, and white residents reacted with hostility, parents stood guard to protect the school and its students (*New York Times*, 1992). Designated an *empowered school* by the Board of Education, the school's principal has unusual powers to hire and transfer teachers, and teachers are given additional free periods for the purpose of curriculum development.

While King Elementary School and Malcolm X Academy Middle School are *neighborhood schools,* to which students are assigned based upon residence, they too enjoy strong support among parents and leaders of Milwaukee's African-American community. School leaders point out that the ultimate goals are to raise test scores, to improve reading, mathematics, and critical-thinking skills, to create positive self-images and patterns of social interaction, and to "inculcate the skills needed by students for self-determination" (Scherer, 1991–92, p. 17). As proof of their effectiveness, school administrators cite higher attendance rates—98 percent attendance in the case of Detroit's Malcolm X Academy (*New York Times*, 1992)—fewer discipline problems, better grades, and improved performance on standardized tests. At the Detroit Malcolm X Academy's "sister" school, the Mae Jemison Academy, which opened in the 1991–92 school year, standardized test scores rose so much and so quickly that the school lost some of its Title I funds. For the most part, however, the schools are too new for the results to be definitive, and the programs remain in their experimental stage. School officials also point out that the long-term effects of the African-American Immersion Schools will not be evident until the children now in elementary school finish high school (ideally, in the same African-American immersion environment) and attend college.

The African-American Immersion Schools have attracted their share of critics. Much of the criticism centers on the curriculum and its Afrocentric perspective. While children do study the experiences and perspectives of other oppressed groups, such as American Indians, the view they receive is not that of the dominant culture. Schlesinger (1992) argues that African-American children are receiving factually unsound information and therefore an inferior education at their separate schools, a criticism he has leveled against those who seek to use Portland's baseline essays as well. (He does not mention, though, that intensive skills-based instruction and strict discipline are also important components of the African-American Immersion Schools.) Both he and Diane Ravitch

(1991–92) attack the move toward a separate curriculum, which they see as potentially disruptive to a unified nation. In Ravitch's words,

> It is not the role of the public schools to teach children the customs and folkways of their ethnic or racial group; that is, as it has always been, the role of the family, the church, and the local community. Nor is it the role of the public school to encapsulate children in the confines of their family's inherited culture. It is the role of the public schools to open children's minds to new worlds, new ideas, new possibilities. (p. 8)

Even though the children attend segregated schools due to residential segregation, the idea of a consciously segregated school, particularly one named after Black Nationalist Malcolm X, frightens many whites. Some fear that the curriculum will fan the flames of racial hatred, that it is not just African-centered, but anti-white as well (*New York Times*, 1992). Others have argued that the schools succeed merely because of their high expectations for the students and that a curriculum affirming the students' culture is neither a necessary nor a sufficient element (Wilson, 1991).

Defenders of the African-American Immersion Schools deny that their approach creates divisions and hatreds. They would like to see the same curriculum and pedagogical methods utilized in all schools. A curriculum that emphasizes the contributions of Africans and African-Americans provides the broadening experience Ravitch advocates as the role of the public schools. In the course of their lives, European-American children and those of other groups have little access to information about the heritage, culture, and contributions of their fellow citizens who are African-American and few incentives to pursue what information is there (Harris, 1992). The pedagogical methods used in the African-American Immersion Schools have, at least initially, proven to be successful with students who have consistently underachieved, posed severe discipline problems, or failed in other situations. If the goal is to produce educated, self-sufficient citizens who can command good jobs in the competitive economy of the next century, schools that combine cultural sensitivity with high expectations may be best suited to attain that goal (Holt, 1991–92).

A different perspective on this issue comes from an examination of nonpublic schools that stress African-American culture and achievement. In 1987, Joan Davis Ratteray and Mwalimu J. Shujaa studied more than two hundred inner-city independent schools throughout the country. (The actual number of these schools exceeds four hundred and may be significantly higher [Ratteray, 1990]). There were several significant items. Some of the schools are more than fifty or one hundred years old. About half are affiliated with religious groups, such as various black churches and the Catholic Church. They are generally smaller than public schools; the average enrollment is 130 students per school, with a student/faculty ratio of 14:1 (Ratteray, 1990). In the schools that had a predominantly African-American student body, Ratteray and Shujaa noted

African culture is a principal force of both public and independent schools serving African-American populations.

a strong African-American cultural presence, even though many administrators did not openly admit such an orientation: "Looking at the pictorial images on the walls, the planned activities, and the ethnic verbal and nonverbal exchanges between teachers and students or administrators and students, there is no question in the minds of most observers who enter the institutions or the classrooms that these are proudly African-American environments" (Ratteray, 1990, p. 201). The independent schools utilized textbooks less often and teacher-made materials more often than their public school counterparts. According to Ratteray, the teachers found textbooks to be deficient in representing African-Americans, and so they created their own materials. Although the study's authors warn of the limitations of quantitative evidence, they do point out that African-American students at independent inner-city schools consistently outperform their peers in the public schools. Parents and school administrators also report fewer discipline problems, greater motivation, and more satisfaction with school (Ratteray, 1990).

Independent schools have enjoyed a long tradition in the United States, and independent African-centered schools have been relatively immune from the kind of criticism suffered by their public school counterparts. In contrast to public schools, independent schools may admit only boys or only girls, may restrict admission to a particular religious group, and may teach religion as part of the curriculum. While some have seen the encouragement of independent schools (and the offering of government-funded vouchers to pay their tuition) as potentially *disuniting*, they are generally not the same critics who have attacked the African-American Immersion Schools for that reason. On the other hand, some have pointed to the independent school admission process, the sacrifice parents make to pay tuition, and the schools' ability to expel problem students as the main reasons for the schools' success. Many of these advantages are also enjoyed by public schools of choice, which require parents to go through an admission process and which often have special powers to select teachers and to transfer both teachers and students who do not conform to the rules.

Schools Serving Other Groups

American Indian. Like African-Americans, American Indians have experienced a school system that devalues them and their culture. Reyner and Eder (1992) argue that from the time American Indians were confined to reservations and their children shipped off to boarding schools, the goal was to eliminate all aspects of Indian culture and to force Indians to take a subordinate place in white society. By the 1920s, the government had to acknowledge that the boarding schools had failed, that the children were returning to their families and communities. The government then began sending Indian children to local public schools, which most attend today (Reyhner & Eder, 1992).

Yet the experience of American Indian children in the public schools has been, for the most part, an unhappy one. Drop-out rates are high, achievement levels low, and Indian children have frequently internalized the belief—often communicated by teachers and the school curriculum—that they are less intelligent than other children (Reyhner & Eder, 1992). These facts have prompted calls for schools that are controlled by Indian educators themselves; a few elementary and secondary schools and a somewhat larger number of two- and four-year colleges have been established to meet the educational needs of American Indian students (Reyhner & Eder, 1992).

Reynor and Eder also describe that the oldest and best-known of the Indian-controlled elementary/secondary schools, the Rough Rock Demonstration School, founded by the Navajo Nation in Rough Rock, Arizona, in 1966. Despite government promises to the contrary, the school has remained severely underfunded and constantly in danger of shutting its doors. Nonetheless, it and another Navajo school, the Rock Point Community School, have pioneered a bilingual/bicultural curriculum that builds upon the heritage and cultural strengths of American Indian children.

The students who come to the Rock Point Community School speak Navajo as their first language, and reading instruction is first conducted in Navajo rather than English. As the students move through the grades, a larger share of the instruction is in English. Students learn to read in English in the second grade. The skills learned in Navajo are transferred to reading instruction in English (Reyhner, 1992). Mathematics and science instruction are also carried out in a culturally appropriate manner. A multisensory approach is used, so that in learning to count and to calculate, children begin by manipulating blocks and other objects. They then discuss the concepts and subsequently move on to abstract problems on worksheets (Davison, 1992). The Rock Point Community School has made a special effort to recruit and maintain Navajo teachers. At first, many of the teachers did not have college diplomas, but the school contracted with the State of Arizona to offer college courses on-site so that the non-degreed teachers could obtain their diplomas and certifications. As a result, only one teacher in the 1987–88 school year was not Navajo (Reyhner, 1992). Studies have shown that when Indian children are taught by Indians, their test scores in reading and language arts and their general achievement levels improve (Reyhner, 1992). The school also works closely with parents and other community members to generate materials and to encourage the achievement of the students.

The results of the Rock Point Community School's efforts are clear. In reading and English grammar, the students outperform all other Navajo students and all other Indian students in the State of Arizona. In mathematics, the eighth-grade students outperform the same groups and score at the national average (Reyhner, 1992). By their senior year of high school, the Rock Point students score above the national average in mathematics (Davison, 1992). Furthermore, the students graduate with fluency in both English and Navajo and are able to contribute to the preservation of Navajo language and culture. Students at the school have produced literary works later published by major presses. Among the creations of the Rock Point school is the anthology of folktales, stories, and poems, *Between Sacred Mountains: Navajo Stories and Lessons from the Land*, edited by Bingham and Bingham and published in 1984 by the University of Arizona Press. Some of the Rock Point students' poems are also included in Virginia Driving Hawk Sneve's acclaimed anthology, *Dancing Teepees: Poems of American Indian Youth* (1989).

The Rock Point Community School and other contract schools that seek to preserve American Indian language and culture have not come under fire to the extent of the African-American Immersion Schools. There are not many schools, and they are small and far from the large urban centers where they might attract media attention. Most critics of bilingual education have focused on programs for Latino students and new immigrants, arguing that those programs prevent Latinos and other immigrants from becoming full participants in the United States economy and society. As described by Reyhner (1992), opponents of bilingual education believe traditional Indian languages have already died out or are on their way to extinction.

Bilingual. The International High School at Middle College in New York City exemplifies a different approach to the issue of bilingual education within a multicultural setting. Dozens of immigrant groups from all over the world have made New York City and the borough of Queens, where the International High School is located, their home. The International High School serves this immigrant population. In order to enroll, teenagers in grades nine and up must have immigrated to the United States within the past four years and score below a certain level on a test of English proficiency (Spain, 1990). The school is a school of choice, with admission determined by lottery, and there is a long waiting list.

In contrast to the Rock Point Community School and the approaches of many bilingual programs, the International High School emphasizes English immersion and intensive instruction in English as a second language. All subject courses are conducted in English. Students may take one class in their native language for the purpose of maintenance, just as students in any high school take a single class in a foreign language. Students are expected to communicate with each other and with the teacher in English. Students are also required to take part in an internship program, working in businesses and public agencies throughout the city. Along with expressing their philosophy of intensive English instruction and usage, teachers point out that it would be impossible to provide bilingual subject-area instruction for the more than thirty languages spoken by the students. This philosophy of English-language immersion has the strong support not only of the parents, who have selected this environment for their children, but also of many immigrant communities as a whole. A major problem of the school, according to officials, is its inability to serve but a fraction of the families who want to attend and the lack of similar programs elsewhere in the city for those families (Richardson, 1993).

Despite its approach to bilingual education, the International High School is very much a multicultural environment. Using the facilities of LaGuardia Community College, the school has a resource-based teaching program that integrates literature and audio-visual materials into the curriculum in all subject areas. Working with the Career Education Department and the Library Media Center, some of the students, as part of their internship, produce a video entitled "Internship: What Is It?" They interview other interns and those who employ them in order to give incoming students a sense of what will be expected of them. Many of the new immigrants are afraid of working in a monolingual environment, and the video helps allay their anxieties. Students also produce a music video in English focusing upon their experience of immigration. This is an interdisciplinary project supervised by the English as a second language (ESL) and social studies teachers and the Library Media Center. At the school, textbooks are not seen as the sole source, or even the most important source, of instruction. Students use trade books and videos, many of which focus upon immigration and cross-cultural issues, and they produce their own materials that are based upon their experiences before, during, and after immigration (Spain, 1990). The materials generated by the students in-house play an important part in instruction, filling in where commercially available materials do not meet the needs of the students, do not speak to their experiences, or do not fit into the philosophy of the school and its curriculum (Spain, 1990).

As in other multicultural programs, cooperative learning is used extensively in the International High School. Projects such as the internship video and the music video on immigration involve the collaboration of several students. In classes students work together on projects and much of the ESL instruction occurs through conversations in small groups. The projects can be quite creative, as the following example from Spain (1990) suggests:

> [One English teacher] spontaneously proposed to the [students] that they play a game and pretend they were getting married in class. They went wild over the idea. The teacher immediately integrated it into the personal development course, having them pair off, find common interests, go on a date, hunt for an apartment, look for a job, and set up a budget, using newspapers, books on survival skills, and periodicals. The students wrote scripts, performed short sketches based on their activities, and eventually had to decide whether to get married, live together, be friends, or separate.
>
> Those who "got married" did so in a mock ceremony that was videotaped. The students dressed up, rehearsed, invited other students and teachers as guests, and held a wedding reception . . . In the course of the project most of the young people underwent deep changes in their relationships with the opposite sex, attitudes toward career and life planning, and their ability to gather information through the use of standard reading materials. (p. 88)

Cooperative learning allows students from many countries and religious traditions to share their experiences; each student receives a thoroughly broadening and truly international education. Cooperative learning also helps students to come to terms with longstanding conflicts related to their ethnicity so that they can work in harmony with others from different traditions. In observing a class, one may find Israelis and Palestinians, Russian Jews, and Muslims from Afghanistan working together on a group project and in the process developing the skills to live peacefully in the diverse nation in which they have settled.

The International High School has achieved extraordinary success in its first decade of existence. Having opened its doors in the 1985–86 school year, it graduated its first class in 1989. Of the original sixty students admitted, fifty-four (90 percent) received their diplomas in four years, a proportion well above that of the city high schools as a whole (Spain, 1990). All of the graduates were accepted to colleges. Discipline problems are virtually nonexistent. Despite the diversity of ethnic and cultural groups represented, few conflicts among students have been reported. In the words of library media specialist Louise Spain, "They may be troubled refugees of war, politics, or economic upheavals, or shy and unassertive as a result of cultural upbringing. What must emerge at the end of their four years in high school is a group of Americanized, English-speaking, college-ready graduates—and it does!" (Spain, 1990, p. 87).

In addition to these schools described, there are countless schools and teachers throughout the country that have responded to the needs of culturally diverse children by offering materials and approaches that are sensitive to those children. While only a fraction of those efforts gain attention in educational journals and the mainstream media, the teachers receive other rewards, most notably the achievement and affection of their students. Teachers who understand the role culture plays in education and offer the perspectives of those outside the dominant culture are helping to make school a less alienating place for children of color at the same time as they are teaching all children to live harmoniously in a diverse society.

❖ Multicultural Education in Teacher Preparation Programs

To prepare teachers to work better with culturally diverse students and to raise all students' awareness of cultural diversity, many states have moved toward requiring courses in multicultural education as part of teacher certification requirements. The 1987 study by Bruce Mitchell found sixteen states and the District of Columbia with multicultural education requirements for teacher certification. Most of the states with such requirements had large culturally diverse populations; among them were Alabama, Connecticut, Illinois, Massachusetts, New Jersey, Ohio, Texas, and Washington State. Some of the states with multicultural education certification requirements were not among those known for large culturally diverse populations, but state officials recognized the need for prospective teachers and their students to know more about the role of culture in education and the diverse groups that make up the United States. Included among these states were Iowa, Minnesota, Nevada, North Dakota, and Utah (Mitchell, 1987). Many states with culturally diverse populations, including California and New York, did not have multicultural education certification requirements in 1987, but have instituted them since.

Multicultural education requirements for teachers can take a number of forms. Some universities have instituted requirements for all students, regardless of academic major. One of those universities is the University of California at Berkeley, which requires all students to take an ethnic studies course that compares the experiences of at least three of the following ethnic groups: African-Americans, Asian-Americans, American Indians, Latinos, and European-Americans. (Wilkerson, 1992). A 1992 survey of approximately two hundred representative universities and two- and four-year colleges found that 34 percent had some sort of general multicultural education requirement (Levine & Cureton, 1992). Students at public colleges and universities on the East and West Coast were more likely to encounter these requirements (Levine and Cureton, 1992). For the most part, the required courses focus on culturally diverse groups within the United States, though some also examine other cultures throughout the world. In some cases, students choose courses in a specific discipline (an education major, for instance, may satisfy the requirement with a course in literature, history, music, or sociology); in others, the course is part of an interdisciplinary core curriculum.

In lieu of, or in addition to, university requirements, teacher education students may be required to take a course in multicultural education offered by the Education Department. Despite that label, some of the courses are quite general; they are essentially ethnic studies courses with general observations on teaching and the schools. Davidman (1990) has criticized such an approach, arguing that these courses have minimal relevance for classroom teachers. Teachers, according to Davidman and Davidman (1988), need concrete guidance in order both to teach culturally diverse students and to teach about cultural diversity in an effective manner:

> We believe that the most practical and powerful way to create multicultural education in the teacher education arena is to utilize a practical definition which can easily be translated into specific teacher behaviors (competencies). We need a conception/definition which simultaneously: (a) can serve as the basis for a course entitled, let us say, "Multicultural Education in the Elementary School"; (b) can be understood and used by university supervisors and cooperating teachers as they provide feedback keyed to behaviors that will help to turn (more or less) monocultural student teachers into multicultural educators; and (c) receive the support of school district administrators and K–12 teachers. The cooperating (or master) teachers, after all, will be asked to model these multicultural competencies, and help their student teachers develop them. (p. 60)

The Davidmans also call for the establishment of different competencies for prospective teachers in elementary, middle, and high school (Davidman & Davidman, 1988).

The Education Department at California Polytechnic State University has instituted an innovative program in multicultural teacher education and supervision. The Department graduates between one hundred and 120 multiple-subject teacher candidates per year (Davidman, 1990). Each student completes two student teaching assignments of one quarter each, allowing the teaching candidate to experience two different schools, with different curriculums, supervising teachers, and student populations. The Davidmans have advocated teaching prospective teachers to research the communities in which they work and to collect demographic data on their students; following that, prospective teachers should explore the various cultures of their students. Teachers should also explore how to teach a multicultural curriculum to children of all cultures (Davidman & Davidman, 1988). To these ends, student teachers must complete a "Classroom Demographic Profile" and a "Typology of Multicultural Teaching" for each of their assignments. Their mentor in this enterprise is the supervising teacher, who has received special training in cross-cultural and multicultural education. On the day they are to be observed by the professor and the supervising teacher, the student teacher also completes a letter of context that explains the lesson in its cross-cultural context and provides information on four to six children in the class that are from a different cultural group than that of the student teacher. The student teacher must describe how rapport has been built with those children and how he/she has tried to promote their success in the classroom (Davidman, 1990).

In their overview of teacher education programs, published in 1992, Jesus Garcia and Sharon L. Pugh describe a great deal of resistance to additional commitments to multiculturalism in university teacher education programs (Garcia & Pugh, 1992). Throughout the university community, conservative scholars and commentators have used the term *politically correct* to ridicule those who support a more inclusive curriculum. Too many professors and students, according to Garcia and Pugh, see multicultural education as a "minority thing," of little relevance to the predominantly white teacher education students, most of whom will see few culturally diverse children in their classes (Garcia & Pugh, 1992). These students and professors show little awareness of the country's changing demographics. In the schools of the future, fewer classrooms will be homogeneously European-American, and the children who sit in those classrooms will be more likely to live and work alongside people of color once they graduate. Garcia and Pugh also point out that multicultural education, "with its multiple perspectives and dialogical communications, is the ideal context in which students can learn to think critically and solve problems" (Garcia & Pugh, 1992, p. 218). With these additional perspectives, students, especially those from the dominant group, are likely to have their basic assumptions challenged and to learn, for example, that textbooks and the mainstream media do not tell the whole truth. When presented with conflicts of any kind, students exposed to a multicultural approach have been taught to see the issue *from both sides*.

The present efforts toward multicultural education—efforts to create a more informed and sensitive staff, to incorporate other perspectives besides the dominant one in the curriculum, to teach techniques for cooperation and conflict resolution among different cultural groups, and to meet the special needs of populations for whom the school experience has been one of alienation and failure—have not occurred without controversy. Yet the staff development project in Columbus, Ohio, the Portland baseline essays, the Human Rights Education Program in the suburban Shoreham-Wading River School District, the various African-American Immersion Schools, the bilingual Navajo-English program at the Rock Point Community School, the International High School in New York City, and the innovative program of practice teaching and supervision at California Polytechnic State University are all steps in the right direction. While the African-American Immersion Schools, the Rock Point Community School, and the International High School have also made progress in boosting the achievement of their special populations, all of the programs provide skills and knowledge that cannot be measured on standardized tests, but are nonetheless necessary if our young people are to think critically, to respect and understand themselves and each other, and to live together in peace.

❖ Summary

During the 1960s and 1970s multicultural education approaches were developed in answer to the increased racial and ethnic consciousness inspired by the Civil Rights movement. However, it is in the 1980s and 1990s that most of the current programs and reforms have appeared. Large states such as California and New York have instituted changes in the curriculum particularly in the area of history and social studies—and in the case of California, new, improved textbooks have been adopted. Both states have experienced controversy in response to these changes.

However, local efforts have been more noteworthy. For example, in Columbus, Ohio, a staff development program has been enthusiastically received by educators. The Portland, Oregon, school district has engaged in curriculum reform that created a nationally recognized series of baseline essays that have become models for other districts. While the essays have evoked controversy, particularly the African-American essays, critics have noted that useful information is also included in the areas of literature, music, and mathematics. The Shoreham-Wading River School District on Long Island, New York, has developed a program which focuses on a broad spectrum of cultural groups and human rights.

Other examples of multicultural education programs include those developed for special populations. In cities such as Detroit and Milwaukee, for example, Afrocentric and African Immersion Schools have been developed for African-American students. Special programs also exist for Latino students. These programs stressing cultural education, parent involvement, and high expectations for students are relatively new and await careful evaluation. However, improved attendance and attitudes of students, and reduction of disciplinary problems have been reported in some programs.

The Rough Rock Demonstration School and Rock Point Community School provide programs for American Indian students. These schools have developed bilingual/bicultural curricula that build upon the heritage and cultural strengths of the children. Impressive productions of literature have been completed at the Rock Point School and students have shown achievement scores at the national average. Unlike the Rock Point Community School, the successful International High School in New York stresses English immersion and English as a second language in their approach to educating a diverse population of students from many different countries.

Many teacher education programs have also subscribed to multicultural education. However, the requirements vary across the country. Some states require courses for certification, while others have no requirements.

Current efforts toward multicultural education in the schools are encouraging, particularly at the local level. Staff development, the incorporation of other perspectives in the curriculum, cooperative learning, and conflict resolution methods and programs that respect the cultures and languages of oppressed groups are promising beginnings. However, a comprehensive approach to multicultural education is the only means for reforming the schools to ensure the empowerment of, participation in, and contribution to the society of all Americans.

❖ CHAPTER 4 **Questions**

1. What are the similarities and differences in the multicultural education approaches of New York and California?

2. Discuss the present, general status of multicultural education at the state and local level. How widespread is its introduction? How comprehensive are those efforts? Give examples.

3. What are the advantages and disadvantages of beginning a multicultural education program with a focus on staff development as in Columbus, Ohio, compared with the emphasis on curriculum reform in Portland, Oregon?

4. Discuss the controversial aspects of the Portland Baseline Essays and identify the strengths of this approach.

5. What are the unique features of the Shoreham-Wading River School District's program for multicultural education?

6. Would you advocate more schools that serve special populations with heavy emphasis on culture? Provide the rationale for your position.

❖ References

Adams, B. S., Pardo, W. E., & Schniedewind, N. (1991–92). Changing "the way things are done around here." *Educational Leadership* (December 1991/ January 1992), 37–42.

Banks, J. A. (1991). Multicultural literacy and curriculum reform. *Educational Horizons, 69* (Spring 1991), 135–140+.

Boateng, F. (1990). Combatting deculturalization of the African-American child in the public school system: A multicultural approach. In K. Lomotey (Ed.), *Going to school: The African-American experience.* (pp. 73–84). Albany, NY: The State University of New York Press.

Browder, L. H., Jr. (1992). Towards a "cultural quota" system in our schools? *International Journal of Educational Reform, 1*(4) (October 1992), 347–355.

Cortes, C. E. (1991). Pluribus and unum: The quest for community amid diversity. *Change, 25* (September/October 1991), 9–13.

Cullinan, B. E. (1989). Latching onto literature: Reading initiatives take hold. *School Library Journal, 35*(4) (April 1989), 27–31.

Davidman, L., & Davidman, P. (1988). Multicultural teacher education in the state of California: The challenge of definition and implementation. *Teacher Education Quarterly, 15*(2) (Spring 1988), 50–67.

Davidman, P. T. (1990). Multicultural teacher education and supervision: A new approach to professional development. *Teacher Education Quarterly, 17*(3) (Summer 1990), 37–52.

Davison, D. M. (1992). Mathematics. In J. Reyhner (Ed.), *Teaching American Indian students.* (pp. 241–250). Norman, OK: University of Oklahoma Press.

Garcia, J., & Pugh, S. L. (1992). Multicultural education in teacher preparation programs: A political or an educational concept? *Phi Delta Kappan, 74*(3) (November 1992), 214–219.

Hare, B. R., & Castenell, L. A., Jr. (1987). No place to run, no place to hide: Comparative status and future prospects of black boys. In M. B. Spencer, G. K. Brookings, & W. Allen (Eds.), *Beginnings: The social and affective development of black children.* NJ: Lawrence Erlbaum Associate.

Harris, M. D. (1992). Africentrism and curriculum: Concepts, issues, and prospects. *Journal of Negro Education, 61*(3), 301–316.

Hilliard, A. G., III. (1990). Limitations of current academic achievement measures. In K. Lomotey (Ed.), *Going to school: The African-American experience.* (pp. 135–142). Albany, NY: The State University of New York Press.

Holt, K. C. (1991–92). A rationale for creating African-American immersion schools. *Educational Leadership* (December 1991/January 1992), 18.

Hostility greets students at black school in white area of Detroit. (1992, December 2). *The New York Times,* p. B12.

King, J. E. (1992). Diaspora literacy and consciousness in the struggle against miseducation in the black community. *Journal of Negro Education, 61*(3), 317–340.

Kohl, H. (1991). The politically correct bypass: Multiculturalism and the public schools. *Social Policy, 22*(1) (Summer 1991), 33–40.

Kozol, J. (1991). *Savage inequalities.* New York: Crown.

Levine, A., & Cureton, J. (1992). The quiet revolution: Eleven facts about multiculturalism and the curriculum. *Change* (January/February 1992), 25–29.

Martel, E. (1991–92). How valid are the Portland baseline essays? *Educational Leadership* (December 1991/January 1992), 20–23.

Massey, D. S., & Denton, N. A. (1989). Hypersegregation in United States metropolitan areas: Black and Hispanic segregation along five dimensions. *Demography, 26*(3) (August 1989), 373–391.

Miranda, A. H., et al. (1992). The implementation of a comprehensive multicultural program. *Journal of Staff Development, 13*(2) (Spring 1992), 2–6.

Mitchell, B. (1987). Multicultural education: A second glance at the present American effort. *Educational Research Quarterly, 11*(4), 8–12.

Myers, W. D. (1985). The Black Experience in Children's Books: One Step Forward, Two Steps Back. In D. McCann & G. Woodard (Eds.), *The Black American in books for children: Readings in racism*, (2nd ed.). Methuen, NJ: Scarecrow Press.

National Commission on Excellence in Education (1983). *A nation at risk.* Washington, DC: U.S. Department of Education.

New York Times, Dec. 28, 1993. Thriving on difference: International high students speak language of learning. p. B1.

O'Neil, J. (1991-92). On the Portland plan: A conversation with Matthew Prophet. *Educational Leadership* (December 1991/January 1992), 24–27.

Ratteray, J. D. (1990). African-American achievement: A research agenda emphasizing independent schools. In K. Lomotey (Ed.), *Going to school: The African-American experience.* (pp. 197–207). Albany, NY: The State University of New York Press.

Ravitch, D. (1991–92). A culture in common. *Educational Leadership* (December 1991/January 1992), 8–11.

Reyhner, J. (1992). Bilingual education. In J. Reyhner (Ed.), *Teaching American Indian students.* (pp. 59–77). Norman, OK: University of Oklahoma Press.

Reyhner, J. & Eder, J. (1992). A History of Indian Education. In J. Reyhner (Ed.). *Teaching American Indian students.* (pp. 33–58). Norman, OK: University of Oklahoma Press.

Scherer, M. (1991–92). School snapshot: Focus on African-American culture. *Educational Leadership* (December 1991/January 1992), 17–19.

Schlesinger, A. M., Jr. (1992). *The disuniting of America.* New York: W. W. Norton and Co.

Sobol, T. (1990). Understanding diversity. *Educational Leadership* (November 1990), 27–30.

Spain, L. (1990). The international high school at LaGuardia Community College: An audiovisual approach to second language acquisition. In E. V. LiBretto (Ed.), *The high/low handbook*, (3rd ed.). (pp. 85–92). New York: R. R. Bowker.

Stevenson, Z., Jr., & Gonzalez, L. (1992). Contemporary practices in multicultural approaches to education among the largest American school districts. *Journal of Negro Education, 61*(3), 356–369.

Wilkerson, M. B. (1992). Beyond the graveyard: Engaging faculty involvement. *Change* (January/February 1992), 59–63.

Willinsky, J. (1990). *The new literacy: Redefining reading and writing in the schools.* New York: Routledge and Kegan Paul.

Wilson, R. (1991). Curricular diversity and academic achievement. *Liberal Education, 77*(1) (January/February 1991), 12–15.

CHAPTER 5

Exceptional Children from Diverse Cultures

Culturally and linguistically diverse students in our schools include many students with mild disabilities and smaller numbers whose disabilities are moderate to severe. These children will be served by both regular and special education since the majority of exceptional students are in regular classes with and without support from special education teachers. Furthermore, the current movement toward *inclusion* seeks to educate all children within the mainstream classrooms.

Culturally and linguistically diverse students in our schools include many students with mild disabilities.

It is important for teachers to understand the issues involving culturally and linguistically diverse students with disabilities. First, these students are overrepresented in special education and this situation has existed for some time. The use of inappropriate assessment instruments and procedures, socioeconomic status, and linguistic and cultural differences have led to misdiagnosis, misclassification, and errors in the placement of these students (Prasse & Reschly, 1986). Males, blacks, and children from households in which the head has not attended college have also been overrepresented (U.S. Department of Education, Office of Special Education and Rehabilitative Services, 1989). In 1987, black students comprised 12.2 percent of the total student population while 24.2 percent of the secondary students in special education classes were black (U.S. Department of Education, Office of Special Education and Rehabilitative Services, 1989). Secondly, the area of assessment and identification of disabilities in children of color has been subject to serious errors due to cultural and linguistic bias in the tests and procedures used. In some school districts, children who are not proficient in English are placed in special education.

Students with limited English proficiency (LEP) are at risk for placement in special education when their language differences are misdiagnosed as language disorders. Language is a key aspect of a student's academic performance and the differentiation of a disorder from a difference is crucial. Many experts in the field point out that the student must be assessed in the primary language as well as English in order to determine if a disorder exists (Cummins, 1986).

Other factors also influence the student's performance. For example, a student who has lost time from school due to absences or disruptions will show delays. As Cummins (1986) has pointed out, it requires approximately two years for a student with LEP to acquire basic communication skills in English. Furthermore, there are other factors to consider:

▌ the length of time in the United States;
▌ the language usage experienced by the student;
▌ the types of classrooms the student has experienced;
▌ the extent to which the evaluators consider factors such as parental views of the student's performance;
▌ the performance of other students with similar backgrounds; and
▌ health and developmental factors.

In a study reviewing current practices used by bilingual speech and language pathologists in California, Langdon (1989) found that their use of documentation was insufficient to establish whether language and academic problems were due to environmental, cultural, or economic differences.

Several landmark cases in special education have resulted from these practices in the past. In the case of *Diana v. State Board of Education* (1970) ,a class action suit was brought on behalf of Latino children in California. These children were placed in classes for children with mental retardation on the basis of their scores on standardized intelligence tests. In a consent decree, the State of California ruled that children

▌ would be tested in their primary language and English if English was not the primary language;
▌ that unfair verbal items would be eliminated from the tests;
▌ that all Mexican-American and Chinese students in classes for children with mental retardation would be re-evaluated using a test in their native language; and
▌ that intelligence tests would be developed that reflected Mexican-American culture and standardized on Mexican-American children. (Ysseldyke & Algozzine, 1984)

In the case of *Larry P. v. Riles* (1979), the issue was overrepresentation of African-American children in classes for children with mental retardation in California. The court ruled that the California State Education Department had to stop the use of intelligence tests to place black students in those classes, that schools in California had to begin to eliminate the disproportionate placement of black students in classes for students with mental retardation, and schools had to reevaluate all black students currently enrolled in such classes (Ysseldyke & Algozzine, 1984).

Despite the significant litigation and legislation, overrepresentation of black and Latino students in special education continues, and segregation and isolation of these students occurs in classes where they are present in disproportionate numbers. However, recent legislation, the

Individuals with Disabilities Education Act (1991), mandates that tests must be culture-fair and that students must be tested in their primary language. This legislation is beginning to show an effect, and in some studies, the number of these students classified with mental retardation is decreasing. It is anticipated that this trend will continue.

❖ The Legal Foundation for Special Education

Federal and state regulations govern the field of special education, assuring a free, appropriate public education to all students with disabilities, ages three to twenty-one. Landmark legislation was passed in 1975, Public Law 94-142, Education of All Handicapped Children Act. That law resulted in major changes in the education of school-aged children with disabilities. For the first time, all students with disabilities ages five to twenty-one were entitled to a free, appropriate public education in the least restricted environment. Recently, Congress reauthorized the law and renamed it The Individuals with Disabilities Education Act or IDEA. The major provisions of the law are shown (Table 5–1) (Smith & Luckasson, 1992).

Special education is defined in the regulations as "specially designed instruction, at no cost to the parent to meet the unique needs of a child with a disability." Individualized instruction may be provided in a continuum of educational settings from the "least (regular classroom) to the most restrictive (homebound) available" (Federal Regulations, 300.14 (a)(1) in Smith & Luckasson, (1992).

In the regulations, the disabilities recognized by the federal government are identified and defined. They include the following, in order of prevalence in the school-aged population (Gearhart, Mullen, & Gearhart, 1993):

- learning disabilities   = 3.62%
- speech handicapped   = 1.72%
- mental retardation   = 0.09%
- emotionally disturbed   = 0.67%
- orthopedic and other health impaired   = 0.17%
- multihandicapped   = 0.15%
- hearing impaired and deaf   = 0.10%
- visually impaired and blind   = 0.04%
- autism and traumatic brain injury   = Data unavailable

Although gifted and talented children are also considered exceptional, based upon their exceptional ability or talent, this population is not included in the regulations or funding. Congress has previously passed legislation, such as the Gifted and Talented Children's Education Act in 1978, which provided incentives to states and local education agencies;

TABLE 5-1 Major Provisions: Individuals with
Disabilities Education Act (IDEA)

1. *Free and appropriate public education (FAPE).* This means that special
   education must be provided to the student without cost to the family and
   student. In addition, the education must be appropriately suited to the
   student's individual needs. Additional funds needed to provide this education
   are shared by the state and federal governments.

2. *Due process rights for parents.* Parents have certain rights under the law that
   must be respected and complied with by the school. These rights include
   the right to examine their child's records, seek an independent, outside
   evaluation, receive a written notice of the school's decision to evaluate their
   child, and consent or object to the school's decision for eligibility, classification, or placement and related services. Parents have the right to make formal
   complaints and receive a due process hearing where an impartial hearing
   officer presides. Parents also have the right to legal counsel, witnesses,
   outside experts who may attend the hearing, and an appeal process.

3. *Individual evaluation.* Non-biased, individualized evaluation must be
   conducted by trained professionals in the child's native language, if needed,
   to determine the child's eligibility for special education services.

4. *Identification and services to all children.* School districts must actually seek
   out and identify all children who may have a disability. Many districts conduct
   a screening program among preschool children in order to comply with this
   provision of the law.

5. *Provision for related services.* When children with disabilities require other
   services in addition to special education, these must be identified and provided without cost to the child and the family. Examples of related services are
   transportation, speech therapy, physical therapy, and counseling.

6. *Individualized education program.* Each student with a disability must have
   an individualized education plan based upon assessed needs. The plan is
   completed by a committee that usually includes a school administrator, the
   prospective special education teacher, the current teacher, the parents of
   the student, and the student. In some school districts an experienced parent
   advocate is also a member. This plan includes the long-term goals and short-
   term objectives to be accomplished during the school year.

7. *Least restrictive environment (LRE).* According to the law, students with
   disabilities, including those in public or private institutions or other care
   facilities, must be educated to the extent appropriate, with students who are
   not handicapped (20 USC Sect. 1412(5) B, in Smith & Luckasson, 1992,
   p. 25). Different interpretations of least restrictive environment are possible.
   However, the current inclusion movement in special education seeks the
   placement of all students with disabilities in the mainstream.

> **SPECIAL BOX 5–1**
>
> The most recent legislation, the Americans with Disabilities Act, was passed in 1990. It protects the rights of individuals with disabilities in employment, public accommodations, transportation, telecommunications, and state and local government operations (Council for Exceptional Children Precis, 1990). In 1992, businesses with more than twenty-five workers were required to change their physical plants to accommodate disabled employees; new buses, trains, and subway cars must be accessible to people in wheel chairs; renovated or new hotels, retail stores, and restaurants must be accessible to people in wheelchairs; and telephone companies have to provide relay services allowing hearing- or voice-impaired people with special telephones to place and receive calls from ordinary telephones (*New York Times*, July 14, 1990).

however, in 1982, this Act was phased out. More recently, the Jacob Javits Gifted and Talented Education Act allocated $8 million for teacher education and sources for identification of gifted children. The Act also established a National Center for Education of the Gifted (Heward & Cavanaugh, in Banks & Banks, 1993).

Despite the fact that gifted and talented individuals exist in every cultural group, children of color are underrepresented in school programs for gifted children. Students who are racially, ethnically, or socioeconomically at risk have been underrepresented in programs for gifted and talented children (Richert, 1987; Van Tassel-Baska, Patton, & Prillaman, 1989). This is due to the identification process and criteria used to place students in these programs. Students' cultural characteristics, values, and approaches to learning must be taken into account (Patton, Prillaman, & Van Tassel-Bask, 1990). While African-Americans make up approximately 16.2 percent of the public school population, they comprise only 8.4 percent of students enrolled in programs for the gifted (Alamprise & Erlanger, 1988, cited in Patton, 1992). In a study on the gifted population, Kirschenbaum in 1988 (in Smith & Luckasson, 1992) found that 2.9 percent of white children received gifted education compared with 1.5 percent of African-Americans, 1.5 percent of Latinos, and 1.1 percent of Native American children. Because identification depends upon the assessment devices and procedures used, schools must improve and expand their identification procedures to include more culturally sensitive devices.

The classification of children with disabilities has led to widespread controversy about the effects of labeling. Labeling identifies an individual child or group according to their classification. Some special educators differentiate classification and labeling. According to Smith and Luckasson (1993), for example, classification is an organized system for the identification and organization of characteristics while labeling is an act that reduces the child or group to the category in which they are placed. There are advantages and disadvantages of categorizing children, (Table 5–2), (Smith & Luckasson, 1992; Ysseldyke & Algozzine, 1990; Lilly, 1992).

The most recent effort to prevent the effects of labeling involves the identification of *children with disabilities* as opposed to *handicapped children*. In this way it is obvious that the disability indicates only one of the groups to which a child belongs. Examples of this important guideline are expressed in the following descriptions: "Danny is a child with a learning disability; Sally is a child with mental retardation."

The provision, in IDEA, for the least restrictive environment views the regular classroom as the ideal environment for all school-aged individuals, and exceptional students must be educated with peers who are not disabled to the maximum extent possible. Thus, the entire school community must be sensitized to acceptance and appreciation of the unique, individual participation of students with disabilities (Salend, 1994). Recently, a movement toward inclusion has begun in the public

---

TABLE 5–2 Advantages and Disadvantages of Labeling Children

Disadvantages:

▮ Teacher expectations may be adversely affected.

▮ Categories do not lead to individual prescriptions.

▮ Labels are of limited use in educational planning.

▮ The child's self-esteem may be negatively affected.

▮ Labels separate the children from their non-disabled peers.

▮ Labels may expose children to a watered down curriculum.

▮ Labels ignore individual differences.

▮ Labels discourage early return of exceptional children to the mainstream.

▮ Stigmas and stereotyping may result.

▮ Possible misidentification may occur.

Advantages:

▮ Names and differentiates among the disabilities.

▮ Professionals can more easily communicate among themselves about various disabilities.

▮ Classification is necessary for research.

▮ Special interest and advocacy groups are more easily formed to lobby for changes or improved services for a disability.

▮ Classification is needed in order to find treatments or cures for a specific disability.

schools. Inclusion is a broad philosophy that has much in common with multicultural education. Both movements aim for the inclusion of all children in the regular or mainstream, educational program and emphasize the positive interdependence, respect, and valuing of all children's unique characteristics and needs in the regular classroom (Dean, Salend, & Taylor, 1993). Schools must make special provisions to support exceptional children in the mainstream classrooms and will also need to provide in-service training programs so that teachers feel more positive and more confident to teach these children. The following suggestions in Special Box 5–2 are examples of guidelines to prepare regular teachers to receive exceptional students in their classrooms.

In many schools, special education teachers are serving as consultants to the mainstream teachers and may work with special students in the classroom. In some programs special education and mainstream teachers are engaged in team teaching. These are exciting developments that will continue to encourage collaboration and cooperation among all teachers for the ultimate goal of educating all children in mainstream classrooms.

SPECIAL BOX 5–2   *Suggestions for Teachers*

▪ Learn about the student's disability.

▪ Learn about special materials.

▪ Determine if any special methods, modifications, or adaptations are needed.

▪ Meet the student prior to receiving that student in your classroom.

▪ Observe the student in the special class or program, if coming to you from a special education program.

▪ Meet with the special education teacher to determine the student's strengths and weaknesses.

▪ Prepare your classroom, if necessary, for the child with physical or sensory disabilities.

▪ Prepare your students to receive the exceptional child.

▪ Assess the new student's skills, if needed.

▪ Discuss expectations for academic and social behaviors with the special education teacher/consultant.

▪ Plan, implement, and monitor instruction in cooperation or collaboration with the special education teacher. Many additional suggestions and activities for the inclusive classroom are available in Salend (1994).

❖ Pre-Referral Interventions

The process of identifying and classifying a child with a disability begins when a teacher, parent, physician, or the child suspects that a disability exists. In many schools, a pre-referral process is used to try to resolve a student's learning or behavior problems and prevent a formal referral for special education. This avoids unnecessary assessment and the risk of misclassification of the student. These interventions are usually conducted by a team that includes special and regular educators and the school psychologist. Steps in the pre-referral process usually include (Gearhart, Mullen, & Gearhart, 1993):

1. a request by the teacher for pre-referral assistance;
2. a conference held by the team in order to delineate the problem and select strategies to resolve the problem;
3. implementation and evaluation of the strategy;
4. a follow-up conference to evaluate the results; and
5. a formal referral if the problem(s) persists.

The pre-referral process is extremely important because many African-American and Latino students are erroneously placed in special education due to learning and/or behavior problems that might be associated with cultural and linguistic differences.

❖ Referral Process

When the pre-referral process does not result in effective interventions, and the child's problems persist, the formal referral for an individual evaluation is used to determine eligibility for special education. The formal process for evaluating children, with the signed consent of the parents, usually consists of the following steps:

- referral;
- evaluation;
- recommendation;
- placement;
- planning conference;
- implementation of the program; and
- annual program review.

A comprehensive re-evaluation is required every three years.

Step 1, a formal, written referral is made to the principal or chairperson of a multidisciplinary committee. Referrals may come from parents, school staff, physicians, judicial officers, or the student. For younger, preschool children, this referral may be made by parents, physicians, social workers, or a child-find service that exists in many states. Parents must always be notified and give their consent for the evaluation.

Evaluation and Recommendation

Step 2, the evaluation process occurs under specific regulations which assure that the testing is non-biased, multidisciplinary, and provided in the child's native language or preferred mode of communication. In this step, testing is conducted to identify a possible disability in a child's physical, sensory, mental, or emotional functioning or to identify a health impairment. The school psychologist, speech pathologist, classroom teacher, nurse, or social worker may be involved in collecting assessment information. This is followed by a recommendation for eligibility, classification, and placement, **Step 3**. The recommendation is made to the Board of Education for that school district.

Placement

The child is then placed in an appropriate regular or special education program, **Step 4**, and this is increasingly the regular educational classroom with or without support from the special education consultant or resource specialist. Parents must give their consent for the placement and the placement must meet the requirement for lease restrictive environment. Special education environments or programs fall into a continuum from least to most restrictive:

- regular classroom with or without support;
- regular class with supplementary instruction (usually in resource room);
- part-time special class;
- full-time special class;
- special school, hospital; and
- home.

IEP Planning

In **Step 5**, the planning conference, instructional decision-making occurs and the individual education program is developed for the child. This plan includes a statement of the child's present level of abilities, annual goals and short-term objectives, and any related services, testing modifications or adaptive physical education needed. Each academic content area has goals and objectives. In addition, transition services needed, the extent of participation in the mainstream, and duration of services are listed. Following completion of the plan and placement in a special education program, the child's IEP is implemented. The IEP must be agreed upon by the school, parents, and the child, when appropriate (Figure 5–1).

It is important to note that there are two additional types of individual plans that exceptional students may have: the Individual Family Services Plan, for infants or toddlers who may have disabilities; and the

Figure 5–1

Pg. 3, 4, 5, etc. Objectives, Evaluation, & Mastery   White Copy: COH / Yellow Copy: Sp. Ed. Tchr. / Pink Copy: Student Folder / Gold Copy: Parent

John Hagarino	000-0000	2/10/75
STUDENT NAME	STUDENT #	DOB

Other Health	USA	2/1
CLASSIFICATION	SCHOOL	TEACHER OR SPECIALIST DATE

Period of Time IEP Covers

BEGINNING DATE 12/1/85 M D Y   UNTIL 12/1/86 M D Y

Annual Goals Copy from Phase I	Short Term Objective Specific Skills, Competencies, Attitudes Expected in Objective Terms	Specific (Supplementary) Method and/or Materials to be Used (Name and Level)	% of Mastery Expected	Means of Evaluation— Degree Specific Name and Level	Results of Evaluation and Degree of Mastery and Date Accomplished	Code +, —, GC
Increase Math Achievement by 6 months	The student will be able to count orally by fives and tens, without assistance, to 100 by the end of the first marking period.	Holt Math 2 Addison-Wesley Math 2	100%	Holt 2 Chapter test eval.		
	Given ten written subtraction problems involving tens and ones with renaming the student will compute the problems by the end of the third marking period.	Taskmaster dittos Level 2	80%			
	Given ten written addition problems involving tens and ones with renaming the student will compute the problems by the end of the second marking period.	Manipulatives— real money Judy clocks	80%	Teacher judgment based on objectives.		
	Shown ten clock settings and given the verbal command, "what time is it?" the student will orally state the correct time to five minute intervals by the end of the fourth marking period.	DLM multi-link cubes number lines charts	80%			
	Shown ten groups of coins valued to a dollar and given the verbal command, "How much is this group worth?" the student will orally state the correct answer by the end of the fourth marking period.		80%			

Forward Copy of Phase II (2 pages) to Chairman COH within 30 Days of Entrance into Program and after final evaluation results but no later than one week before closing of school.

Individual Transition Plan, for adolescents through age twenty-one who are attending school and also for those who have recently left school (Smith & Luckasson, 1992).

Implementation and Program Review

Step 6, Implementation and program review, refers to evaluation of the plan or program that must be conducted at least annually. The student's classification and placement, related services, or the academic program may be changed. In addition, goals and objectives for the coming year may be changed at the annual review. Each student must be reevaluated every three years using Steps 2 through 6. This is to ensure that the student continues to meet eligibility requirements for special education and returns to the regular mainstream classroom as soon as possible.

❖ High Incidence Disabilities

The largest groups of students with disabilities include those with learning disabilities, speech/communication disorders, mild mental retardation, and emotional/behavior disorders (Gearhart, Mullin, & Gearhart, 1993). These are referred to as high incidence disabilities. Each group will require some modification of instructional materials and methods. However, each individual student will have unique, individual characteristics in learning and behavior that teachers must identify through careful assessment.

Learning Disabilities

Students with learning disabilities comprise the largest group of all exceptional children with (mild) disabilities. These are students of average intelligence or better who show a significant difference between their measured potential for learning and their actual achievement. The federal government's definition of a learning disability is:

> . . . a disorder in one or more of the basic psychological processes involved in understanding or in using language, spoken or written, which may manifest itself in an imperfect ability to listen, think, speak, read or write, or do mathematical calculations. The term includes such conditions as perceptual handicaps, brain injury, minimal brain dysfunction, dyslexia, and developmental aphasia. The term does not include children who have learning problems which are primarily the result of visual, hearing, or motor handicaps, of mental retardation or emotional disturbance, or of environmental, cultural, or economic disadvantage." (U.S. Office of Education, 1977, p. 65083)

Students with learning disabilities form a heterogeneous group whose only common characteristic is the discrepancy between their potential and achievement. Each student with a learning disability must be treated as an individual with appropriate assessment and program planning.

The cause of learning disabilities is unknown although researchers have investigated factors such as biochemical, neurological, environmental, and genetic causes. Some of the students may demonstrate problems with inattention, spatial orientation, clumsiness, gross and fine motor problems, and perceptual difficulties. Some researchers have also found difficulties in social perception among this group of children (Lerner, 1988; Wanat, 1983; Leigh, 1987; Bryan & Bryan, 1986).

Dyslexia. Reading is a difficult area for many students with learning disabilities. At the elementary level, the focus may be remedial reading or compensatory strategies. At the secondary level, compensation is the priority and it will be helpful for the teacher to consider taping the material or having a peer or the resource teacher read to the student. It is also possible to provide curriculum content material at a lower level so the student receives the same information that the regular text provides, but at a lower level of difficulty. A term closely associated with learning disabilities is *dyslexia*. The term has been defined as "a medical term referring to disorder in reading, presumably due to some form of neurological dysfunction. It is also known as specific reading disability and the terms are used interchangeably" (Vellutino, 1979, p. 63).

Hyperactivity. Another term closely associated with learning disability is hyperactivity. It has been referred to as the single, most common disorder in children (Silver, 1990). However, the terms should not be used synonymously. Hyperactivity is now referred to as Attention Deficit/Hyperactivity Disorder as classified in DSM-III, the diagnostic manual used by physicians. Several proposals are under consideration by the U.S. Congress to include ADHD as a disability under IDEA. Although hyperactivity has a long history in the field of learning disabilities, at this time it is presumed to be a neurological disorder that affects the child's ability to control his or her level of motor activity, distractibility, or short attention span, and impulsivity (Silver, 1990). Secondary problems that have been identified include: learning problems, aggressiveness and antisocial behavior, and poor self-concept or self-esteem (Leigh, 1987). About 10 to 20 percent of all students with learning disabilities have ADHD (McKinney, Montague, & Hocutt, 1993). About 15 to 20 percent of children and adolescents with learning disabilities have ADHD (Silver, 1990).

While the intervention for learning disabilities is usually special education, treatment for ADHD may include several interventions: behavior management, family counseling, and the use of medications such as Ritalin. According to Silver (1990), about 80 percent of children and adolescents with ADHD show significant improvement after taking medications that decrease motor activity level, distractibility and impulsivity,

SPECIAL BOX 5–3   *Suggestions to Teachers*

The following suggestions are general. All students with learning disabilities have individual characteristics and needs that will determine the most appropriate teaching strategies to be used.

1. Use cooperative learning whenever possible so that students can help each other with such tasks as writing, reading, and spelling.

2. Tape lectures so that individual students who have difficulty taking notes may do so more slowly.

3. Provide written outlines of lectures.

4. When information must be memorized, help students by providing mnemonic devices.

5. Use a variety of instructional modes—demonstrations, tapes, films, models, lectures.

6. Vary the forms of seat work given. Use a lesson plan format that provides a great deal of guided practice before independent seat work is assigned.

7 Teach a variety of meta cognitive strategies—self-monitoring, self-instruction, and self-evaluation.

8. Provide activities for overlearning and use of a lot of prompts and cues to increase error-free responding and practice by students.

_____

(Ysseldyke & Algozzine, 1990)

and increase attention span and reflectivity. In the classroom, teachers often use behavior management strategies for children whose ADHD is not well-controlled by medication or other interventions.

It is easy to confuse cultural characteristics of behavior with ADHD. Children from cultures with a behavioral style that is more physical and active will sometimes become a challenge to a teacher who emphasizes *in-seat learning* and low levels of verbal interactions among students. In the teacher's perception, such a child may appear to be hyperactive.

Speech and Communication Disorders

Children from poverty, children who speak dialects or those who speak different languages are often at risk for being misdiagnosed as language disordered. In addition, school personnel, through ignorance, may judge the language of these children as sub-standard or inferior. Anastasiow, Hanes, and Hanes (1982) have studied the language of Anglo, Puerto Rican and black children in poverty and have pointed out that it is difficult to obtain an accurate assessment of language in children from poverty conditions because: (1) the children may be more timid to speak in the presence of adults; (2) they may not understand that they are to "do their best" on a test; and (3) they may remain less verbal in the classroom.

Those researchers developed a Sentence Repetition Task to study the influence of dialect. When children who speak a dialect are asked to repeat sentences, they will shift the phonology and syntax of the sentence into the correct form of their own dialect. This translation process is interpreted as a reflection of normal intellectual function (Anastasiow, Hanes, & Hanes, 1982).

This is a valuable demonstration of the children's ability to comprehend standard English sentences and to translate the sentences into their language structures. Examples of sentences from the Sentence Repetition Task are shown with their most common dialect changes (Table 5–3).

The table also shows some examples of phonological and grammatical forms identified in language of low-income, inner-city children (Baratz, 1969; Labov, 1972; in Anastasiow, Hanes, & Hanes, 1982).

Speech Disorders. The second largest group of children with disabilities has communication disorders (speech/language disorders). Two major classifications occur in speech/language disorders. Some children may have only speech disorders such as difficulties with the correct articulation or speech sounds, or disorders in voice where the pitch or loudness may be abnormal; others may have problems with fluency and stuttering, or dysfluency, may occur. Fluency involves the rate and flow of speech.

TABLE 5–3 Examples of Phonological and Grammatical Forms in the Language of Low-Income, Inner-City Children (Baratz, 1969; Labov, 1972, in Anastasiow, Hanes, & Hanes, 1982, pp.57–58)

---

1. "He walk" for "He walks." (omission of s in third person singular)

2. "Mary husband" for "Mary's husband." (omission of possessive)

3. "Two coat" for "Two coats." (omission of plural s)

4. "She walks" for "She is walking." (omission of copula and duration indicator)

5. "She a cook" for "She is a cook" or "She's a cook." (omission of copula)

6. "Muss" for "Must." (simplified final consonant cluster)

7. "Den" for "Then." (fricative th /O/ and /O/ become /d/ in initial position)

8. "Boo" for "Book." (weakening of final plosives)

9. "Everyday she be walking" for "Everyday she walks." (use of be as duration indicator)

Disordered speech attracts attention by being sufficiently deviant from normal speech, interferes with communication, and adversely affects communication for the speaker or listener (Gelfand, Jensen, & Drew, 1982, in Gearhart, Mullin, & Gearhart (1993).

Language Disorders. The second major type of disorder in communication is in language. Children may have problems with form, content or use of language. Form is concerned with the rules that govern our use of oral language. It includes rules for phonology, morphology, and syntax. Phonology includes rules for sound combinations in English; morphology involves rules for the structure of words—the way that basic meaning is formed by parts of words; syntax refers to the rules that govern the grammatical forms of language.

Both Speech and Language Disorders. Some students have both speech and language disorders. While intervention is primarily the responsibility of the speech/language clinician, teachers can model appropriate speech and language, be aware of the level of language difficulty in a given task, allow sufficient time for students to respond to questions and volunteer ideas, and simplify oral directions. Other tips for regular teachers offered by special education teachers include creating a supportive environment and allowing students to practice skills in the classroom that they have worked on in therapy. Teachers can also make language an important part of classroom instruction, providing many opportunities for students to express themselves and listen to others throughout the school day. Many materials are available to assist the teacher in these objectives and some teachers are using a process approach to written language which also facilitates verbal expression. Additional suggestions are in Special Box 5–4.

Bilingual Students. It is necessary to be especially cautious in working with students who are learning English. Language differences must be differentiated from language disorders. It appears to be easy for schools to misclassify these students. However, when unbiased, individual assessment conducted by an individual who speaks the home language of the student results in the determination that the LEP student has a language disorder, that student may be served in a bilingual special education program. These programs combine special education and bilingual education.

Black English. African-American students who speak Black English are also at risk for misdiagnosis. Black English represents a language difference as opposed to a disability. Black English is a dialect of English which has been influenced by British and American English and English-based pidgin from sixteenth century West Africa (Ovando, 1993). Pidgin refers to a simplified communication used between people with different languages. Black English developed among the slaves principally in the

SPECIAL BOX 5–4 *Helpful Suggestions for Teachers*

A. Model interactive communication
(other students can also benefit and model)

B. Modify instructional style
1. Limit directions to 1-2 steps
2. Give essential information in short statements—keep subject close to verb
3. Avoid indirect commands and either/or statements
4. *Show* students what to do rather than tell them
5. To help with expression
    a. Allow extra time to respond
    b. Ask them to act out what they cannot express verbally
    c. Gently encourage them to continue when they begin to communicate
    d. Reduce anxiety
        (1) select one-word answers
        (2) raise hand when a statement is true
        (3) answer early

Southern states, where, from the late 1700s until the early 1900s, the majority of the black population lived. In the twentieth century, the language spread throughout the United States as blacks began to migrate to large urban centers in the north.

Black English is a sophisticated language with its own rules, structures, styles, and functional patterns (Ovando, 1993). In addition, the contexts in which it is used are culturally determined and highly specific. The language may be used in situations where joking, teasing, boasting, scolding, and encouraging are appropriate; however, the relationship and status of the speakers are very important.

The use of the verb "to be" has different rules in Black English than in American English. The verb is usually dropped entirely where it might be contracted in American English. For example: "Mary fat; he talking; she singing." The verb "to be" is also used in Black English to denote continuous action as in "He be walking everyday" or "She be eating all the time." Examples are shown of the sentence repetition where meaning is conveyed and appropriately understood by the listener (Table 5–4).

Students who speak Black English at school run the risk of being considered deficient in their language by teachers who are ignorant of the language. Some teachers may even feel intimidated by the use of Black

TABLE 5–4 Examples of Sentences from the Sentence Repetition Task (Anastasiow, Hanes, & Hanes, 1982, pp. 58–61) and Most Common Dialect Changes

American English	Black English
1. He was tied up.	He got tied up.
2. She isn't a good singer.	She ain't no (ain't a) good singer.
3. Where can he do what he wants?	Where can he do what he want?
4. Then he went to the movies by himself.	Then he went to the movie by himself.
5. She said, "Whose toys are those?"	She say, "Whose toy are those?"
6. Although I want ice cream I bet I'm not going to get any.	Although I want ice cream, I ain't gonna (not gonna) (I'm not gonna) get any.
7. He runs home quickly after school because he has a bicycle to ride.	He run home quickly after school because he have a bicycle to ride.
8. The teacher will give you a smile when you have finished your work.	The teacher be giving you a smile when you finish your work.
9. Joe is good when he feels like it.	Joe be good when he feel like it.
10. I asked him if he did it and he said he didn't do it.	I asked him if he did it and he say he didn't do it.

English from male adolescents who joke and jive with each other. It is important to recognize the value and authenticity of the language and to appreciate that the students are not language deficient but simply language different. Teachers may find it helpful to integrate Black English into their conversations with students once they have established rapport (Franklin, 1992). This is not to imply that teachers should try to imitate the students' speech or language. Rather, it consists of the teacher's natural and appropriate use of expressions or terms that can convey meaning and understanding of Black English. The use of such vocabulary, after establishing rapport, can make important connections with students and contribute to positive relationships. Franklin makes the following general recommendations for teaching African-American students with disabilities:

- Use "real world" learning activities.
- Use varied stimuli.
- Present lessons at a rapid pace.

- Use small group and peer tutoring activities.
- Use techniques that incorporate body movement.
- Provide instructional activities that include music, singing, and movement.
- Promote verbal interactions and divergent thinking in problem-solving.
- Use cooperative learning.

Mental Retardation

The third largest group of students with disabilities has mental retardation. Mental retardation is mild for the majority of the exceptional children in this classification and can be remedied with special assistance (Smith & Luckasson, 1992). Mental retardation is defined as:

> . . . substantial limitations in present functioning. It is characterized by significantly subaverage intellectual functioning, existing concurrently with related limitations in two or more of the following applicable adaptive skill areas: communication, self-care, home living, social skills, community use, self-direction, health and safety, functional academics, leisure, and work. Mental retardation manifests before age nineteen. (AAMR Ad Hoc Committee on Terminology and Classification, in Hallahan & Kauffman, 1994)

Problems in attention may occur in this group and the children will require help with selective attention and time on task. Task analysis is frequently used in teaching this group. In this method, a task is broken down into small, sequential steps that are taught one step at a time to mastery. Tasks may be cognitive/academic social or perceptual-motor.

Memory may also be a problem. Students with mental retardation may have short- and long-term memory deficits. They may not correctly remember facts or the sequence may be incorrect. It is important to emphasize material to be remembered and to help the student *over learn* through a great deal of practice.

Generalization is another limitation of students with mental retardation; students are unlikely to benefit from incidental learning and will require direct instruction in the task to be learned. Teachers must *teach* for generalization by teaching the skill in several contexts or environments.

Children with mental retardation have often suffered the stigma that comes with this label. In some school settings, the children are referred to as *retards*. In fact, any special education student may be referred to in this manner in schools where sensitivity and understanding are lacking. It is important for teachers to be sensitive to this situation and to teach positive acceptance of differences.

Great progress with these students is being made through early intervention at the pre-school level. The effects of the disability can be greatly limited and sometimes prevented thought this early recognition. Community-based instruction has also shown promise when instruction is given in the natural environment for a particular skill.

See suggestions for the teacher in Special Box 5–5.

Emotional/Behavior Disorders

The next largest group of students includes those with emotional disturbance or behavioral disorders.

SPECIAL BOX 5–5 *Suggestions for Working with Students with Mental Retardation*

1. Set goals that are realistic for the individual and the community in which s/he lives.

2. Assign tasks that are
   (a) personally relevant;
   (b) carefully sequenced from easy to difficult; and
   (c) allow the learner to be highly and frequently successful.

3. Recognize the individual strengths and weaknesses, provide incentives for performance, and establish necessary rules for behavior.

4. Explain required tasks in terms of concrete concepts.

5. When giving instructions, be specific: "John, go to the principal's office, give this sheet to Mrs. Smith and come back."

6. After giving specific steps, briefly summarize the instructions: "Remember, John,
   (a) Go to the principal's office,
   (b) Give this sheet to Mrs. Smith and
   (c) Come back."

7. When giving instructions, ask what is to be done:
   "John, tell me what you are to do?"

8. When praising, be specific, not general:
   "John, you did a good job taking the absentee sheet to Mrs. Smith. You went directly to the office and you came straight back."

9. When praising, emphasize "you" rather than "I."
   ("I" encourages dependence on the teacher).

According to the federal definition, children with emotional disturbance "exhibit one or more of the following characteristics over a long period of time and to a marked extent, which adversely affects educational performance:

1. an inability to learn that cannot be explained by intellectual, sensory, or health factors;
2. an inability to build or maintain satisfactory interpersonal relationships with peers and teachers;
3. inappropriate types of behavior or feelings under normal circumstances;
4. a general pervasive mood of unhappiness or depression; or
5. a tendency to develop physical symptoms or fears associated with personal or school problems.

The term includes children who are schizophrenic. The term does not include children who are socially maladjusted, unless it is determined that they are seriously emotionally disturbed" (IDEA, 1990).

A current debate in the field involves the definition and classification of children with emotional disturbance. One group has criticized the vague criteria present in the federal definition that makes identification of children difficult. Many of the criteria cannot be translated into objective measures of emotional disturbance versus normal behavior: For example, "over a long period of time and to marked; an inability to build or maintain satisfactory interpersonal relationships; or general, pervasive mood of unhappiness" (IDEA, 1990). These expressions may receive different interpretations by different persons. How severe must the child's condition be to meet the definition? Another problem with the definition is that some professionals consider the term *emotional disturbance* a misnomer. The identification of a child with a disability in this area really depends upon observed behavior. Thus, many programs use the term *behavior disorder* in preference to emotional disturbance. The third issue with the definition is that it excludes the children who are *socially maladjusted* and makes it impossible to obtain special education services for them.

The Council for Children with Behavior Disorders, the major organization for professionals who work with these children, has proposed a new definition which is under consideration and controversy for replacing the current federal definition. CCBD has presented the following reasons for change in the definition (CCBD Newsletter, Feb., 1993)

1. the current definition in which "seriously" is used as a qualifier is overly restrictive and unfair;
2. the criteria for eligibility in the current definition are confusing and at times arbitrary;

3. the proposed definition focuses directly on the child's responses in school settings and places this response in the context of appropriate age, ethnic, and cultural norms;

4. the proposed criteria for eligibility are clear and concise; and

5. the proposed definition is clear and reflects current research and practice in the area.

The proposed definition is more useful to educators and other service providers and will more appropriately identify children who should receive special education services at their school.

The proposed definition is (CCBD Newsletter, Feb., 1993):

(1) as used in section 602 (a) (1) of the Individuals with Disabilities Education Act (20 U.S.C. 1401 (a)(1):

    (A) The term "emotional or behavior disorde" means a disability that is—

        (i) characterized by behavioral or emotional responses in school programs so different from appropriate age, cultural, or ethnic (group);

        (ii) more than a temporary, expected response to stressful events in the environment;

        (iii) consistently exhibited in two different settings, at least one of which is school-related; and

        (iv) unresponsive to direct intervention applied in general education, or the condition of a child is such that general education interventions would be insufficient.

    (B) The term includes such a disability that co-exists with other disabilities.

    (C) The term includes a schizophrenic disorder, affective disorder, anxiety disorder, or other sustained disorder of conduct or adjustment, affecting a child, if the disorder affects educational performance as described in paragraph (i).

Students with emotional disturbance/behavior disorders have special needs in the areas of behavior and learning. Their emotional disability interferes with their ability to learn and they are, on average, two years below grade level in academic subjects. Therefore, interventions must include both academic and social/emotional strategies. As for other students with disabilities, these students require careful, individual assessment to determine their specific needs and to plan an appropriate program.

Interventions differ among programs for these students and are based upon different theoretical/philosophical views in the field. These include behavioral, psychoeducational, ecological, and biophysical perspectives. Some of these interventions have been successful with many students and their progress has been encouraging. Interventions include:

behavior management programs, aggression replacement training, social skill training, and remediation of academic problems; however, much more progress is needed for this population in order to significantly raise achievement levels, reduce the drop-out rate, prevent continued aggressive behavior, and assure long-term participation in the society as independent, responsible adults.

Suggestions for the Teacher. Students with emotional disabilities have complex problems, which include both academic and social needs. Students in the mainstream may require counseling or other supportive services. Effective interventions have been identified that help these students to achieve and progress in accordance with their abilities. Some of these include: behavior modification strategies, cognitive strategies, contracts, hands-on learning activities, and computer-assisted instruction. Close cooperation between the regular and special educator can result in satisfactory progress for the student.

❖ Other Disabilities

Smaller groups of students with other "low incidence" disabilities include: hearing impaired and deaf; multihandicapped; orthopedic and other health impaired; visually impaired and blind; and autism and traumatic brain injury.

Hearing Impaired and Deaf

Some disabilities have led to the formation of specific cultures. Individuals with hearing impairment have developed a cultural identity that seeks to preserve and respect the essential characteristics of the group and to resist intervention. Some characteristics include the use of manual communication and opposition to such surgical intervention as cochlear implants. In a recently televised segment, "Sixty Minutes" (Nov. 8, 1992) presented a family that had experienced opposition expressed by members of the deaf community to its decision to have a cochlear implant for its daughter.

Students with a hearing impairment are divided into two groups: The hard-of-hearing and deaf.

Hearing Impaired. A hearing impairment, whether permanent or fluctuating, which adversely affects a child's educational performance, but which is not included under the definition of *deaf*.

Deaf. A hearing impairment which is so severe that the child is impaired in processing linguistic information through hearing, with or without amplification, and which adversely affects educational performance. (Federal Register, 1977, p. 42478, in Gearhart, Mullen, & Gearhart, 1993).

Students who are hard-of-hearing have sufficient hearing to benefit from the use of a hearing aid which permits them to understand the oral communication of others. Students who are deaf have an impairment that is so severe that they cannot hear even with a hearing aid. Some students have prelingual deafness—occurring before they developed language; others have post lingual deafness—in which they lost their hearing after developing language. One in ten children with prelingual deafness has at least one parent who is deaf (Smith & Luckasson, 1992). These children will learn manual communication/sign language in early childhood or a combination of oral and sign language. "The 90 percent of these children who have hearing parents have greater difficulty acquiring language because the parents do not use a total communication approach as early as possible" (Smith & Luckasson, 1992).

Hearing loss may be either conductive or sensorineural. Conductive losses are due to blockage or damage in the outer or middle ear, resulting in a mild to moderate disability. Many conductive losses can be corrected by surgery or other techniques. Sensorineural losses are more severe, caused by damage in the inner ear or auditory nerve, and cannot be corrected through surgery or other medical treatment. Conductive losses are more common in young children.

Causes of hearing impairment include various illnesses and injuries, heredity, and infectious diseases. Four major causes are:

1. maternal rubella or German measles. When a pregnant woman contracts German measles, the child may be born with profound hearing loss, visual impairment, mental retardation, or other disabilities;
2. meningitis, which affects the central nervous system (the coverings of the brain and spinal cord are the meninges) and often causes a profound hearing loss. This is the most common cause of post-natal deafness in school-age children and a major cause of sensorineural deafness;
3. otitis media, an infection of the middle ear which can be treated with antibiotics; and
4. heredity.

There are over 150 identified types of genetic deafness. A more recently identified cause of hearing impairment in some children is a virus, the cytomegalovirus or CMV. Teachers need to know the cause and severity of hearing loss in order to understand the student's problems and instructional needs.

Three different approaches are used to teach students with hearing impairments: the oral approach, manual communication, or total communication. In the oral (speech) approach, children are taught to use their residual hearing—whatever hearing is available to them after the loss, speech reading and speech—to receive and send communications; the manual approach involves teaching the child finger spelling or the

American sign language, which is a language in itself; total communication uses both oral and manual communication.

The educational placement of these students depends on the severity of the hearing loss, the availability of speech, and the availability of local programs and support services. The committees on special education or a multidisciplinary team responsible for placement decisions would recommend a program placement for the student. Educational programs must provide intensive instruction in communication for these students. Telecommunication and assistive devices are making it easier for this group to make progress in school and in the community.

Professionals involved in the diagnosis and treatment of individuals with hearing losses include the audiologist, who is responsible for the measurement of the type and degree of loss, and the speech pathologist or speech/language teacher, who provides the treatment for students with this disability.

The Parents' Role. Parents vary in their views of hearing impairment, particularly with respect to the approaches used to teach their children. Parents who favor the oral approach want the child to appear no different from children without the impairment. Any approach that makes

---

SPECIAL BOX 5–6 *Suggestions for the Teacher*

1. Give the student an appropriate seat where s/he can be close to you and removed from the noise.

2. Model positive behavior and attitude toward the child (for the other students in your classroom). Provide information for the class on hearing impairments.

3. Assign a buddy for the student to help with communication of classroom activities.

4. Face the student when speaking.

5. Use written information to accompany oral presentations. Write important assignments, words, messages on the board.

6. Be familiar with the student's hearing aid and verify that it is working each day.

7. Confer with other professionals (speech pathologist, special education teacher) for answers to questions and suggestions.

8. Work carefully with the student's interpreter or notetaker to maximize effectiveness of instruction.

(Cartwright, Cartwright, & Ward, 1989)

their child stand out as *different* is opposed. Other parents accept the manual approach and/or total communication with the belief that communication is the priority for the child and any approach that helps the child communicate with others is to be employed. When parents of opposing views discuss the merits of each approach, the debate can become quite intense, reflecting their strong feelings about this issue.

Suggestions for the teacher are in Special Box 5–6.

Multihandicapped

IDEA defines multihandicapped as:

> . . . concomitant impairments (such as mentally retarded—blind, mentally retarded—orthopedically impaired, etc.) the combination of which, causes such severe educational problems that they cannot be accommodated in special education programs solely for one of the impairments. The term does not include deaf-blind children. (Sect. 300.5(5))

Students with multihandicaps have more severe disabilities and will not often be placed in the regular classroom. Although the inclusion movement seeks to bring all students into the mainstream, the intensity of special needs in this population will make it difficult to serve them in the mainstream. Nevertheless, individuals with multiple impairments must also be educated in the least restrictive, environment possible.

Orthopedic and Other Health Impaired

In IDEA, orthopedic impairment is defined as:

> . . . a severe impairment which adversely affects a child's educational performance. The term includes impairments caused by congenital anomaly (e.g. clubfoot, absence of some member, etc.), impairments caused by disease (e.g., poliomyelitis, bone tuberculosis, etc.), and impairments from other causes (e.g., cerebral palsy, amputations, and fractures or burns which cause contractures. (Sect. 300.5(b))

Other health impaired means:

> . . . having limited strength, vitality or alertness, due to chronic or acute health problems such as a heart condition, tuberculosis, rheumatic fever, nephritis, asthma, sickle cell anemia, hemophilia, or diabetes, which adversely affects a child's educational performance. (Sect. 300.5(7))

Major types of physical disabilities and health impairments include: (1) neurological impairments; (2) neuromuscular diseases; and (3) impairments of health and diseases. Children with health impairments are limited in strength and energy and require ongoing medical attention. Those with physical disabilities have a problem with structure and function of the body. States and school districts will have guidelines for teachers who work with these children in the mainstream, particularly for infectious diseases such as the HIV or the AIDS virus.

Some health impairments are found in specific racial/ethnic groups. Sickle cell anemia, for example, affects one in four hundred African-Americans and one in ten carry the trait (Gearhart, Mullin, & Gearhart, 1993). The anemia is named for the sickle-shaped red blood cells which are fragile, elongated, and rapidly destroyed in the body. Children with sickle cell anemia may suffer *crises* when oxygen is reduced. Treatment involves bed rest, antibiotics, fluids, non-aspirin pain killers, and sometimes transfusions. No cure exists at this time (Gearhart, Mullin, & Gearhart, 1993).

In addition, certain medical procedures required in the classroom, such as catheterization and medication, will need guidelines for teachers who must monitor them. In some cases teachers will perform certain procedures such as assistance in the bathroom. Coordination among the student, physician, school nurse, and family will be needed.

Special Adaptation. Some of the considerations for these students will include preparation for unavoidable absences. The teacher will need to identify ways to help the students keep up with the class. The use of close-captioned TV, telephone, home books, and tutoring may be used. Students who are subject to seizures will require knowledge and understanding by the teacher and emergency provisions to assist the student. Teachers will also require training in how to assist students with paralysis and in wheelchairs. Teachers of these students will need to work in close coordination and cooperation with other professionals. The physical environment may require modification for a student with physical impairments and assistive devices may be needed for mealtimes. The teacher will also need to consider other appropriate adaptations and modifications in the classroom which may be required for students with orthopedic and other health impairments.

Visually Impaired and Blind

Visually Impaired. A pupil with a visual handicap which, even with correction, adversely affects a child's educational performance. The term includes both partially seeing and blind children.

Types of visual impairments include: (1) disorders of the eye—myopia, hyperopia, and astigmatism; (2) disorders of the eye muscles—strabismus and nystagmus; (3) disorders of the cornea, iris, and lens; (4) disorders of the retina; and (5) damage to the optic nerve. Individuals with visual impairment vary widely in visual efficiency, which determines the type and extent of visual aids needed. In order to determine a child's eligibility for services, school districts often use the amount of visual acuity. For example, in some districts visual acuity between 20/70 and 20/200 in the better eye with correction is required to be eligible for special educational services.

The causes of visual impairment may be congenital or acquired. It is estimated that almost 50 percent of children with blindness have hereditary causes. Some of the more common causes include dry eyes, trachoma, gonorrhea, measles, and eye injuries.

Most students with visual impairments are educated in the mainstream classrooms where they have the regular curriculum along with their sighted classmates. A professional specialist in visual impairment provides consultation to the teachers and recommends aids for the student. These may include the availability of braille. Minor modifications in teaching can help the students with mild to moderate impairments make good progress in the regular classroom. Some suggestions for teachers include:

1. Repeat orally any information given on the board.
2. Enlarge information to be presented with the overhead projector.
3. Prepare handouts using enlarged print.
4. Address students by name to get their attention.
5. Audiotape lessons for use at home.

Autism and Traumatic Brain Injury

The most recent additions to the list of disabilities that qualify students for special education are autism and traumatic brain injury. Although autism involves atypical behaviors, it is separate from emotional disturbances or behavior disorders.

Autistic. A pupil who manifests a behaviorally defined syndrome which occurs in children of all levels of intelligence. The essential features are typically manifested prior to thirty months of age and include severe disturbances of developmental rates and/or sequences of responses to sensory stimuli, of speech, of language, of cognitive capacities, and of the ability to relate to people, events, and objects (Part 200 Regulations, New York State).

Considered a low-incidence disability, the disorder affects only about four in every ten thousand children (Batshaw & Perret, 1986, in Smith & Luckasson, 1992). Characteristics of the disorder include severely disordered thinking, communication, and behavior. Language may be abnormal or absent; interpersonal relationships are dysfunctional, if present, and ritualistic movements and self-injurious behavior frequently occur.

Understanding of the causes and classification of autism have changed as research has progressed. In the 1940s, Kanner (1943) attributed it to the aloof, hostile behavior of parents and it was considered a mental illness. However, most recently it is understood as a severe language disorder associated with brain damage. In PL94-142, it was classified with physical impairments and, finally, in IDEA is in a single category. These

> **SPECIAL BOX 5–7** *General Suggestions for Teachers*
>
> ▌ Help all of your students to understand and accept children with disabilities in your classroom.
>
> ▌ Use opportunities to foster positive interaction between non-disabled students and those with disabilities.
>
> ▌ Use instructional approaches that address individual needs and learning styles.
>
> ▌ Confer with special education teachers to obtain suggestions for instructional and behavior management in the classroom.
>
> ▌ Allow necessary adapted or modified instruction for students with disabilities.
>
> ▌ Use cooperative learning structures. These structures can address the major aims of multicultural education and assure the positive integration of students with disabilities.
>
> ▌ Teach tolerance and acceptance of the differences that these children bring to the classroom along with cultural and linguistic differences.
>
> ▌ Collaborate and team teach with special education teacher when possible.

children need an appropriate educational program which includes speech/language, behavior modification, counseling, and family support. In some school districts, students with autism may attend regular classes with sufficient support. The number may increase as we move toward including and educating all children in the mainstream.

Traumatic Brain Injury. Due to medical advances and new technology, many children survive such accidents as automobile and cycle accidents, falls, and near drownings. Child abuse and other forms of violence can also result in traumatic brain injury.

These children are now eligible for special education services. When they have sufficiently recovered to return to school, many require assistance to relearn basic skills and can make progress with the assistance of special educators and related service providers. It is encouraging to see such progress, and teachers can benefit from watching the child's small steps toward accomplishing objectives.

In summary, mainstream teachers will teach children and adolescents with disabilities who belong to diverse cultural and linguistic groups. Teachers can facilitate the progress of these students in many ways.

Parents can make a difference.

Working with Parents

It is important for teachers to understand the cultural differences that families experience with regard to disabilities in their children. Child-rearing practices and family roles, views on disability, and views of medicine, sickness, and sexuality are all subject to culturally different views.

Child-rearing practices have been discussed and will be further discussed in Chapter 11. Family structure determines if the extended family is depended on for support and assistance with child-rearing. A family having a child with a disability that relies on an extended family for support will experience difficulty if they live far away from the extended family and cannot find other support. Special help will be needed by refugee families and families that have recently immigrated. These families will need to find support groups and special help to manage their child who has a disability. Teachers can make referrals to agencies that sponsor support groups. These resources should be compiled by teachers.

While some families believe in early intervention and the benefits of early childhood programs, others view a disability as due to fate, even spiritual, and may accept the disability without concern or attribute it to misfortune or bad luck (Smith, 1993). In this case, intervention by an outsider may not be acceptable and a member of the extended family or a cultural network may be sought for assistance (Smith, 1993). Other families may find direct intervention too intrusive since they are trying to save face. A community liaison can be helpful.

The family's views on medicine, sickness, and sexuality will also vary. Mainstream views on sickness, health-care professionals, drugs, and surgery may conflict with the family's cultural values. Some families may employ healers, elders, herbs, massage—traditional and non-traditional methods—in response to their child's disability. Healing may be practiced as holistic medicine by traditional healers after years of study and training. The teacher can respect the family's cultural preferences, be sensitive to cultural conflicts, and be prepared to make important referrals when needed.

❖ Summary

Children of diverse cultures and languages who live in conditions of poverty are at high risk for disabilities. Thus, many children of color will have various disabilities that have been classified by the federal government. These include learning disabilities, mental retardation, emotional disturbance, speech and language impairment, hearing impairment, orthopedic and health impairment, and small numbers who may have multiple handicaps, autism, and traumatic head injury. Since all children with disabilities are entitled to a free, appropriate public education in the least restrictive environment, most students with disabilities will be educated in regular classrooms. Teachers' knowledge and understanding of these students will help to promote positive relations with their peers, enhance their self-esteem, and assure academic progress. Individuals with disabilities, like other oppressed groups, have suffered prejudice, discrimination, and ostracism in society. Though major changes have occurred with the passage of PL 94-142 (1975) and the recent Americans with Disabilities Act (1990), this population continues to struggle for the right to full participation in American society.

The largest groups of students with disabilities includes those with learning disabilities, speech/language impairment, mental retardation, and emotional disturbance. Those with learning disabilities share the primary characteristic of a discrepancy between their potential and academic achievement. These students require remedial and compensatory strategies. Reading is a major area of difficulty for this group and specialized teaching approaches are available. Some children with learning disabilities are also hyperactive and may require intervention for this problem. With appropriate individualized instruction, students with learning disabilities can accomplish their goals and objectives.

Children whose primary language is not English are sometimes at risk for misclassification as speech/language impaired. It is important to distinguish between language disorders and language differences. Children who speak Black English may also be misdiagnosed when educators are ignorant about and unappreciative of Black English as a language, with its own structure and rules. Communication disorders include both speech and language impairment. Students may have problems in articulating sounds, fluency or pitch, and volume of their speech; or they may have difficulty in one or more of the components of language. Strategies are available to teachers that will facilitate the ability of these students to express themselves in the classroom.

Mental retardation is characterized by limitations in intellectual functioning accompanied by impairment in adaptive behavior. The definition serves to prevent misclassification of some children who score below average on intelligence tests, but function at age-appropriate levels in communication, self-care, home living, health, and other areas of daily life.

These children may have problems in attention, memory, abstract thinking, and generalization. They may need extensive practice to master academic tasks. However, early intervention and effective teaching have shown excellent results in prevention of failure and acquisition of basic skills.

Children with emotional disturbance comprise the fourth largest group of students with disabilities. The federal definition for this classification is under discussion for changes to make it less vague, easier to accurately classify students, and more inclusive of students with behavior problems. The needs of these students include both academic and behavioral interventions. Approaches that are available vary according to the theoretical perspective upon which they are based. Some interventions are derived from behavior modification and others from psychodynamic theories. Children and adolescents with emotional disabilities can make progress when individualized programs address their specific need for interventions that consider culture, language, learning approach, strengths, and weaknesses.

Smaller groups of students include those with sensory impairment, physical disabilities and other health impairment, autism, and traumatic head injury. Modifications in the classroom environment, instructional methods, and materials will be required for these students. Additionally, specially trained personnel serve students with sensory impairment and more severe disabilities. Classroom teachers can cooperate and collaborate with other professionals who serve these students and express sensitivity in their work with culturally/linguistically diverse students and their families.

In addition to cultural and linguistic differences, students with disabilities also have special characteristics and needs related to their impairment. Teachers can help these students to realize their potential through knowledge and understanding of the students' special instructional needs, and a commitment to modifying and adapting instruction when needed. Consultation and collaboration with the special educator will help to identify the excellent resources available to teachers, including practical and effective methods for teaching.

❖ CHAPTER 5 **Questions**

1. How do culture and language play a role in misdiagnosis and errors in the classification of children of color in special education?
2. Which provision in the Individuals with Disabilities Education Act (IDEA) protects the rights of parents and children? How is this implemented?
3. The individualized education program (IEP) specifies the education to be received by a student with disabilities. What are the contents of this program/plan?
4. Why should teachers in regular classrooms have knowledge and understanding of the types of disabilities in the school-aged population and methods and materials to teach these students?
5. What is the basis for public disinterest in and opposition to funding programs for gifted students?
6. Explain the underrepresentation of children of color in the gifted/talented population of school-aged children.
7. How should a teacher respond to a student's use of Black English in the classroom?

❖ **References**

Anastasiow, N., Hanes, M. E., & Hanes, M. L. (1982) *Language and reading strategies for poverty children*. Baltimore: University Park Press.

Banks, J. A., & Banks, C. A. (Eds.). (1993). *Multicultural education: Issues and perspectives*, (2nd ed.). Boston: Allyn and Bacon.

Benton, A. L., & Pearl, D. (Eds.). (1979). *Dyslexia: An appraisal of current knowledge*. New York: Oxford University Press.

Bryan, T., & Bryan, J. (1986). *Understanding learning disabilities*. Palo Alto, CA: Mayfield.

Cartwright, G. P., Cartwright, C., & Ward, M. (1989). *Educating special learners*. Belmont, CA: Wadsworth.

Council for Children with Behavior Disorders (CCBD) Notice of Inquiry on EBD terminology. *CCBD Newsletter*, Feb. 1993.

Cummins, J. (1986). Empowering minority students: A framework for intervention. *Harvard Educational Review, 56*(1), 18—36.

Dean, A., Salend, S., & Taylor, L. (1993). Multicultural education: A challenge for special educators. *Teaching Exceptional Children, 26*(1), 40-43.

Franklin, M. (1992). Culturally sensitive instructional practices for African-American learners with disabilities. *Exceptional Children, 59*(2), 115-122.

Gearhart, B., Mullen, R. C., & Gearhart, C. (1993). *Exceptional individuals: An introduction*. Pacific Grove, CA: Books/Cole.

Hallahan, D., & Kauffman, J. (1994). *Exceptional children: An introduction to special education*. Boston: Allyn and Bacon.

Langdon, H. (1989). Language disorder or difference? Assessing the language skills of Hispanic students. *Exceptional Children, 56*(2), 160-167.

Leigh, J. (1987). Adaptive behavior of children with learning disabilities. *Journal of Learning Disabilities, 20*(9), 557-562.

Lerner, J. (1988). *Learning disabilities: Theories, diagnosis, and teaching strategies.* Boston: Houghton Mifflin.

Lilly, M. S. (1992). In W. Stainback, & S. Stainback (Eds.), *Controversial issues confronting special education: Divergent perspectives.* Boston: Allyn and Bacon.

McKinney, J. D., Montague, M., & Hocutt, A. (1993). Educational assessment of students with attention deficit disorder. *Exceptional Children, 60*(2), 125-131.

Ovando, C. (1993). Language diversity and education. In J. Banks & C. Banks (Eds.), *Multicultural education: Issues and perspectives,* (2nd ed.). Boston: Allyn and Bacon.

Patton, J. (1992). Assessment and identification of African American learners with gifts and talents. *Exceptional Children, 59*(2), 150–159.

Patton, J. M., Prillaman, D., & Van Tassel-Baska, J. (1990). The nature and extent of programs for the disadvantaged gifted in the United States and territories. *Gifted Child Quarterly, 34*(3), 94-96.

Paul, J. L., & Simeonsson, R. J. (1993). *Children with special needs: Family, culture, and society,* (2nd ed.). Fort Worth, TX: Harcourt, Brace, Jovanovich.

Prasse, D., & Reschly, D. J. (1986). A case of segregation, testing or program efficacy? *Exceptional Children, 52*(4), 333-346.

Richert, E. S. (1987). Rampant problems and promising practices in the identification of disadvantaged gifted students. *Gifted Child Quarterly, 31*(4), 149-154.

Salend, S. (1990). *Effective mainstreaming.* New York: Macmillan.

Salend, S. (1994). *Effective mainstreaming: Creating inclusive classrooms,* (2nd ed.). New York: Macmillan.

Silver, L. B. (1990). Attention deficit-hyperactivity disorder: Is it a learning disability or a related disorder? *Journal of Learning Disabilities, 23*(7), 394-397.

Smith, C. (1993). Cultural sensitivity in working with children and families. In J.L. Paul & R.J. Simeonsson (Eds.), *Children with special needs: Family, culture and society.* Fort Worth, TX: Harcourt, Brace, Jovanovich.

Smith, D. D., & Luckasson, R. (1992). *Introduction to special education: Teaching in an age of challenge.* Boston: Allyn and Bacon.

Stainback, W. & Stainback, S. (Eds.). (1992) *Controversial issues confronting special education: Divergent perspectives.* Boston: Allyn and Bacon.

Van Tassel-Baska, T., Patton, J., & Prillaman, D. (1989). Disadvantaged gifted learners at risk for educational attention. *Focus on Exceptional Children, 22*(3), 1-16.

Vellutino, F.R. (1979) Toward an understanding of dyslexia: Psychological factors in specific reading disability. In A.L. Benton, & D. Pearl (Eds.), *Dyslexia: An appraisal of current knowledge.* New York: Oxford University Press.

Wanat, P.E. (1983). Social skills: An awareness program with learning disabled adolescents. *Journal of Learning Disabilities 16*(1), 35–38.

Ysseldyke, J., & Algozzine, B. (1984). *Introduction to special education.* Boston: Houghton Mifflin.

Ysseldyke, J., & Algozzine, B. (1990). *Introduction to special education,* (2nd ed.). Boston: Houghton Mifflin.

CHAPTER 6

Cooperative Learning for Diverse Classrooms

Why Cooperative Learning?

In schools and classrooms across the country, at this time, it is possible to find students with disabilities rejected by their peers, and separated according to racial and ethnic groups. Even in desegregated schools, students may be tightly segregated as they seat themselves in classes or at lunch in the school cafeteria. In some settings, there may be peer pressure on those students who venture outside the group for friendships and interactions. Clearly, the teacher in these situations will be challenged to promote intergroup respect, understanding, and positive relations. Cooperative learning has been found effective in accomplishing these goals (Slavin & Oickle, 1981; Slavin, 1983; Kagan, 1989; Slavin, 1984; Slavin, 1985; Slavin, 1977; Slavin, 1979; Ziegler, 1981; Holt, 1993).

Furthermore, as Parrenas and Parrenas (1990) have found, as children progress through school they choose fewer friends from other racial and ethnic groups. Racial tensions continue through middle and high school and may continue to increase if preventive measures are not taken. There is a need for educators to identify methods that will promote positive interracial and interethnic relations among students of diverse cultural groups.

While interracial and interethnic pressures or conflicts may be absent or reduced in small, rural schools, socioeconomic and religious diversity can be equally challenging for the teacher. Students will need to learn acceptance and tolerance of the diversity that exists. Those from low socioeconomic groups or unfamiliar religious groups can face ostracism, ridicule, and failure in the classroom. Cooperative learning will help these students to enjoy belonging to the class, gain the respect and appreciation of their class members, and experience academic success. Regardless of the nature and extent of diversity in a school or classroom, all students need to learn appreciation and respect for their differences and skills for cooperation with others.

Linguistic diversity among students also calls for attention to promoting positive relationships between these students and others as well as between students and staff. As Holt (1993) has noted, linguistic diversity will include students with varied levels of proficiency in English. These students include those whose primary language is English; students with limited English proficiency (LEP) whose primary language is other than English; and students who are fluent English proficient (FEP) with a primary language other than English (Holt, 1993). Teachers will need to identify strategies that will promote mutual support and help students to acquire content and language. As Holt has noted, "cooperative learning is a key strategy for LEP students because it enhances interactions among students and dramatically improves achievement" (Holt, 1993, p. 3). Recent research on students with limited English proficiency has identified those factors that are important for school success. These include: promoting positive relationships between students and staff and among students themselves in addition to improving curriculum content; supporting students' primary language and culture; and enhancing communication and interactions between parents and educators (Holt, 1993). Cooperative learning integrated with multicultural/minority education has been recommended (Holt, 1993). Wong-Fillmore in Cummins (1993) reported that Latino students learned significantly more English in classrooms where reciprocal interaction with teacher and peers was promoted. Cooperative learning provides these opportunities.

❖ What is Cooperative Learning?

Cooperative learning has been defined as small group instruction in which students work together to maximize their own learning and that of their peers (Johnson, Johnson, & Holubec, 1990). In contrast with traditional, competitive classrooms, in cooperative classrooms children work together to accomplish shared goals and they reach their goals only if others in the group also reach theirs (Table 6–1). Cooperation results in every student's success (Johnson, Johnson, & Holubec, 1990). It is based upon a set of beliefs and principles that closely agree with the aims of multicultural education. Cooperative tasks can foster cooperation, interdependence, intercultural understanding, and positive peer interactions. Both academic and social skills can be learned cooperatively. The principles and beliefs on which this approach is based include the following:

Principles of Cooperative Learning

1. Leadership is distributed in the group. All students are capable of performing leadership tasks; the teacher does not choose a leader for the group.
2. Heterogeneous groups are more effective. Ascher (1986) has noted that cooperative learning methods capitalize on the heterogeneous students of many urban schools. It has been found that cooperative learning fosters greater student gains in heterogeneous groups. The groups may be randomly selected or chosen by the teacher.
3. Positive interdependence is learned and valued. Children need to recognize and value dependence upon one another; strategies are used to create interdependence:
    ▮ group and individual accountability are established;
    ▮ materials must be shared by the students;
    ▮ members of the group create a product; and
    ▮ all members of the group receive a reward, which is the same for everyone.
4. Social skills are taught and learned. The teacher defines and discusses social skills and observes the processes with the students.
5. Group autonomy is important. Students become more self-sufficient when they solve their problems with minimal input from the teacher.

Components of Cooperative Learning

The essential components of cooperative learning are:

▮ positive interdependence;
▮ face-to-face promotive interaction;

TABLE 6–1 What is Cooperative Learning?

Traditional, Competitive	Cooperative
Students compete with each other.	Students cooperate.
Focus is on the individual.	Focus is on the group; students learn to help the group.
Some students dislike those who are always "first," who always gain recognition.	All students achieve and are recognized; students like each other.
Some students win and others lose.	
Students try to do better than everyone else.	All students "win."
	Students help all to succeed.
Students do not learn the value of interdependence.	Interdependence and individual accountability are learned and valued.
Cooperative social skills are not learned.	Cooperative skills are learned.
The teacher is the only leader.	
	All students may be leaders; leadership is shared.

- individual accountability;
- interpersonal and small group skills; and
- group processing.

Johnson, Johnson, and Holubec (1990) point out that positive interdependence is the essence of cooperative learning. Positive interdependence exists when the students perceive that they "sink or swim together." The responsibilities of each student are to learn the assigned material and ensure that all members of their group learn it. This leads to the realization that they must coordinate their and their groupmates' efforts to complete a task. Academic gains of individuals have been positively correlated with this approach (Kagan, 1989).

Interdependence. Kagan (1989) notes that there are strong, intermediate, and weak forms of interdependence. When the success of each group member is not likely to contribute to that of others, or when the success of the group is not likely to depend upon the success of individuals, positive interdependence is weak. An intermediate form of interdependence exists when the success of each member contributes to the success of all members, but an individual could succeed on his own. Strong, positive interdependence occurs when the success of every individual is impossible without the contribution of each member, and the success of a group or team is not possible without the success/contribution of each individual. The type of interdependence created by the teacher will have a strong effect on the encouragement and help that group members give each other and the extent of their cooperation.

Positive interdependence can be created by the structure of the task or the reward. For example, the teacher can structure the task so that a single product is completed by the group or a randomly selected individual paper is taken as the group score. The group grade or group product must hold each individual accountable for a contribution or achievement gains will not consistently occur (Slavin, 1983). There are several forms of accountability. Reward accountability makes each student accountable for knowing the contribution of every student to the product or grade. For example, if each student takes a test and the group grade is based on the sum or average score, every student must know the score obtained by each group member.

Interaction. Face-to-face promotive interaction is the notion that students must promote and encourage each other to learn and succeed. It refers to the interaction and verbal exchanges among students that are promoted by positive interdependence.

Accountability. Task accountability occurs if each student is made accountable to the group for his/her portion of the project (Kagan, 1989). There are several ways that the teacher can arrange task accountability. For example: (1) each student could receive a grade on her portion of the project or product; (2) each could be held responsible for a unique aspect of the project; or (3) the group could not move on until everyone completes the task at the present level or center (Kagan, 1989). Individual accountability can also be structured for such activities as listening or participating in a discussion. Examples of these activities will be available in Chapter 7.

Group Skills. Interpersonal and small group skills are developed when students work in small groups. These skills must be taught by the teacher in order for high-quality functioning to exist. The students must get to know and trust one another, communicate accurately and unambiguously, accept and support each other, and resolve conflicts constructively. The development of social skills can be fostered through modeling, role-playing, observation, reinforcement, processing, and practicing specific skills. Modeling involves learning through imitation. Models (either peers or adults) demonstrate the appropriate behavior, while students observe and imitate.

There are many instructional materials available for teaching social skills. Two examples are programs in which modeling and role-playing are key components, *Skillstreaming the Elementary School School Child*

TABLE 6–2 Group II: Friendship-Making Skills

Skill 25: Apologizing

STEPS	NOTES FOR DISCUSSION
1. Decide if you need to apologize for something you did.	Discuss how we sometimes do things for which we are later sorry. Apologizing is something we can do to let the other person know we are sorry. It also often makes us feel better. Emphasize sincerity.

2. Think about your choices:
  a. Say it out loud to the person.
  b. Write the person a note.
	Discuss when it is best to use verbal or written ways to apologize.

3. Choose a good time and place.	Discuss how to choose a good time: apologize soon after the problem. The student may want to be alone with the person for a verbal apology.
4. Carry out your best choice in a sincere way.	Discuss the body language and facial expression associated with sincerity.

SUGGESTED SITUATIONS

School: You are late for a class.

Home: You accidentally break something.

Peer group: You said something cruel because you were angry, or you had planned to do something with a friend but you have to go somewhere with your parents instead.

COMMENTS

It may be beneficial to discuss how difficult it might be to apologize. Discussion of how a person might feel before apologizing (e.g., anxious, afraid) as well as how a person might feel receiving the apology (e.g., relieved, less upset or angry) may make students more willing to try.

SOURCE: Skillstreaming the Elementary School Child: A Guide for Teaching Prosocial Skills (pp.) by E. McGinnis and A.P. Goldstein, 1984, Champaign, IL: Research Press. Reprinted by permission.

(McGinnis & Goldstein, 1984) and *Skillstreaming the Adolescent* (Goldstein, Sprafkin, Gershaw, & Klein, 1980). In these programs, social skills are clearly defined with specific steps to be taught.

For example, one of the "Friendship-making Skills" in McGinnis and Goldstein is the skill, "Apologizing." The teacher would teach the skill in the following steps:

1. Decide if you need to apologize for something you did.
2. Think about your choices.
   a. Say it out loud to the person.
   b. Write the person a note.
3. Choose a good time and place.
4. Carry out your best choice in a sincere way.

See the complete plan for teaching the skill (Table 6–2). This is a good skill to teach at the beginning of the school year or when an appropriate incident occurs in the classroom.

Group Processing. Group processing is the final component of cooperative learning. As directed by the teacher, the groups express feedback on group members' actions that were helpful or not helpful and make decisions concerning actions to continue or to change. This component will encourage students to improve their functioning in future groups (Johnson, Johnson, & Holubec, 1990). Processing consists of having students review their group activity. Questions about helping could include: "Did I give help when needed?" or "Did I ask for help when needed?" Processing questions concerning praising might be: "What praise did I give?" "What praise did I receive?" and "What praise felt good?" (Kagan, 1989).

Kagan (1989) includes an additional key element of cooperative learning, team-formation, which is especially important in a multicultural classroom. Students of diverse cultural and linguistic groups will learn to work harmoniously and cooperatively with each other when the class functions as teams. The formation of teams will be discussed more extensively later.

❖ How Effective is Cooperative Learning?

Cooperative learning has been effective in raising academic achievement levels as well as promoting positive interpersonal, interracial, and interethnic relationships (Johnson, Johnson, & Holubec, 1984; Slavin & Oickle, 1981; Ziegler, 1981; Holt, 1993; Slavin, 1979, 1983, 1984, 1985).

Johnson, Johnson, Holubec, and Roy (1984) have conducted many studies on cooperative learning. In an analysis of 122 studies conducted between 1924 and 1981, they found that cooperative learning experiences

Cooperative learning promotes positive interpersonal, interracial, interethnic relationships.

tended to promote higher achievement than competitive and individualistic learning. This was true across all ages and subject areas and most tasks (Parrenas & Parrenas, 1990). Johnson and Johnson (1984, p.15) identified factors that contribute to the effectiveness of cooperative learning. These include:

1. the discussion process, in which controversies and conflicts that arise can motivate children to achieve, retain the material learned, and learn the material in greater depth;
2. increased peer feedback, support, and encouragement of learning;
3. the exchange of ideas which leads to enriched learning in the heterogeneous group; and
4. the liking/positive feelings for each other that develops among students in the group.

Cooperative learning has also been effective in teaching higher-level thinking skills: critical thinking, positive attitudes toward the subject area, and motivation to learn (Johnson, Johnson, & Holubec, 1984). However, the most important accomplishment with relevance for the multicultural classroom is that cooperative learning has been related to students' psychological health in the areas of emotional maturity, a strong personal identity, and basic trust and optimism about people (Johnson, Johnson, & Holubec, 1984). Those authors point out that constructive socialization is promoted in the cooperative learning experiences. This finding is of critical importance in the classroom where children of different cultural and linguistic groups need to learn to socialize, to like each other, and to respect themselves and others.

It is also important to teachers in multicultural classrooms that all children reach high levels of achievement. Slavin (1983) analyzed forty-six studies on cooperative learning. Higher achievement with cooperative learning was shown 63 percent of the time; 33 percent showed no difference; and 4 percent showed higher achievement for traditional approaches. Slavin found that in studies using group rewards for individual achievement, 89 percent showed gains.

Another important finding for those interested in multicultural education is that, in cooperative learning, students will learn to see things from more than one perspective. They will learn to *walk in another's shoes*. This involves the ability to understand how another student views and reacts to a situation. It is referred to as social perspective-taking. As opposed to egocentrism, Johnson, Johnson, and Holubec (1984) found

> . . . cooperative learning experiences tend to promote greater cognitive and affective perspective-taking than do competitive or individualistic learning experiences. (p. 21)

Self-esteem, relationships with school personnel, and positive expectations toward future interactions with students are also promoted by cooperative learning.

Kagan (1989) has noted that cooperative learning has resulted in improved race relations among students in integrated classrooms. In studies involving students from grades three through twelve, cross-ethnic friendships showed greater improvement in cooperative learning classrooms than in the control classes (Slavin, 1983). Slavin (1979) also found in one study that students in the traditional classroom listed 9.8 percentof their friends as from a different race as compared with 37.9 percent in the cooperative classroom.

Positive outcomes resulting from the use of cooperative learning have been noted for racially/ethnically mixed students (Slavin & Oickle, 1981). Their 1981 study of 230 racially mixed students found that after using heterogeneous cooperative learning groups, African-American students achieved greater academic strides than their Caucasian counterparts. The authors of this study attribute these outcomes to attitudinal differences among the students. They believe that African-American students, while holding fewer stereotypes about Caucasians, are *cooperatively predisposed*, and Caucasian students, who have more stereotypes about their ethnically diverse peers, are *competitively predisposed*. Whatever the attitude, the authors found that once both groups of students became more accepting of differences, understanding became the precursor of cooperation. This, in turn, facilitated learning, achievement, and successful completion of tasks, while building a foundation of mutual respect among students.

Angry (1990) described a problem that existed at the middle school level in a Florida community. Students were having difficulty in positive communication. Students from varied ethnic groups were feeling alienated and unable to work together. Problems also existed in discipline, gang violence, fist fights, and class disruptions.

Students were unaware of cultural differences that prevented mutual respect and understanding. They preferred to work with their own ethnic group and referred to other groups with negative comments. A student survey was completed and objectives and instructional techniques were chosen.

With twelve weeks of cooperative learning, basic facts about the various ethnic groups, and cultural understanding, students demonstrated positive changes in working with peers from different cultural groups, reduced their feelings of alienation, and increased cooperation with others.

Based upon an educational philosophy called *Cooperative Pluralism*, Nakagawa (1991) developed a collection of materials for elementary level instruction in which cooperative learning was blended with multicultural education. Practical strategies for teachers were included, which emphasize interrelationships rather than culture-specific learning activities. Nakagawa points out that culture is not a "laundry list of traits and facts" and she is concerned about the effect of emphasizing differences among cultures (p.19). She cautions that in multicultural education the school must stress cultural pluralism and move from "me" to "we." Her multicultural education program emphasizes interrelationships in cooperative groups and includes five goals: self-identify, diversity, ideals, interdependence, and interpersonal relationships.

According to Parrenas and Parrenas (1990), studies have shown that a cooperative learning approach called *Student Learning Teams* can also lead to increased positive race relations among students. Those authors reviewed the use of cooperative learning for educationally disadvantaged and limited English-speaking students. They found that cooperative learning can help to eliminate ethnocentrism and racism and help students learn important social skills. However, the approach was effective only when it met two conditions: (1) group goals and (2) individual accountability should be incorporated in the learning activities. The group must be aware of the goals and understand that they will succeed through group effort; and everyone must contribute to the effort. In addition, they must understand that the group will succeed if each individual is held accountable, and that *freeloaders* will not be tolerated. Some examples of cooperative learning methods that incorporate group goals and individual accountability are: student teams (Slavin, 1986); team-games tournament (Devries & Slavin, 1978); cooperative reading and composition

(Stevens, Madden, Slavin, & Parnish, 1978); and team-assisted individualization in math (Slavin, 1978). These will be described in Chapter 7.

Ascher (1986) noted that cooperative learning methods were valuable for urban schools since they foster better student achievement than individualistic methods, increase cross-ethnic friendships, improve students' self-esteem and positive attitudes toward other students in the school. However, when studies conducted elsewhere were replicated in the San Diego elementary and secondary schools, results were insignificant. Earlier studies had found significant positive effects of cooperative learning such as cross-ethnic friendships and academic learning. The authors suggested that the disappointing outcomes for San Diego might be due to the brief time period used and inconsistencies in the implementing the program (Davis, 1994).

Several studies have demonstrated that the use of cooperative learning also enhanced the integration of students with disabilities with other students (Putnam, Rynders, Johnson, & Johnson, 1989; Slavin, Stevens, & Madden, 1988; Taymans, 1989). A study using the Cooperative Integrated Reading and Composition (CIRC) model to teach reading, writing, and language arts (Slavin, Stevens, & Madden, 1988) demonstrated that cooperative learning techniques enhanced student performance for handicapped and non-handicapped students in the same classroom, especially in reading comprehension. In addition, when cooperative learning was combined with direct instruction, the performance of the students increased even further.

Cooperative learning can enhance the integration of students with disabilities.

Taymans (1989) asserts the mainstreamed, learning disabled students who have difficulty keeping pace with their peers in terms of achievement are generally at risk of eventually dropping out of school due to a lack of academic and social success. Cooperative learning provides interventions that enable learning disabled students to reach a higher success rate in academic, social, and vocational areas. When students become invested in each others' learning and dependent upon one another, they feel a greater acceptance from their peers and are less frustrated by academic failures. Because all groupmates are concerned with achieving a common outcome, each student has a fair chance to succeed. In the case of a learning disabled, mainstreamed student, self-esteem often improves. In addition, other group members are encouraged to be more accepting and tolerant of individual differences.

Research has demonstrated that cooperative learning experiences stimulate handicapped students' performances in academic activities and in school-related social situations (Johnson & Johnson, 1983; Johnson & Johnson, 1986; Madden & Slavin, 1983; Putnam et al. 1989; Sharan, 1980; Slavin et al. 1988). Another important outcome of this research is that the non-handicapped student's performance is enriched as well. Slavin et al (1988) explains that this has valuable implications for the mainstreaming of handicapped students in regular education. They believe that from the perspective of special and remedial education, the fact that non-handicapped students are benefiting from cooperative learning is more likely to encourage regular education teachers to incorporate this strategy into their classrooms. Thus, this will help mainstreaming achieve its full potential.

❖ How Do You Begin?

The Role of the Teacher

The teacher's role is different in a classroom where children are engaged in cooperative learning experiences. As compared with competitive or individualistic learning structures, teachers have to employ major strengths in structuring cooperation among students (Johnson, Johnson, & Holubec) (Table 6–3).

The teacher shares authority with the students during cooperative learning experiences while holding them accountable for their learning and/or product. The teacher's role is that of a consultant and manager. However, in some situations the teacher might give direct instruction in a skill or concept while being careful not to interfere with the groups' work or discussions. In other situations, the teacher might observe and record students' questions, comments, or verbal interactions. The stu-

TABLE 6–3   Roles and Responsibilities of the Teacher

1. Clearly state the lesson objectives .

2. Make decisions
    a.   Size of group
    b.   How to assign students to groups
    c.   How to arrange the room
    d.   How to assign roles to students

3. Explain the task, goal, and purposes to students
    a.   Be sure that positive interdependence is structured in the task
    b.   Be sure that individual accountability is structured in the task
    c.   Select and explain to students the criteria for successful completion of the task
    d.   Clarify expected student behaviors

4. Monitor the groups' functioning
   Suggestions: (Johnson, Johnson, & Holubec, 1987)
    a.   Provide immediate feedback and reinforcement
    b.   Encourage students to explain and elaborate
    c.   Reteach or expand teaching
    d.   Observe group skills that have been mastered
    e.   Praise and encourage good group skills
    f.   Note group skills that you need to teach
    g.   Learn interesting things about students

5. Process group functioning with students

6. Provide closure

7. Evaluate student learning

dents may also be given feedback on the functioning of their group. The teacher's responsibility will vary in designing the lesson content or structure, depending upon the approach used. Intrinsic motivation is the goal of many teachers and external rewards for motivation are not often used.

A cooperative classroom will bring different types of rewards and satisfaction to the teacher. Teaching and learning are shared with the students so they teach one another and help each other to solve problems. Teachers find satisfaction in the positive outcomes of cooperation and collaboration in the classroom. They recognize the value of small group learning and the growth of independence and responsibility in the students. Teachers are freed from always lecturing and directing the students. Management tasks are reduced since there is less concern about keeping the students quiet. It is also important to remember that achievement gains will bring both teacher and student satisfaction. Furthermore, some researchers have pointed out that cooperative classrooms may be more compatible with some minority students, and result in higher achievement due to the compatibility of classroom structure with their cultural values. This may be due to the fact that cooperative classrooms are more appropriate for field-sensitive learners. Mexican-American, American Indian and African-American students, for example, have been identified as field-dependent learners (Ramirez & Casteneda, in Nieto, 1992). Field-sensitive learners prefer to learn in social settings in cooperation with others. Context and materials that have social content are also important to these students (Nietro, 1992).

However, teachers should continue to use some competitive and individual learning tasks, because students should not have "only" cooperative learning experiences. In reality, they must learn to compete, cooperate, work individually without comparison with others, and maintain flexibility. However, the goals and objectives of multicultural education can best be achieved through an educational approach that fosters interracial and interethnic harmony, positive interdependence, and cooperation among heterogeneous classmates. Although we cannot predict the types of jobs our students will have or the kind of environment in which they will live and work, we do know that those environments will be characterized by widespread diversity among the many persons who inhabit them.

❖ Approaches to Cooperative Learning

There are several approaches to structuring cooperative learning for your classroom, Special Box 6–1.

Prepackaged Curriculum

The teacher can use a general procedure for any type of task or a prepackaged curriculum approach. One example of a prepackaged program is *Finding Out*, which contains group learning activities for science and math. The program is available in English and Spanish and is useful for classrooms where students are learning English as a second language. While the program has been found effective by some researchers (DeAvila, Duncan, & Navarette, 1987), Johnson, Johnson, and Holubec (1984) note that prepackaged programs generally do not work. Those authors offer a general procedure for structuring cooperative learning tasks across a variety of subject areas. The complete procedure addresses skills needed by teachers (Table 6–4).

SPECIAL BOX 6–1 *Cooperative Learning Approaches*

1. Prepackaged curriculum

2. Jigsaw (Eliot Aronson, 1978)

3   Student learning teams (Slavin, 1980)

4. Team-Games-Tournaments (D. DeVries, 1973)

5. Learning together (Johnson & Johnson, 1987)

6. Co-op, Co-op (Spencer Kagan, 1989)
    Round table, (1989)
    Round robin, (1989)

7. Student-teams-achievement divisions (STAD, Slavin, 1980)

Three Approaches

Among the most familiar structures are *Jigsaw, Student Learning Teams* and *Teams-Games-Tournaments*.

Jigsaw. The original designers of Jigsaw were Eliot Aronson and colleagues at the University of Texas and later at University of California at Santa Cruz (Aronson, Blaney, Stephan, Sikes, & Snapp, 1978). Jigsaw was originally developed as a means of making students interdependent. Each would have a part of the whole, which made sense alone, but the other parts are needed for mastery of the total lesson. For example, in a unit on Puerto Rico, one student would receive information on the geography, another student would have the economy, another the history, and so on. All of the information would be required to master the entire unit. In the original method, students are organized into teams of six. Each team member first reads her unique section. Then members in each group, who have studied the same section, meet and discuss it. Next, they return to their teams and take turns teaching their teammates about their sections. Interdependence is assured since team members must learn about other sections from their teammates. Modifications of Jigsaw include four to five members where students read a common narrative and then receive a topic on which to become an expert. Meeting in groups and teaching teammates follow. Students then take individual quizzes which are added together to give them scores. The highest-scoring teams are recognized in a class newsletter (Slavin, 1985).

TABLE 6–4 Skills Needed By Teachers (Johnson, Johnson, & Holubec, 1984)

1. The teacher specifies objectives for the academic and cooperative skills for the students to learn. The objectives should be stated in measurable terms.

2. Decisions are made on how groups will be selected and the number of students per group.

3. The classroom is arranged for small group learning.

4. Materials are planned so that interdependence will be promoted.

5. The teacher assigns roles for students in the group.

6. The academic task is explained to the students.

7. The teacher structures positive interdependence and individual accountability through distribution of the materials or rewards.

8. Intergroup cooperation is structured.

9. Evaluation criteria are explained to the students so that they understand what is required for success.

10. The desired behaviors are clearly stated to the students.

11. Students' behavior in the groups is monitored by the teacher.

12. The teacher intervenes to give assistance with the task or to teach a cooperative skill when necessary.

13. The teacher provides closure for the lesson.

14. The teacher evaluates student learning.

15. Processing is conducted with the students to evaluate how they functioned.

Student Learning Teams. Student learning teams have been found to increase learning more than traditional methods in sixteen to twenty-one studies conducted throughout the world (Slavin, 1989). Steps in the method include: teacher teaches the group, teams study together, a test is given to individual members, scores are added to form team scores, and the team with the highest score is recognized.

Team-Games-Tournaments. Teams-games-tournaments are the same as student learning teams except for the quizzes. In place of quizzes, academic game tournaments are used. Students compete with members of other teams. Games consist of simple, relevant questions based upon the academic content. Each table has three students, each from a different team, and plays the game, which often consists of numbered questions on a ditto sheet (Slavin, 1989). Relevant multicultural content can be used in any of the above structures.

Co-op, co-op, and student teams-achievement divisions are described in Chapter 7.

Schniedewind and Davidson (1981) also suggest teaching formats that teachers may use. These include:

- partners;
- peer teaching;
- group projects;
- jigsaw;
- cross-age projects;
- learning centers;
- board games;
- co-op card games;
- treasure hunt; and
- research project.

Some authors recommend choosing an academic lesson using familiar skills as the first cooperative activity. (Social skills will also be learned since they are an integral part of cooperative tasks.) Examples of academic tasks that use familiar skills may be studying spelling or vocabulary for intermediate students; matching colors with their names for primary students; labeling bones of the body at the junior high level; and naming the components of a short story in a high school classroom (Dishon & O'Leary, 1984).

Learning Together

The following material will expand on each of the fifteen steps outlined in Table 6–4.

Step 1. The teacher begins by specifying objects—both academic and collaborative. An example of the academic objective could be to say: "Identify Europe, Asia, America, and Africa on the maps." Next, the teacher develops the learning task needed to accomplish this objective and any prerequisite learning activities that will be provided for the entire class, before group work begins.

Academic objectives should be appropriately matched with the student's level of ability and entry level skills. It may be necessary to analyze the learning task (break it down into small, sequential steps) so that objectives can be specified for each step, and students' knowledge and understanding of cooperation and collaboration can be assessed. Collaborative skills are related to the goals of cooperative learning. Some examples are: encouraging each other to share ideas, and accepting and giving constructive criticism (Schniedewind & Davidson, 1987).

Step 2. After instructional objectives are written, the teacher will need to make decisions about the selection, size, and composition of the groups. Johnson, Johnson, Holubec, and Roy, (1984) have noted that groups tend to range in size from two to six members. They point out certain advantages and limitations of larger groups. For example, as group size increases, the number of ideas, expertise, abilities, minds available for brainstorming, and hands to carry out the work also increase. However, it takes more time for everyone to have a chance to speak, to keep all members on task, and to reach consensus. The shorter the time period available, the smaller the group should be, according to Johnson et al. Usually, the group size will depend on the nature and quantity of materials available. Those authors recommend that beginning teachers start with groups of two or three and increase the group size as students become more skilled and experienced.

Group Heterogeneity. In assigning students to groups, heterogeneity is the preferred structure as noted earlier. Groups should reflect the diversity in the class-racial/ethnic, linguistic, disability, socioeconomic, religious, gender, and ability levels. Task-oriented and non-task-oriented students should also be placed together. When the teacher selects the groups, they will usually be more heterogeneous than student-selected groups. This is due to the fact that students will usually choose friends much like themselves to work within a group. Students can, however, participate in the selection process by listing who they would like to work with and placing them in a group with one person from their list with others chosen by the teacher (Johnson et al., 1990).

Another technique is to have student list three persons with whom they would like to work. After reading all the lists, the teacher can build groups around children who were not chosen. Thus, each group may include one isolated student with several other supportive, skilled students. This procedure could be used to help students with a disability, for example, before other students are ready to positively accept their differences. Random assignment of students to groups can also be used.

In answer to the question of how long groups should remain together, there is no absolute answer. Groups may remain together throughout the school year or may be changed frequently, but it is important that they are together long enough to be successful. In a multicultural classroom, it will be helpful for students to work cooperatively with everyone in the class in order to build positive interracial/intercultural harmony.

Step 3. The next consideration is arrangement of the classroom. Group members need to sit in a circle, close enough to make eye contact and communicate easily without interrupting other groups. Everyone should be seated at the same level—equality is achieved in this way. Schniedewind and Davidson (1987) point out that teachers can organize and maintain the room for small group learning by placing the desks or tables in clusters to accommodate three to five students; or they may prefer the traditional arrangement that can be rearranged as needed. The second choice requires clear, firm directions so that the change can be made quickly and efficiently with a minimum of disorder. It's a good idea to teach a set of procedures for this change to minimize the amount of time required.

The time required for the learning activity must also be determined so that there will be sufficient time for directions, group work, correcting/checking papers, and processing. While at first a cooperative learning activity may require more time than traditional activities, as students become familiar with procedures for cooperative learning, lessons should move more quickly (Schniedewind & Davidson, 1987). It will be helpful to set a time limit for an activity and stick to it. Students should be reminded that they receive no reward for finishing first, the goal is to cooperate and do a good job. Schniedewind and Davidson (1987) recommend that when activities are short, completing a worksheet, for example, the last question should be open-ended so that those who finish first will have other activities to complete. Those authors also remind us that some students may need *catch up time* in the weekly schedule to finish their work.

Step 4. The next step involves planning/selecting materials so that positive interdependence is created. This may be accomplished through interdependence of resources, accountability, or rewards. The teacher can create resource interdependence through careful distribution of limited materials by: (1) giving only one copy of the material to the entire group; (2) giving each student a part of the material, in jigsaw fashion where everyone receives one part of the materials and all parts are needed to complete the task; or (3) giving each student a resource material which must be synthesized with that of the other members.

Accountability interdependence can be established through the teacher's method for evaluating each group's product or accomplishment. Some examples of this approach include: one paper to grade for the entire group; randomly calling on one student to give the group's response; or checking and grading individual work and adding all the scores together for the group grade. Evaluation criteria are needed in advance and these should be shared with students before the group work begins. Reward interdependence can be created by the manner in which the teacher rewards students for meeting the criteria. Rewards must be carefully used so that students can clearly relate them to group functioning. For that reason, everyone in the group should receive a reward or no one should be rewarded. Dishon and O'Leary (1984) suggest that if students are working cooperatively in groups, rewards should not be given, but if needed initially, should be withdrawn as soon as students begin to work together cooperatively.

Step 5. Interdependence can also be ensured in the group by assigning interconnected roles to students. For example, each group can have:

1. a summerizer-checker who sees that everyone understands the task and can summarize when needed;
2. a researcher-runner who gets materials for the group and communicates with the other groups;
3. a recorder to write the groups' decisions and edit the final report;
4. an encourager who reinforces each member's contribution; and
5. an observer to monitor the group's collaborating.

The Teacher's Role. The teacher will also need to determine if students possess the social skills that are needed for small group work and will need to teach these skills, if necessary. These skills include:

1. checking for understanding in order to find out who understands and who doesn't;
2. involving everyone in making decisions;
3. sharing ideas and information;
4. encouraging each other; and
5. checking for agreement.

(Dishon & O'Leary, 1984). Steps in teaching social skills include:

1. defining the skill and rationale for learning it;
2. modeling/demonstrating how to do it;
3. having students practice the skill;
4. giving feedback on students' performance by others in the group/class;
5. processing with the students about learning the skill; and
6. having students continue to practice the skill until it is mastered.

Examples for assessing and teaching social skills may also be found in Goldstein et al., (1984) as noted earlier.

Step 6. In the next step, the teacher explains the academic task to students. This step involves a clear description of the task and an explanation of the purpose, objectives, and relevant concepts and the procedures for completing the task.

Steps 7 and 8. Following the explanation, the teacher should verify that positive interdependence, individual accountability, and intergroup cooperation have been carefully structured. These are key components of cooperative learning that were discussed in Step 4.

Step 9. Evaluation criteria are explained to students in this step. The objectives of the lesson should determine the criteria. For example, if individual differences are involved, the criteria may be set for each student such as, "Johnny will complete fifteen additional problems without error;" "Mary will correctly compute twenty-five additional problems." Variation could also exist in the number of spelling words that each student will learn. In addition, the teacher could set criteria for the entire class in this way so that class cooperation is promoted.

Step 10. Next, desired student behaviors are specified by the teacher. Johnson, Johnson, and Holubec (1984) suggest that the teacher specify a few behaviors for each lesson. Their examples are such behaviors as: evaluating ideas instead of people or listening carefully to what each student has to say.

Steps 11 and 12. After discussing appropriate behavior with the students, the teacher is ready to monitor the groups and intervene when needed. To intervene, the teacher may need to provide assistance with the task or to teach collaborative skills. However, intervention should be avoided whenever possible so that students are not disrupted in their work and can learn to solve their own problems. Cooperative/collaborative skills are taught and learned like any other skills. These ideas were discussed earlier in the chapter. The reader will also find detailed discussion in Johnson, Johnson, and Holubec (1984).

Steps 13, 14, and 15. Providing closure to the lesson is one of the final steps. A summary of the content learned and its application is usually covered in this step. This step is followed by the evaluation of student outcomes. The teacher evaluates the quantity and quality of student learning using the evaluation criteria previously discussed. In addition, the teacher discusses with students how well the groups functioned. Processing is an essential, important component of cooperative learning. In this final step, students review their functioning as a group. They evaluate the manner in which they completed the task and the social skills that they used in the process. This includes judging, discussing, and planning (Dishon & O'Leary). Examples given by those authors include: "Some ways we checked our facts . . ." "We practiced by . . . ," etc. This process helps students to plan future group work and evaluate what worked and what didn't work.

To process social skills, students may analyze how they worked together as a group; what they learned that can be applied to other group sessions; and goals that can be set for the next group session.

All of the above are important elements that should be incorporated in the teacher's lesson plan. Guidelines for writing lesson plans for cooperative learning activities may be found in Dishon and O'Leary, (1984), and Schniedewind and Davidson, (1987). The latter text also includes many activities and tips for teachers in a lesson plan format.

❖ Cooperative Learning in the College Classroom

It is helpful to use cooperative learning in college classrooms where students in preservice teacher education programs can experience it firsthand. Assignments can be easily structured for cooperative learning groups. Mack (1993) describes the use of cooperative pairs of students selected from different ethnic, racial, and gender groups to examine a common textbook from different perspectives. Students were given a choice of partners (who had to be from a different population group), text, and population.

In the outline provided for the project, Mack asked students to give: (1) initial individual responses to the text; (2) a collaborative, critical study of the text; (3) a collaborative synthesis; and (4) concluding responses to the study as a whole.

Other activities that have worked well are: class projects such as curriculum development (units of instruction); discussion of a topic which is summarized and presented to the entire class. Additional activities are listed (Table 6–5).

TABLE 6–5   Suggestions for Using Cooperative Learning in the College Classroom

---

1. Have students complete assigned projects together in small working groups of two to four students.

2. Have students discuss a topic in small groups and choose an individual to present the summary of ideas and positions.

3. Students can work in collaborative pairs to conduct research.

4. Base groups can be formed at the beginning of the semester to complete assignments, study for tests, and serve as support and encouragement throughout the semester.

5. Have students develop questions for class discussion.

6. Groups of three to four students can identify main issues or points in reading assignments and present them to the class.

7. Students can exchange views on sensitive issues in small groups and decide what to share with the entire class.

8. Groups can evaluate instructional materials and report to the class; evaluate studies or articles in professional journals; observe in certain types of classrooms; try out teaching methods and present results to the class.

❖ Potential Problems

Problems have developed when students have had very different approaches to completing assignments; great distance between their homes so that joint meetings for library work and discussions are difficult; extreme differences in their time available for study and school assignments—often due to extensive job commitments; and different priorities in their personal and career objectives. It is sometimes necessary for the instructor to play a mediating role and help in seeking solutions to the problems.

The teacher may face certain types of problems in trying to begin cooperative learning in the classroom. Students may resist the small group organization or participating in collaborative activities. When this occurs, Schniedewind and Davidson (1987) suggest beginning cooperative learning in small groups with which the teacher is already working. Assigning a short, well-defined task and goal may also be helpful.

Secondly, teachers may find it difficult to manage the varied levels of skills in the heterogeneous groups. A solution to this problem may be found in assigning different parts of a task according to ability levels of the students. Those who are at a high level can be assigned more challenging parts of the task or faster students can help those who are slower.

Another problem may be the off-task behavior of some students. Teachers may need to arrange procedures for dealing with interpersonal problems of students, providing orientation when new students enter, and monitoring the noise level in the room. For problems such as name-calling and put-downs, classroom rules and activities may be needed to build students' self-esteem. Rules should be developed by the student in order to be most effective.

When students lack skills to help each other in the group, the teacher will need to teach helping skills using role-playing and discussions. Examples of these skills include: encouraging each other to participate; expressing support and acceptance; asking and giving help; and explaining, clarifying, and summarizing what has been discussed.

❖ Two Cooperative Classrooms

Mr. Smith

Mr. Smith's fifth-grade class is described as an inclusion class at his elementary school. It includes twenty-nine students, fifteen of whom are identified special education students. Three other students are described as below average in academics. Mr. Smith, the regular education teacher, and Miss James, the special education teacher, work together as a team, full time in the classroom.

It is impossible to notice any distinct differences among these students. When observed, they resemble regular fifth-graders, eager and enthusiastic about learning. The special education students cannot be identified among the twenty-nine children. This is really what inclusion means— including all children in the mainstream educational program. The benefits are obvious; children accept each other and work together easily. The classroom atmosphere is charged with energy, enthusiasm, and positive feelings.

Mr. Smith does things in his classroom that give positive recognition to all students. Each day, one student receives a standing ovation upon entering the classroom. Children literally stand on their chairs to applaud.

The classroom is permanently arranged for cooperative learning groups—small tables where three students usually sit. Occasionally groups are as large as five and students quickly arrange the extra chairs.

The morning schedule begins with the pledge at 9 AM following by a standing ovation for one student.

The morning schedule today includes the following activities:

9:00 AM   Pledge
            Standing ovation for a student

9:15 AM   Literature period

            Teacher reads to students from the story "Weasel."
            Most students are seated on the floor in a corner of the
            room; others remain in their seats to listen.

9:30 AM   Teacher prepares students for transition to a meeting in
            their Base Groups.

            Base groups are mainly for support and encourage-
            ment. They remain together throughout the school year.
            The specific activities conducted in the base groups are
            shown in Special Box 6–2.

9:45 AM   Group meeting ends. Teacher calls all students to the
            front of classroom. They line up and are counted off in
            fours. Each "number" receives a list of five different
            words. Four students, numbered one to four, are seated
            at each table.

            The groups will work with vocabulary from the story (on
            the lists handed out). Each student will "teach" five
            words to the group. Students review the method they
            will use to teach the words. They have obviously had
            previous experience in this.

            Because directions are very important, Mr. Smith insists
            that everyone is listening "times two," a signal for both
            eyes and ears, as he delivers the following directions:

1. First, define the words for your group.

2. Next, help them if they don't understand. (Teacher asks class, "What are some ways that you can help if someone doesn't understand a word?") Students give suggestions such as "use it in some sentences."

3. When everyone knows all five words, there is a sign-off sheet to complete, guaranteeing that everyone knows them.

4. The teacher again reviews the procedures and checks students' understanding.

Mr. Smith monitors the groups throughout the activity, clapping several times and apologizing whenever he must interrupt. Several times he interrupts when the noise level is too high. He asks the class, "How can you keep the noise level down?" Students suggest, "leaning in toward the center of the table to talk to each other," "Don't talk at the same time." Everyone is enthusiastically engaged in the assigned activity. Occasional laughter and words of praise are heard among the students.

10:40 AM   Activity ends.

SPECIAL BOX 6–2   *The Procedures for Base Group Meetings*

Opening tasks—Ask and Answer (Beginning of school day)

1. How are you today? What's the best thing that's happened to you since our last class session?

2. Are you ready for today's classes?

3. Did you do all your homework? Is there anything that you don't understand?

4. What if _____ happens today?

Closing tasks—Ask and Answer (Meeting at end of day)

1. Do you understand today's work? What help do you need to finish it?

2. What are three things you learned today?

3. Will you get all of your work done tonight?

A Morning with Miss Jones' Class

Miss Jones, the regular fifth-grade teacher, and Miss Brown, the special education teacher, work together in an inclusive classroom. However, Miss Brown divides her day between this class and a fourth-grade classroom. There are twenty-seven fifth-graders including six students who are classified with disabilities.

Miss Jones describes her class as having been "totally out of it" at the beginning of the school year. Students were unable to behave appropriately either socially or academically. At present, the students have developed guidelines for behavior which are integrated into the schoolwide assertive discipline behavior management system. Cooperative behaviors are rewarded through this system, primarily for the teams of the entire class. Desks are arranged in clusters for small groups. The following schedule is organized this morning for cooperative learning in Miss Jones' classroom:

9:00 AM	Students begin the day in their base groups where they check off homework on a special form. They consult each other on accuracy, neatness, and completeness. The base groups chose names at the beginning of the school year and the names are posted on banners hanging from the ceiling. Each banner hangs above the base group's location.
	Job cards are picked up from a holder on the bulletin board. Jobs include attendance, lunch count, pledge leader, office messenger, line leader, pencil sharpener, windows, etc. Some jobs are completed at this time.
9:15 AM	Pledge
9:15–9:30 AM	Planning assignments for the day—how they will be completed (in base groups).
9:30–10:15 AM	Students work together to complete a worksheet on vocabulary comprehension for a recent story. Miss Jones has organized the groups based on a reasonable range in reading levels. Miss Jones gives directions for the worksheet:

1. Pronounce the words.
2. Know the meanings.
3. Use the words in a sentence.
4. Consult the partners to complete the worksheet.

(The special education teacher takes two students out of the classroom for reading instruction. Miss Jones explains that this was necessary due to the extremely low reading level of the students.

Miss Jones interrupts groups to review procedure when needed. She also gives points for appropriate behavior—"being on task"—both team points and class points. A student is called to post the points on a wall chart.

Miss Jones intervenes when students are having difficulty with academic or social challenges. (Some students are having snacks such as apples or dried fruit at this time as they work with group members.)

10:15 AM   Reading ends. Students select one team member to bring completed paper to the teacher.

10:20 AM   Math. Groups change again. Miss Jones gives the directions for math.

Students are working on a project for which they are to develop a name and menu with prices for their new restaurant.

Miss Jones reviews with them, "What can you say to be encouraging?" Students volunteer suggestions.

Groups continue to work on the project while Miss Jones and Miss Brown monitor, giving help when needed.

11:00 AM   Students line up to leave for art.

❖ Summary

Cooperative learning has been found effective for promoting positive interracial and interethnic relations among students from diverse cultural and linguistic groups. It is also effective for students with limited English proficiency. Cooperative learning has been defined as small group learning in which students help each other to assure that everyone learns and succeeds. They accomplish shared goals and objectives through interdependence and individual accountability. Positive interdependence, fact-to-face promotive interaction, individual accountability, interpersonal and small group skills, and group processing are the essential components of cooperative learning.

The effectiveness of cooperative learning approaches has been shown in numerous studies. Academic achievement levels as well as positive interpersonal, interracial, and interethnic relationships have been improved through its use. Higher-level thinking skills, critical thinking, positive attitudes toward the subject area, and motivation to learn are additional results. Furthermore, several studies have shown that the use of cooperative learning facilities the integration of students with disabilities in a regular education classroom. Both students with and without disabilities have shown improved academic performances and non-handicapped students became more accepting and tolerant of individual differences.

The teacher's roles in a cooperative classroom include planning and organizing groups, monitoring groups functioning, and processing with the students how the groups have functioned. The teacher serves as consultant and manager and shares some authority with the students.

Cooperative learning can also be used in the college classroom and serves to prepare teachers in its use. College students can often complete more meaningful assignments, in greater depth, when they work in groups. Preliminary discussion of complex or sensitive questions can often be conducted more easily in small groups where everyone can participate and shy students are less inhibited. Support, encouragement, and mutual assistance on difficult assignments and topics can be shared. Equal distribution of work and individual responsibility can be problems at this level.

Among younger students problems also arise which involve inappropriate behavior, lack of participation, and variation in skills in heterogeneous groups. However, studies have shown that African-American and other students who are field sensitive do very well in cooperative learning. In fact, the benefits of cooperative learning in teaching students how to live with and value the diversity in our society far outweigh any problems that may arise.

❖ CHAPTER 6 **Questions**

1. Briefly explain why cooperative learning is a promising approach to use in teaching about diverse cultures and teaching to diverse cultures in the classroom.

2. How can cooperative learning benefit students with limited English proficiency?

3. In what important respects does cooperative learning differ from traditional, competitive learning?

4. Slavin and Oickle (1981) described African-American students as "cooperatively predisposed." What did they mean by this expression?

5. Some studies have shown that cooperative learning can help to reduce ethnocentrism and racism and increase cross-ethnic friendships. Explain and identify the components of cooperative learning that could produce these results.

6. What, in your opinion, are the most important challenges to the teacher in using cooperative learning? Suggest how these challenges can be met.

❖ **References**

Angry, R. (1990). *Enhancing ethnic relations through teaching multicultural education in the secondary schools.* Miami, FL: Nova University.

Aronson, E., Blaney, M. Stephan, C., Sikes, J., & Snapp, M. (1978). *The jigsaw classroom.* Beverly Hills, CA: Sage Publications.

Ascher, C. (1986). *Cooperative learning in the urban classroom.* ERIC/CUE Digest No. 30. New York: ERIC Clearinghouse on Urban Education.

Cummins, J. (1993). Empowering minority students: A framework for interventions. In L. Weis and M. Fine (Eds.), *Beyond silenced voices: Class, race and gender in United States schools.* Albany, NY: State University of New York Press.

Davis, B. (1984). *Evaluation of the race/human relations program: A study of cooperative learning strategies.* San Diego, CA: San Diego City Schools, Planning, Research and Evaluation Division.

DeAvila, E., Duncan, S. E., & Navarette, C. (1987). *Finding out/Describumiento.* Compton, CA: Santillana Publishing Co., Inc.

DeVries, D., & Slavin, R. E. (1978). Teams-games-tournaments: Review of ten classroom experiments. *Journal of Educational Research and Development in Education, 12:* 28-38.

Dishon, D., & O'Leary, P. W. (1984). *A guidebook for cooperative learning: A technique for creating more effective schools.* Holmes Beach, FL.: Learning Publications, Inc.

Goldstein, A. P., Sprafkin, R. P., Gershaw, N. J., & Klein, P. (1980). *Skillstreaming the adolescent: A structured learning approach to teaching prosocial skills.* Champaign, IL: Research Press.

Holt, D. (1993). *Cooperative learning: A response to linguistic and cultural diversity.* Language in education: Theory and practice. Washington, DC: ERIC Clearinghouse on languages and linguistics.

Johnson, D. W., & Johnson, R. T. (1986). *Cooperation and competition,* New York: Longman.

Johnson, D. W., Johnson, R. T., & Holubec, R. (1987). *Structuring cooperative learning: Lesson plans for teachers.* Edina, MN: Interaction Book Co.

Johnson, D. W., Johnson, R. T., & Holubec, E. J. & Roy, (1984). *Circles of learning: Cooperation in the classroom.* Alexandria, VA: Association for Supervision and Curriculum Development.

Johnson, D. W., Johnson, R. T., & Holubec, R. (1984). *Circles of learning: Cooperation in the classroom.* Alexandria, VA: Association for Supervision and Curriculum Development.

Johnson, D. W., & Johnson, R. T. (1983). The socialization and achievement crisis: Are cooperative learning experiences the solution? In L. Bickman (Ed.), *Applied Social Psychology Annual 4.* Beverly Hills, CA: Sage Publications.

Kagan, S. (1989). *Cooperative learning resources for teachers.* San Juan Capistrano, CA: Resources for Teachers.

McGinnis, E., & Goldstein, A. P. (1984). *Skillstreaming the elementary school child: A guide for teaching prosocial skills.* Champaign, IL: Research Press.

Mack, T. (1993). Acquiring a multicultural perspective through the use of collaborative pairs. Paper presented at annual meeting, College English Association, Charlotte, NC. April, 1993.

Madden, N., & Slavin, R. E. (1983). Mainstreaming students with mild handicaps: Academic and social outcomes. *Review of Educational Research, 53:* 519-569.

Nakagawa, M. (1991). *A call for cooperative pluralism: From me to we.* Olympia, WA: Office of State Superintendent of Public Instruction.

Nieto, S. (1992). *Affirming diversity: The sociopolitical context of multicultural education.* New York: Longman.

Parrenas, C. S., & Parrenas, F. Y. (1993). *Cooperative learning, multicultural functioning and student achievement.* In L. M. Malave (Ed.), annual conference journal, Proceedings of the National Association for Bilingual Education Conference, Tucson, AZ, p. 181-189.

Putnam, J. W., Rynders, J. E., Johnson, R. T., & Johnson, D. W., (1989). Collaborative skills instruction for promoting positive interaction between mentally handicapped and non-handicapped children. *Exceptional Children, 55*(6), 550-557.

Schniedewind, N., & Davidson, E. (1987). *Cooperative learning: cooperative lives. A sourcebook of leaning activities for building a peaceful world.* Dubuque, IA: William C. Brown.

Sharan, S. (1980). *Cooperation in education.* Provo, UT: Brigham Young University.

Slavin, R. E., (1986). *Educational psychology: Theory into practice.* Englewood Cliffs, NJ: Prentice Hall.

Slavin, R. E., & Oickle, E. (1981). Effects of cooperative learning teams on student achievement and race relations: Treatment by race interactions. *Sociology of Education, 54*: 174-180.

Slavin, R. E. (1978). Student teams and achievement divisions. *Journal of Research and Development in Education, 12*: 39-49.

Slavin, R. E. (1988). *Student team learning: An overview and practical guide,* (2nd ed.). Washington, DC: National Education Association.

Slavin, R. E. (1983). When does cooperative learning increase student achievement? *Psychological Bulletin, 94*: 429-449.

Slavin, R. E. (1984). Team assisted individualization: Cooperative learning and individualized instruction in the mainstreamed classroom. *Remedial and Special Education, 5*(6) 33-42.

Slavin, R. E. (1985). Cooperative learning: Applying contact theory in desegregated schools. *Journal of Social Issues, 41*(3), 45-62.

Slavin, R. E. (1977). *Student learning team techniques: Narrowing the achievement gap between the races.* Baltimore: Center for Social Organization of Schools, Johns Hopkins University Report No. 228.

Slavin, R. E. (1979). Effects of biracial learning teams on cross-racial friendships. *Journal of Educational Psychology, 71*: 381:387.

Slavin, R. E. (1989). Cooperative learning and student achievement. In R.E. Slavin (Ed.), *School and classroom organization.* Hillsdale, NJ: Erlbaum.

Slavin, R. E., Stevens, R. J,. & Madden, N. A. (1988). Accommodating student diversity in reading and writing instruction: A cooperative learning approach. *Remedial and Special Education, 9*(1), 60-66.

Stevens, R. J., Madden, N., Slavin, R. E., & Parnish, A. M. (1987). Cooperative integrated reading and composition: Two field experiments. *Reading Research Quarterly, 22*, 433-454.

Taymans, J. M. (1989). Cooperative learning for learning disabled adolescents. *The Pointer, 33*(2), 28-32.

Ziegler, S. (1981). The effectiveness of cooperative learning teams for increasing cross-ethnic friendships: Additional evidence. *Human Organization, 40*: 264-268.

CHAPTER 7

Cooperative Learning Activities

The activities presented are to serve as examples for integrating multicultural education into the traditional curriculum. It is expected that teachers will be able to develop many additional activities that will result in curriculum reform. Many of the following activities have been selected from a variety of sources which are carefully identified. In other instances, the activities have been developed by the authors. Your evaluation or reactions to the activities are encouraged.

Cooperative learning activities for helping students to get acquainted, build positive classroom climate and teams, acquire collaborative skills, and achieve academic objectives are included. A lesson plan format is used, which covers the important aspects of cooperative learning discussed earlier. Although decisions on group size, assignment of students to groups, assignment of student roles, and room arrangement must always be decided, in many of the lesson plans that follow, these decisions are left to the judgment of the teacher. In addition, plans for monitoring and processing are included in some activities to serve as models or examples for the teacher. It is expected that the teacher will complete the lesson plan for each activity.

❖ Activities to Help Students Get Acquainted

At the beginning of the school year the teacher can use such well-known routines as students interviewing each other about how they spent the summer, their career-vocational goals, a famous person whom they would most like to be, or other interesting topics that are then shared with the class. Other activities include NAME TEST, geared to the age of the student, in which each (older) student gives the names of all the students introduced before, and adds his or her name to the list. For younger students, a ball can be tossed between students in a circle. The person tossing the ball gives his or her name, the person receiving it adds his or her name, and passes it to yet another until all have been introduced.

❖ Team-Building and Class-Building

The needs and characteristics of the students will determine the amount and type of team-building activities needed. In a very diverse classroom, extensive team-building and class-building activities may be needed in order to help students: (1) build a team identity, (2) experience mutual support, (3) value individual differences, and (4) develop synergy (Kagan, 1989). Kagan points out that while team-building helps to create a positive sense of unity in the team, class-building aims at providing networking among the entire class and helps students to see themselves as members of the entire class. Class-building results mainly from creating class goals and engaging in class-building activities and structures. Some of the goals that teams work for should be class goals, each team contributing to a class project or earning points that contribute to the class goal.

Co-op Co-op is a special activity for class-building (Kagan, 1989). The philosophy of the activity is that the goal of education is to foster the natural curiosity, intelligence, and expressiveness of students through producing a group product and sharing the product with the entire class.

The name Co-op Co-op refers to the cooperation within the team followed by cooperation within the entire class. Kagan views it as a means of operationalizing the ideas of John Dewey.

The essential elements of Co-op Co-op are to have students work together in small groups to "advance their understanding of themselves and the world, and then to provide them with the opportunity to share that new understanding with their peers" (Kagan, p. 14:5). The specific steps consist of:

1. a student-centered class discussion to stimulate the expression of students' interest in a subject to be covered;
2. selection of student learning teams;
3. team-building and cooperative skill development;
4. team topic selection: After team identity and communication skills are sufficiently developed, the team chooses a topic to work on that is related to its interests and the subject or unit;
5. minitopic selection: Each team distributes a part of the topic chosen to each member;
6. minitopic preparation: After subdividing the team topic into minitopics, students work individually on their minitopics. Preparation may involve library work, collecting data, interviewing, etc;
7. minitopic presentations;
8. preparation of team presentations; and
9. team presentations;
10. evaluation: Team presentations are evaluated by the class, individual contributions to the team effort are evaluated by teammates, and individual write-up or presentation of the minitopic is evaluated by the teacher.

To build team identity, the teacher may also have students choose team names, team banners, logos, cheers, or handshakes. Group projects such as doing a mural, formations, fun problems, or games may also be used. Team names may be chosen immediately after teams have been formed. Three rules are used: (1) each team member must have a say, (2) no decision can be reached unless everyone consents, and (3) no member consents to the group decision if she has a serious objection (Kagan, 1989).

Roundtable and Roundrobin (Kagan, 1989) are activities in which students take oral or written turns, respectively, in contributing to the group. A single piece of paper and pen are passed from student to student on the left in Roundtable (around the table). The same procedure is used to make oral contributions in Roundrobin. Roundtable can be used in many different subject areas and for different purposes in a lesson. For team-building, an example of its use is to make as many different words as possible from the work cooperation.

Fun problems, games, projects, and brainstorming can also be used for team-building. Another activity that can be used is the lesson "Esteem through Silhouettes."

ACTIVITY

Subject Area: Language Arts "Esteem through Silhouettes"

Grade Level: 1–6

Objectives:
- Students will build self-esteem through silhouettes.
- Students will learn their unique traits.

Teacher Decisions:
- *Group size*: 4 members, so that racial, ethnic groups, sexes, etc., are represented
- *Student roles*: Teacher judgment
- *Room arrangement*: Teacher judgment

Materials:
- Four pieces of paper and a pencil for each group
- Black construction-paper silhouettes previously prepared
- White chalk (the teacher holds these)

Lesson Format:
1. Tell the students "We're going to play the Roundtable game. It's a way to brainstorm. The paper will go around and around at each table while each member writes down an idea on the paper."
2. Check for understanding.
3. Say "Today you will write down special things that describe each team member. Everyone is different and special."
4. "Each team will have two minutes to write down ten things about each teammate."
5. "You will play the game four times so that you can make a list for each teammate. Everyone plays."
6. "If someone needs help, call out the word. Keep the paper moving. Spelling does not count."
7. "Each team that gets ten points in two minutes can earn a bonus point."
8. Check for understanding.

Positive Interdependence: Extra points can be earned for cooperating.

Individual Accountability: Each student must write down an answer when the paper is passed to her.

Criteria for Success: Each team with ten items about each person gets an extra point each round.

Monitoring: Encourage all to participate.

Processing: Give feedback. Ask students to give feedback on what went well. Teacher chooses four things from each list that are most special. Teacher writes these in white chalk on the silhouettes.

Evaluation:
▋ Task achievement
▋ Group functioning
▋ Notes on individuals
▋ Suggestions for next time

Source: Dimas, M. (1990). In M. Male, & M. Anderson (Eds.), *Fitting in: Cooperative learning in the mainstream classroom.* San Francisco: Majo Press. Reprinted with permission.

❖ Cooperative/Collaborative Skills

The teacher must be certain that the skills required for small group learning are acquired by students. In classes where it is necessary to teach these skills, Schniedewind and Davidson (1987) have developed exemplary activities. According to those authors, in order to learn successfully in small groups, students must:

1. Recognize and appreciate their diverse skills and talents.
2. Be able to cope with evaluation by their peers.
3. Avoid put-downs.
4. Recognize and value their interdependence.
5. Learn to see things from diverse perspectives.
6. Learn to reach consensus.
7. Solve their own problems.
8. Achieve academic gains.

The following activities can be used to teach these skills.

ACTIVITY

Subject:	Language Arts "Roles To Make or Break a Group"
Grade Level:	Elementary
Objectives:	▪ Student will increase their understanding of the different roles people play in groups.
	▪ Students will increase their understanding of how each role helps and hinders a group from accomplishing its task.
	▪ Students will increase their understanding of how each role makes others in the group feel good or bad.
	▪ Students will get an opportunity to have a structured group discussion.
Teacher's Decisions:	▪ *Group size:* 7-9
	▪ *Group assignment:* Teacher judgment
	▪ *Student roles:* As directed for the activity
	▪ *Room arrangement:* Teacher judgment

Materials:
- Four copies of Observer worksheets for each group
- Copies of Participant worksheet for each student
- Three copies of each chair sign
- Single chair for each student placed in three circles of seven to nine chairs each

Lesson Format:

1. Use the chair signs to explain to students that "We each may play different roles during a discussion." Discuss each term/role and its effect on the group.

2. The class is divided into groups of seven or nine students. Helpful and not helpful roles are alternated.

3. Give each student a Participant worksheet. Give each observer an Observer worksheet. Review the roles with students and have them cross out any role not being used.

4. Each group will have discussion (concurrently) focused on one of the topics suggested for discussion or another chosen by the teacher. Whomever is sitting in a chair will play that role in terms of contribution to the discussion and style of participating.

5. Every three minutes each student moves one chair over and takes a new role. Include the Observer role in rotation. Observers fill out an Observer worksheet in each group. Each Observer receives a new worksheet.

6. After four rotations, stop and have each group talk about the activity. Students discuss the roles in the order listed on the Participant worksheet.

(The class can gather as a whole to review the discussion questions.)

Suggested Topics for Discussion:

1. How we can cooperate to welcome and work with the new (non-English speaking or other student from a culturally/linguistically different group) in our class.

2. How we can work together to make life easier and more satisfying for the secretaries in our school.

3. What we can do about the trash thrown in the public park near the school?

4. Other appropriate topics chosen by the teacher.

Monitoring and Processing:

1. During the discussion, observe to see that whomever is sitting in a certain chair is playing that role in terms of contribution to the discussion and behavior.

2. Every three minutes call out "Clockwise" and each student moves one chair over, taking on a new role.

3. After students have completed (approximately) four rotations, stop and have the group talk about the activity.

4. Have students discuss some of the following questions and have the observer in each group fill out the Observer worksheet.

Questions:

1. Which roles did you like playing? Why?

2. Which roles did you not like playing? Why not?

3. What role is typical for you? How helpful, or not helpful, is that role to you? To others?

4. Were there any roles that surprised you in terms of how helpful or harmful they were to the group decision-making? To people's feelings? Explain.

5. Which roles does this class need more of in order to do cooperative discussion and tasks successfully? How could we get people to play those more often?

6. Which roles does this class need fewer of? How could we work together to get rid of some of those roles?

Source: Schneidewind, N., & Davidson, E. (1987). *Cooperative learning: Cooperative lives. A source book of learning activities for building a peaceful world.* Dubuque, IA: William C. Brown. Reprinted with limited permission.

Roles To Make Or Break A Group Worksheet

OBSERVER

Role	Classmate in Role	Description
Idea-Giver		
Peacekeeper		
Encourager		
Clarifier		
Distractor		
Silent One		
Teaser		
Dominator		

Roles to Make or Break a Group Worksheet

PARTICIPANT

When I played the _____ role, I said or did _____

_____

_____

I felt _____ about

myself and _____ about other group members.

When I played the _____ role, I said or did _____

_____

_____

I felt _____ about

myself and _____ about other group members.

When I played the _____ role, I said or did _____

_____

_____

I felt _____ about

myself and _____ about other group members.

Usually in a group I play the _____ role. I feel _____ about

that. Another role I would like to play is _____ because _____

_____ . A role I don't want to play is _____ ,

_____

_____

_____

ACTIVITY

Subject Area: Language Arts "Put-Downs Don't Really Make it Better"

Grade Level: Elementary

Objectives:
- Students will increase their awareness of why put-downs happen; why we and others use them.
- Students will identify realistic alternatives to put-downs.
- Students will work cooperatively to create a product which can be shared with others.

Teacher Decisions:
- *Group size*: 4-5
- *Group assignment*: Heterogeneous
- *Student roles*: Teacher judgment
- *Room arrangement*: Teacher judgment

Materials:
- One Situation Card for each group
- Alternatives worksheet for each group

Lesson Format: Part A

1. Read a Situation Card to the entire class.
2. Divide the blackboard into three columns: "Turning my bad feelings in on myself," "Turning my bad feelings out on others," and "Changing the situation to get rid of my bad feelings."
3. Have students brainstorm on possible ways to deal with the situation you just read. List those ideas in the correct columns. If a column is blank, try to get suggestions for it.
4. When there are few ideas in each column, discuss the pros and cons of each for each student involved in the situation.

Questions for Discussion:

1. What is a put-down?
2. What do put-downs do for the person making the put-down? What does the person making the put-down want it to do for her?
3. What do put-downs do for the person being put down?
4. Why do people put other people down?
5. Instead of putting someone else down, what happens if you put yourself down? If you do that inside your head? If you say it aloud?

6. What makes some people put themselves down when they feel bad while other people put others down?

7. When you are in a situation where you are tempted to put yourself down, or put someone else down, what are some alternatives?

8. What do you have to do in a situation in order to end up feeling good? What can you do so other people end up feeling good?

9. How can you change a situation so no one is put down? Why is that hard?

Part B

1. Divide the class heterogeneously into groups of four to five students. Give each group a Situation Card.

2. Students are given ten minutes to plan skits which show the situation dealt with by each of the three methods above.

3. Each group presents the three versions of its skit to the class.

4. Each group discusses and answers the alternatives, but for another group's skit. Assign these to cover each skit.

5. Discuss the Alternatives worksheet for each skit.

6. Each student receives credit for the activity if each person in his group participates in planning and presenting a skit and each person contributes to a signed Alternatives worksheet that is handed in. Each group member signs the Alternatives worksheet to show agreement.

Source: Schniedewind, N., & Davidson, E. (1987). *Cooperative learning: Cooperative lives. A source book for learning activities for building a peaceful world.* Dubuque, IA: William C. Brown. Reprinted with limited permission.

Put-Downs Don't Really Make it Better Worksheet

SITUATION CARDS

1. Evan is finishing his history report. He looks over at Benji's and sees that it is longer than his. He also thinks that it looks better. He then looks at Adam's and sees that it has lots of spelling mistakes and is very messy.

2. Jason is playing ball with Joey and Danny. He looks up and sees Jamal walking along the top of the playing field fence. Jamal never even wavers. Jason goes to try and can't even boost himself up onto the fence.

3. Jeffrey works for two hours on a cover for the class calendar. He erases a lot and smudges his picture. The teacher says he would like to use the picture if Jeffrey will copy it over. Jeff refuses, and in fifteen minutes, Belle draws one which is used.

4. Arjuna comes in with a new coathook that he can't put up himself. He goes over to Dexter, who is finishing his math homework, and asks if he'll put it up. Dexter says, "No." Then he goes to Elaine, who is talking with a new student. She says, "No." Then he goes over to Rebecca, who is drawing.

5. Rachel is typing a story into the computer. Every time she tries to load her disk, the computer says, "Atari: Memo Pad." After the fourteenth try she knocks the disk onto the floor. Next to her the whole time are three students playing PacMan on another computer.

Put-Downs Don't Really Make it Better Worksheet

ALTERNATIVES

1. List the characters in the situation. _____

   _____

2. Which character was feeling bad about himself or herself? Why? _____

   _____

3. In the version where that character turned those feelings inward, what did he or she
   do? _____

   _____

4. How did the character feel afterward? _____

   _____

5. How did the others react? _____

   _____

6. How did they feel? _____

   _____

7. In the version where the character turned those bad feelings out on others, what did
   he or she do? _____

   _____

8. How did that person feel afterward? _____

   _____

9. How did the others react? _____

   _____

10. How did they feel? _____

    _____

11. In the version where the character tried to change the situation, what did she or he
    do? _____

    _____

12. How did that person feel? _____

    _____

13. How did the others react? _____

    _____

ACTIVITY

Subject Area: Language Arts "Controversy is Constructive"

Grade Level: Elementary

Objectives:
- Students will learn the positive value of controversy.
- Students will work creatively with controversy in a group.

Teacher Decision:
- *Group size*: 5
- *Group assignment:* Heterogeneous groups
- *Student roles:* Teacher judgment
- *Room arrangement:* Teacher judgment

Materials:
- None

Lesson Format:

1. Take ten minutes to define and talk about controversy with the whole class. Explain that controversy is a conflict of ideas. In group work, controversy is inevitable and positive! When people have different ideas, it's important to listen carefully to each other's ideas. You may criticize other student's ideas without criticizing them as people. For example, you might strongly disagree with some of your friends about how to spend the group's limited money letting people know more about pollution in the local community. Even though you might disagree regarding the use of the money, you still like the people in your group.

2. Ask students to think about this situation. As a class, brainstorm all the ways of solving this problem.

3. Ask students to write down what they think is the best way to solve this conflict.

4. Divide students into heterogeneous groups of five. Tell them that, as a group, they are to decide which two ways of solving the problem the group feels would be most effective. First, each student is to state his No. 1 choice, with the reason why. After all people in the group have had a chance to talk, the group then tries to reach a decision as to which are the two best solutions. Allow about ten minutes.

5. Return to the whole class and report decisions.
   - What solutions did each group choose and why?
   - What are some strengths and weaknesses of the different solutions?
   - How can we use some of these ideas when we have conflicts in our class?

**Monitoring and
Processing:**

1. How many different solutions did your group have? Was there controversy—a conflict of ideas?

2. Did you listen carefully to each person and her reason before you began debating? If not, why?

3. How convincing were other people's reasons for their choices? Did these reasons convince you to change your mind?

4. How did the group finally resolve the conflict of ideas?

5. Are you pleased with the result? If so, why? If not, why? Conclude by reminding the students that they will often have differences of opinion with others. They will often disagree on ideas. Write on the board or on oak-tag:

Controversy is Positive and Healthy

_____, even though I disagree with you about
     (name)

_____, I accept you as a person.
      (idea)

Conclude by having each student say this to anyone in his group with whom he disagreed.

Source: Schneidewind, N., & Davidson, E. (1987). _Cooperative learning: Cooperative lives. A source book for learning activities for building a peaceful world_. Dubuque, IA: William C. Brown. Reprinted with limited permission.

ACTIVITY

Subject Area: Language Arts "Coming to Consensus"

Grade Level: Elementary

Objectives:
- Students will acquire the skill of coming to a consensus.
- Students will have the opportunity to make real-life decisions as a group by consensus.

Teacher Decisions:
- *Group size:* Variable
- *Group assignment:* Teacher judgment
- *Room arrangement:* Teacher judgment

Materials:
- Copies of Consensus Guidelines worksheet
- Chart paper
- Markers
- Paper and envelopes
- Stamps
- Use of telephone
- Telephone books

Lesson Format:
1. Explain to students the field-trip policy of your school district. This may include a specific number of trips per year, cost of trips, use of transportation, and so forth. Tell them that they, instead of you, will decide on the trip or trips. List district-mandated conditions on chart paper and post in front of the room. Add any nonnegotiable conditions.
2. Review brainstorming. Then brainstorm on guidelines that should be used for the group to decide on field trips. Be sure to include reasons for field trips, money, distance conditions, and so forth. After class brainstorms, correct any factual errors.
3. Then, the class brainstorms on possible places for this year's trip. After you have a reasonably long list, open it up for discussion. Students should give pros and cons of all the ideas. They ask each other questions regarding the suggestions which some know more about than others.
4. Pass out Consensus Guidelines worksheet. Read with the class. Explain any confusing points. Explain that, in this case, there is no reason to reach an immediate decision. Consensus is often a slow process, not good for emergencies, but useful when it is important for everyone to be satisfied.

5. The class continues discussion on field trip possibilities with the idea of reaching a consensus. At this stage, they should come up with a list of all possibilities which might be realistic—all ideas that some people strongly like and that no one strongly hates. It is appropriate to have between three and seven ideas.

6. Divide the class into as many groups as there are possible trip ideas. Avoid large groups by having two groups work on one place, if necessary. Each group researches a different possibility. This research can include making phone calls to places, writing letters, getting written materials, inquiring on costs and transportation, figuring out relevance to curriculum, speaking with classes who have been to the places before, and so forth.

7. After the groups have had enough time to complete their research (probably several weeks later), hold another class discussion. Each group presents its information, not pushing its ideas, but providing all the necessary facts. Then open discussion to the whole class on all the possibilities. Review consensus guidelines. Make a chart for each possible place, listing pros and cons of each idea. Work toward a consensus.

Questions for Discussion:

1. Were you able to reach consensus? What helped or hurt your reaching a consensus? In what ways did you like using consensus? In what ways did you like using consensus, rather than a vote, to try to reach this decision? In what ways did you dislike it?

2. In what ways will a field trip be more successful if the decision is reached by consensus? In what ways might it be less successful?

3. What satisfied you about working toward consensus rather than voting? What frustrated you?

4. How attached to (or turned off to) the idea that you researched did you get? Why? How strong were your feelings about that idea compared to your feelings about the other ones?

5. The larger a group, the harder it often is to reach consensus. What small groups are you in at school, or outside school, in which consensus might be used to reach a decision?

Example: Field Trip Guidelines:

1. Must be related to something we're studying

2. Can't be more than one hour away

3. Can't cost more than $2 each for admission and transportation

4. Can't have furry animals since Tony and Belle are allergic

Coming to Consensus Worksheet

CONSENSUS GUIDELINES

Consensus is a way of working together as a group to reach a decision with which everyone is comfortable. It is informal discussion involving talking things through, understanding what other people are saying and feeling, and trying to work out decisions that are acceptable to everyone. Everyone must be part of the decision and satisfied with it. When a decision is reached, the group shapes it and puts it into words which everyone understands. Here are some helpful attitudes in consensus:

Unity:	trying to come up with things the whole group can accept.
Cooperation:	understanding that the needs, feelings, and ideas of everyone are important.
Openness:	checking our own beliefs and changing them if new ideas make us feel differently.
Diversity:	bringing out disagreement and seeing value and truth in what everyone says.
Creativity:	coming up with new ideas.
Patience:	working until we find something acceptable to everyone.
Respect:	recognizing that everyone has rights, whether they agree with us or not.

Source: Schneidewind, N., & Davidson, E. (1987). *Cooperative learning: Cooperative lives. A source book for learning activities for building a peaceful world*. Dubuque, IA: William C. Brown. Reprinted with limited permission.

❖ Activities for Academic Skills

Multicultural education must be integrated in all areas of the curriculum if it is to be truly effective. It is particularly important to integrate the areas of mathematics, science, and technology, which are less likely to receive the addition of ethnic holidays, heroes, and cultural contributions so often added to the social studies curriculum. Addison-Wesley has recently published a set of readings and activities, *Multiculturalism in Mathematics, Science and Technology: Readings and Activities* (1993). This material provides useful examples of the integration of multicultural education in these areas.

The following lesson plans can serve as examples of curriculum in the various content areas in which multicultural education has been integrated. It is hoped that teachers can use these examples to plan many additional lessons.

ACTIVITY

Subject Area:	English
Poetry Lesson:	Children's poem by Langston Hughes
Background:	▪ Langston Hughes, African-American poet, playwright, and novelist, is one of the most outstanding American writers of the 20th century. He was born in Joplin, Missouri, in 1902 and was educated at Lincoln University in Pennsylvania and Columbia University in New York.
	▪ Langston Hughes traveled widely to such countries as Mexico, Africa, Europe, China, Japan, Spain, and Russia.
	▪ He was an important leader in the Harlem Renaissance of the 1920s and wrote many poems about Harlem. He has given us many wonderful poems. Some of the best known are "I, Too" and "What happens to a dream deferred?" Langston Hughes died in 1967.
Grade Level:	Elementary
Objectives:	▪ Students will read and interpret a poem.
	▪ Students will answer four questions about the poem.
	▪ Students will experience the group process.
Teacher Decisions:	▪ *Group size:* 4
	▪ *Group assignment:* Heterogenous groups
	▪ *Student roles:* Observer; recorder
	▪ *Room arrangement:* Teacher judgment
Materials:	▪ A copy of the poem, and discussion questions for each student
	▪ Suggested poems: Dreams; Grandpa's stories; The Blues
Lesson Format:	Students are to work together to answer the four questions on the poem. They will turn in only one set of answers on which they must all agree. They are to sign the agreement form to indicate agreement with an understanding of the group's answers. They should make certain that everyone has had the opportunity to give his or her opinion/contribution.
Questions for Discussion:	1. What is the message of the poem?
	2. What emotions is the poet expressing?

3. What do you think about the message that is given?

4. What are key words in the poem?

Positive Interdependence: Everyone must agree with the answers and one grade will be given. They must help each member to understand the questions and answers.

Individual Accountability: The teacher will randomly call on group members to explain and give the reasons for their answers.

Criteria for Success: Answers will be graded on how well they are explained and supported. Students must work together until they all agree that the reasons are logical and clear.

Monitoring: Teacher circulates among the groups, occasionally asking students to explain answers already agreed upon. Praise, cooperation, and other group skills demonstrated.

Processing: How well did we work together? What can we do to improve the process next time? Were you satisfied with the paper that your group handed in?

Source: Adapted from Johnson, D., Johnson, R., & Holubec, R. (1987). *Structuring cooperative learning: Lesson plans for teachers.* Edina, MN: Interaction Book Co. Adapted with permission.

ACTIVITY

Subject Area: Social Studies "Ancestors Day"

Grade Level: 3–8

Objectives:
▪ Students will learn about and gain respect for their ancestors and culture;
▪ Students will share their research with the class.

Teacher Decisions:
▪ *Group size:* 3
▪ *Group assignment:* Teacher judgment
▪ *Student roles:* Recorder, encourager, others as needed
▪ *Room arrangement:* Teacher judgment

Materials:
▪ None

Lesson Format: In groups, students will:
1. Develop questions to ask and answer.
2. Decide how they will obtain information.
3. Decide how they will share with the class.
4. Decide how they will invite some ancestors "to speak to the class" (great grandparents, great aunts, etc.)

Positive Interdependence: Each group will receive one grade for the report to the class. The report will be given in panel format. Students will help each other practice and prepare for the entire class presentation.

Individual Accountability: Each student will write a separate report on ancestors. In the group, students will listen, review, and offer suggestions for the class presentation.

Time Required: Ongoing project for two to three weeks with time allotted each day or several times weekly according to the teacher's judgment.

Monitoring: Monitor student participation and skills. Intervene to teach or reteach skills when needed. This can also be done as "whole class" instruction.

Processing: Help students evaluate how their group functioned, what they learned from this activity, and what they would like to change next time in order to improve group cooperation.

ACTIVITY

Subject Area:	Social Studies "Indian Children"
Grade Level:	2-3
Objective:	▪ Students will read and comprehend the poem.
Teacher Decisions:	▪ *Group size:* 3
	▪ *Group assignment:* Teacher judgment
	▪ *Student roles:* Recorder, reader, encourager
	▪ *Room arrangement:* Teacher judgment
Materials:	▪ A copy of the poem and questions for each group
Lesson Format:	1. Students will read and discuss the poem, "Indian Children," in their group (after studying Indians in Social Studies).
	2. The reader will read the poem to the group.
	3. The group will discuss the questions and, when they agree on the answers, the recorder will write the group's answers.
Monitoring and Processing:	Monitor student participation and roles. Process with the students how the group functioned, what they would change the next time, and if they have additional questions about American Indian children.
Source:	Male, M., & Anderson, M. (Eds.), (1990). *Fitting in: Cooperative learning in the mainstream classroom*. San Francisco: Majo Press. Adapted with permission.

Indian Children
by Annette Wynne

Where we walk to school each day
Indian children used to play—
All about our native land,
Where the shops and houses stand.

And the trees were very tall,
And there were no streets at all,
Not a church and not a steeple—
Only woods and Indian people.

Only wigwams on the ground,
And at night bears prowling 'round—
What a different place today
Where we live and work and play!

QUESTIONS

1. How was life different for the Indians? _____

   _____

   _____

2. How was the land different when the Indians lived here?_____

   _____

   _____

3. What do you think is the most important line in the poem? (Be able to defend your

   choice.) _____

   _____

   _____

To Group Members: When you sign your name for the answers to these questions, it means that you have participated in the assignment and understand the questions and the answers. You also must agree with the answers and be able to explain them.

ACTIVITY

Subject Area: Science "Chemicals from Nature: Dr. Eloy Rodriguez, expert in isolating chemicals from herbs"

Grade Level: 6-8

Objectives:
- Students will learn about the plants used for their medicinal qualities in some countries and cultures.
- Students will learn about a famous scientist, Dr. Eloy Rodriguez and his work.
- Students will conduct critical thinking.

Teacher Decisions:
- *Group size:* 5
- *Group assignment:* Students number off one to five for each group
- *Student roles:* Reader, checker, recorder
- *Room arrangement:* Teacher judgment

Materials:
- Various herbs: yerba, buena, mint, oregano, cinnamon bark, chamomile (obtained by the teacher)
- Individual copies of Questions for Critical Thinking
- Students could bring various herbs from home to show to the class

Lesson Format:
1. Each group receives one set of materials to read and hand in.
2. Group members choose a reader, who reads the material to the group.
3. Each group member is responsible for the answer to one question, assigned according to her/his number.
4. The group chooses a recorder, who writes the responses on the form to be handed in.
5. The group-chosen checker reads answers to the group and verifies agreement.
6. Everyone must agree on each response and one grade for the group is given.

Monitoring and Processing:
1. Intervene to provide help with reading, spelling, and writing.
2. Observe to see that roles are appropriately performed.

3. Note any questions raised by students for later class discussion.

4. Discuss with students additional roles that were needed.

5. Discuss questions raised during the reading.

6. Discuss how well the groups cooperated and how they could improve the next time they do a similar activity.

Evaluation: Answers are complete and accurate, based upon the material read.

Source: From Addison-Wesley. *Multiculturalism in mathematics, science and technology: Readings and activities*. Copyright 1993 by Addison-Wesley Publishing Company. Reprinted by permission.

Chemicals From Nature

Eloy Rodriguez

Is there "chemistry" between Latin-American herbology, pharmaceutical companies, and chimpanzees? Dr. Eloy Rodriguez, a Mexican-American professor of biology and chemistry, investigates such questions in his laboratory and in the field. Since the 1970s, Dr. Rodriguez and his colleague, Dr. Manuel Aregullin, have researched and isolated chemicals from plants. Often, they first learn of the beneficial properties of plants from various experts ranging from their grandparents to resourceful chimpanzees.

Through his family and community, Dr. Rodriguez recognized the long-established knowledge of herbology in his Latin American heritage. Knowledge of the medicinal qualities of plants in the southwestern United States, the Caribbean, Central America, and South America was first developed by the indigenous people of these areas and then adopted by the Spanish. The use of herbs to cure a variety of illnesses indicates the presence of medically effective chemicals in the plants. Some of these herbs, such as mint, oregano, cinnamon bark, and chamomile, may be familiar to you. Dr. Rodriguez and Dr. Aregullin are experts at isolating the effective chemicals in such herbs.

Although clues usually come from the medicinal-plant knowledge of indigenous people, medicinal plants can also be found by observing the behavior of animals. A recent clue came from the eating habits of wild chimpanzees in Tanzania. An anthropologist observed that chimpanzees showing signs of illness collected and ate special leaves. He sent a sample of these leaves to Dr. Rodriguez. From these leaves, Dr. Rodriguez and his colleagues isolated a rare chemical called thiarubrine-A, and learned that it has strong antibiotic properties. It is interesting to note that this same chemical has been found in a medicinal plant used by native people in Canada.

Once a chemical such as thiarubrine-A has been isolated from a plant, it can serve as a "lead" or model chemical for a pharmaceutical company to synthesize or create artificially. These synthetic chemicals are tested and often developed into medical drugs. Synthetic drugs or medicines from pharmacies are much stronger than chemicals originally found in nature. Dr. Aregullin has observed that nature rarely produces strong toxic chemicals; herbal remedies tend to be more gentle and nontoxic. However, Dr. Rodriguez cautions that any remedy should be from a reliable source and if people who know little about herbal medicines "just go out and pluck, they're going to get themselves into problems."

QUESTIONS FOR CRITICAL THINKING

1. Think about the times when you have had indigestion, a cold, the flu, a sore throat ,or some other minor ailment. Are there any herbal or "family" remedies you commonly use at such times? List them and explain their use.

_____

_____

_____

2. How do you think indigenous people of North and South America first discovered the medicinal qualities of plants?

_____

_____

_____

3. Some people think herbal remedies are better for your body than commercial pharmaceuticals. What are some arguments for and against this point of view?

_____

_____

_____

4. Why do you think Dr. Rodriguez and Dr. Aregullin chose to spend their careers researching the medicinal herbs used by Latinos and other cultures?

_____

_____

_____

5. Dr. Rodriguez warns that people who "just go out and pluck" herbs are going to have problems. What are some problems that could occur if people gathered herbs for medicine without expert advice?

_____

_____

_____

ACTIVITY

Subject Area: Science "What Makes Different Skin Colors?"

Grade Level: Elementary–Jr. High

Objectives:
- Students will understand that there is a scientific reason for different skin colors.
- Students will be able to explain the role of melanin in skin color.
- Students will be able to identify four other pigments in the skin.

Teacher Decisions:
- *Group size*: 4
- *Group assignment*: Teacher judgment
- *Student roles*: Reader, checker, recorder (if needed)
- *Room arrangement*: Teacher judgment
- *Time required*: Several class periods

Materials:
- *The Color of Man* by Robert Cohen—This book contains a picture of a magnified skin cell with melanin particles
- Microscope and stained slides of skin cells, if available
- Films, videotapes

LessonFormat/ Learning Activities:
- In groups of four, students will research the answers to the questions below and additional questions that they raise.
  1. How do some people practice discrimination based on skin color?
  2. How is skin color passed on to children?
  3. What happens when parents are of two different races?
- If the teacher has microscope and slide available, students can be shown the cells.

Positive Interdependence: Each group is responsible for answers to all questions. One grade will be given to each group. A written report/answers will be turned in by a student from each group.

Individual Accountability: Each member of the group is responsible for the answer to one question. The group must agree on each answer after discussing and evaluating it.

Criteria for Success:
- All questions must be answered and written.
- One complete paper is due from each group.

Monitoring: Check for group functioning, individual participation.

Processing: Discuss with students: What else would we like to know? Who might help us to find out? How did our group work together? What could we do better next time?

ACTIVITY

Subject Area:	Social Studies "Who Is This Famous Person?"
Grade Level:	7-8

Objectives:
- Students will be able to match famous names in American history with their accomplishments.
- Students will appreciate the contributions of persons from diverse cultural groups.

Teacher Decisions:
- *Group size:* 3-4
- *Group assignment:* Random; students will line up and count off 1 to 3. Each number will receive one or two biographical sketches. Each group will consist of students numbered 1 to 3. Groups must be heterogeneous, balanced.
- *Student roles:* Teacher judgment
- *Room arrangement:* Teacher judgment
- *Time required:* Several class periods

Materials:
- Biographical sketches prepared by teacher: A single page on a famous American Indian, Puerto Rican, Japanese-American, Chinese-American, and African-American

Lesson Format: Students will work in groups of three or four to learn basic facts about accomplishments of famous people in U.S. history. This activity will help students learn about and appreciate their accomplishments and prepare for a test.

Positive Interdependence: Each student is responsible for learning all of the information. Numbers one, two, and three must share their information by reading to the group, assuring that everyone understands, and summarizing the most important facts.

Individual Accountability: Individual grades will be given on a test. Grades will be averaged to obtain a final group grade.

Criteria for Success: Each group must receive a total of 90%.

Expected Student Behavior: Students will share information sheets, ask questions, help each other to understand the information, and summarize important facts to be retained.

Monitoring: Observe students to see that everyone is working together, roles are performed, praise is given for cooperation and helping, and to see if intervention is needed. Monitor noise level.

Processing: Ask students if they cooperated. How could they improve cooperation? Learning the information? Helping all to understand? What are their perspectives on the events and accomplishments described?

Evaluation: Matching test prepared by teacher.

Source: Adapted from Male, M., & Anderson, M. (Eds.). (1990). *Fitting in: Cooperative learning in the mainstream classroom*. San Francisco: Majo Press. Adapted with permission.

ACTIVITY

Subject Area: Language Arts and Social Studies

Title: What are the causes of interracial and intergroup conflict? What can individuals do to promote better understanding among people?

Grade Level: 6-8

Objectives:
- Students will learn research and interviewing skills.
- Students will learn/understand some of the causes of intergroup conflict.
- Students will learn some of the ways to contribute to better understanding among people in their school and community.

Teacher Decisions:
- *Group size:* 3-5
- *Group assignment:* Heterogeneous, reflecting class composition
- *Student roles:* Teacher judgment
- *Room assignment:* Teacher judgment
- *Time required:* 3-4 days

Materials:
- Newspaper articles and school and community examples of conflict collected by teacher and students
- Interview questions for each student (see lesson format)

Lesson Format:
1. The class will read and discuss the newspaper and other examples of intergroup conflicts.
2. The teacher will present to the class the general guidelines for interviewing.
3. Each group will brainstorm three to four interview questions on (1) the cause of interracial and intergroup conflict, and (2) what can individuals do to promote better understanding among people. Each group will agree on the three best questions. One member will hand in the group decisions.
4. The teacher will list all questions and the whole class will discuss them and vote on the four best questions to use in the interview. Each student will have a copy of the questions.
5. Students will practice asking each other the questions.
6. Each group member will interview five people including family members, neighbors, students, and teachers (two days).

7. Results will be recorded by each student on the interview form.

8. Groups will discuss and compile the results. One student will be selected to report the results to the class.

9. Each group will select one member to record the suggestions on what individuals can do to promote better understanding among people.

10. All suggestions will be combined, printed, and distributed throughout the school.

Monitoring: Monitor group functioning to see that all students are participating. Intervene to assist with vocabulary or other skills.

Processing: Discuss how the groups function and what they could do to improve. Ask what they learned about interviews and what they would like to learn.

Evaluation:

▋ Interviews were conducted successfully according to guidelines and questions.

▋ Some causes of interracial and intergroup conflict in the school and community have been identified.

▋ Ways to promote understanding among groups have been identified.

▋ Written expression of interview results has been legibly and correctly completed.

ACTIVITY

Subject Area: Social Studies "Sexual Harassment (Case of Supreme Court Justice Clarence Thomas)"

Grade level: 6-8

Objectives:
- Students will understand the role of Congress in the confirmation process of presidential appointments.
- Students will understand the term sexual harassment.
- Students will debate the two sides of the confirmation hearing.
- Students will prepare an essay on how they would have voted and why and provide defense of the position.
- Students will learn the definition of sexual harassment and identify examples of the different age levels and situations.

Teacher Decisions:
- *Group size:* Teacher judgment—at least one male and one female
- *Group assignment:* Teacher judgment
- *Student roles:* Teacher judgment
- *Time required:* 2 days

Materials: Preliminary information presented to the entire class by the teacher:
- Summary of the appointment-confirmation process
- Summary of the Thomas hearing
- Definition and appropriate examples of sexual harassment
- Prepared questions for each student to ask

Lesson Format:
1. Students will work in pairs—answering questions and defending position.
2. Students will be organized into two debate teams—pro and con.
3. Students will role-play the hearing (if possible).
4. Students will prepare an essay.

Monitoring: Monitor students' participation and need for assistance.

Processing: Process the activity with students—what they learned, how their group functioned, and the ease with which they could express their position. Have them identify additional terms and concepts that they would like to learn about in the future.

Evaluation: Each pair will hand in an essay for a grade. Evaluate the quantity and quality of student learning in academic and social areas.

ACTIVITY

Subject Area: Music and Social Studies

Grade levels: 7-8

Objectives:
- Students will analyze words of the song, "My Country Tis of Thy People You're Dying"
- Students will identify emotions expressed in the song.
- Students will identify historical events in the song.

Teacher Decisions:
- *Group size:* 2-3
- *Group assignment:* Random
- *Student roles:* Recorder, checker, additional roles as needed
- *Room arrangement:* Teacher judgment

Materials:
- Copy of recording by Buffy St. Marie of the song, "My Country Tis of Thy People You're Dying"
- Copies of the words to hand out to each student

Lesson Format: Each student will identify historical events in the song and the emotions expressed. Students will also identify the event or part of the song that they found most powerful or upsetting and explain why. Each individual member will be responsible for one stanza of the song. The group will discuss, clarify, and prepare its analysis to present to the class.

Monitoring and Processing: Monitor student behavior and need for assistance. Process group functioning with the students.

Evaluation: One grade for each group. Evaluate quantity and quality of student learning.

Source: Adapted from Filor, A. M. (1992). *Multiculturalism*. New York: New York State Council of Educational Associations.

ACTIVITY

Subject Area: Language Arts and English

Grade Levels: 7-8

Objectives:
▪ Students will read a passage from *Bury My Heart at Wounded Knee.*
▪ Students will identify literal, interpretive, and applied meaning of the author's statements.

Teacher Decisions:
▪ *Group size:* 3-5
▪ *Group assignment:* Random
▪ *Student roles:* Recorder
▪ *Room arrangement:* Teacher judgment

Materials:
▪ Copies of the passage for each student
▪ Copies of the checklists for each student

Lesson Format:
1. Each student will read and check her/his reactions to the statements.
2. Each group must reach consensus on the answers. The recorder completes column marked "Group" on the checklist.
3. The entire class will discuss the reading and choose an appropriate title for the passage.

Monitoring and Processing: Monitor group function and need for assistance. Discuss additional questions raised by students. Discuss how well the groups functioned.

Evaluation: Teacher judgment

Source: Adapted from Filor, A. M. (1992). *Multiculturalism*. New York: New York State Council of Educational Associations.

Helinmot Tooyalaket (Chief Joseph) of the Nez Perces

The earth was created by the assistance of the sun, and it should be left as it was . . . The country was made without lines of demarcation, and it is no man's business to divide it . . . I see the whites all over the country gaining wealth, and see their desire to give us lands which are worthless . . . The earth and myself are of one mind. The measure of the land and the measure of our bodies are the same. Say to us if you can say it, that you were sent by the Creative Power to talk to us. Perhaps you think the Creator sent you here to dispose of us as you see fit. If I thought you were sent by the Creator I might be induced to think you had a right to dispose of me. Do not misunderstand me, but understand me fully with reference to my affection for the land. I never said the land was mine to do with it as I chose. The one who has the right to dispose of it is the one who has created it. I claim a right to live on my land, and accord you the privilege to live on yours. (p. 300)

Brown, D. (1970). *Bury My Heart At Wounded Knee*. New York: Bantam Books.

Based on the statements by Chief Joseph, place a check mark beside the statement(s) with which you agree in the column marked *you*. The recorder in your group can place a check mark beside the statement(s) with which the *group* agreed.

LEVEL I: LITERAL MEANING What did the author say?

You		Group
_____	It is no man's business to divide up the land	_____
_____	White men were sent by the Creator to exterminate Indians.	_____
_____	Whites wanted to give Indians worthless land	_____
_____	Indians love Mother Earth.	_____

LEVEL II: INTERPRETIVE MEANING What did the author mean?

You		Group
_____	Indians live in harmony with nature and do not try to control it.	_____
_____	Chief Joseph hated white people.	_____
_____	Chief Joseph did not believe in private ownership of real estate.	

_____   Chief Joseph was a Christian.   _____

_____   Indians had more right to the land than whites. _____

_____   Indians hate white people.   _____

LEVEL III: APPLIED MEANING What principle applies?

You   **Group**

_____   The Lord giveth and the Lord taketh away.   _____

_____   Human dignity is not bounded by culture.   _____

_____   Live and let live.   _____

CIRCLE ONE OF THE FOLLOWING AS AN APPROPRIATE TITLE FOR THIS ARTICLE:

Cultural Clash

Dignity

Hostility

Arrogance

Other: _____

ACTIVITY

Subject Area: Music "Ethnic Music"

Grade Level: 4–8

Objectives:
- Students will enjoy a variety of music from different ethnic/cultural groups.
- Students will acquire basic information on various ethnicities.
- Students will acquire vocabulary related to music, musicians, and their countries of origin.

Teacher Decisions:
- *Group size:* 2 for research activity; 4 for teams
- *Group assignment:* Teacher judgment
- *Student roles:* Reader, recorder, reporter for teams, additional roles as needed
- *Room arrangement:* Teacher judgment
- *Time required:* 2-3 days

Materials:
- Recordings of such songs as "Volga Boatman," "O Solo Mio," "Sometimes I Feel Like a Motherless Child," "La Cucharacha," Reggae, Israeli music—ten-twenty selections (chosen by teacher)
- Lists of ethnic groups to be studied, e.g., Sioux, Jamaican, Vietnamese, etc. (chosen by teacher)

Lesson Format:

Part I	Pairs will research ethnic groups and give reports.
Part II	Teams will be formed to guess "mystery musical selections." (Guess the cultural group).
Part III	Several musicians from the community will be invited to speak to the class.
Part IV	A program could be planned to which parents and other classes are invited.

Monitoring and Processing: Monitor student participation and behavior. Intervene to provide task assistance.

Evaluation:
- The team with the highest score wins chocolate kisses—one point for each selection correctly guessed. (Part 2)
- Group grades for reports.
- Quiz on vocabulary terms.

Source: Adapted from Filor, A. M. (1992). *Multiculturalism*. New York: New York State Council of Educational Associations.

ACTIVITY

Subject Area: Language Arts "Ethnic Origin of Words"

Grade Level: 6-8

Objectives:
- Students will understand that words we use come from different languages of the world.
- Students will teach two words to a group.
- Students will learn new words of diverse ethnic origin.

Teacher Decisions:
- Group size: 4
- Group assignment: Count off one to four; each number receives two words.

Materials:
- Lists of words of Spanish, Indian, French, African origin—places, structures, and objects for example

Lesson Format: Teacher distributes words. Each group will research the origin of eight words.

Postivie Interdependence:
- Each student teaches her two words to the group, completes the research, and shares results with group.
- Every member must know origin and meaning of eight words.

Individual Accountability: Each student is responsible for two words of the eight.

Monitoring: Monitor student participation and behavior. Intervene to give assistance when needed.

Processing: Process group functioning with the students.

Evaluation: Each student will take a quiz on the word origins and meaning of the words. Individual scores will be added to form group scores. Only group scores will be given. Record any additional words that students suggest for future learning.

Source: Adapted from Filor, A. M. (1992). *Multiculturalism*. New York: New York State Council of Educational Associations.

ACTIVITY

Subject Area:	Language Arts "Illustration of a Story"
Grade Level:	3-4

Objectives:
- Students will illustrate interpretation of the story and its characters.
- Students will show creative thinking.

Teacher Decisions:
- *Group size:* 3
- *Group assignment:* Random—counting off
- *Room arrangement:* Teacher judgment

Materials: One of the following stories:
- Kraus, J. (1992). *Tall boy's journey*
- Thomas, J. C. (Ed.). (1990). *A gathering of flowers: Stories about being young in America*
- Wilken (1989). *Rosie the cool cat*
- Birdseye (1988). *Airmail to the moon*

Lesson Format:
1. Teacher reads the story to the entire class.
2. Discuss the story with the class.
3. Explain to students that they will listen to the story and decide in their groups on a picture that they will create about the story.

Positive Interdependence: The group will agree upon and be able to explain one picture. Each group will receive one piece of drawing paper and one box of crayons. Students must agree on what they will draw and who will draw what before the group begins.

Individual Accountability: Each must share ideas and make a contribution to the picture. Each student must take a turn explaining something in the picture to the class.

Criteria for Success: Completed picture by the class.

Expected Behaviors: Everyone will work together—share creation and drawing of the picture.

Monitoring: Listen for agreement and sharing. Intervene to help, if needed.

Processing: How did the group decide on what to draw and who would draw what? How did students share ideas? How could they improve the process next time?

Evaluation: Creativity in pictures and understanding and interpretation of the story. Group functioning. Sensitivity to content and characters in the story.

Source: Adapted from Whitson, N. (1987). Creative thinking. In Johnson, R.T., Johnson, D. W., & Holubec, E. D. (Eds.), *Structuring cooperative learning: Lesson plans for teacher*. Edina, MN: Interaction Book Co.

ACTIVITY

Subject Area:	Language Arts, Art, and History "Commemorative Postage Stamps"
Grade Level:	3-8
Objectives:	▍ Students will research a famous Asian-American, African-American, Native American, Latino-American or other ethnic American.
	▍ Students will learn about commemorative postage stamps—how they are selected, who is the artist, or how artists are selected to create the stamps.
	▍ Students will create a commemorative stamp for the famous person they have researched.
Teacher Decisions:	▍ *Group size:* Pairs
	▍ *Group assignment:* Students pair according to interests
	▍ *Student roles:* Teacher judgment
	▍ *Room arrangement:* Teacher judgment
	▍ *Time required:* 2-4 days
Materials:	▍ Teacher and students will bring any commemorative stamps they own to the class to show.
	▍ Students will need a variety of resource materials designated in the school library or in the classroom library, if possible. They may also obtain suggestions from families, neighbors and friends.
	▍ Students will visit the local Post Office to see and hear about collecting commemorative stamps.
Lesson Format:	Each pair will research a famous person from one of the groups above and compose an essay on the person. Both members must agree on the accuracy and quality of the essay. After the essay is completed, they will plan and produce a commemorative stamp.
Monitoring and Processing:	Monitor noise level, student sharing and behavior. Intervene to provide assistance for spelling and other needs. Process group functioning with the students.
Evaluation:	Evaluate quantity and quality of student learning. Evaluate essays for factual information included and depth.
Source:	Adapted from Filor, A. M. (1992). *Multiculturalism*. New York: New York State Council of Educational Associations..

ACTIVITY

Subject Area: Language Arts "Book Report"

Grade Level: Elementary

Objectives:
- Each group will read a book, write and present a book report to the class. Books can be chosen from the following list:
  1. *Many lands, many stories: Asian folktales for children.* Retold by David Conger. Tuttle Publishers, 1987.
  2. *Back in the beforetime: Tales of the California Indians.* Edited by Jane L. Curry. McElderry Publishers, 1987.
  3. *The Cowtail Switch and other West African stories.* By Harold Courlander and George Herzog. Henry Holt, 1987.

Teacher Decisions:
- *Group size:* 4, randomly assigned.
- *Group assignment:* Groups will complete two book reports
- *Student roles:* Reading manager, presentation manager, checker-encourager, writer
- *Time required:* Approximately 5 class periods (45 minutes each)
- *Room arrangement:* Desks should allow students to face each other so that they can read and discuss quietly

Materials:
- Book for each group member
- One book report form for each group

Lesson Format: *Task*—Each group is told to read a book and then write and present the book report to the class. Groups read together during the reading time given in the classroom and fifteen minutes three times weekly for homework.

The reading manager: Sets the pace of the group, monitors the progress, assures that everyone completes the assignment together.

Positive Interdependence: Each member reads the book so that each can contribute to the written report.

Evaluation is Based On:
- 50% equal contributions of all members
- 25% written report
- 25% class preparation

Individual Accountability:	▌ Each student receives an individual grade based on teacher's observation and opinion of checker/encourager. ▌ Each group that receives 80% or more gets a free period on Friday.
Monitoring:	Teacher monitors participation and cooperation throughout the assignment.
Processing:	How did the group work together? What worked best to complete the task? How could the process be improved next time? How could the assignment be improved?
Source:	Adapted from Lamond, D. (1990). Book reports. In Male, M., & Anderson, M. (Eds.), *Fitting in: Cooperative learning in the mainstream classroom*. San Francisco: Majo Press.

Book Report Form

Title of Book_____

Author_____

Publisher_____ Year _____

1. Who are the main characters and what are their roles?

CHARACTER	ROLE

2. How does the story begin? _____

    _____

3. Is there a conflict or problem developed? Briefly describe it._____

    _____

4. How does the story end?_____

    _____

5. What is the favorite part of each member of the group? _____

    _____

6. What is the reaction to the story of each member of the group? _____

    _____

7. Would the group recommend the book to others? Why? Why not? _____

    _____

ACTIVITY

Subject Area:	Language Arts and Social Studies "Cartoons and Comics: Stereotypes and Caricatures"
Grade Level:	6-8
Objective:	Students will be able to define and identify stereotypes and caricatures in cartoons and comic strips.

Teacher Decisions:
- *Group size:* 2
- *Group assignment:* Teacher judgment
- *Student roles:* Recorder, checker
- *Room arrangement:* Teacher judgment

Materials:
- Cartoons and comic strips on transparencies
- Overhead projector
- Cartoons and comics brought in by students

Lesson Format:

1. Write definitions of stereotype and caricature on the board and show examples in cartoons and comics.

2. Point out examples of positive (without stereotypes) and negative cartoons and comics that show persons from diverse racial and ethnic groups.

3. Discuss with the students where the humor is found in the cartoons and comics. Point out examples where humor exists without the use of stereotypes.

4. Each group will choose a cartoon or comic strip to write about in a paragraph. They will identify any stereotypes or caricatures. These will be presented to the class by a member of each group.

5. Discuss with the students the difference between caricatures and stereotypes.

6. Individual students can be called on to present reasons for the group's conclusion.

Monitoring and Processing: Check for understanding of the terms and intervene to clarify or refer students to written definitions on display (board). Check for additional teaching needed. Process group functioning with the students and their reactions to and application of things learned.

ACTIVITY

Subject Area: Math "Solving Word/Story Problems"

Grade Level: Elementary/Jr. High

Lesson Objectives:
- Students will be able to cooperatively solve word problems. Every student will be able to find correct solutions to word problems.
- Students will appreciate the value of cooperating with others.

Teacher Decisions:
- *Group size:* 4
- *Group assignments:* Have students count off one to four; all ones are in a group, all twos, and so on
- *Student roles:* Assigned randomly and students help each other with the roles.
  - Reader: to read problem aloud to the group
  - Recorder: to write down computations and answers
  - Checker: to check to make sure that all group members understand how to solve each problem
  - Observer: to record actions of each member on an observation sheet; does not contribute to solving problem
- *Room arrangement:* Teacher judgment

Materials:
- One set of word problems for each group taken from real community problems, issues, and activities. If the students attend a neighborhood school, the teacher can easily develop these from his knowledge of and involvement with the community. If the students come from several communities, problems, issues, and events can be contributed/shared by the students.

  Example: Fifty Hmong families from Southeast Asia have recently moved into the community. If each family has four school-aged children, how many new children will come to our schools?

  (Other lessons can involve learning about the country, culture and language of the new families. Prejudice and discrimination can also be discussed with respect to these differences.)

Lesson Format: 1.   Each group receives a set of word problems and one answer sheet that is handed in.

2.   All students in a group will receive the grade for the group.

Monitoring and Processing: Monitor group functioning and students' skills. Note need for instruction in any skills. Process how the groups functioned.

ACTIVITY

Subject Area: Math "A Class Quilt"

Suggested Grade Level: 2-3

Objectives:
- Students will use fractions: halves, and fourths.
- Students will make quilt patterns representing their family or culture.
- Students will solve problems in arranging patterns.
- Students will learn about other families and cultures.

Teacher Decisions:
- *Group size:* 4
- *Group assignment:* Teacher judgment
- *Student roles:* Teacher judgment
- *Room arrangement:* Teacher judgment
- *Time required:* 2-3 days

Materials:
- 4 x 4 squares of paper
- Crayons
- Glue
- Bbutcher paper
- Quilts from home to show the class—brought in by teacher and students
- Solid 4 x 4 squares

Lesson Format:
1. Explain to the students that they will make a class quilt which consists of one-half solid color blocks and one-half "their special design" blocks.
2. Each group will work together to create and assemble two blocks. Each block will consist of two solid squares and two patterned squares. (Groups will be given the solid color squares which were cut out earlier.)
3. Students should be encouraged to ask for help at home in creating a pattern that represents their family or culture.
4. When all members agree on the arrangement they have chosen, they will be ready to bring it to the large butcher paper to glue.
5. Discuss with the class the overall arrangement of a block that consists of four squares—two solid colors and two patterned.

6. Talk about halves and fourths and show the fractions on the board.

7. Have each group complete the question sheet and turn it in.

8. When all groups have completed their blocks, glue all to the butcher paper to make the class quilt.

Monitoring: Monitor the groups for noise level and understanding of one-half and one-fourth. Intervene to teach/reteach.

Processing: Process group functioning with the students.

Source: Adapted from Burk, D., Snider, A., & Symonds, P. (1991). *Project-based math for second grades*. Portsmouth, NH: Heinemann.

ACTIVITY

Subject Area: Math "Measurement: Our Size"

Grade Level: Elementary

Objectives:
- Students will learn to measure.
- Students will use a measurement tool.
- Students will compare their measurements.
- Students will note similarities and differences.

Teachers Decisions:
- *Group size:* 2
- *Group assignment:* Students of different racial/ethnic groups, gender, and abilities
- *Student roles:* Teacher judgment
- *Room arrangement:* Teacher judgment

Materials:
- "Our size" lab sheet
- Measuring tools

Lesson Format:
1. Students will work in pairs to complete the lab sheet.
2. The unit of measurement is left to teacher judgment—inches or centimeters. It is important that students write the unit of measurement with each number.
3. The grade level will determine the measuring device used and the vocabulary. Non-readers will need pictures and oral directions.
4. Students will compare their measurements and report to the class on which measurements are different and which are the same (or similar).

Monitoring: Monitor for special problems—embarrassment (obesity, for example), or physical disabilities, disagreement on measurements. Try to have students settle disagreements.

Processing: Process with the students the group functioning, comparisons, and what they learned.

Source: Davidson, N. (Ed.). (1990). *Cooperation learning in math: A handbook for teachers*. Metro Park, CA: Addison-Wesley. Reprinted by permission.

OUR SIZE

Name _____

Name_____

How tall? _____

How tall? _____

Head size? _____

Head size? _____

Waist size? _____

Waist size? _____

Wrist size? _____

Wrist size? _____

Length of foot? _____

Length of foot? _____

Width of
thumbnail?_____

Width of
thumbnail?_____

ACTIVITY

Subject Area: Language Arts "Show and Tell"

Grade Level: Elementary

Objectives:
- Students will share cultural objects from home or family experiences—something that they feel is special or very important to them.
- Students will learn about other families and cultures.

Teacher Decisions:
- *Group size:* 2
- *Group assignment:* Teacher judgment
- *Student roles:* Teacher judgment
- *Room arrangement:* Class seated in circle; pairs turn to face each other.

Materials:
- None

Lesson Format:
1. The teacher explains that partners will share what they brought and what they have to say about it.—Each will have a turn (about five minutes).
2. Then some boys and girls will tell the class about something that their partner brought or told them. (Teachers will choice) Partners will be asked to agree that the description is accurate.

Monitoring: Monitor noise level. Monitor and reinforce good listening behavior. Give a signal for pairs to switch.

Processing: Process with the students how the activity could be improved next time. Discuss with them the importance and appreciation of a good listener.

Source: Adapted from: Winget, P. (Ed.). (1987). *Integrating the core curriculum through cooperative learning. Lesson plans for teachers.*

It is possible to design many learning activities that integrate multicultural education and cooperative learning. It requires the creative use of students' communities, cultural, and linguistic backgrounds and relevant instructional materials. The following examples are presented as a small sample. It is hoped that each teacher will create many more.

Suggestions for using students' cultural/linguistic backgrounds in the classroom:

Mathematics

1. Frame word problems in community references.
2. Use examples drawn from the community to teach concepts.
3. Teach about mathematicians from diverse cultures.
4. Invite adults from diverse cultures to speak to students about their jobs or careers in mathematics.
5. Use textbooks and other materials that include people and examples from diverse cultural/linguistic groups.

Science

1. Use examples and analogies from local community/environment.
2. Invite adults from diverse cultural/linguistic groups to talk about their careers in science.
3. Build a lesson around a famous scientist such as Dr. Charles Drew, and African-American who was a pioneer in blood plasma research.
4. Have students conduct cooperative research on a community environmental problem.

History/Social Studies

1. Use parallel examples taken from the local communities of students.
2. Use community issues and problems to design a lesson.
3. Invite families of students to participate in relevant discussions, e.g., the Korean War experience, Vietnam, the presidential election, in order to present diverse perspectives.
4. Use artifacts, buildings, statues in the community to illustrate, reinforce concepts, issues, or historical events.
5. Have students trace the history of their community cooperatively:
   – Use the library.
   – Interview community members, organizations.
   – Tour the community with students and take photographs.
   – Visit community sites, if possible.

English/Language Arts

1. Use the language of your students in instruction.

2. Teach the literature of diverse groups and compare perspectives when possible.

3. Use storytelling from various cultures—have students bring stories to school.

4. Invite community members for storytelling.

5. Assign students to interview community issues, problems, needs, or activities.

6. Assign writing projects about community issues, problems, needs, or activities.

7. Invite members of diverse cultural/linguistic groups to speak about jobs in the media—journalists, screenwriters, television reporters.

❖ Summary

Cooperative learning activities can be designed for every area of the curriculum. Activities are also available to help the teacher build team and class cohesion. It is also possible to teach the skills needed by students to function in small groups. Such important cooperative skills as how to reach consensus, see things from different perspectives, avoid put-downs, and solve problems can be taught to students through appropriate activities. These are skills that can be used throughout life in a diverse society where cooperation and collaboration are always in demand.

Through following a series of planning steps for lessons, the teacher can use cooperative learning to teach respect for each individual's strengths and contributions. Respect for and appreciation of diversity can be learned. Teachers are encouraged to become familiar with a wide variety of resources, including the community, which can aid them in planning learning activities that accomplish the goals and objectives of multicultural education.

❖ CHAPTER 7 Questions

1. Develop three cooperative learning activities in arithmetic for children in second grade.
2. What are the benefits of heterogeneous groups in a classroom of diverse cultural and linguistic groups of students.
3. Briefly describe some general monitoring activities for the teacher.

4. Obtain a traditional lesson plan of your own or from another teacher and change it to a cooperative learning activity.

5. What are some of the social skills that you would evaluate at the end of a cooperative learning activity?

❖ References

Brown, D. (1970). *Bury my heart at wounded knee.* New York: Bantam Books.

Burk, D., Snider, A., & Symonds, P. (1991). *Math excursions 2: Project-based math for second grades.* Portsmouth, NH: Heinemann.

Davidson, N. (1990). *Cooperative learning in math: A handbook for teachers.* Menlo Park, CA: Addison-Wesley.

Dishon, S., & O'leary, P. W. (1984). *A guidebook for cooperative learning: A technique for creating more effective schools.* Holmes Beach, FL: Learning Publications, Inc.

Filor, A. M. (1992). *Multiculturalism.* New York: New York State Council of Educational Associations.

Johnson, D., Johnson, R., & Holubec, R. (1987). *Structuring cooperative learning: Lesson plans for teachers.* Edina, MN: Interaction Book Co.

Kagan, S. (1989). *Cooperative learning resources for teachers.* San Juan Capistrano, CA: Resources for Teachers.

Mack, T. (1993). *Acquiring a multicultural perspective through the use of collaborative pairs.* Paper presented at the annual meeting of the College English Association, Charlotte, NC.

Male, M., & Anderson, M. (Eds.). (1990). *Fitting in: Cooperative learning in the mainstream classroom.* San Francisco: Majo Press.

Multiculturalism in mathematics, science, and technology: Readings and activities. (1993). Menlo Park, CA: Addison-Wesley.

Schniedewind, N., & Davidson, E. (1987). *Cooperative learning: Cooperative lives. A source book of learning activities for building a peaceful world.* Dubuque, IA: William C. Brown.

Winget, P. (Ed.). (1987). *Integrating the core curriculum through cooperative learning: Lesson plans for teachers.* Sacramento, CA: State Department of Education, Special Education Division.

CHAPTER 8

Multicultural Materials and the Whole Language Approach

Like cooperative learning, the *Whole Language movement* and its many variants offer special opportunities for both teaching culturally diverse children and incorporating instruction about diverse cultures for all children. While cooperative learning allows children of different backgrounds to interact and to learn from each other, the Whole Language movement gives teachers the chance to incorporate a wide variety of print and nonprint materials into the curriculum. Teachers have gone beyond basal readers and textbooks, with their many limitations in the presentation of cultural information, and brought in trade books, videos, and computer programs. In its stress upon writing as a key component of reading instruction, whole language has allowed children of all cultures to generate their own knowledge and to "publish" it for their peers. (Occasionally, such books have been published for the wider market as well.) Finally, the emphasis of the Whole Language movement upon "reading and writing across the curriculum" has led to a more interdisciplinary approach in social studies and the sciences, with trade nonfiction and historical fiction being used to teach about world cultures and the problems they face today.

Despite this progress, the Whole Language movement remains vaguely defined, and the existence of a whole language curriculum is no guarantee of multicultural content or culturally-sensitive instruction. In most classrooms, teachers are modifying whole language principles to suit their own needs. Though many see whole language as a fad, trade books are making their way into classrooms in increasing numbers, and even publishers of basal readers are picking up on the trend, incorporating more complete stories by noted children's-book authors.

This and Chapters 9 and 10 focus on the intersection between the Whole Language movement and multicultural education. This chapter provides an overview of whole language and related movements as well as criticisms and modifications that have been made in real-world classrooms. This chapter also analyzes the shortcomings of traditional basal readers and textbooks, with respect to their presentation of diverse cultures, and discusses similar issues with respect to trade books and nonprint materials. Finally, this chapter suggests ways in which the teacher can increase his or her cultural awareness and ability to incorporate quality multicultural materials into a pure or modified whole language approach.

Chapter 9 focuses exclusively on the selection of print and nonprint materials about diverse cultures. Overall goals of selection are examined, as well as specific criteria that can be used. These criteria are explored in greater depth, with examples from recently published trade books, videos, and computer programs, so that teachers can become more adept at choosing materials and avoiding (or supplementing) those that contain outdated interpretations or reinforce stereotypes. Chapter 9 also describes the need to take a critical approach when using any work, whether it be a textbook, a "classic" that may not conform to current standards of cultural sensitivity, or a nonprint material.

Chapter 10 offers some strategies for incorporating multicultural content into the curriculum at various levels. The chapter critiques the current approach, which focuses too often upon the most superficial aspects of culture—holidays, food, and crafts—and relies too heavily, especially in the early grades, upon the illustrated folktales that dominate trade publishing. The chapter describes alternative models and programs that are currently being implemented, as well as suggesting ways in which teachers can work together and learn more about successful programs elsewhere in the country.

❖ What is Whole Language?

The term *Whole Language* has been applied to a number of movements with a similar set of elements. Among the other terms associated with whole language are the *New Literacy* (Willinsky, 1990), the *Shared-Book Experience* (Holdaway, 1979), and *Writing Across the Curriculum* (Willinsky, 1990). In its theory and practice, whole language has been somewhat broadly (and vaguely) defined (Barrera, 1992); however, there are some common elements that set it apart from traditional approaches that are based upon textbooks, basal readers, and programmed instruction kits.

The first of these elements is the use of trade books in the classroom as opposed to basal readers, with the purpose of making "language instruction meaningful to children by giving them an active role in the learning process and by integrating the various aspects of language (listening, speaking, reading, and writing) instruction" (Fox, 1992, p. 168). While basal readers and their associated worksheets break down the various elements of reading, such as phonics, vocabulary, and word recognition, trade books approach them as a unified, inseparable whole. Thus, trade books are more capable of attracting the student's interest and communicating the true meaning of the written word (Willinsky, 1990). Kenneth Goodman, one of the principal theorists of the Whole Language movement, has argued that reading cannot be taught as a set of discrete, isolated skills; in separating the process, meaning is lost (Goodman, 1985). Trade books—books that have grown out of the author and illustrator's creative process—can recapture that meaning (Willinsky, 1990). Furthermore, trade books, with their varied styles, approaches, and points of view, are more capable of fostering "active critical thinking" in the content areas than textbooks (Kalb, 1989; Fox, 1992). Proponents of using trade books in the classroom call upon teachers to work with school library media specialists and public librarians to help select books, develop lesson plans, and promote books to the students; in some cases, school library media specialists have team-taught units with classroom teachers (Cleaver & Taylor, 1983; Loertscher, 1988).

While most teachers in the primary grades focus mainly upon reading instruction, proponents of whole language assert the importance of oral expression as well. The skills of speaking, listening, and storytelling are seen as crucial to reading and must be developed first in the early grades and then alongside more advanced reading instruction (Fox, 1992). This is particularly true, Fox argues, for American Indian and other culturally diverse students, who may have experienced a rich oral tradition, but who see the school's traditional approach as foreign to their experience (Fox, 1992). Oral expression has also been seen as a means of preserving the dual language abilities of students who are in a bilingual education program or learning English as a second language (Reyhner-B, 1992).

Writing is a key element of the Whole Language movement. According to Willinsky, "this emphasis upon writing signals to students that they are primarily engaged in the construction of meaning rather than serving as empty jugs waiting to be filled . . . The image of reading as simply a receptive and decoding skill has itself been purged of its passivity in favor of an active reader constructing meaning in a transactional process." (Willinsky, 1990, p. 30). This writing can take many forms, from the "prewriting" of kindergartners to an interdisciplinary secondary school curriculum that emphasizes writing in all content areas, including science and mathematics (Willinsky, 1990). Through writing, students gain the power to interpret and, ultimately, to evaluate critically what he or she has read (Willinsky, 1990).

Writing also allows students to draw upon their own experiences and to bring into the classroom the stories of themselves, their family, and their community (Fox, 1992). Schools can utilize professional writers to show students the process of writing (Willinsky, 1990). Alternatively, they can bring in parents, grandparents, or other older people in the community, interview them, and let students write histories based upon those interviews (Fox, 1992). With the emergence of lively and easy-to-use desktop publishing programs, such as Bank Street Writer and Microsoft's Creative Writer, students can write, illustrate, and publish their own books. Children in bilingual classrooms can generate bilingual publications and publish works in Spanish, Creole, or traditional Indian languages (Reyhner-B, 1992).

Writing in a whole language curriculum may be independent writing, in which the student chooses the topic and form, or controlled writing, in which the topic and form are determined by the teacher (Fox, 1992). Through controlled writing, students receive direct instruction in penmanship, spelling, grammar, and written expression, but these exercises should be balanced with those allowing more freedom of expression (Fox, 1992). The process of editing and publishing can be a shared enterprise, with elements of cooperative learning brought into the whole language experience (Butler, 1991).

While there is always an element of teacher direction in any curriculum, another principal element of whole language is student choice in the materials to be read. With a wide variety of trade books in the classroom and a close relationship between classroom and library, students will be able to experiment with a number of literary genres and select their favorites. Thus, students will become engaged in the process of evaluating books, answering their own questions, and developing their preferences (Willinsky, 1990).

Many schools have implemented programs of sustained silent reading, in which both students and staff read books of their choice for a regular period of time each day; these programs have been shown to increase reading comprehension among students (Reyhner-C, 1992). By including teachers and other staff with the students in sustained silent reading, the program offers positive examples for students. There are no tests on what is read during this period; the goal is to allow students to experience the pleasure of reading on their own (Willinsky, 1990).

A final element of whole language is the incorporation of nonprint materials in the reading curriculum and in the various content areas. Films and videos of children's literature are often used to broaden the language experience; students can also compare the book and film version of the same story. Skits and plays, storytelling, and music are other examples of nonprint language-related activities (Fox, 1992). Because published folktales have their roots in the oral tradition, storytelling, music, and dramatics work particularly well with that genre (Hoffman, 1992). More recently, computer software and multimedia programs have been incorporated into the whole language approach. Through nontechnical authoring programs such as HyperCard, both teachers and students have been able to produce their own multimedia scripts, combining the written word with sound and pictures. More powerful computers and mass storage devices, such as laser discs and CD-ROMs, have given computer graphics the same realism and appeal as commercial videos. A news article published at the end of 1993 observed that more than 80 percent of all schools in the United States utilize the *Carmen Sandiego* series to teach history, geography, and science (Thomas, 1993). Other popular programs, such as *The Oregon Trail* and *SimCity*, offer more complex simulations, allowing the students to experience a situation firsthand and requiring them to absorb a wide variety of information in order to make decisions.

Attractive reading centers will encourage students to pick up books on their own.

❖ Critiques and Modifications of the Whole Language Approach

Like its counterpart, cooperative learning, whole language has come under fire from some quarters. A principal concern with any innovation, whole language included, is its impact upon student achievement, as measured by standardized tests. While it is generally agreed that subjective factors, such as a child's increased motivation and enjoyment of reading, are important, most researchers and educational administrators are more concerned with the kind of objective and quantifiable information that standardized tests provide.

So far, the statistical evidence on the effectiveness of whole language, as measured by standardized tests and other quantitative studies, is incomplete and contradictory (Willinsky, 1990; Chall, Jacobs, & Baldwin, 1990; Heymsfeld, 1989). Because whole language is a relatively new approach in the United States, long-term studies do not exist. In New Zealand, where a whole language approach has been in place on a national level for three decades, the literacy rate is among the world's highest (Willinsky, 1990). However, New Zealand and the United States are distinct societies, and a host of other factors besides curricular approaches would account for the differences in literacy (Special Box 8–1).

Other studies focus exclusively on specific age groups or populations. Jeanne Chall cites an analysis by Stahl and Miller that pointed to benefits of whole language at the kindergarten level. In first grade, though, the test scores were higher for students who had instruction in phonics (Chall, Jacobs, & Baldwin, 1990). Chall, Jacobs, and Baldwin's own study of low-income students, not separated by race or ethnicity, found a variety of approaches to be the best. In the early years, intensive phonics instruction helped students to decode and recognize words better (Heymsfeld, 1989). However, reading involves a variety of skills, and an approach that benefits word recognition may have a negative effect upon vocabulary building and a student's ability to read for meaning. As Chall, Jacobs, and Baldwin (1990) describe,

> The effects of structure by grades and by above-average and below-age readers suggest further insights. First, what seems to be effective for reading and vocabulary development in the lower grades may not be effective in the later grades. For example, a single-skills emphasis (that is, less variety in practice) was beneficial for third-graders' word recognition, but had a negative relation with seventh-graders' word recognition gains. Similarly, although focused reading instruction produced greater gains in comprehension among the younger children, it did not produce expected gains among seventh-graders. In addition, seventh-graders in classes with a high level of teacher direction of activities and selection of materials had lower gains in reading comprehension compared to seventh-graders in classes where more freedom of choice of materials and activities was found. (p. 119)

Other researchers have pointed out the critical role of learning styles, observing that some children do better with intensive phonics instruction in the early grades, while others in the same classroom learn better with a more holistic approach. Effective teaching thus combines a variety of approaches, including phonics, instruction in specific skills, and a modified whole language approach using trade books and less structured writing (Heymsfeld, 1989).

Despite the criticisms, Chall and other major researchers in the field of reading see benefits in moving toward a more holistic approach based upon trade books and extensive practice in writing. (Chall, Jacobs, & Baldwin, 1990). The whole language approach is particularly effective in

SPECIAL BOX 8–1   *What Accounts for National Literacy*

New Zealand has perhaps the most developed implementation of whole language in the world, and proponents of whole language cite New Zealand's high literacy rate as evidence of the method's success. However, sociologists cite a number of factors that account for a country's high literacy. In fact, educational methods have far less to do with the literacy rate than any of the factors described below:

▌ universal, free, and compulsory education for all ethnic and racial groups
▌ relatively little income disparity

The overall wealth of the country is less important than the disparities of income between rich and poor. Where there is greater inequality, people generally have less access to education and less motivation to stay in school. At the same time, disparities in educational attainment tend to reinforce income disparities.

▌ relative equality between men and women

Where there is gender equality, girls receive the same education as boys. However, in societies where women have few opportunities and little power, girls may not attend school or may drop out years before their brothers. Literacy among women may be actively discouraged by fathers and husbands.

▌ low immigration

Even if immigrant children attend and complete school, their parents may have had few educational opportunities in their country of origin, thereby depressing national literacy rates.

All of the above factors point to a favorable literacy situation for New Zealand.

building students' interest in reading in a variety of content areas (Willinsky, 1990; Chall, Jacobs, & Baldwin, 1990). Moreover, it is also useful in building vocabulary and increasing student knowledge of word meanings, skills that become ever more important as students move from elementary to middle school and beyond (Chall, Jacobs, & Baldwin, 1990). Low-income or "at-risk" students can reap special benefits from a modified whole language program. The 1990 study by Chall, Jacobs, and Baldwin on literacy and language development among low-income children describes decoding and overall reading skills in the early years that are comparable to their more advantaged peers. Between fourth and seventh grades, however, the low-income children's ability falls off in comparison to their peers; this occurs first for below-average-ability students, but eventually occurs for almost all low-income students. The chief culprit, according to the researchers, is the students' limited vocabulary, lack of exposure to books outside of school, and reduced access to enriching and challenging literature. Unlike middle-class youngsters, poor youngsters of all cultural backgrounds are less likely to have books at home that

Using trade books in the classroom can help students considered "at risk."

would give them anything beyond the basal readers and textbooks used in their classrooms (Chall, Jacobs, & Baldwin, 1990; Reyhner-C, 1992). Jon Reyhner's observations, though focused upon American Indian students, could be applied generally (Reynor-C, 1992).

> It is up to the teacher to introduce students to literature beyond the bits and pieces that appear in basal readers. Children from the dominant culture can often learn to read well in spite of the school because their parents recognize the need for providing reading material in the home, and encourage their children to utilize public and school libraries. For Indian students, whose parents may be less familiar with books and libraries, the teachers' role in providing interesting literature for their students is especially critical if the students are to learn to read fluently and succeed in school. (p. 165)

For at-risk students in particular, the statistics on whole language show some benefits over other methods, both among preschool and primary-grade children (Willinsky, 1990), and among children beyond the third grade (Chall, Jacobs, & Baldwin, 1990).

In spite of the criticisms of a pure whole language curriculum and the absence of long-term statistical proof for its overall superiority, its elements are being incorporated into growing numbers of classrooms in the United States. Implementations of whole language range from "reductionist programs that use literature mainly as a pragmatic vehicle for teaching reading and writing skills, to expansive programs that are holistic and treat literature as a powerful way of knowing about oneself and the world" (Barrera, 1992, p. 227). In some cases, it is one of a variety of approaches used to accommodate the diverse learning styles within a classroom. Many teachers use trade books to supplement the basal reader, while other teachers have dispensed with the basal reader altogether or use it only sparingly. In content areas such as social studies and science, trade books—both fiction and nonfiction—are used almost exclusively in some classrooms; most classrooms still rely on the textbook, with trade books as a supplement or a source of alternative perspectives.

Ultimately, a teacher's incorporation of the elements of whole language will depend upon a variety of factors, not the least of which is the school's overall openness to new approaches. Some schools have adopted whole language as a dominant model, and teachers in this happy situation can count on the support of other teachers and the school library media center (Kalb, 1989). Funds in these schools are available for the purchase of trade books and nonprint materials. In some schools, there is a standardized curriculum that may or may not include trade books. At the Malcolm X Academy Middle School, a Milwaukee middle school geared to the needs of African-American children, the reading curriculum is skills-based; integrated into it, however, are works of fiction, nonfiction, and folklore highlighting the African-American experience. Other schools may provide such a standard curriculum, but one entirely based upon basal readers and textbooks; in those cases, teachers will have to take the initiative to bring in trade fiction and nonfiction as well as non-print materials.

❖ The Promise of Whole Language in Presenting Diverse Cultures

For teachers with culturally diverse student bodies, or teachers who seek to present to their students the diversity of the human experience, the whole language approach, in either pure or modified form, has a potential far beyond that of traditional approaches (Willinsky, 1990). Most obviously, the whole language approach offers the wide range of culturally diverse perspectives that are available in trade books and non-print materials (Barrera, 1992). In addition, Willinsky argues that the *new literacy* (his term for a Whole Language-based program) alters the power balance of the classroom in favor of the students; students can choose their own reading, and through writing become active creators rather than passive recipients of information (Willinsky, 1990). This is particularly essential for children of color, whose encounters with traditional teachers and traditional methods of reading instruction have been, more often than not, a source of conflict, repression, and humiliation (Ogbu, 1990). As a result, schools seeking a more inclusive curriculum, one that meets the needs of culturally diverse children, have turned to elements of whole language. It has been incorporated into the curricula of the Afrocentric schools, and Indian educators have openly embraced the movement (Fox, 1992).

Problems of Basal Readers and Textbooks

Those who work with culturally diverse populations have long criticized basal readers. A 1992 study by Jon Reyhner indicates long-standing dissatisfaction with the representation of American Indians in both basal readers and U.S. history textbooks. Among the complaints registered over the years were the portrayal of American Indians as savages, illustrations of superficial and stereotypical features such as headdresses and war paint, the overemphasis on traditional crafts, and the almost exclusive preoccupation with white, middle-class characters (Reyhner-A, 1992). The "perfect" world of the white, middle-class youngsters in the basal readers may seem disturbing and upsetting to those who do not live the same picture-book lives, as Pueblo Indian researcher Joseph H. Suina has described:

> The Dick and Jane reading series in the primary grades presented me with pictures of a home with a pitched roof, straight walls, and sidewalks. I could not identify with these from my Pueblo world. However,

it was clear I didn't have these things and what I did have did not measure up . . . I was ashamed of being who I was and I wanted to change right then and there. Somehow it became so important to have straight walls, clean hair and teeth, a spotted dog to chase after. I even became critical and hateful toward my bony fleabag of a dog. I loved the familiar and cozy surroundings of my grandmother's house, but now I imagined it could be a heck of a lot better if only I had a white man's house with a bed, a nice couch, and a clock. In school books, all the child characters ever did was run around chasing their dog or a kite. They were always happy. As for me, all I seemed to do at home was go back and forth with buckets of water and cut up sticks for a lousy fire. "Didn't the teacher say that drinking coffee would stunt my growth?"..."Did my grandmother really care about my well-being?" (p. 298)

While basal readers have improved since the Dick and Jane series to which Suina was exposed, problems remain. Reyhner points out a continuing rural bias in portraying American Indians, even though a majority of American Indians now live in metropolitan areas; also overrepresented are Indians living in the Southwest (Reyhner-A, 1992). Although renowned author/illustrators of color such as Pat Cummings and Eloise Greenfield have contributed to basal readers, most of those involved in the creation of basal readers and other structured reading programs come from the dominant culture and have little awareness of other cultural experiences. The constraints inherent in basal readers—a controlled vocabulary, fixed structure, and limited length—work against the complex portrayal of another culture. Thus, the aspects most likely to appear are the most superficial ones—the Chinese New Year, noncontroversial Indian heroes such as Pocahontas and Sacajawea, and watered-down versions of the life of Martin Luther King, Jr. and George Washington Carver. When children of color appear in the stories, which they do with less frequency than their white counterparts, they are most often portrayed in universal situations. The settings are predominantly suburban and middle class; only the faces are different. Finally, there is a tendency for children from a variety of culturally diverse backgrounds to appear in the same story—along with children with disabilities—in one "politically correct" whole. This attempt to lump all the "different" children together does not allow any one child's experience to be explored in any depth. Readers of color may also see it as demeaning in its trivializing of cultural diversity and its negation of the children's distinct backgrounds. Given the fact that many children of color are from low-income families and may have less access to other books at home, the shortcomings of basal readers become even more significant.

Subject-area textbooks suffer from many of the same problems as basal readers. In textbooks of previous decades, for example, American Indians were portrayed as brutal savages, the enemies of white settlers who allegedly brought civilization to the West (Reyhner-A, 1992). In dealing with other racial and ethnic issues, Cameron McCarthy and others have noted a "tendency to avoid complexity and conflict" (McCarthy, 1990, p. 123).

McCarthy argues that textbooks, in portraying the African-American experience, focus almost exclusively on slavery; yet they fail to show the cruelty and violence that characterized that institution. Nor do the textbooks give a significant account of the many instances of slave rebellion and resistance, which are described for adults in Vincent Harding's *There Is a River* (1983) and for young adult readers in William L. Katz's *Breaking the Chains* (McCarthy, 1990).

The Council on Interracial Books for Children (1980) described a wide range of bias in social studies and mathematics textbooks, from the absence of illustrations featuring girls and children of color in the math books to history books that ignore the perspective of any group outside the mainstream. Furthermore, textbooks have been slow to incorporate changing events and interpretations; as late as 1983, almost no world geography textbooks contained information about the conflicts in Central America and the U.S. government's involvement on the side of right-wing forces (McCarthy, 1990). As McCarthy has observed,

> Indeed, educators and textbook publishers have, over the years, trotted out a particularly cruel fantasy about the story of civilization and this society—one in which the only knowledge worth knowing and the only stories worth telling are associated with the heirs of Greece and Rome. Within this frame of reference, art, architecture, music, science, and democracy are all portrayed as the fertile products of Europeans and their Caucasian counterparts in the United States. (p. 120)

Advantages of Trade Books and Nonprint Materials

In presenting diverse cultures, fiction, nonfiction, and folktales published as trade books offer a number of advantages over basal readers and textbooks. The first of those advantages is the sheer number and variety of the books in existence. With more books available, children have a better chance of reading about a wide range of cultural experiences; no longer are they confined to the single tale in a basal reader.

Many of the multicultural trade books now published have been written or illustrated by someone from that cultural group. These books offer role models for children from the same group and have a better chance of reflecting the perspective of that group, as opposed to the dominant perspective. In 1965, a study by Nancy Larrick showed African-American characters in only 6.7 percent of the fifty-seven hundred trade books published between 1962 and 1964 (Larrick, 1965). Virtually none was written by an African-American author. The books that did feature African-American characters often relegated them to marginal roles and portrayed them in distorted and stereotypical ways (Chall, Radwin, French, & Hall, 1985). By the early 1990s, the situation had improved significantly. In the previous decade, small presses brought into print the works of distinguished authors and illustrators of color, including Eloise Greenfield, Jan Spivey Gilchrist, Wade and Cheryl Willis Hudson, Gary Soto, Nicholasa Mohr, and Joseph Bruchac; in doing so, they challenged the major publishers to become more inclusive (Miller-Lachmann, 1992). In 1985, only eighteen children's books published by major presses were written or illustrated by African-Americans (Cooperative Children's Book Center, 1986). In 1992, that number had risen to ninety-four, with an increase as well in the number of American Indian, Latino, and Asian-American authors (Cooperative Children's Book Center, 1993).

The trade fiction, folklore, and nonfiction that is now available to children spans age groups, interests, and reading abilities. African-American preschoolers and kindergartners can hear Angela Shelf Medearis' excellent *Our People*, see Michael Bryant's compelling, realistic illustrations, and learn that, " . . . our people came out of slavery with nothing but hope, but our people became anything they wanted to be. Some were politicians, some started businesses, and some became teachers and doctors. Our people farmed the land, and some went out to the wild, wild West" (Medearis, 1994). Students offered a choice in their reading materials may choose a multicultural sports novel such as Walter Dean Myers' *Hoops* (1983), mystery novels such as Rosa Guy's Imamu Jones series, or a host of romance novels with culturally diverse characters and perspectives. Many multicultural novels are written for reluctant readers or those reading below grade level. Others are geared to readers for whom English is a second language. Among the trade books available are bilingual books and those in Spanish or other languages; the publishing of books in Spanish is a growing area for publishers of children's books today.

Trade books in social studies and the sciences—both nonfiction and fiction—offer perspectives beyond those in the textbook as well. Many of them explore a particular topic in depth; that topic may not be covered in textbooks or may receive no more than a paragraph in passing. The subtitle of William L. Katz's *Black Indians: A Hidden Heritage* (1986) tells it all; few textbooks explore the African-American presence in the West or the alliances between African-Americans fleeing slavery and the Indian Nations of the Southeast that were trying to keep their land and their way of life. In the form of a novel, Cynthia DeFelice's *Weasel* (1990) describes how the U.S. government in the early nineteenth century used mercenaries and pathological killers to eliminate the Indians east of the Mississippi; once the Indians were gone, the mercenaries turned on the settlers and their families.

In addition, trade books have been the first to respond to fast-breaking events around the world as well as new interpretations of those events. Even though textbooks in the first half of the 1980s contained little information about events in Central America, there were at least a half-dozen trade books for middle and high school readers to fill the gap. Published by both large and small presses, these books reflected a wide range of viewpoints (Miller-Lachmann, 1992).

By using a whole language approach that incorporates nonprint as well as print materials on diverse cultures, teachers can go beyond textbooks and basal readers in other ways. Feature films, dramatizations of children's books, and documentaries offer alternative perspectives in a format that appeals to young people. One film that has been used in Spanish and social studies classes at the high school level is *El Norte* (1984). It is the story of a Guatemalan Indian brother and sister who flee to the United States after family members are killed and try to build new lives in Los Angeles. Music provides another source of cultural information. Blues, rap, and salsa are examples of genres that are created by and reflect the perspectives of African-Americans in the South, urban black teenagers, and immigrants from the Spanish Caribbean. Eloise Greenfield's picture book *Nathaniel Talking* (1989) uses the style and rhythms of rap and the twelve-bar blues to tell Nathaniel's story of his life. This outstanding book, published by a small press, can serve as a starting point for children to learn about musical forms and to set their own stories to music. Storytelling is a major element of Native American culture (Hoffman, 1992). Using it in the classroom can help Indian children to rediscover their roots at the same time as it emphasizes to non-Indian children the role of the oral tradition in a non-European society.

The Role of Writing in Teaching about Culture

Despite growing support of multicultural books in the world of juvenile publishing, there are still groups for which little or no information exists in trade books, textbooks, or basal readers. This is the case not only for subgroups of the principal minority groups—such as Haitian-Americans, Dominican-Americans, and various Indian Nations—but also for Arab-Americans and many nationalities of European-Americans. Here, the writing component of whole language serves an additional purpose—the recording of a group's experience in the United States. By interviewing or surveying family and community members and then writing the results, students can create knowledge about their own and other groups. Children can also write their own stories for the benefit of their younger siblings and future generations. Children's creative writing is a means of combining their imagination with the everyday realities they experience; these stories serve as a useful counterpart to the homogenized and idealized worlds portrayed in basal readers. Writing can also serve as a means of challenging the perspectives offered in textbooks as youngsters write from their own experiences and utilize the insights of older members of the community.

Among new immigrants and bilingual children, writing allows for the preservation of native-language skills (Edelsky, 1991). In the case of

American Indians, writing in the native language is also a means of preserving languages that may otherwise die out. Among the writing projects that have been initiated in classrooms on Indian reservations are tribal language dictionaries, the transcription of traditional stories into the tribal language, the captioning of pictures, the translation of published stories in English, and the creation of original stories in the tribal language (Reyhner-B, 1992).

❖ A Promise Unfulfilled

Despite the immense resources available in trade books and nonprint materials and the potential of language-related activities such as writing, storytelling, and dramatics, the implementation of a whole language curriculum does not guarantee a multicultural one. In fact, in the wrong hands, trade books, nonprint materials, and classroom activities can actually reinforce stereotypes and inhibit cultural understanding. Furthermore, larger issues—patterns of interaction in the classroom, strategies for using the materials, and relations between the school and the larger community—influence the outcome of any whole language approach, particularly when it is used with culturally diverse students (Barrera, 1992).

Even though a whole language curriculum is in place, the trade books used may not present a diversity of cultures. Rosalinda Barrera describes one such program in New Mexico. The school she describes, a K–6 elementary school in a working-class/lower/middle-class zone in a metropolitan area, had a student population that was 65 percent Latino, with most of those Mexican-American; 3 percent American Indian; 2 percent African- American; and 30 percent European-American. Eighty per cent of the teachers, however, were European-American, with 20 percent Latino. The school had fully implemented a whole language approach (Barrera, 1992):

> The program is characterized by extensive use of children's literature for reading and writing instruction, rather than traditional school textbooks; curricular integration that fuses language arts instruction and content area instruction (e.g., science, social studies, math); a process writing component that promotes classroom publication of child-written texts; and ongoing qualitative assessment of children's language and literacy largely through teacher observation and conferencing. (pp. 228–229)

All of the instruction was in English, with 10 percent of the students receiving supplementary English as a second language instruction. (Barrera, 1992).

In spite of the children's diverse cultural backgrounds and the innovative nature of the curriculum, the trade materials to which the children were exposed reflected a striking lack of cultural diversity. Many of the books had been published in New Zealand, as the school had exchanged books with a sister school in that country. Even so, there were no books on the indigenous Maori; most of the books featured white, upper/middle-class characters, or were animal stories. Virtually all of the authors and illustrators were European-American or white New Zealanders (Barrera, 1992). Other language activities also failed to reflect the surrounding community's linguistic and cultural diversity. While the superficial aspects of food, holidays, costumes, and crafts received attention, few community members came into the school to share their stories and perspectives. The invited authors and storytellers were, like the books, predominantly European-American (Barrera, 1992).

Barrera expresses concerns as well about the methods used in language and literature teaching, which she believes subordinates the students' culture and feelings to the dominant perspective, as defined by the school, its predominantly European-American faculty, and the limited range of texts they make available to the students (Barrera, 1992):

> . . . the language and literature activities that are conducted reflect the school culture primarily—the acceptable ways of telling stories, of responding to the literature, of talking about books, of asking questions about the materials, and so forth, are those of the teachers and the mainstream culture. It appears that the children's personal and shared meanings are overshadowed by the meanings in commercial literature . . . The organizing patterns of the literature become the ways children structure their own texts. In essence, it is the language and culture reflected in the school literature that counts, whereas the language and cultural backgrounds of the students are largely ignored in instruction. (p. 231)

Barrera's case study stands out because of the absence of multicultural materials and the teachers' lack of awareness of how cultural issues can inform other language activities, such as oral response to the literature, storytelling, and writing. As she points out, one's personal and cultural background plays an important role in the development of thought and language. The process of thinking and speaking—both individual and culturally determined—in turn influences the way that both children and teachers respond to the literature. Teachers who are not aware of this issue may interpret a child's silence as lack of knowledge or preparation, may dismiss a response that is not offered in standard English, or may determine that, given response is incorrect or unacceptable. Even if a child's response reflects prejudices within his or her culture, these prejudices must first be aired in order to be ultimately countered.

Other problems occur when the materials and methods used are outdated and actually reinforce stereotypes. Until the late 1960s, the number of published African-American authors for children could be counted on the fingers of one hand (Sims, 1982). While the European-American author Ezra Jack Keats has been widely acknowledged as a skilled and sensitive creator of books about people of color, other authors—highly-regarded at the time—were not so sensitive or talented (Feelings, 1991). Unfortunately, some of those books published in previous decades won awards and were well-loved by white, middle-class children who had little opportunity to learn about those cultures firsthand. When those children became teachers and administrators (not to mention, parents), they embraced the books of their youth.

Claire Bishop's *The Five Chinese Brothers* (1938), which has been reprinted many times and is widely available today, "pivots on the premise that all Chinese look alike" (McCunn, 1988, p. 51). The book's cutesy, stylized illustrations do little to dispel stereotypical images of Chinese and Chinese-Americans. Another highly regarded older work by a European-American author, Rachel Isadora's *Ben's Trumpet* (1947), features an uncaring and disorganized family that feeds into common perceptions about the African-American family both in the early twentieth century and now (Feelings, 1991). Leo Politi wrote dozens of books about various cultural groups, most notably Mexicans and Mexican-Americans, between the 1940s and the 1970s. His works portrayed those cultures as exotic, with illustrations of *sombreros*, *huaraches* (sandals), and other surface, stereotypical, and often inaccurate elements that reflected a tourist's conception of the culture (Cortes, 1992; Miller-Lachmann, 1992). Stereotypes in trade book portrayals of American Indians have been particularly pervasive and persistent (Slapin & Seale, 1992). Even today, an otherwise exemplary multicultural book, Mary Hoffman and Caroline Binch's portrayal of a black child in Great Britain, *Amazing Grace* (1991), features "playing Indian," with the correspondingly stereotypical dress and behavior (Kruse, 1992). Such books, if used in a whole language curriculum, could become a source of humiliation and ridicule for children of color at the same time as they reinforce white children's distorted views of other cultures in the United States and around the world.

Another problem for whole language curricula is the potential for ignoring the linguistic diversity of the students. This includes not only the absence of books and language-related activities in Spanish, Korean, Chinese, Creole, or traditional American Indian languages, but also the inability to recognize and work with the linguistic patterns of Black English, American Indian English, or Caribbean dialects. The latter is an area of great controversy, for many minority educators have argued for the teaching of mainstream English in the schools, while others have pointed to the need to preserve and explore the dialects spoken within the minority community (Lee, 1994; Leap, 1992). William Leap's study of Ute Indian students points to gains in oral expression when students are allowed to speak in their dialect; "there are no instances," he reports, "of the stereotyped 'silent Indian student,' reluctant to engage in academic-related discourse within a formal interview setting" (Leap, 1992, p. 148). For low-income African-Americans, for whom speaking in class discussions is less of an obstacle, some language-related activities in which Black English is permitted may have the effect of making school seem less alienating at the same time as children learn to make choices about when to use Black English and when to use standard English (Lee, 1994). Teachers should also be aware that Black English is generally spoken only in low-income communities and only in certain situations; most middle-class African-Americans use standard English and insist their children do so as well (Lee, 1994).

Dialect also becomes an issue in selecting and using multicultural books, as many folktales and contemporary stories are written using a pure or modified dialect. Depending on their skill and cultural awareness, teachers who offer the books and, especially, read them aloud, can capture the rhythm and beauty of the original words, or they can make the words demean and ridicule the cultural group (Hoffman, Payne, & Smith, 1992). In no case should teachers read aloud a book in dialect when they do not feel comfortable using the dialect, though they may make that book available for children to read aloud or silently (Hoffman, Payne, & Smith, 1992). (If children read the book aloud, they too should be made aware of the importance of reading the dialect correctly, lest classmates be hurt or other cultures become the source of jokes.) Finally, teachers who use books written in dialect must be certain that the language is used authentically. In addition, if the characters from only one cultural group and no others use dialect, dialect becomes a source of negative stereotyping; books of this type should be avoided (Miller-Lachmann, 1992).

In terms of selecting and using multicultural materials and developing language-related activities for bilingual students, the same care must be taken as for monolingual students. Many of the books available in translation for Spanish-speaking students are hardly multicultural. The *Clifford, the Big Red Dog* series is one example of a translated series that has been widely used; the Spanish version features the same suburban setting and universal story line as its English counterpart. A translation into Spanish is no guarantee that Latinos or any other group will not be stereotyped within a book; thus, the same criteria for selection apply to all materials in other languages. Other books have errors in the translation. When using Spanish translations from mainstream publishers or importing Spanish-language books from other countries, teachers need to be aware of differences between the Spanish spoken in Spain, that spoken in Latin America, and differences among the various Latin-American countries (Edelsky, 1991). Teachers who offer books featuring the Spanish spoken in Spain and insist that their students speak that way are certain to alienate students from Mexico, Puerto Rico, or the Dominican Republic (Edelsky, 1991). Likewise, care must be taken in offering books in French to students from Haiti or initiating language-related activities in French. While many upper-class Haitians do speak French, and it is used in Haitian schools, most Haitians are predominantly Creole-speaking (Edelsky, 1991). Sadly, there are few published books in Creole; thus, teachers and students must work together to create instructional materials. The situation for other language groups may resemble one of the above extremes, or it may fall somewhere in the middle.

The pitfalls of selecting multicultural books are many, and they pose a special problem for teachers whose own inter-cultural awareness may be limited (and may have been shaped by the outdated and inaccurate images presented during their youth). Barrera uses the term *cultural gap* to refer to "a void in teachers' knowledge bases about culture as it relates to literacy and literature" (Barrera, 1992, p. 227). As a result of this cultural gap, teachers may avoid units that require them to select materials on unfamiliar cultures, or they may stick to "safe" materials, such as award-winning folktales. Teachers who want to reach out to their students of color and provide a solid culturally diverse curriculum for all students can take steps to improve their knowledge base, both about the cultures themselves and about the materials that are available. Because of their own cultural gap, teachers may assume that, when given a choice of books (as students are in a whole language program), students will only read about children like themselves. Students may need encouragement to pick up a book about children whose way of life is unfamiliar to them, but teachers often underestimate students' curiosity about the world and their willingness to read good books about other cultures (Rochman, 1993).

❖ Bridging the "Cultural Gap"

The Whole Language movement can enhance multicultural awareness and understanding only if teachers are able to bridge the cultural gap. The teacher's own background should not be an obstacle to understanding. In the words of renowned literary critic Henry Louis Gates, Jr., "[a]ny human being sufficiently curious and motivated can fully possess another culture, no matter how 'alien' it may appear to be" (Gates, 1992, p. xv). The following are some practical suggestions for teachers seeking to increase their own multicultural awareness and their ability to select materials and develop instructional strategies:

1. Inform ourselves by means of books for adults.

There is a significant and growing body of literature—both fiction and nonfiction—by and about African-Americans, American Indians, Asian-Americans, and Latinos as well as about every region of the world. These books offer insights into cultures with which we may be unfamiliar— their history and current situation and the perspectives of those who are part of those cultures. Many of the books cited in earlier chapters, such as Ronald Takaki's *Strangers from a Different Shore* and *A Different Mirror*,

Earl Shorris' *Latinos*, Russell Thornton's *American Indian Holocaust and Survival* and *The Autobiography of Malcolm X* can serve as a starting point. *Global Voices, Global Visions: A Core Collection of Multicultural Adult Books* (Miller-Lachmann, 1995), is a recently published bibliography that offers an annotated list of recommended titles and an overview of issues and publishing trends concerning the above four minority groups and the other regions of the world. Other good sources for recommended adult multicultural books include *The New York Times Book Review*, *Multicultural Review*, and the multivolume *Reader's Adviser* (Sader, 1994), as well as specialized literary biographies focusing on individual groups.

2. *Learn about the body of multicultural children's books that are available and how one can evaluate forthcoming books.*

Chapter 9 offers criteria for selecting multicultural children's books for use in the classroom. It expands upon the criteria found in *Our Family, Our Friends, Our World: An Annotated Guide to Significant Multicultural Books for Children and Teenagers* (Miller-Lachmann, 1992). That book also contains evaluations of more than one thousand titles published between 1970 and 1990, organized by region of the world. For the United States, there are separate chapters on books—fiction, nonfiction, and series books—about African-Americans, Asian-Americans, Latinos, and Native Americans. Each of the chapters has been compiled by an expert in the area who also works with young people as an author, teacher, or librarian.

Other excellent bibliographies and analyses of multicultural children's literature include *The Multicolored Mirror: Cultural Substance in Literature for Children and Young Adults* (1991), which grew out of a multicultural literature conference organized by the Cooperative Children's Book Center in Madison, Wisconsin, and *Against Borders: Promoting Books for a Multicultural World* (1993), which offers content analyses and strategies for using outstanding works of multicultural fiction and personal narrative in the classroom. For books in Spanish and those about the Latino experience, a valuable source is Isabel Schon's *A Hispanic Heritage* (1988).

Periodicals geared to librarians are useful sources for evaluating new multicultural books. Among the most respected are *Booklist*, *School Library Journal*, *Bulletin of the Center for Children's Books*, *The Horn Book*, and *Voice of Youth Advocates*. Users should note, however, that *School Library Journal* and *Voice of Youth Advocates* use outside reviewers, while the other three have in-house reviewers. Outside reviewers, especially, can vary from cultural insiders, who might offer insights even experienced and knowledgeable in-house reviewers lack, to those with very little background. Articles in each of these journals may provide bibliographies and insights into a body of literature, such as illustrated folktales or books in Spanish. *Booklist*, *School Library Journal*, and *Bulletin of the Center for Children's Books* review books published for preschoolers through high schoolers (*Booklist* reviews adult books also). *The Horn Book* specializes in books up through junior high, and *Voice of Youth Advocates* only reviews books written for or appropriate for the secondary level.

These five periodicals review all types of children's books, not just multicultural ones. Two periodicals, however, specialize in multicultural literature. One is *Multicultural Review*, which covers children's as well as adult books and is particularly useful for its special articles, essays, and bibliographies. The second source is the *Interracial Books for Children Bulletin*, published by the Council on Interracial Books for Children. Both of these publications feature reviewers from the cultural groups portrayed in the books, and often they (particularly the *Interracial Books for Children Bulletin*) have been the most detailed and critical in examining recently published books.

3. Work with colleagues and the school library media specialist to develop methods of teaching multicultural literature.

Chapter 10 will expand upon this topic. However, the school library media specialist is a valuable resource for selecting materials, integrating print and nonprint materials, and incorporating the library and library skills into the curriculum. The study by Chall, Jacobs, and Baldwin (1990) indicates positive effects of library visits in the areas of reading comprehension and vocabulary. As part of their training, most school library media specialists with recent masters' degrees have been exposed to multicultural children's literature and criteria for their selection.

Other colleagues can also assist in developing units. With the emphasis upon reading and writing across the curriculum, subject teachers are working more closely together. Teachers of music, art, and computer have their expertise to contribute. Even for monolingual teachers, bilingual teachers are an important resource, for they often have a firsthand understanding of the cultural group to which English-only as well as bilingual students belong. Teachers of all cultural groups should not hesitate to rely upon each other, and by working together they provide a model of cooperation for their students.

4. Be aware of nonprint sources and what they can contribute.

Nonprint materials are an integral part of the whole language approach and should be used along with trade books. Louise Spain's essay in *The High-Low Handbook*, third edition, describes the successful use of a multimedia program for intensive English as a second language instruction at the International High School in New York City. She points out that video adaptations of literary works offer both an enticing introduction and help in understanding the print works for those with limited English proficiency. In all subject areas, videos and other media offer access to the subject matter through a variety of senses. Among the videos most often used at the International High School are *Eyes on the Prize* (a documentary of the Civil Rights movement), *West Side Story*, *Stand and Deliver* (the inspiring story of a mathematics teacher and his Latino students at an inner-city high school in Los Angeles), and *El Norte* (the story of two teenagers, Maya Indians, fleeing to the United States to escape persecution) (Spain, 1990).

In addition, teachers can use movies, music, and art to develop their own awareness. The films of Spike Lee, for instance, encompass a wide range of African-American experiences for adult viewers. Other sensitive and well-made films may not be appropriate for classroom use, but can help teachers gain greater understanding and sensitivity. The holistic approach of whole language is not just for students, but also for teachers seeking to inform themselves about their own and other cultures.

School Library Journal reviews non-print as well as print materials, and *Booklist* and *Multicultural Review* also publish articles from time to time. *The New York Times* regularly covers feature films, music, and art by people of color, though most of its coverage is of materials for adults.

5. Look for language-related activities that go beyond food, holidays, and crafts.

Too often what passes for multicultural activities in schools is superficial—food, holidays, crafts, costumes, and simple songs. Teachers need to work together to develop more imaginative activities that explore cultures in greater depth. Often, people in the community can be a source for program ideas, and by bringing community people in, the school can strengthen its ties to the surrounding neighborhood and to the parents who live in the neighborhood. Chapter 10 discusses this issue in more detail.

6. Develop alternatives for teaching about cultures for which few or no print materials exist.

Students, their parents, and members of the community can themselves become publishers, historians, and experts using this strategy. By writing down the information gained from the community, teachers have materials that can be used and expanded upon by future classes, and over time, the school becomes a repository for information on how the community has changed over the years. Chapter 10 offers suggestions for incorporating this idea into the curriculum.

7. Use the knowledge and resources of the public library and cultural institutions in the community.

The public library is often a source for information and programming. Many public librarians have worked in the community for a long time and have initiated successful after school, summer reading, and adult education programs. The Queens Borough Public Library's New Americans Project sponsors video productions, cultural activities, and a wide variety of classes for the many immigrant groups that make their home in the borough of Queens in New York City. A joint project of the New York Public Library and the community school board in the Washington Heights neighborhood of Manhattan—a predominantly Dominican-American neighborhood—has helped children to write their own stories about the immigrant experience and to generate other materials in the absence of published ones.

8. Find out about resource centers around the country that can help evaluate materials and develop programs.

Teachers need not "reinvent the wheel." Many resource centers exist to help teachers in a specific area of the country or with information about specific cultural groups. These resource centers may publish resource lists, sponsor workshops, discussion groups, and conferences, or offer people to consult with individual schools and districts. The Cooperative Children's Book Center at the University of Wisconsin is one such resource center. Though limited for the most part to helping teachers and librarians in Wisconsin, it works in a number of areas, though its areas of strength include multicultural children's literature and intellectual freedom. The Multicultural Resource Center at the Baldwin School in Bryn Mawr, Pennsylvania, is one of four centers that offer resources on multicultural curricula and instruction to independent schools across the country. Africa Access, located in Silver Springs, Maryland, publishes lists of resources and selection criteria focusing exclusively on Africa. While it serves schools and libraries across the country, it is an example of a resource center that specializes in a single region or cultural group. The Coalition for Indian Education in Albuquerque, New Mexico, is involved in program development and advocacy for Indian students. For teachers of Latino and Spanish-speaking bilingual students, there is the Center for the Study of Books in Spanish for Children and Adolescents at the California State University at San Marcos. Each of these centers, and many others across the country, can assist teachers with materials and instructional strategies.

❖ Summary

Whole language is difficult to define. However, it is characterized by the integration of reading and writing across the curriculum; the use of trade books and a wide variety of print and nonprint materials; the extensive use of writing taught as a process; and student-centered instruction.

The effectiveness of whole language with respect to student achievement is yet to be firmly established. However, an approach that emphasizes meaning, that promotes children's interest in reading, and motivates them to read offers definite advantages. The extensive use of trade books, for example, opens a wide world of information and understanding through the variety of materials. In addition, children of color whose learning style is field-sensitive, holistic, and context-oriented can benefit from a whole language approach.

In contrast to basal readers and traditional textbooks, trade books are available which present many cultures, varied perspectives, and varieties of language. Furthermore, many trade books are written by members of the cultural group about which they write and can be more authentic. There are excellent examples of multicultural literature available in the wide selection of trade books. However, these books must be carefully chosen so that they make a positive contribution to the knowledge and understanding of a culture. Teachers will need to review books carefully or obtain dependable reviews by others in order to make good choices.

Another element of whole language that is available for multicultural education is the emphasis on writing. Children and their families can record experiences within their cultural group that can be shared with others. This can capture rich sources of information and reaffirm respect for the cultural experiences of children.

In addition to the need for careful review of books, teachers will need to become more skilled in selecting and developing instructional materials and more aware of multicultural content and requirements. Resources are readily available to accomplish these aims.

❖ CHAPTER 8 **Questions**

1. Discuss the major elements of whole language.

2. What are the elements of whole language that most clearly address cultural differences among students?

3. Defend the use of some basal readers and textbooks in the classroom.

4. How can teachers provide instruction in basic skills for some students when using a whole language approach?

5. What are some of the cautions in using whole language in multicultural education?

6. How could a teacher evaluate her use of whole language in teaching reading and writing?

❖ References

Barrera, R. (1992). The cultural gap in literature-based literacy instruction. *Education and Urban Society*, 24(2) (February 1992), 227–243.

Butler, S. (1991). The writing connection. In V. Froese (Ed.), *Whole language: Practice and theory* (pp. 97–146). Boston: Allyn and Bacon.

Chall, J. S., Radwin, E., French, V. W., & Hall, C. R., (1985). Blacks in the world of children's books. In D. McCann & G. Woodard (Eds.), *The Black American in books for children: Readings in racism*, (2nd ed.). Methuen, NJ: Scarecrow Press.

Chall, J. S., Jacobs, V. A., & Baldwin, L. E. (1990). *The reading crisis: Why poor children fall behind*. Cambridge, MA: Harvard University Press.

Cleaver, B. P., & Taylor, W. D. (1983). *Involving the school library media specialist in curriculum development*. Chicago: American Library Association.

Cooperative Children's Book Center. (1986). *CCBC choices 1985*. Madison, WI: Cooperative Children's Book Center.

Cooperative Children's Book Center. (1993). *CCBC choices 1992*. Madison, WI: Cooperative Children's Book Center.

Cortes, O. G. de. (1992). Hispanic Americans. In L. Miller-Lachmann, *Our family, our friends, our world: An annotated guide to significant multicultural books for children and teenagers* (pp. 121–154). New Providence, NJ: R. R. Bowker.

Council on Interracial Books for Children. (1980). *Guidelines for selecting bias-free textbooks and storybooks*. New York: Council on Interracial Books for Children.

Edelsky, C. (1991). *With literacy and justice for all: Rethinking the social in language and education*. New York: The Falmer Press.

Feelings, T. (1991). Transcending the form. In M. V. Lindgren (Ed.), *The multicolored mirror: Cultural substance in literature for children and young adults* (pp. 45–57). Fort Atkinson, WI: Highsmith Press.

Fox, S. (1992). The whole language approach. In J. Reyhner (Ed.), *Teaching American Indian students* (pp. 168–177). Norman, OK: University of Oklahoma Press.

Gates, H. L., Jr. (1992). *Loose canons: Notes on the culture wars*. New York: Oxford University Press.

Goodman, K. S. (1985). Unity in reading. In H. Singer & R. B. Ruddell (Eds.), *Theoretical models and processes of reading*. Newark, DE: International Reading Association.

Heymsfeld, C. (1989). Filling the hole in whole language. *Educational Leadership*, (March 1989), 65–68.

Hoffman, A., Payne, S., & Smith, R. (1992). African Americans. In L. Miller-Lachmann, *Our family, our friends, our world: An annotated guide to significant multicultural books for children and teenagers* (pp. 25–91). New Providence, NJ: R. R. Bowker.

Hoffman, E. (1992). Oral language development. In J. Reyhner (Ed.), *Teaching American Indian students* (pp. 132–142). Norman, OK: University of Oklahoma Press.

Holdaway, D. (1979). *Foundations of literacy*. Sydney: Ashton Scholastic.

Kalb, V. (1989). Curriculum connections: Literature. *School Library Media Quarterly*, (Spring 1989).

Kruse, G. M. (1992). No single season: Multicultural literature for all children. *Wilson Library Bulletin*, (February 1992), 30–33+.

Larrick, N. (1965, April 11). The all-white world of children's books. *Saturday Review*.

Leap, W. L. (1992). American Indian English. In J. Reyhner (Ed.), *Teaching American Indian students* (pp. 143–153). Norman, OK: University of Oklahoma Press.

Lee, F. R. (1994, January 5). Lingering conflict in the schools: Black dialect vs. standard speech. *The New York Times*, p. A1.

Loertscher, D. (1988). *Taxonomies of the school library media program*. Englewood, CO: Libraries Unlimited.

McCarthy, C. (1990). Multicultural education, minority identities, textbooks, and the challenge of curricular reform. *Journal of Education, 172*(2), 118–129.

McCunn, R. L. (1988). Chinese Americans: A personal view. *School Library Journal, 34*(June/July 1988), 50–52.

Medearis, A. S. (1994). *Our people.* New York: Atheneum.

Miller-Lachmann, L. (1992). Introduction. In Miller-Lachmann, *Our families, our friends, our world: An annotated guide to significant multicultural books for children and teenagers.* New Providence, NJ: R. R. Bowker.

Ogbu, J. (1990). Literacy and schooling in subordinate cultures: The case of black Americans. In K. Lomotey (Ed.), *Going to school: The African-American experience* (pp. 113–131). Albany, NY: The State University of New York Press.

Reyhner, J. (1992a). Adapting curriculum to culture. In J. Reyhner (Ed.), *Teaching American Indian students* (pp. 96–103). Norman, OK: University of Oklahoma Press.

Reyhner, J. (1992b). Bilingual education. In J. Reyhner (Ed.), *Teaching American Indian students* (pp. 59–77). Norman, OK: University of Oklahoma Press.

Reyhner, J. (1992c). Teaching reading responsively. In J. Reyhner (Ed.), *Teaching American Indian students* (pp. 157–167). Norman, OK: University of Oklahoma Press.

Rochman, H. (1993). *Against borders: Promoting books for a multicultural world.* Chicago: American Library Association.

Sims, R. (1982). *Shadow and substance: Afro-American experience in contemporary children's fiction,* (2nd ed.). Chicago: NCTE/ALA.

Slapin, B., & Seale, D. (Ed.). (1992). *Through Indian eyes: The native experience in books for children.* Philadelphia: New Society Publishers.

Spain, L. (1990). The international high school at LaGuardia Community College: An audiovisual approach to second language acquisition. In E. V. LiBretto (Ed.), *The high/low handbook,* (3rd ed.) (pp. 85-92). New York: R. R. Bowker.

Suina, J. H. (1988). Epilogue: *And then I went to school.* Hillsdale, NJ: Erlbaum, (Quoted in Lawrence Reyhner-A, 1992) .

Thomas, A. (1993, December 31). School courses weave in software. *The Christian Science Monitor*, p. 9.

Willinsky, J. (1990). *The new literacy: Redefining reading and writing in the schools.* New York: Routledge and Kegan Paul.

CHAPTER 9

Selecting Multicultural Materials for the Classroom

General Principles

Even if they allow students to choose their own books to read in the classroom, teachers must select which books go into classroom collections, just as the school library media specialist must select which books are added to the library's collection. Teachers are also in a position to promote certain books and to make others required reading. Thus, teachers seeking to include multicultural books in their curricula must be able to judge which books contribute to students' understanding about their own and other cultures and which books merely reinforce misconceptions and stereotypes.

Literary quality has often been used as a standard for choosing books. Among the elements taken into account in defining literary quality for works of fiction are the coherence of the plot, the depth of the characterizations, the seamless flow of the writing, the delineation of the setting, and the handling of the principal themes. Evaluators of picture books examine the quality and style of the illustrations, their use of color, their relation to the text, and their appeal to young children. Principal concerns in evaluating nonfiction are accuracy, balance, currency, the clarity and appeal of the writing, the quality of the illustrations, and the presence of finding aids such as indexes and the table of contents (Miller-Lachmann, 1992). To reflect accurately our diverse society and the global village to which we belong, however, books must do more than simply be well written and attractively and appropriately illustrated. In the words of children's book author and poet Eloise Greenfield (1985),

> The books that reach children should: authentically depict and interpret their lives and their history; build self-respect and encourage the development of positive values; make children aware of their strength and leave them with a sense of hope and direction; teach them the skills necessary for the maintenance of health and for economic survival; broaden their knowledge of the world, past and present, and offer some insight into the future. These books will not be pap—the total range of human problems, struggles, and accomplishments can be told in this context with no sacrifice of literary merit. We are all disappointed when we read a book that has no power, a story that arouses no emotion, passages that lack the excitement that language can inspire. But the skills that are used to produce a well-written racist book can be used as well for one that is antiracist. The crucial factor is that literary merit cannot be the sole criterion. A book that has been chosen as worthy of a child's emotional investment must have been judged on the basis of what it is— not a collection of words arranged in some unintelligible but artistic design, but a statement powerfully made and communicated through the artistic and skillful use of language. (p. 21)

How, then, can teachers distinguish between a "well-written racist book" and "one that is antiracist," that seeks to build awareness, tolerance, and mutual respect? In writing specifically about the education of American Indians, Ricardo L. Garcia and Janet Goldenstein Ahler (1992) point to four basic principles that can be applied to any cultural group:

> Ethnocentrism and racism are the root causes for the many stereotypes and biases pertaining to American Indians. To discourage these prejudices, the following generalizations should be kept in mind: Indian groups are (1) similar, (2) different, (3) diverse, and (4) ongoing social realities. (p. 28)

European-American children can learn a great deal by reading books by and about people from other cultures.

1. Cultural groups are similar.

Books that are chosen for the classroom and used in the curriculum should emphasize the similarities among all people, regardless of their cultural group. Human beings have the same needs, the same capacity for love, hatred, friendship, and altruism, the same developmental stages and fundamental conflicts. Even when they read about different cultures, children should be able to see basic similarities between themselves and the individuals in the book. For example, the short story collection for teenage readers *A Gathering of Flowers: Stories about Being Young in America*, edited by Joyce Carol Thomas (1990), features stories by African-American, American Indian, Asian-American, Latino, and European-American writers, all touching upon the struggles of being a teenager, searching for one's identity, and/or experiencing the pains of first love.

2. Cultural groups are different.

While showing basic similarities, books should not make all children seem exactly the same, with only the color of the faces distinguishing them. Cultures are distinct, and they provide the framework within which people experience universal emotions, conflicts, and developmental issues. The books teachers give their students should show, in a positive, though increasingly complex, way, the uniqueness of each way of life. The authors in *A Gathering of Flowers* do not all tell the same story, for each of the characters approaches adolescence with the perspective of his or her own cultural milieu. While the transition from childhood to adolescence or adulthood is a universal stage, rites of passage differ, as do various cultures' definitions of what "adolescence" is. In acknowledging the differences among cultures, we must also acknowledge their different histories, including the legacies of oppression and racism. Denying cultural differences and the fact that they, at times, have led to racism only perpetuates racism. Furthermore, by denying culturally diverse children the uniqueness of their culture, as was done to American Indian children in the boarding schools of the late nineteenth and early twentieth centuries, we destroy an important part of their identity.

3. Cultural groups are diverse.

Stereotyping consists of the assignment of a set of characteristics to everyone in a given racial or ethnic group. Stereotypes not only exaggerate cultural differences, they assume all members of the group share those differences, regardless of individual personality, family background, socio-economic status, and membership in a sub-group. Books for children should portray the uniqueness of each individual and the diversity within every cultural group. American Indians, for example, may belong to one of hundreds of Nations, may live on a reservation, in an urban area, in a small town, or in a suburb, and may be of any combination of mixed race. As discussed in earlier chapters, there is no single heritage or experience that can be called "African-American," "American Indian," "Asian-American," "Latino," or "European-American." Diversity within cultural groups should be reflected both within books and in the combination of books that a teacher selects.

4. Cultural groups are ongoing social realities.

All cultures evolve over time, and books should reflect those changing conditions. Few societies today can be characterized as purely "traditional;" all are in various stages of change and modernization. The immigration experience—one common to many culturally diverse children in the United States today—tends to speed up that process. Books that do not take those changes into account widen the sense of difference, reinforcing the stereotypes of outsiders, and appearing inauthentic to members of the group. While folktales have much to offer in helping children to understand the values, concerns, and imaginative traditions of each culture, a curriculum based entirely on folktales fails to communicate how cultures have evolved through the centuries. In portraying the process of a culture's evolution, it will be necessary to use more than one book. Some books deal with the process of change itself and how the characters or personages cope with it, while others portray a single moment in time, focusing on the rural, the urban, the traditional, the historical, or the contemporary.

The Need for a Variety of Books

It is a tall order to ask for a single book to communicate the universality, distinctiveness, diversity, and evolution of a cultural group. Hazel Rochman (1993) writes, "[i]f you think that the book you're promoting is the only one kids are ever going to read on a subject—about the pioneers or about Columbus or about the Holocaust or about apartheid—then there's intense pressure to choose the 'right' book with the 'right' mes-

Students should be offered a wide variety of books about a given culture so that one book does not carry the weight of the entire culture.

sage" (p. 20). The book has to communicate so much, so flawlessly, that its literary impact and appeal to young people may get lost in the message, if such a "perfect" book can be found at all. Keeping in mind the four general principles, teachers have the obligation to make available a variety of books, which as a collective unit portray cultures and their individual members in all their complexity. Taken together, for example, all of the novels for grades four to six published in recent years that feature African-Americans show characters in a variety of situations and settings, in the past and present. In addition, by providing a number of choices and incorporating several books about a group into the curriculum, teachers can help students to comprehend the nature and scope of diversity and to develop their critical abilities in comparing each of the treatments. Even a flawed book can be used, both for what it does contribute and for teaching children to become more informed and critical readers.

❖ Specific Criteria for Selection

Given these general principles, as well as the need for a variety of treatments, there are specific criteria teachers can use in deciding which books will be chosen for classroom use and which will be given a more significant place in the curriculum. While judgments on individual books, and how they meet the criteria, may differ, most experts on multicultural literature agree that certain features distinguish good multicultural books from ones that are outdated, stereotyped, and ultimately hurtful to members of the group who may read it. Nonetheless, several issues discussed below have spawned a great deal of controversy, most notably the question of balance and the ability of authors who are not part of a culture to write about a culture.

The first group to develop and disseminate widely a set of criteria for choosing multicultural books was the Council on Interracial Books for Children. Formulated in the 1970s, the flyer "Ten Quick Ways To Analyze Children's Books For Sexism And Racism" reached more than 200,000 librarians, educators, and parents by 1980 (Council on Interracial Books for Children, 1980). The CIBC followed it up with *Guidelines for Selecting Bias-Free Textbooks and Storybooks* (1980), which offered analyses of sexism, racism, handicapism, ageism, and classism in the basal readers, textbooks, and trade books that were available at the time, along with specific criteria for evaluating the portrayals of African-Americans, Asian-Americans, Latinos, and Native Americans. That publication also criticized the cultural and political biases of history textbooks.

Though directed at those who work with children, "Ten Quick Ways To Analyze Children's Books For Sexism And Racism" also sought to teach children how to examine their own books. The CIBC urged readers to "check the illustrations" for stereotyped images, tokenism (defined as faces that look exactly like white faces, except for the color), and the depiction of people of color in passive, subservient, or dependent roles. In suggesting to "check the story line," the CIBC alerted readers to people of color who must possess extraordinary abilities in order to succeed, who have to be infinitely understanding and forgiving, and whose stereotypical "problems" are solved by white people. Readers were encouraged to "look at the lifestyles" for stock portrayals, to "weigh the relationships between people" for the balance of power and the depictions of family relationships, to "note the heroes" for an excessive concentration upon "safe" heroes valued by the dominant culture, but less respected within their own community, and to "consider the effects on a child's self-image." On the controversial issue of the author's or illustrator's background, the CIBC urged readers to analyze the jacket copy for evidence of an outsiders' qualifications to write or illustrate the book and also to "check out the author's perspective"—whether it reflects the views of the dominant culture or those of minority groups. Finally, the CIBC asked readers to "watch for loaded words" and to "look at the copyright date," although, they pointed out, a recent copyright date is no guarantee of cultural sensitivity (Council on Interracial Books for Children, n.d.).

During the 1980s, a number of books written for teachers and librarians offered additional analyses and criteria for specific ethnic groups, along with lists of recommended works. One of the most widely read was Rudine Sims' *Shadow and Substance: Afro-American Experience in Contemporary Children's Fiction* (1982). Sims described three types of books about African-Americans, the "social conscience" books written by whites that were filled with stereotypes and inauthentic elements, the "melting pot" books, in which African-Americans occupied roles indistinguishable from their white counterparts, with no discussion of the race issue, and "culturally conscious" books, which presented the African-American characters within the context of their culture and community (Sims, 1982). Since the publication of *Shadow and Substance*, Sims has observed an improvement in the quality of books about African-Americans, stemming, primarily, from the fact that more authors and illustrators from that group have broken into print and are portraying the vast diversity of the African-American experience, from an African-American perspective (Sims-Bishop, 1991).

The most important book to analyze children's books about American Indians published during the 1980s was Beverly Slapin and Doris Seale's *Books Without Bias: Through Indian Eyes* (1988), which also included essays by prominent American Indian authors, such as Michael Dorris. That book has been revised and updated and is now entitled *Through Indian Eyes: The Native Experience in Books for Children* (1992).

For Asian-Americans and Asian cultures (except for India and the Pacific Islands), a good source is Esther C. Jenkins and Mary Austin's *Literature for Children about Asians and Asian-Americans: Analysis and Annotated Bibliography, with Additional Readings for Adults* (1987). Although the bibliography in this older book is out of date, the book's most important contributions are its discussion of selection criteria, its suggestions for using the books in the curriculum, and its checklists for evaluating multicultural units.

A good source for detailed, critical evaluations of books about Latin America and the Latino experience is Isabel Schon's *A Hispanic Heritage: A Guide to Juvenile Books about Hispanic People and Culture*. This title is in fact a series, each volume of which covers books published in a given time period; the fourth volume came out in 1993 and covers books published between 1987 and 1992. Each volume contains a discussion of general themes and specific criteria, updated as new issues have emerged.

Working with twenty area specialists on the general multicultural bibliography *Our Family, Our Friends, Our World*, Miller-Lachmann (1992) identified a number of major issues that teachers and librarians should take into account when evaluating fiction and nonfiction about both global cultures and minority cultures within the United States. Although the bibliography did not include folktales or nonprint materials, the same principles for evaluation can be applied to them as well. What follows is a discussion of the key issues and criteria that can be applied to all multicultural materials, including the criteria teachers should look for in examining each type of work (fiction, nonfiction, folktales, and nonprint materials) for the different age levels.

Accuracy and Authenticity

Accuracy is a major concern when evaluating any work of nonfiction. A treatment that contains false or distorted information is inaccurate, as is one that has significant omissions. A book may suffer from glaring errors in scholarship, or there may be the kind of minor errors that point to a pattern of careless research and presentation. There is a tendency for biographies and other works of nonfiction to leave out a heroic person's failings or any kind of negative and unpleasant information. In the early grades, teachers may prefer an overly positive treatment of culturally diverse groups and their heroes, just as few picture-book biographies of mainstream heroes such as George Washington and Thomas Jefferson discuss their flaws. In the later grades, however, children deserve to know the truth, even if it raises difficult dilemmas or is at times unpleasant. Books for older children and teenagers should also contain source notes and otherwise offer models of scholarly research for students.

Standards of scholarship should apply as well to folklore about diverse cultures. In evaluating a picture-book folktale or a collection for older children, the teacher should look for clear and descriptive source notes and, if necessary, go to the original source to check a work's authenticity (Hearne-A, 1993). Too many books have no source notes at all, and teachers should not be fooled by notes that merely describe the culture or claim the author heard stories (but not necessarily this particular story) from family members or friends in a given region (Hearne-A, 1993). Beyond citing the source, folktales should "respect the source," offering young readers not only an adaptation that preserves the spirit of the original, but which is also an accurate portrayal of the culture from which the tale comes (Hearne-B, 1993). When an author uses literary or artistic motifs from one culture in a folktale from another, such as Kiswahili words in a tale from West Africa or Southwestern Pueblo-inspired art in a tale from the Sioux, the result is not folklore but "fakelore" (Hearne-B, 1993, p. 36).

In fiction, the issue of authenticity is closely tied to that of accuracy. Authenticity involves the accurate portrayal of characters' thoughts and emotions, cultural details, and events in the recent and more distant past. For example, the African-American characters in Bruce Brooks' *The Moves Make the Man* (1984) and Mildred D. Taylor's *Roll of Thunder, Hear My Cry* (1977)—both historical novels that take place in the South—confront racist humiliations and threats. The protagonist in *The Moves Make the Man* hardly reacts at all, which some African-American reviewers have pointed out as unrealistic, while the characters in Taylor's novel, and its companion works featuring the Logan family and friends (*Let the Circle Be Unbroken*, *The Road to Memphis*, *Song of the Trees*, *The Friendship*, and *Mississippi Bridge*), respond with a wide and complex range of emotions, from anger to calculated submissiveness to pride in their ability to flourish despite the odds. Checking the authenticity of a work of fiction is often far more difficult than verifying footnotes, references, and source notes in nonfiction and folklore. If a teacher is unfamiliar with the culture, he or she will need to rely upon trusted review sources, bibliographies, fiction and nonfiction for adults, and the advice of friends and colleagues who are cultural insiders.

The Avoidance of Stereotyping

Stereotypes are sweeping general statements about a culture and the individuals that are part of it. Most stereotypes are negative, though positive stereotypes, such as the portrayal of Asian-Americans as a model minority also exist. Stereotypes in print and nonprint materials are hurtful even when they seem positive, for they deny the uniqueness of each group member. Unfortunately, stereotyping remains common in books and other materials about culturally diverse groups.

In nonfiction, the broad generalizations that constitute stereotyping may be made directly, such as the linking of all Arabs to terrorism or the description of Brazilians of African heritage as happy-go-lucky. They may be made through illustrations, as when all members of a certain group are shown as living in poverty. It is a common practice in books about other countries for authors to describe a national character, but the books should show a range of people and their outlooks as well.

With picture books of all kinds, folktales, concept books, and original stories, illustrations are a major place where stereotypes occur. Illustrators who stereotype make all the characters from a given group look alike, with exaggerated features that make those same characters look "different" from everyone else. *The Five Chinese Brothers*, with its uniformly vacuous faces, yellow skin, and slanty eyes, is a primary example. Stereotyped illustrations of African-Americans give members of this group big lips and identical skin tone and facial features. Illustrations are also stereotyped if they associate characters from a given group with a stock set of objects (*sombreros*, *huaraches*, and *burros* for Mexicans and Mexican-Americans, for example) or activities (such as taking a *siesta* under a palm tree).

Fiction texts are fraught with the potential for stereotyping. Stereotypes can occur in characterizations when general social, occupational, behavioral, and physical attributes assigned to the group dominate and the characters fail to emerge as fully realized individuals. Secondary and minor characters—who are less developed in general—tend to suffer from stereotypes more than the main protagonist, and teachers should therefore examine carefully any book with a main character who is white and a sidekick (or an antagonist) who is a person of color. Teachers should make sure that the books they offer do not all place people of color in secondary or minor roles, even if the characters are fully developed.

Stereotypes can occur in the plot when the characters from a given group play roles that are considered "typical" of that group. If a novel presents all of the African-American characters as involved in the drug trade, it is an example of stereotyping. So are novels that portray Mexican-Americans as migrant workers and Asian-Americans who gain the attention of classmates because of their good grades. For American Indians, the stereotyped roles include the "noble savage" who shows white people how to live simply and respect the environment, and the "savage savage" who attacks settlers' homes and takes their scalps. In addition to giving people roles and actions that are stereotyped, books may resolve conflicts in a stereotyped manner. If whites (or in the case of books set in other countries, Americans) solve the characters' problems or if the characters learn they must act more like people in the dominant culture in order to succeed, the plot reinforces stereotypes. For instance, several books published in recent years featured female Asian-American characters, all model students, who found happiness by learning to socialize and flirt with boys.

Settings of novels may reinforce stereotypes. Not all African-Americans live in ghettos, and less than 50 percent of American Indians live on reservations, but a disproportionate number of the novels published for children have these settings. Teachers should make sure their classroom collections represent a variety of settings, and books that do take place in overrepresented settings (urban ghettos, reservations, migrant farm communities for Mexican-Americans) are free from other elements of plot and characterization that would lead readers to believe these are the only living conditions for those cultural groups. Similarly, the themes of multicultural novels should be as diverse as the people themselves. Not all books about a given group should deal with resisting pressure to join a gang, for instance, and not all books about gang-related themes should be filled with African-American and Latino characters. Issues and problems do not face members of one group only, and they do not face all members of the group. Finally, teachers should look critically at books that have characters speak in stereotyped language. Dialect should be used correctly, not as how a member of the dominant culture might imagine it to be used (the classic ridicule of the Italian accent or Black English is a perfect example), and the same dialect, the same way of speaking, should not characterize all the members of a racial or ethnic group.

Appropriate Language

The correct and non-stereotyped use of dialect is one of several issues related to the appropriateness of language in a book, video, or computer program. The language itself should be authentic. The folktale *Sebgugugu the Glutton* (1993), retold by Verna Aardema, was marred by the appearance of Zulu expressions in a tale from Rwanda, where Zulu is not spoken. The computer program *Discover the World II* (1992) featured the indigenous people of West Africa speaking Kiswahili, which is one of several major languages spoken in *East* Africa; there are some three dozen languages spoken in West Africa, but definitely not Kiswahili. (A common mistake, incidentally, is to call the language Swahili. Swahili refers to the ethnic group. The language, Kiswahili, is spoken by the Swahili, but also by other ethnic groups in East Africa.)

Words in other languages, as well as words in dialect, should appear correctly in print or on video, as should the expression of those words, that is, the way they are used in the course of the story. Words in other languages or in dialect should be integral to the story, not just superficial elements and certainly not presented in a way that makes the speakers seem exotic or less intelligent. Examples of books that use dialect well, as an eloquent, authentically rendered means of expressing a story in a time, a place, and a community are Patricia McKissack's *Mirandy and Brother Wind* (1988), Virginia Hamilton's *The People Could Fly: American Black Folktales* (1985) (which uses modified dialect and is accompanied by a tape featuring Hamilton and actor James Earl Jones), and Rita Williams-Garcia's *Blue Tights* (1988). While teachers may not feel comfortable reading aloud a work written in an unfamiliar dialect, an increasing number of books have accompanying cassette tapes.

For students in bilingual programs, language is an important, though often neglected, issue. Translations should be idiomatic, consistent with the way the language is spoken in the students' countries of origin. A careless or poor translation for bilingual students implies that the students themselves are inferior.

Terminology should be up-to-date and free from pejorative expressions. Specialists in African Studies have called attention to the use of words such as "tribe" (to refer to ethnic groups in Africa), "hut" (to refer to African dwellings), "Bushmen" and "Hottentots" (to refer to the Khoi and San of southern and southwest Africa), "primitive," "savage," and "native" (Afolayan, Kuntz, & Naze, 1992). These terms, imposed by Western colonialists, connote inferiority. Often terminology changes with time; an example is the emergence of the term *African-American* in lieu of *Afro-American*, which gained prominence in the 1970s. Teachers can keep abreast of issues related to terminology by reading current articles and reviews.

Finally, language with respect to racial and ethnic issues should be age-appropriate. In her review of Jeri Ferris' *Arctic Explorer: The Story of Matthew Henson* (1989), school library media specialist April Hoffman (Hoffman, Payne, & Smith, 1992) makes the following point:

> She [Ferris] presumes too much sophistication on the part of her young readers. Children believe what they read, especially when it is in a "true fact" book. Two sentences, meant to be ironic, are not clarified and sound blatantly racist if taken literally. They are "He was the wrong color," and "As usual, Matt ate with the crew, not with the other expedition members." Examples such as these point to the need for extra sensitivity in writing and editing books on Black Americans for elementary-age readers. (p. 44)

Younger elementary-age children are likely to take a statement like "He was the wrong color" literally and assume the subject really was the wrong color. They are also likely to be upset by racial epithets and other expressions of prejudice. Most picture books do not contain such epithets, but many books written in chapter format—both fiction and nonfiction—do. Teachers should take into account the maturity level of the class before making such books available, so that the books do not hurt children who read them or cause less tolerant classmates to repeat the words. Frank language is common in young adult books, which offer a greater deal of realism for teenage readers. Epithets may be used in young adult books that deal with racial or ethnic issues, but like any other type of profanity, the epithets should not overshadow the story or seem to exist mainly for shock value. Books that use such words should be examined carefully for their overall treatment of racial issues.

The Author's Background

The issue of the author's background has perhaps led to more controversy than any other in the evaluation of multicultural children's books. There are those who believe the background in not important as long as the story is authentic, and to conduct extensive background searches to determine an author's qualifications itself reeks of racism (Rochman, 1993). Others argue that writing about a culture of which one is not a part is extraordinarily difficult; "there are more barriers and greater barriers to success in recreating, picturing, or explaining that which is not part of one's heritage" (Kruse, 1992, p. 31).

Essentially, both sides are correct. Writing, and the writing of fiction in particular, involves both experience and imagination. Without experience—gained from being raised in the culture, living within the culture or community for an extended period of time (as former journalist Suzanne Fisher Staples did before writing *Shabanu: Daughter of the Wind* (1989), her novel about a twelve-year-old girl living in the Cholistan Desert of Pakistan), or studying the culture extensively with the help of those who are part of it (as Linda Crew did for *Children of the River* (1989), a novel about an immigrant teenager from Cambodia)—a novel cannot convey the complex nuances. In past years and even today, books written by outsiders suffer from superficiality, stereotyping, and inauthenticity in characterization, language, setting, plotting, and theme. Too often, the outside writer or illustrator imposes his or her own cultural perspective upon the material. Examples of this are illustrators who either draw stereotypical racial features or Caucasian ones with colored-in faces, and authors who highlight aspects of life of interest to the dominant culture, but of little significance to the culture being portrayed. Characters in books about other countries may be tourists from the United States making superficial observations or having "typical" tourist experiences; often, these books have more to do with issues facing the tourist characters than with the country or its people. For instance, Will Hobbs' *Changes in Latitudes* (1988) is a compelling tale of a family falling apart while on vacation, but its portrayal of Mexico is inaccurate and patronizing.

While an author or illustrator from the culture is at an advantage, the proper background is no guarantee of authenticity and depth. Cultural groups are diverse; problems may arise, for instance, when a middle-class author writes about those from his or her culture who live in poverty. Authors from a culture may not be willing to display the culture's "dirty laundry;" for example, the Chilean photographer who authored the series book *We Live in Chile* (1985) made no mention of the repressive dictatorship under which his country suffered for more than a decade.

Ultimately, writers and illustrators rely upon the imagination in the rendering of their work. The most talented writers of all races and ethnic groups call upon the imagination to produce memorable and compelling works of fiction, not only about their own culture, but also about any other culture with which they empathize. In an interview with Hazel Rochman (1993), one of those writers, Nobel Prize winner Nadine Gordimer, discussed this issue:

> When I went back to South Africa in 1990, I interviewed Nadine Gordimer for *Booklist* at her home in Johannesburg. I asked her if she felt

that as a white she could write about the black experience, and how she answered those who said she was using black suffering. She got angry. "How does a writer write from the point of view of a child?" she said. "Or from the point of view of an old person when you are seventeen years old? How does a writer change sex?" (p. 22)

Nonetheless, Rochman warns,

And yet ... only gifted writers can do it, write beyond their own cultures. Fiction and nonfiction are full of people [characters and personages] who don't get beyond stereotype because the writer cannot imagine them as individuals. Traveling to foreign places—or reading about them—isn't necessarily broadening. Many tourists return from their experience with the same smug stereotypes about "us" and "them." Too many books about other countries, written without knowledge or passion, take the "tourist" approach, stressing the exotic, or presenting a static society with simple categories. Some writers who try to tackle a country's complex political and social issues seem to think that in a book for young people it's fine to do a bit of background reading and then drop into a country for a few weeks, take some glossy pictures, and go home and write a book about it. (pp. 22–23)

In sum, the content of the work itself is the most important issue. Works by authors from the culture itself are more likely to portray the culture authentically, and they are more likely to reflect its perspective. Yet to categorically exclude works because of the author's background would exclude some compelling, well-written works that bring a culture and its people to life (Special Box 9–1).

The Book's Perspective

The issue of perspective is closely tied to that of background. Essentially, perspective refers to the work's point of view, the way it sees, portrays, and interprets events. Most of what is available in basal readers, textbooks, trade books, and other materials reflects the perspective of the dominant culture. For example, nonfiction about other countries tends to examine those countries from the point of view of United States foreign policy or, as Rochman (1993) has observed, as a tourist focusing upon a "journey."

If the book takes a tourist approach ... then you get the kind of nonfiction photo-essay so common in children's literature, where the pictures are arranged so that the child—usually attired in national dress—goes on a "journey," a journey that allows the book to include some colorful scenery and local customs. (p. 23)

Given the pervasiveness of this tourist perspective, it is small wonder that a disproportionate share of stories set in other countries—both fiction as well as nonfiction—feature a child who takes some sort of trip.

SPECIAL BOX 9–1 *False Pretenses and the Background Dilemma*

Since its original publication in 1976, Forrest Carter's *The Education of Little Tree*, which claimed to be the autobiography of a young boy raised in the mountains of Tennessee by his Cherokee grandparents, has been embraced by teachers everywhere for its simple, poignant description of the boy's way of life. From his grandparents, Little Tree learns about Cherokee culture, traditional wisdom, his own family's roots, and survival skills. He also witnesses and experiences the cruelty of racism.

American Indian educators, among others, praised the book's authenticity. Thus, it came as a surprise when a *New York Times* op-ed article by historian Dan Carter (no relation) revealed its author to be Asa Earl Carter, a former Klansman and speechwriter for George Wallace (Carter, 1991). Toward the end of his life, Asa Earl Carter turned to writing novels and advocating for environmental issues. Dan Carter could find no records of the existence of Little Tree or his grandparents.

Despite the revelations, most of those who had recommended *The Education of Little Tree* for middle school readers continued to do so. Ginny Moore Kruse argued that "[t]he book itself arouses empathy for Little Tree and respect for his culture, regardless of whether or not its author's ancestry was, in part, Cherokee and whether or not the author had a lifelong respect for people of races other than white and American Indian" *(Kruse, 1992, p. 31).* In *Our Family, Our Friends, Our World,* (Miller-Lachman, 1992), the book's category was changed from nonfiction to fiction, and the following assessment was made:

> New information about the book's origins do not diminish the literary quality or the narrative power of the work. Nor has Dan Carter challenged the accuracy of the presentation. Yet it is not autobiography, but rather a carefully crafted work of fiction from a man who appears to have rewritten his life as well. (p. 174)

The controversy that erupted over *The Education of Little Tree*, and over dozens of other books whose authors allegedly misrepresented themselves and their backgrounds, points to the ability of some authors to write convincingly about a culture to which they do not belong—so convincingly, in fact, that they are believed to be part of the culture. Ultimately, teachers must evaluate the work itself, rather than the author's birth certificate, in selecting a multicultural book for classroom use.

The dominant perspective emerges in other ways. Works of fiction may portray people of color as "just like" members of the dominant group or only successful if they "make it" in the dominant society (Council on Interracial Books for Children, 1980). Folktales, too, can be adapted from the perspective of the dominant culture if the topic chosen or the retelling reflect European-American values rather than those of the original culture. For instance, *Nobiah's Well* (1993), by Donna Guthrie, bills itself as "a modern African folktale." This tale contains a child character who teaches his foolish and hot-tempered mother a lesson about concern for all living creatures. While many European fairy tales feature cruel adults who receive their comeuppance from children, this is not characteristic of folklore from anywhere in Africa.

When the perspective is that of another culture besides the dominant one, the results can be eye-opening. For instance, most books about opposition to slavery before the Civil War focus upon the white abolitionists; in truth, most of those who helped slaves escape were black (Hoffman, Payne, & Smith, 1992). Patricia and Fredrick McKissack's biography *Frederick Douglass: The Black Lion* (1987), which is written from an African-American perspective, points out that had the British won the Revolutionary War, slavery would have been abolished in 1833. Those from the dominant culture may not consider this issue, but it was central to the lives of the slaves and their descendents (Hoffman, Payne, & Smith, 1992). Michael Dorris' short novel *Morning Girl* (1992) portrays an Indian family living on an island in the Caribbean late in the fifteenth century. Most of the novel is about Morning Girl's relationship with her younger brother, but at the end, Columbus and his men arrive, and readers witness the "discovery" from the perspective of those whose civilization he destroyed.

Writers of African-American, American Indian, Asian-American, and Latino descent have played a crucial role in exposing young readers to diverse perspectives. Faith Ringgold's picture book *Tar Beach* (1991), which grew out of her famous "story quilt," looks at the George Washington Bridge and its construction from the perspective of a child whose father helped build the bridge, but because of his race received few rewards. The child imagines herself flying over the bridge and "owning" it, owning the building of the union that denied her father membership, and owning the ice cream factory, so that she and her family could eat ice cream for dessert every day. Yoko Kawashima Watkins' *So Far from the Bamboo Grove* (1986) and Sook Nyul Choi's *Year of Impossible Goodbyes* (1991) are autobiographical novels for teenage readers that explore the World War II Japanese invasion of Korea and its aftermath from two different perspectives—the Japanese (Watkins) and the Korean (Choi). Another path-breaking autobiographical novel that garnered praise for its unique perspective is Lyll Becerra de Jenkins' *The Honorable Prison* (1988), which describes a family, in an unnamed South American country, forced into a bleak internal exile because of the father's opposition to the country's dictator. While some novels by culturally diverse authors contain autobiographical elements, others are family stories handed down from generation to generation. Elizabeth Fitzgerald Howard's picture book *Aunt Flossie's Hats (and Crab Cakes Later)* (1991) is based upon the life of Howard's own aunt and offers the collective memories of a middle-class African-American family living in Baltimore earlier in the century. James Berry digs further back into his Jamaican family's roots to tell the harrowing tale of an African father and son brought to the West Indies as slaves. His young adult novel *Ajeemah and his Son* (1992) describes how the two were separated, on plantations only miles away, but never able to communicate with each other, given new names, and treated with arbitrary, relentless cruelty; the book also shows Ajeemah's eventual triumph after emancipation—his marriage to another slave and their beginning of another family in freedom. Books such as Ringgold's, Watson's, Choi's, Jenkin's, Howard's, and Berry's are rich and vivid in their portrayal of the past from the perspective of their own and their family's experiences. In these cases, the author's background is key to the story, offering readers a view that would not be available had the author not come from that culture, that family, that community.

The Concept of Audience

Closely tied to the issue of perspective is the author's concept of his or her audience. Books that reflect the dominant perspective are usually written for what is believed to be a general audience, though in past years some (such as the "social conscience" books derided by Sims) were directed at groups that did not conform to dominant values (Sims, 1982). That general audience has often excluded people of color, as they have been left out of the books or presented in stereotypical ways.

Today, most multicultural materials, including those by authors and illustrators of color and from culturally diverse perspectives, have been directed to a broad audience. The books touch upon universal conflicts and themes and are generally written in standard English. Nonetheless, they may contain revelations disturbing to members of the dominant culture, as they very well should. White readers may be shocked and upset by Mildred D. Taylor's portrayal of racism in the South before the Civil Rights movement or the cruelty experienced by children who participated in the movement, as documented by Yvette Moore's young adult novel *Freedom Songs* (1991) or the real-life memoirs of Sheyann Webb and Rachel West Nelson, *Selma, Lord, Selma* (1980). These books offer different messages to white and African-American children; middle-school classes with mixed student bodies can benefit from a discussion of how books and films may affect different audiences differently.

An increasing number of books by African-American authors about the African-American experience are being directed primarily to African-

American readers. One of the first to do this was Rita Williams-Garcia's *Blue Tights* (1988). Written in modified street slang, this novel for young teenagers focuses on African-American issues and concerns—physical characteristics such as skin tone, hair, and body type, divisions between African-Americans based upon national origin (West Indies vs. the United States) and social class, African dance, and the Black Muslims. There are universal elements as well, such as the protagonist's need for love, her decisions about sexual activity, and the painful process by which she learns to accept and respect herself. Another important book, directed to African-American preschoolers and kindergartners, is Angela Shelf Medearis' *Our People* (1994), in which the young protagonist learns about the accomplishments of her culture from her much-admired father.

Directed first and foremost to readers from the author's own cultural group, these books are enormously valuable in classrooms with students from that group, who can finally experience an author speaking to them personally. In addition, the books have much to say to young people from all cultures. More than any other type of work, they tell us which issues are of most importance to the group portrayed. Through these books (as well as nonprint materials such as videos and music), children can learn empathy, the ability to imagine themselves as someone else or someone from another culture, and to try to understand the work's content from that perspective. Just as the Whole Language movement urges children to be meaning-makers through their own experiences and the materials they encounter (Willinsky, 1990), multicultural materials directed to a specific group give children a chance to step into another culture in order to create meaning. Children of color must do this all the time when reading basal readers, textbooks, and books from the perspective of the dominant culture; it is a process that children from the dominant culture should experience also if they are to develop sensitivity and the capacity for empathy.

Integration of Cultural Information

In evaluating books and nonprint materials, teachers should examine how cultural information is incorporated into the story. If the entire point of the story is to communicate aspects of the language, culture, and social or political situation, the power of the narrative is lost, and the work comes to resemble a textbook or dry instructional filmstrip or video. The excessive focus upon cultural details, at the expense of the story, tends to turn details into exotica, for they are not a natural part of unfolding events. Teachers should make sure that the role of cultural elements in the character or personage's life is presented realistically as well as unobtrusively. The processes of urbanization and assimilation have reduced the place of distinct cultural elements and practices in the lives of many people throughout the world. At the same time, people are not all alike; the role of culture and how it changes under changing conditions cannot be ignored.

Balancing the need to inform a diverse audience with the need to maintain the flow of the narrative can be tricky. An author must know both the subject and the audience. One book that attains this balance is Frances Temple's *A Taste of Salt* (1992). Set in contemporary Haiti, the story features teenagers Djo, one of Jean-Bertrand Aristide's supporters, and Jeremie, the girl who visits Djo in the hospital and records his story after he is badly burned by anti-Aristide thugs. Temple, a United States citizen who has lived and worked in Haiti, holds the reader's interest with Djo and Jeremie's story, played out against the backdrop of Haiti's first election. The youngsters struggle against poverty, fear, and ignorance, and they learn to stick together in order to survive and to change their country for the better. Temple's book does more than expand upon today's headlines; through appealing characters with whom the reader can easily empathize, through their conflicts—some of which are unique to Haiti and some of which are common to all teenagers who believe in a cause and who grow to love each other despite their initial differences—she gives the reader a sense of time, place, and culture. Fortunately, an increasing number of novels for young readers succeed in portraying an unfamiliar setting unobtrusively and with a parallel focus upon what is universal in the human condition.

Currency of Facts and Interpretations

Before selecting multicultural books or nonprint materials for classroom use, teachers should check the copyright date and make sure that materials already in use are still current. Events change very quickly. Soon after the publication of *A Taste of Salt*, Aristide was deposed and forced into exile by the military, a fact that does not invalidate the book, but does require additional attention when the book is used. The same holds for the large and generally excellent body of fiction in print about life in South Africa under the recently ended apartheid regime. Teachers should keep up with current events both in the United States and abroad in order to know when events change the situation described in a contemporary novel, work of nonfiction, or documentary film.

Checking the copyright date may not be enough, however. Many works of nonfiction, especially those in series, are revised from time to time. Some revisions are thorough, others cosmetic. With the latter, facts may be changed, but the interpretations from the previous decades remain—sometimes along with the outdated photos.

Balance and Multidimensionality

Teachers usually look for balance, for the even-handed presentation of both sides of an issue, especially when evaluating nonfiction. While a balanced presentation may consist of the equal presentation of both sides within the same work, in the style of the Opposing Viewpoints series published by Greenhaven Press, teachers will most likely want to select a variety of individual works, each of which offers a different perspective or viewpoint. Given the mainstream bias of most textbooks, trade books from the perspective of African-Americans, American Indians, Asian-Americans, and Latinos themselves offer the best opportunity to present the other side. Well-researched nonfiction works that provide a perspective that is often lacking in textbooks include William L. Katz's *Breaking the Chains: African-American Slave Resistance* (1990) and Virginia Hamilton's *Many Thousand Gone: African-Americans from Slavery to Freedom* (1993), both of which describe vividly the conditions of slavery and more widespread slave resistance than textbooks generally acknowledge, and Simon Ortiz's *The People Shall Continue* (1988), a picture book for younger readers that describes American Indian history from an Indian perspective in the style of traditional storytelling.

Works of fiction are rarely objective; the best of them make their case with passion and skill, leaving a lasting impression with the reader. Mildred D. Taylor does not balance the racists in *The Friendship* (1987) with very many tolerant whites, though in *Mississippi Bridge* (1991) and other works she does highlight a white youngster who reaches out to the Logans despite pressure from his family and community. Those who oppose the immigration of refugees from the war-torn nations of El Salvador, Guatemala, Haiti, or elsewhere will find food for thought in Fran Leeper Buss' *Journey of the Sparrows* (1991). Written with the assistance of Salvadoran refugee advocate Daisy Cubias, this simple, lyrical novel for intermediate readers describes a twelve-year-old girl's journey to Chicago after her father is murdered in El Salvador and her equally harrowing trip back to bring her baby sister to safety. Frances Temple's *Grab Hands and Run* (1993) explores the same topic by means of a Salvadoran brother and sister who make the perilous journey alone to Canada.

Often issues do not have only two sides, but are complex and multidimensional. Teachers should make sure all sides are represented and that students are aware of the complexities. For instance, *So Far from the Bamboo Grove* and *Year of Impossible Goodbyes* present two different perspectives on the same event, but they are not, by any means, the only stories to be told. Brenda Wilkerson's *Not Separate, Not Equal* (1987) goes beyond the two-sided debate regarding school integration in the 1950s to explore the impact of integration upon a teenager who does not need any more complications in her life. The protagonist's parents have recently died, a favorite black teacher at her old school is fired for lack of a degree, and the six integration pioneers are set upon by a racist as they travel to and from school; as a result, the protagonist wonders if desegregation is really worth the price. Wilkerson's is an African-American perspective, but one that makes readers aware of the sacrifices African-American children made and continue to make in the name of racial equality and understanding.

Illustrations

Illustrations play a prominent role in picture books, including folktales and nonfiction for young readers. Cover illustrations are also a principal "selling point" for first chapter books and intermediate and young adult fiction. When children are given a choice of books to read, they often pick those with the most attractive covers. A multicultural book with an unattractive cover may require a lot of "pushing" before a child or teen will give it a chance.

Various other criteria apply to illustrations: They should be accurate and authentic and not offer stereotypical images of people of color. Facial features should be drawn without exaggeration or grotesque elements that may lead to ridicule of people of color. People of the same ethnic or cultural group should not all look the same. Too many picture books and folktales continue to portray certain cultures, such as American Indians, in exotic garb or in festival clothing at inappropriate times. They may be pictured as engaging in stereotypical activities or behaviors. Like the text, illustrations should portray the diversity of everyday life, as it exists (or existed) at the time of the story. Particularly in trade nonfiction and series works, teachers should look for reproductions or photos that are recycled from book to book and photos or other pictures characteristic of one ethnic group being used in a book about another, such as pictures of the Hopi Indians used in a book about the Navajo.

❖ Selecting Nonprint Materials

The ten concerns just described also apply to nonprint materials such as filmstrips, videos, cassettes, and educational software. With videos especially, visual images play a much greater role. Teachers should be aware of the expressions and body language portrayed in the video, the authenticity of clothing and objects, and the importance of portraying people from the culture in a variety of roles. Nothing in the video should be used to demean a people or to portray them as inferior. This is a particular danger with group shots, which strip the individuality from the subjects and make it more likely that they will appear savage or exotic; individual shots and close-ups should predominate. For animation, the same artistic standards apply as for static illustrations; unfortunately, many animators do not portray people of color realistically, but rather pick out and exaggerate a single feature. The language used by characters should be authentic. American Indians have pointed out the ridiculously inaccurate use of tribal languages in the western movies of decades past. Dialogue and voice-over narratives should present the perspective of the group itself.

Recent years have seen many changes in the use of audio-visual materials. Old-fashioned filmstrips have declined in popularity as videos

It is important to select authentic nonprint materials.

have gained. Most schools now own VCRs and monitors and have access to libraries of current and classic works. Teachers who want to make televised documentaries and dramas available to their students may do so, as long as copyright restrictions are strictly observed. Many works now considered "classic," such as the Walt Disney Studios adaptation of *Pinocchio*, are in fact filled with stereotyped images of non-white people. Teachers might want to avoid such "classics" or, depending upon the maturity of the class, discuss them critically both before and after the showing. In general, the more current the work is, the more likely it is to display greater cultural sensitivity, though there are enough exceptions to warrant a teacher's previewing the work first.

Music can contribute a great deal to a child's understanding of his/her own or another culture. Both traditional/folk music and contemporary musical expressions should be utilized. For instance, a thorough presentation of African-American music would include gospel and spirituals, blues, jazz, and hip-hop (rap). The need to cite and to respect the source—so important for separating folklore from "fakelore" (Hearne-B, 1993)—holds true for folk music. Whenever possible, teachers should provide the original or the closest version to the original in terms of historical period, performer, and adaptation. For bilingual classes, music is a particularly good source for other-language activities. The choices are plentiful, particularly for cultures (such as the Dominican Republic and Haiti), where there are few materials in print. Teachers should be able to understand and interpret the content of the music before bringing it to class. For many cultures, traditional musical forms are shunned by young people, and in some cases, certain types of music—Mexican *mariachi* music, for instance—has become a stereotypical aspect of the culture, while other types of music receive little attention.

Music is not the only aural medium making its way into classrooms. An increasing number of books are being put to tape, and storytellers are recording and distributing folktales. If a reading or storytelling makes use of dialect, that dialect should be authentic. Storytellers should offer the source for their tale either on the tape itself (the best approach) or prominently in the printed matter that accompanies the cassette. Standards for adapting a story authentically on cassette are the same as for an adaptation in print.

Educational software is a new and thriving area, and one where more attention needs to be given to cultural content. Several popular painting and writing programs feature settings around the world. Unfortunately, the settings contain stereotyped objects and outdated terminology; several programs offer an "African hut," for example. One program, described earlier, has a generic African speaking Kiswahili. All of the programs that have elements from Africa treat the continent as if it were one country. American Indians fare little better. Few allow the child to play the role of the Indians and to see the events from their perspective. This makes a program like *Pilgrim Quest* especially frustrating. Settlers are supposed to negotiate with neighboring Indians, but without their point of view, the Indians appear foreign, exotic, and savage. Even as

Educational software is a new area that needs more attention in terms of cultural diversity.

SPECIAL BOX 9–2 *A Sample Reading List*

The Malcolm X Academy Middle School is a Milwaukee middle school that offers a curriculum geared to the needs of the African-American students who live in the district. Because many of its students read below grade level, the reading curriculum is heavily skills-based. Basal readers are used, as are computer programs that offer drills and immediate feedback. Nonetheless, the curriculum does include novels and nonfiction about the African-American experience, most of them from an Afrocentric perspective. The following is the 1993–1994 school year reading list for all three grades, with the themes covered and the books used:

Grade 6 Reading List

I. Who Am I?/My People
Sounder
Song of the Trees
Sister
My Side of the Mountain
Talk About a Family
Aeson: Tales of Aethiop the African

II. Entrepreneurship and Community/Social and Political Responsibility
George Washington Carver
Historic Black Women (Empak Publishing Co.)
Historic Black Pioneers (Empak)

III. Values/Rites of Passage
The Island of the Blue Dolphins
Abdul and the Designer Tennis Shoes
Circle of Gold
Aesop: Tales of Aethiop the African
The Golden Pasture

Grade 7 Reading List

I. Who Am I?/My People
The Cay
Aesop: Tales of Aethiop the African (Part II)
Slake's Limbo
The Shimmershine Queen
The Upstairs Room

II. Entrepreneurship and Community/Social and Political Responsibility
Fast Sam, Cool Clyde, and Stuff
Black Scientists and Inventors (Empak)

III. Values/Rites of Passage
Where the Red Fern Grows

Sour Land
Circle of Gold
Phillip Hall Likes Me, I Reckon, Maybe
The People Could Fly

Grade 8 Reading List

I. Who Am I?/My People
The Magical Adventures of Pretty Pearl
I Know Why the Caged Bird Sings

II. Entrepreneurship and Community/Social and Political Responsibility
Corey
Freedom Crossing
The Night Journey

III. Values/Rites of Passage
The Pearl
Blue Tights
Won't Know 'Til I Get There
The Moves Make the Man
The Secret of Gumbo Grove
Tales of an Ashanti Father

Not all the books on this list are about the African-American experience. Others are written by authors who are not African-American. You might want to find out which books are not about the African-American experience and discuss why they might have been included on this list.

Other books have aroused controversy for their portrayal of African-Americans. Using reviews and annotated bibliographies, discuss what the controversies were about and whether or not you would have included the book on the list.

Most of the books on the list are classics that have been written before 1990. Choose a book for intermediate or young adult readers, published for the first time since 1990, that you would add to the list and justify your decision. Be sure to indicate the grade level and theme under which it would fit.

acclaimed a program as *The Oregon Trail* gives scarce attention in the game itself to the Indians who inhabited the western states; there is certainly no mention that the land was once theirs or that they might have once attacked settlers and travelers to defend it. The manual in the educational version does contain this kind of information, but teachers do not use the manuals as much as they should, and programs from many publishers do not contain such a comprehensive educational version. Indians in the program are uniformly friendly; one even helps the wagon across the river in exchange for three sets of clothing. Without the additional information in the manual, this otherwise excellent program contributes its share to the noble savage stereotype.

By its nature, software is limited in its complexity by hardware constraints—memory and hard disk drive space. Still, laser discs and CD-ROMs, which are appearing in more and more schools, permit greater complexity and depth. It remains to be seen whether the software will take advantage of the new hardware to present multicultural issues in a more sensitive and authentic manner.

❖ Some Parting Words

In evaluating books for classroom use, teachers may wonder if different criteria should be used depending upon the ethnic composition of the class. Works that portray the contributions of culturally diverse groups and feature strong protagonists from those groups help to build the self-esteem of children from those groups. At the same time, those works help to build tolerance, acceptance, and respect on the part of children who are not part of the group. With a teacher's guidance, children from other cultures will be able to find experiences in common, for the experience of oppression and racism has not been limited to one race, religion, or ethnic group.

By the same token, a work that would be deemed hurtful or inappropriate to children from one ethnic group is hurtful and inappropriate for all. If a teacher believes the stereotyped illustrations in a picture book might humiliate Asian-American children, for example, why should that book be used in a class in which no Asian-American students are present? Such a book would only reinforce other children's stereotyped images of Asian-Americans, and it would become a source of ridicule *in abstentia*. As children mature, they gain the ability to look critically at books and other materials they encounter in the classroom; no longer do they believe everything they see and read. At this point, teachers can make available works that are flawed, biased, inauthentic, or stereotyped, in order to encourage students to become critics and to recognize the need for a culturally sensitive approach. The point at which this process occurs varies among students and may depend as well upon the dynamics of the class. However, by middle school, teachers should be prepared to offer problematic materials and to take a more critical stance toward those materials (Henderson, 1991).

Finally, many of the trade books discussed are, like most textbooks and basal readers, published by the major presses. Other books cited come from small and alternative presses. During the early 1980s, alterna-

Small presses are an important source of multicultural books.

tive presses were the most committed to bringing multicultural authors and books into print. Among the most important of the small and alternative presses were (and continue to be) Children's Book Press, which publishes folktales and original stories with a focus on the Asian, Latin-American, and Latino experience; Just Us Books, which concentrates on nonfiction about Africa and African-Americans; Black Butterfly Press, which publishes picture books by African-American authors and illustrators, and Lee & Low, a recently established house that publishes books on a vide variety of multicultural themes. In addition, smaller publishing houses with a more regional (rather than national) distribution have made available a number of books about groups—particularly the Indian Nations—for which very little is in print otherwise.

❖ Summary

General principles for selecting quality books for classroom collections emphasize the presence of a positive portrayal of cultural groups. This includes showing that cultural groups are similar, are different, are diverse, and are evolving. Specific criteria have been provided by several organizations. Some of these are: (1) checking illustrations for stereotypes, tokenism, and people of color in passive, subservient roles; (2) checking the story line; (3) looking at the lifestyles portrayed; (4) analyzing the book cover; (5) watching for loaded words; and (6) checking the copyright date. The author suggests checking accuracy and authenticity; the author's background; the book's perspective; integration; and balance and multidimensionality in the characters and story.

❖ CHAPTER 9 **Questions**

1. Explain the need to portray members of cultural groups as both similar to and different from others in books chosen for multicultural classrooms.

2. What are the dangers in books that focus on the exotic aspects of a culture?

3. How can a teacher solve the problem of presenting variety in the portrayal of a culture?

4. Criteria for selection of multicultural literature presented in *Our Family, Our Friends, Our World* include accuracy and authenticity in the story or writing. How can a teacher who is unfamiliar with a specific culture apply this criterion?

5. What is the dilemma involved in checking the author's background? How would you resolve it?

6. The particular perspective of a book is very important in the portrayal of a given culture. Would you reject a book if the perspective was not balanced—presented from more than one point of view? What is an alternative?

❖ **References**

Afolayan, M., Kuntz, P., & Naze, B. (1992). Sub-Saharan Africa. In L. Miller-Lachmann, *Our family, our friends, our world: An annotated guide to significant multicultural books for children and teenagers* (pp. 417–443). New Providence, NJ: R. R. Bowker.

Carter, D. (1991, October 4), The transformation of a Klansman. *The New York Times*, p. A31.

Council on Interracial Books for Children (1980). *Guidelines for selecting bias-free textbooks and storybooks.* New York: Council on Interracial Books for Children.

Council on Interracial Books for Children (n.d.). *Ten quick ways to analyze children's books for sexism and racism.* New York: Council on Interracial Books for Children.

Garcia, R. L., & Ahler, J. G. (1992). Indian education: Assumptions, ideologies, strategies. In J. Reyhner (Ed.), *Teaching American Indian students* (pp. 13–32). Norman, OK: University of Oklahoma Press.

Greenfield, E. (1985). Writing for children: A joy and a responsibility. In D. McCann & G. Woodard (Eds.), *The Black American in books for children: Readings in racism* (2nd ed.). Methuen, NJ: Scarecrow Press.

Hearne, B. (1993a). Cite the source: Reducing cultural chaos in picture books, Part one. *School Library Journal, 39*(7) (July 1993), 22–27.

Hearne, B. (1993b). Respect the source: Reducing cultural chaos in picture books, Part two. *School Library Journal, 39*(8) (August 1993), 33–37.

Henderson, V. (1991). The development of self-esteem in children of color. In M. V. Lindgren (Ed.), *The multicolored mirror: Cultural substance in literature for children and young adults* (pp. 15–30). Fort Atkinson, WI: Highsmith Press.

Hoffman, A., Payne, S., & Smith, R. (1992). African Americans. In L. Miller-Lachmann, *Our family, our friends, our world: An annotated guide to significant multicultural books for children and teenagers* (pp. 25–91). New Providence, NJ: R. R. Bowker.

Kruse, G. M. (1992). No single season: Multicultural literature for all children. *Wilson Library Bulletin* (February 1992), 30–33+.

Miller-Lachmann, L. (1992). *Our families, our friends, our world: An annotated guide to significant multicultural books for children and teenagers.* New Providence, NJ: R. R. Bowker.

Rochman, H. (1993). *Against borders: Promoting books for a multicultural world.* Chicago: American Library Association.

Sims, R. (1982). *Shadow and substance: Afro-American experience in contemporary children's fiction* (2nd ed.). Chicago: NCTE/ALA.

Sims-Bishop, R. (1991). Evaluating books by and about African-Americans. In M. V. Lindgren (Ed.), *The multicolored mirror: Cultural substance in literature for children and young adults* (pp. 31–44). Fort Atkinson, WI: Highsmith Press.

Willinsky, J. (1990). *The new literacy: Redefining reading and writing in the schools.* New York: Routledge.

CHAPTER 10

Strategies for Using Multicultural Materials

In addition to selecting multicultural materials, teachers need to know how to incorporate those materials into the curriculum. Even well-chosen materials can lead to stereotyping and misinformation if used incorrectly. Teachers also experience a variety of constraints in using multicultural materials, including limited budgets and the restrictions of a standardized curriculum.

❖ Problems with the Current Approach

Problem One: The Time of Year

At present, multicultural materials tend to be used in schools at certain times each year. Teaching about American Indians tends to occur in October and November, coinciding with the holidays of Columbus Day and Thanksgiving. Teachers often introduce materials about African-Americans in January and February because of the birthday of Martin Luther King, Jr. and Black History Month. Also receiving attention during January and February are books about Asian and Asian-American culture, particularly as they relate to the lunar new year (Yeh, 1991). Although introducing multicultural content to coincide with holidays is better than not introducing it at all, it does have the effect of marginalizing the culture. Why is there a single Black History Month (and the shortest month at that!)? Why not black history all year long? The history of each cultural group belongs in the curriculum throughout the year, as part of our unique, but shared, American history. Multicultural materials should be offered at all times, not just during holidays that call attention to the culture.

Problem Two: Superficial Aspects

At the same time, when diverse cultures are taught, the focus still tends to be on the most superficial aspects of the culture—the holidays, clothing, food, and crafts. Holidays are an important aspect of each culture, revealing its conception of the life cycle, the annual cycle, and key historical events. Yet holidays are not ordinary days, and to concentrate upon them obscures the elements of daily life, past and present. Holiday costumes are not what people within the culture wear every day, but children get the sense that people in other cultures wear unusual clothing because of the excessive focus upon holidays. Clothing, food, and crafts pose a different problem. While most cultures tend to celebrate the same holidays over time (an exception is Kwanzaa, an African-American celebration that was created in 1966 and has been gaining acceptance ever since), clothing, food, and crafts have undergone changes as a result of modernization, immigration, and other larger societal changes. A focus upon traditional clothing, food, and crafts often means a focus upon a way of life that no longer exists except as a show for tourists. Teachers must be aware of what traditional practices have changed and how they have changed in order to avoid giving children a tourist's view of a culture. Teachers also need to explore activities that go beyond the superficial aspects of culture to reveal the richness and diversity of daily life within the culture.

Problem Three: Reliance upon Folktales

Finally, the present approach to teaching other cultures places too much emphasis upon published folktales. Unfortunately, a disproportionate percentage of multicultural books published, particularly in the picture book category, are folktales. Even for intermediate readers, collections of folktales are beginning to dominate, especially in books about Africa (Miller-Lachmann, 1994).

While folktales are important and should be offered to children, the problems of relying too heavily upon folktales in a multicultural curriculum are fourfold. Assuming the tale is verifiable and presented in an authentic manner—that it is folklore and not "fakelore"—it still emphasizes the traditional and the rural. Many folktales are animal stories or take place in nature. Without other alternatives, they give the impression that the culture is an entirely rural one even at present, and that there are only a few people, all of whom live together in harmony with the animals. As traditional stories, these tales offer insights into the roots of a culture and its core values, as they have been handed down through the generations, but they do not tell us much about how people in the cultures live today.

Secondly, folktales tend to emphasize the exotic aspects of the culture, what is unusual or strange about it. Illustrations of folktales frequently feature traditional or festival dress (or the artist's conception of it), and often the folktales chosen for publication are those that portray the most "picturesque" or exotic sub-groups within a culture rather than the largest or most influential.

A third problem with folktales about unfamiliar cultures is that readers are more likely to believe that certain imaginative or supernatural elements occur in real life. Folklore from all cultures has a strong element of fantasy, but what children recognize as fantasy in European folktales may be perceived as real in tales from Africa, Latin America or Southeast Asia. In evaluating John Steptoe's acclaimed adaptation *Mufaro's Beautiful Daughters* (1987), Nigerian folklore expert Michael Afolayan warned of this problem and gave the example of the "'competition call' made by the beautiful women of the region to the king," as "one such example of an imaginary device" (Afolayan, Kuntz, & Naze, 1992, p. 429).

Finally, folktales from other cultures are likely to be misinterpreted when viewed through the lens of the dominant culture, leading to further distortions. When publishers and authors choose tales to adapt, they often choose on the basis of current issues in United States society. One that has occupied the forefront in recent years is the environment and its protection. Certainly the rise in environmental consciousness has fueled interest in American Indian folklore and culture, at the peril of reinforcing the image of American Indians as noble savages living at one with nature, far from the corruption of civilization. Africans, too, have suffered from the noble savage stereotype, as communicated in folktales. Verna Aardema's adaptation of a Rwandan tale in *Sebgugugu, the Glutton*

(1993) features a character who is punished for his greed, represented in part by his efforts to obtain more cattle. Reading this didactic tale, one gets the impression that people in Rwanda (or elsewhere in Africa) do not believe in individual enterprise or in amassing private property. Nothing could be further from the truth in a society in which, traditionally, the size of one's herd is the principal measure of wealth.

The following suggestions and strategies are offered in order to combat the problems detailed above: the tendency to focus upon multicultural issues merely during holidays and Black History Month; the concentration upon the most superficial aspect of culture, such as holidays, food, crafts, and clothing; and the overreliance upon published folktales in presenting diverse cultures through literature. Each of the strategies can be used in some form on any grade level from kindergarten through high school; as a result, the general outline of the strategy will be described rather than specific course outlines and lesson plans. Each of the strategies is a composite of programs being used currently in schools around the country.

❖ Multiculturalism Across the Curriculum

One of the major tenets of the Whole Language movement, as it has been adapted by schools, is the teaching of literature and writing across the curriculum (Willinsky, 1990). Teachers of social studies and science are using fiction to explore issues, while math teachers are having children

Library displays can give both teachers and students ideas for further study.

write about the role of numbers in their own lives. Because so much of multicultural literature presents the history of diverse cultures in the United States and around the world, there is a natural connection between this literature and the disciplines within social studies. Though less obvious, there are also connections between writings about diverse cultures and the disciplines of science, mathematics, art, and music.

Science

Science is an area that can be explored using the insights of diverse cultures within the United States and around the world. In discussing the origins of the universe and humankind, teachers can offer students creation myths from a variety of cultures. One very good collection for intermediate readers is Virginia Hamilton's *In the Beginning: Creation Stories from Around the World* (1988). Environmental issues lend themselves to a multicultural approach. Students can explore various cultures' conception of the environment, or they can read about current environmental controversies as they affect different cultures. Given the wide availability of folktales from different cultures on environmental themes, these would serve as a starting point for exploring traditional perspectives. For American Indians, some good choices would be Caron Lee Cohen's *The Mud Pony: A Traditional Skidi Pawnee Tale* (1988) and Paul Goble's *Her Seven Brothers* (1988), an adaptation of a Cheyenne myth. From the Miskito Indians of Central America, there is the cautionary tale *The Invisible Hunters* (1987), adapted by Harriet Rohmer, Octavio Chow, and Morris Viduare. This book, like all of the folktales and contemporary picture-book stories published by Children's Book Press, is a bilingual edition, in this case English and Spanish. From African cultures, some good folktale selections on environmental themes are Rosa Guy's adaptation of *Mother Crocodile* (1981), which comes from the Oulouf tradition of Senegal in West Africa, and *The Orphan Boy* (1991), a Maasai tale from East Africa adapted by Tololwa Mollel. From the Aboriginal culture of Australia comes Dick Roughsey's *The Giant Devil-Dingo* (1973), which presents the concept of the Dreamtime and offers many parallels with American Indian legends.

Contemporary books about environmental issues as they relate to diverse cultures allow children to see how cultures have adapted traditional beliefs to the challenges of the present. Often indigenous groups have led the fight for the preservation of the land, but the issues are often complex. For elementary school children in second or third grade and up, there is *Red Ribbons for Emma* (1981), a photo-documentary that describes a Navajo Indian woman's struggle to prevent a coal company from mining on reservation land. Middle school readers will appreciate Brent Ashabranner's *Morning Star, Black Sun: The Northern Cheyenne Indians and America's Energy Crisis* (1982), which takes an interdisciplinary approach in presenting the complicated issues surrounding Indian land rights and resource extraction. As Ashabranner shows, the Northern Cheyenne have at times chosen the promise of economic development over the preservation of the environment. The rain forests of Austrialia are the subject of Jeannie Baker's picture book *Where the Forest Meets the Sea* (1988), which is distinguished by its attractive, original, and creative art work. Young children who use this book may be inspired to create their own collages from nature, thus combining the disciplines of art and science. For slightly older readers, George Ancona's *Turtle Watch* (1987) is a photo-documentary that describes how scientists in Brazil have worked with the local community to preserve the endangered sea turtles. There are a number of books as well for elementary and middle school readers about individual scientists of color who have received scant attention in traditional science textbooks.

SPECIAL BOX 10–1   *An Interdisciplinary Gold Mine*

While multicultural materials are plentiful in the fields of language arts and social studies, teachers often have a hard time finding materials and lesson plans in the sciences. Two sources that use a multidisciplinary approach, combining the study of science with American Indian history and folklore, are *Keepers of the Earth: Native American Stories and Environmental Activities for Children* (1988) and *Keepers of the Animals: Native American Stories and Wildlife Activities for Children* (1991). Created by folklore scholar Michael Caduto and Abenaki storyteller, writer, and publisher Joseph Bruchac, with introductions by N. Scott Momaday and Vine DeLoria, Jr., these two volumes offer a comprehensive portrayal of various American Indian cultures as they regarded the natural world. For the American Indian cultures, science, as we understand it, was part of everyday life, for humans, animals, and the rest of the natural world existed in an interdependent relationship. Each culture had its own way of interpreting that relationship, just as Western scientists have developed their own rules for the way the universe works. Using these two volumes, teachers and students can gain an understanding of how scientific concepts are developed through observation and how various cultures come to think about the world around them.

   Keepers of the Earth and *Keepers of the Animals* are geared to adult readers, who will find within their pages not only information related to the sciences, but also instruction in the art of storytelling and how to use traditional folktales in teaching about American Indians. Caduto and Bruchac provide lists of activities for a variety of ages, from preschoolers to adolescents and adults. Teachers can also obtain a Teacher's Edition, which provides specific lesson plans and workbook activities. For students in the elementary grades, an anthology of the stories themselves is also available.

Mathematics

An interdisciplinary, multicultural approach to the study of mathematics would certainly utilize books that highlight the achievements of the Aztecs, the Chinese, and various ethnic groups in Africa who devised complex calendars and number systems. Books on the pyramids in Egypt and Latin America can be combined with demonstrations. Through statistics, math can be combined with social studies in increasingly complex ways. Students can learn to represent population growth or other numerical information in textbooks and trade books by means of graphs, pie charts, and pictographs. Students can also become the collectors of statistics within their classroom and community, finding out, for instance, how many parents speak another language besides English or where the people who live on their street or in their building were born. These findings can then be represented visually. As students become the "statisticians" of their community, they develop a personal interest in the study of mathematics, and their findings become part of the permanent record of the community.

Art and Music

Art and music are important elements of any interdisciplinary approach. Students can evaluate and compare the artistic styles of folktales within or among cultures. Live or video presentations of artists and craftspeople offer insight into how a particular culture's art is created. Through music, children can learn about different musical instruments, rhythms, and melodies. Listening to the lyrics of folk and contemporary music—either in the original language or in translation—children learn about the traditional stories and mores of a group, or they can learn about political and social conflicts today. Children in bilingual classes can work with their counterparts to translate lyrics from their native language into English. Music and art can also be used in the process of creating a video documentary about a given culture or about various cultural perspectives upon a specific issue, such as immigration or the environment.

A Specific Example

An example of an ambitious multidisciplinary program on cultural diversity, which began in 1991–1992 and is ongoing, is that which took place at a Philadelphia-area middle school, the Stetson Middle School. This school, which has a diverse student body of European-Americans, African-Americans, Latinos, and Asian-Americans, divided the year into five segments. During those segments, students studied the contributions of American Indians, European-Americans, African-Americans, Asian-Americans, and Latinos, as well as current issues facing each of these groups, as part of each of their subject-area classes. In addition to their regular subject-area curriculum, each class completed a project—a bulletin board, a meal for the class, a play, a sculpture. Several times during the year, a locker area was turned into a tropical rain forest that illustrated the animals inhabiting that region of Latin America or Asia and some of the environmental issues surrounding the rain forest. Finally, students and staff videotaped the different class offerings for each segment and edited the videotape into a collage of their year (Bishop, Bender, & Kowalchik, 1993).

Obviously, such a grand undertaking requires the cooperation of many subject-area teachers as well as the school library media specialist and the administration. In fact, any interdisciplinary multicultural approach will require cooperation among teachers. In the elementary grades, where students remain with one teacher throughout most of the day, coordination is simpler; the classroom teacher may need to work only with the music, art, or library media specialist. At the middle school level, a number of teachers will need to come together for a fully multi-disciplinary approach. For this to happen, there generally has to be support at the top, on the part of the principal, for the necessary meetings to take place and the materials to be obtained. Even without such broad support, teachers can work together with colleagues in one discipline to coordinate readings and in-class activities. Natural alliances can occur between the language arts teacher and the social studies teacher, or between either one of those subject-area teachers and the school library

Students participate enthusiastically in the creation of their own bulletin boards.

media specialist. Even a limited interdisciplinary approach, such as the introduction of multicultural novels in a social studies class and biographies in a language arts class, is easy to accomplish and can have a major impact upon students' understanding of the topic.

❖ Using the Community to Teach About Cultures

In schools where there is a great deal of diversity, the outside community can play a major role in teaching the children about their own and each others' culture. Even in schools that are entirely European-American, there may be Jewish children and children from a variety of nationalities, who might have immigrated during different times in the country's history. Much can be gained by inviting people from the community—parents, grandparents, religious leaders, political leaders, artists, and others—into the classroom to offer their insights and experiences. In the first place, a stronger school-community partnership strengthens the community's—and by implication, the parents'—commitment to the school, leading to higher achievement. As Comer and others have noted, children of color are particularly well-served by a school and a community that work together (Comer, 1980).

Bilingual students and students from other language traditions benefit when their parents and others from the community offer programs in their native language, and where the maintenance and preservation of the native language is reinforced (Cummins, 1986). For instance, the school can work with American Indian communities to preserve and create materials in tribal languages that, without the support of the schools, would otherwise die out within a few generations (Reyhner-B, 1992).

Other groups with a relatively small presence in the United States may not have access to many published works about their experiences; bringing people from the community into those schools will validate those students' cultural experiences and help others in the school to learn more about their classmates. As an example, the Connecting Libraries and Schools Project (CLASP) of the New York Public Library has worked with teachers and school library media specialists for grades K–8 to provide materials for the predominantly Dominican-American student body of Community School District 6. In the absence of those materials, the public librarians have supported initiatives by teachers, parents, and community organizations to generate locally produced materials. The public library has also sponsored multicultural music, storytelling, puppetry, and drama programs, some held in the school building and some at the library branch.

Teachers and administrators who want to involve the community in the education of their culturally diverse students have a number of options, each offering an increasingly greater level of participation. The school can invite parents to speak to a class, and it can seek grants to bring local writers, artists, storytellers, puppeteers, and musicians to the school. Through programs sponsored in part through New York City's three public library systems, some of the city's most prominent writers for children, including Walter Dean Myers, Rita Williams-Garcia, Jacqueline Woodson, Yvette Moore, and Nicholasa Mohr have returned to schools, where they once attended as students, in order to speak and lead writing workshops. In social studies classes, the community's political and religious leaders may be invited; science teachers may want to bring in people from the health-care field, scientists, or inventors.

In addition to bringing community figures into the classroom, teachers can send their students out into the community to conduct interviews with parents, grandparents, and others, and to do research on the com-

Astronaut, Dr. Mae Jemison speaking at the Mae Jemison Academy, Detroit, MI. Used with permission.

munity. As a group, the class can decide what kinds of cultural and historical information it wants to collect, who to interview, what questions to ask, and how to deal with problem situations. As described in an earlier section, the interviews and other information collected may be analyzed statistically in math class, while the students could use their social studies class to examine the issues raised, their language arts class to write up the interviews, and their art class to represent the information visually. Beyond collecting interview information, older students could use the school and public library to research their community via newspaper articles and local history materials. All students, kindergarten and up, can write and illustrate their own stories, and as their skills improve, they can write and illustrate their family's history, the results of their first-person research (interviews and surveys), and their findings from sources in the library. Teachers can adjust their requirements and expectations to the abilities of the students, demanding increasing sophistication as the students move from grade to grade. The written work may be in English, in the student's original language, or in a bilingual edition.

A principal step in the creation of the community record is its publication. Before publication, however, the students' writing should be edited and revised into something resembling a "conventional final copy" (Edelsky, 1991, p. 32). Students learn a great deal, both about the mechanics of writing and how to communicate to the audience, when they read and help to edit each other's work as opposed to relying solely upon the suggestions of the teacher (Edelsky, 1991). While many younger students create homemade books which may be stapled together, attached by brads, or spiral bound, the personal computer has made the publication process easier while adding new capabilities. The best programs make it possible for students to input text with little assistance, and either add clip art illustrations provided by the program or ones created by the students themselves. Ambitious teachers with a special interest in desktop publishing can take those works and go on to create very professional-looking publications, with four-color graphics and scanned photographs. Alternatively, interactive texts can be created using HyperCard or other authoring programs.

School-generated documents in languages other than English can be translated into English, or writings in English can be translated into the other languages offered at the school. With the cooperation of bilingual and English-only teachers, the classes can work together on the translation. This makes the works more accessible, reinforces English and other-language skills among both groups, and counters the isolation that bilingual students frequently feel, as their program often leads to resegregation within the school. (See Chapter 3 for a discussion of resegregation and how it relates to bilingual students.)

Finally, the *published* works can be circulated within the school and maintained in the library media center as part of the school's resources.

Schools may also want to make contact with other schools in the local area or in distant parts of the country to share publications. In this way, students from a different culture, within the same city or far away, can learn about another community, another experience. Students from diverse cultural backgrounds will also gain more awareness of and respect for each other if they read their counterparts' personal, family, and community stories. As the popularity of pen pals attests, when children read about personal experiences from other children, these experiences become more real and compelling. Thus, teachers who are engaged in family and community history projects should explore setting up sister school relationships with schools that serve a different population.

❖ The In-Depth Teaching of a Culture Through Literature

Most strategies for teaching about cultures, including those previously described, involve activities that can be pursued in addition to the regular curriculum. While a day or a week here and there may be devoted to creating the class project or putting together the individual, family, and community histories, the rest of the time may consist of the standard curriculum, as structured by basal readers and textbooks. (On the other hand, the rest of the curriculum may be a multicultural one as well.)

Norton's Five Phases

The five-phase model described by Donna Norton offers a sequence geared to the older elementary and middle school level that is, in fact, an integral part of the reading curriculum. A teacher could devote as little as a few weeks or as much as a full year to explore the cultural traditions of one or more groups. However, Norton insists that the sequence be completed with each group before going on to the next, in order to avoid giving students an incomplete picture of each group's experience from its beginning to the present day (Norton, 1990).

While Norton argues for the importance of folklore and mythology, she sees them as components of a broader curriculum that includes nonfiction, biography, historical fiction, and contemporary fiction. Because folklore represents the oral traditions of a group, its earliest history, its explanations of the origins of the universe and humankind, and its core values, it should be studied first. Afterward, students can identify the same themes and values as they appear in other works of literature (Norton, 1990). Both Phase I and Phase II in Norton's scheme focus upon folklore and mythology.

Phase I.   Phase I consists of general instruction in the oral tradition along with a review of its different forms—myths, legends, folktales, and fables (Norton, 1990). As part of this first phase, students read a sampling of tales from a broad cultural group or region, such as Indians from the United States and Canada, Indians of Latin America and the Caribbean, people from Africa, South Asia, East Asia, Southeast Asia, and the indigenous groups of Australia, New Zealand, and the Pacific Islands. This sampling should familiarize children with the major themes and types of stories characteristic of the broad group or region, including creation myths, transformation tales, trickster tales, and family tales. (Norton, 1990). At the end of this phase, teachers should help students summarize and state some generalizations about the tales and their telling that can be tested during Phase II, when the class explores the oral tradition in one or two sub-groups (Norton, 1990).

Phase II. With Phase II, students begin to recognize for themselves the diversity within cultures. Either in small groups or as an entire class, students read extensively in the folklore, legends, and mythology of several Indian Nations or ethnic groups in Latin America, Africa, Asia, and the Pacific (Norton, 1990). In this way, students can compare the values and world views of more than one group to note their commonalities and differences. Students may also examine two versions of the same tale, interpreted by different cultures, or two approaches to telling and illustrating a tale from one particular tradition. In doing this, students learn to critique the authenticity of a tale and its presentation. For example, after receiving a background in the principal values and themes of African folklore and then focusing more specifically on tales from East Africa, students will be able to identify inauthentic elements in tales such as *Nobiah's Well.*

They can also see the extent to which cultures in a given region may influence each other and how contact between two very distinct cultures, such as the Aztecs and the Spaniards (see John Bierhorst's *Doctor Coyote: A Native American Aesop's Fables* [1987], for instance), may be reflected in the folklore of one or both. Similarly, students can see how the process of migration from one place to another affects the oral tradition and how it has evolved in the various places to which groups have moved. This is especially true for West African folklore, in its various incarnations in Africa and among those sent from there to slavery in the United States, in the Caribbean, and in the coastal regions of Brazil. Thus, students learn that the oral tradition is not static; through the centuries and even today it changes in response to wider events.

Phase III. In Phase III of Norton's program, students get a sense of the events that have affected each group's existence. Here, students read a variety of nonfiction and biographical accounts (Norton, 1990). There is an emphasis upon autobiographies and personal narratives at this stage; as the writer is a product of his or her own culture, these firsthand accounts often reflect the issues raised by works in the oral tradition. The ancient teachings are a part of the subject's consciousness, and what happened in later life is often interpreted through these teachings. Other subjects come to question traditional ways or reformulate them to suit contemporary situations. Nonfiction and biography can be used together to explore the individual's impact upon larger events and to place the individual in the context of his or her group's history. Of all the types of literature, this is the one most often utilized to show how cultures change over the years. At the same time, the students' knowledge of the values and beliefs of the culture—gained through the study of myths, folktales, and legends—can help them to evaluate whether a work of nonfiction or biography is told from the perspective of the group or from the perspective of an outsider who knows very little about the culture (Norton, 1990; Dorris, 1979).

Phase IV. Norton's fourth phase has students read historical fiction, with the goal of teaching them to evaluate its authenticity in light of traditional literature and nonfiction and to see how the authors—both from within the group and outside it—bring events to life through plot, setting, characterization, theme, and language (Norton, 1990). Students can discuss how historical fiction, as opposed to traditional literature and straight history, can contribute to our understanding of a group and the issues facing it at a given moment in time. Author Katherine Paterson has pointed out that the time period and subjects chosen for a work of historical fiction says as much about the writer's culture at the time the book was written as it does about the subject's (Paterson, 1993). Students can thus identify the writer's concerns in writing the book and how that may have affected the time period chosen and the portrayal of the culture.

Phase V. After reading traditional literature, nonfiction accounts, and historical fiction, children are ready to explore contemporary poetry and fiction. They can examine how traditional values have persisted to the present day by comparing themes in the first two phases to those in the fifth, and final, one (Norton, 1990). Poetry relies heavily upon cultural symbolism and imagery from a given setting, and a study of traditional motifs is thus essential to its understanding. Some novels contain a great deal of symbolism, and most evoke a setting that claims to be authentic. Contemporary literature also reveals the results of change and the current conflicts experienced by group members. These works, more than any other, offer a sense of how young people from the group live today. Teachers should provide a broad range of contemporary literature in order to give students a needed awareness of the diversity of situations—social, economic, and geographical—in which members of the group may find themselves. As in the case of other forms of literature, students can use what they have learned previously to check the authenticity of the works and to compare the content and style of poems and novels by members of the group to those of outsiders who are writing about the group (Norton, 1990).

SPECIAL BOX 10–2 *Activities Surrounding Picture Book Illustrations*

Different authors have adapted the same or similar folktales in different ways. The illustrations of those folktales, particularly in picture books, represent a variety of styles as well. Some illustrators have chosen realistic representations of the people and settings, while others attempt to replicate the motifs and styles of art from the culture itself. Still others offer illustrations that reflect the artist's own unique style and background.

Teachers with an interest in art—particularly teachers in kindergarten, first, and second grades—can use the following interdisciplinary language-related activity with their students:

Choose a variety of illustrated folktales from the same or similar traditions. For example, a selection of folktales from southern and southeastern Africa may include John Steptoe's *Mufaro's Beautiful Daughters*, Ashley Bryan's collection *The Ox of the Wonderful Horns and Other African Folktales*, and Barbara Knutson's *Sungura and Leopard*. After hearing the books read aloud, children can evaluate the illustrations for themselves and discuss which ones they like best and why. Teachers can help the children identify cultural elements and to classify the illustrations as traditional or realistic. As shown in the photograph on page 345 from a first-grade class, students can then write about which story and which illustration they prefer, and they can illustrate their own writing in their own style.

Variations on this exercise include combining folktales and contemporary picture book stories, such as, in the case of southern Africa, Niki Daly's *Not So Fast, Songololo*, Catherine Stock's *Where Are You Going, Manyoni?*, or Dianne Stewart's *The Dove*, illustrated by Jude Daly. Students can discuss whether the illustrations of contemporary stories vary more in style than those of folktales and whether certain artistic styles and elements in the illustrations (such as traditional dress and certain objects) are more typical of one type of story or the other. Students can keep count of certain animals and objects in illustrations of folktales and contemporary stories.

❖ Limitations of Funding and Standardized Curriculums

Teachers who seek to implement one or more of the previously mentioned strategies may encounter resistance on the part of administrators or other factors beyond their control. Two major constraints are the standardized curriculums in many school districts—curriculums that emphasize textbooks and basal readers and *"teaching to the tests"*—and funding limitations that prevent the purchase of additional materials.

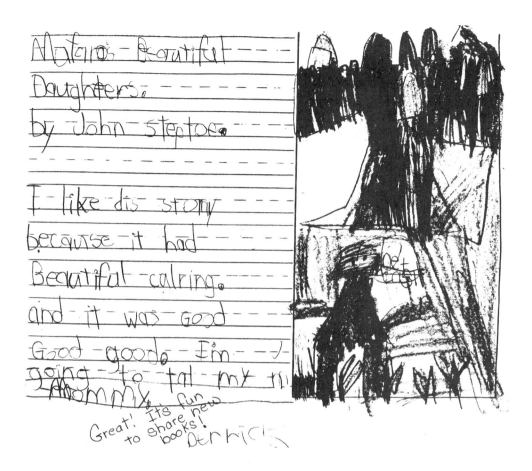

Mufaro's Beautiful
Daughters.
by John Steptoe.

I like dis story
because it had
Beautiful calring.
and it was good
Good good. Im
going to tal my m
Mommy.

Great! Its fun
to share new
books!
Derrick

By using their time efficiently, teachers can create opportunities to present multicultural materials in addition to the prescribed basal readers and textbooks. Most schools do allow some flexibility and teacher choice, though any additional materials may have to be approved by a supervisor. In a number of states, teachers who seek to offer multicultural materials in lieu of or in addition to a standardized skills-based curriculum have a state mandate that encourages or requires greater inclusiveness.

Under these circumstances, teachers take the *"additive" approach*, annexing multicultural materials an to an already established curriculum that has little cultural diversity (Lynch, 1989). Such an approach is far from ideal—most experts in multicultural education believe the materials should be an integral part of the curriculum—but it may be the only option a teacher has. However, there are ways a teacher can present the material to make it more a part of the regular curriculum.

Many basal readers today do contain some culturally diverse selections, though for the most part, the selections have very little cultural content. Nonetheless, they may provide a starting point for more in-depth explorations. Since many selections are written by established authors, teachers can assign trade books by the same author. This allows students to see how, in a different context, the author's work has much to say about the group to which he or she belongs. Alternatively, thematically organized basal readers offer teachers the opportunity to present books about other cultures that touch upon those themes. For a theme on the family, for example, there are many possibilities, though teachers should be careful not to offer only books about stereotypical (and stereotypically dysfunctional) family situations for a given cultural group. Trade books offered in addition to basal readers should reflect a diversity of family (and other) experiences, among all groups, including European-Americans.

Like basal readers, textbooks can serve as a starting point for a multicultural approach. Here, multicultural materials should offer a different perspective. Few textbooks present the Indian response to Columbus' voyage or to the encroachment of white settlers upon their land and their way of life. The books may state that the Indians were defeated, and even that the treatment of them was cruel, but the Indian voices themselves are absent. The same is generally true for African-Americans, Asian-Americans, Latinos, and recent immigrants, who in fact may have little or no coverage at all. By offering a different perspective from the mainstream one in textbooks, trade books and other materials show students what a perspective is and how events can be seen from more than one. Children develop a more critical attitude toward what they read and an ability to interpret events from the point of view of someone else. These are important lessons for any child, and particularly for children from the dominant culture who may have few opportunities to do so otherwise.

Finally, budgetary constraints may make it difficult for teachers to use materials besides those already in the classroom. Many teachers report spending their own money to make books and other materials available to their students. Other solutions involve the cooperation of the school library media specialist, other teachers, and the local public library. In a growing number of urban areas, programs such as the Library Power Project are helping to stock school library media centers with materials that reflect the ethnic composition of the school. State Departments of Education or Public Instruction may provide materials free of charge or at reduced cost. The public library may also be able to assist with multiple copies of paperback works as well as films and videos. A group of teachers can work together to share a limited number of materials, organizing their units so that materials can rotate among them.

❖ Finding More Information

The strategies outlined in this chapter are only a few of what can be done to incorporate multicultural materials into the curriculum. Teachers drawing up grade-specific lesson plans need not have to do everything by themselves. This kind of information is available through resource centers and often through state Departments of Education. District and regional bodies may also have this kind of information. In New York City, for instance, entire curriculums, with unit outlines, lesson plans, and sample tests, are published in paperback book form. In addition, teachers should contact resource centers, many of which can supply lesson plans for one or more cultural groups. Some resource centers are affiliated with the School of Education at a major university. Others (particularly for independent schools) are located at individual schools. In other cases, the resource centers are affiliated with ethnic group organizations, such as the Southern Poverty Law Center (which publishes the magazine *Teaching Tolerance*) or the Navajo Curriculum Center at the Rough Rock Demonstration School. By contacting major ethnic cultural and political organizations, teachers will eventually be directed to a resource center or curriculum outreach office.

Resource centers often sponsor conferences, as do statewide teachers' associations. Those seeking a more inclusive curriculum should attend those conferences, since teachers with already established and successful programs frequently hold workshops and are available to advise others. With any of these sources—state or district curriculum guides, guides provided by resource centers, and other teachers' successful programs—teachers need to look critically at what has been done and adapt those resources to the level of the class and the teachers' own knowledge and needs. Nonetheless, teachers—even those with successful units—must keep current in order to respond both to changing events and issues and to the wealth of materials that are being created each day.

❖ Summary

Multicultural materials should be used as an ongoing part of the curriculum throughout the school year. Overemphasis on the more superficial aspects of culture—holidays, foods, arts, and crafts—should be avoided. Overemphasis on the use of folktales can also present a problem when the tales present only the past of a culture, overemphasize one setting or type of environment, or present only the exotic aspects of a culture.

The whole language philosophy promotes teaching reading and writing across the entire curriculum. There are many choices in literature available that will allow teachers to integrate cultural information to mathematics, science, art, music, and other areas. The library media specialist, art and music teachers, and the computer instructor can assist the teacher in identifying materials and activities. Community resources are also available to teachers in the form of visiting lectures, artists, musicians, and craftspeople.

Many resources are available to teachers who are committed to multicultural education integrated throughout the curriculum. Teachers, in this way, can contribute to a future society in which we can all live together in cooperation, mutual respect, and recognition of our differences, and in harmony as Americans.

❖ CHAPTER 10 **Questions**

1. What suggestions could you give to a teacher who wants to use multicultural activities in the classroom, but doesn't know how to begin?

2. What are the problems that can occur when teachers rely exclusively upon folktales to teach about diverse cultures? How does Norton's five-phase approach address this problem?

3. Briefly describe a lesson or unit in which environmental issues could be studied as related to diverse cultures. Give examples of several objectives and learning activities.

4. What are some examples of community resources that you might use in the above unit or lesson?

5. Why should teachers avoid overemphasis on holidays, heroes, foods, arts, and crafts in teaching about diverse cultures?

6. Discuss the importance of integrating multicultural material in the areas of math, science, and technology.

❖ **References**

Afolayan, M., Kuntz, P., & Naze, B. (1992). Sub-Saharan Africa. In L. Miller-Lachmann, *Our family, our friends, our world: An annotated guide to significant multicultural books for children and teenagers* (pp. 417-443). New Providence, NJ: R. R. Bowker.

Bender, E., Bishop, J., & Kowalchik, L. A. (1993, November). *Caught between two worlds: Multicultural literature and film in the middle school classroom.* Presented at Our Multicultural World: 13th Delaware Valley Young Adult Librarians conference. Media, PA

Comer, J. P. (1980). *School Power.* New York: The Free Press.

Cummins, J. (1986). Empowering minority students: A framework for intervention. *Harvard Educational Review, 56* (1), 18-36.

Dorris, M. (1979). Native American literature in an ethnohistorical context. *College English, 41,* 147-162.

Edelsky, C. (1991). *With literacy and justice for all: Rethinking the social in language and education.* New York: The Falmer Press.

Lynch, J. (1989). *Multicultural education in a global society.* New York: The Falmer Press.

Miller-Lachmann, L. (1994). The folktale flood: Multicultural publishing aAcross genres. *School Library Journal, 40*(2) (February 1994), 35-36.

Norton, D. (1990). Teaching multicultural literature in the reading curriculum. *The Reading Teacher, 44*(1) (September 1990), 28-40.

Paterson, K. (1993, June). *Is that book politically correct: Truth and trends in historical literature for young people.* Presented at the American Library Association 112th annual conference. New Orleans, LA.

Reyhner, J. (1992). Bilingual Education. In J. Reyhner (Ed.), *Teaching American Indian students* (pp. 59-77). Norman, OK: University of Oklahoma Press.

Willinsky, J. (1990). *The new literacy: Redefining reading and writing in the schools.* New York: Routledge and Kegan Paul.

Yeh, P. (1991). Publishers' Perspective. In M. V. Lindgren (Ed.), *The multicolored mirror: Cultural substance in literature for children and young adults* (pp. 67-76). Fort Atkinson, WI: Highsmith Press.

CHAPTER 11

The School-Home-Community Partnership

This chapter has been written with certain assumptions. First, parental involvement in the education of children of color is essential since studies have shown that this leads to increased achievement (Clark, 1983). Secondly, it is especially important for parents from low-income families to be involved in the schools in order to improve the relevance, quality, and equity in the education of their children. Third, the information included in this chapter represents an introduction to important cultural differences that educators need to understand and appreciate. It is hoped that the reader will be motivated to learn more about the groups discussed.

Parental involvement in the education of children of color is essential.

Most importantly, it is assumed that the reader will understand the danger in generalizing the characteristics of the various cultural groups discussed. There are always differences among families in any given culture due to a variety of important factors. Socioeconomic level, the level of acculturation, length of time in the United States, English proficiency level, and the education level of parents will result in distinct differences among families in a cultural group. The reader should keep these factors in mind while reading about the cultural differences that influence a child's academic and social behaviors in school-family relationships.

In order to provide authentic parental viewpoints on the school-home relationship, the author interviewed parents from different cultures. Some of the interviews included in the chapter may appear "too exemplary to be true;" however, parents' responses to structured questions have been given verbatim whenever possible. The questions posed to each parent are shown (Table 11–1).

TABLE 11–1 Parent Interview Format

Background information:
- Date
- Name
- Location
- Number of children, ages, grade level
- School district/region

TABLE 11–1 continued

I Length of time in area
I Length of time in the United States
I Native country
I Primary language

Interview questions:
1. What would you like your child's teacher to know about your language and culture?

2. What kind of training should teachers have to work with children and families from different cultures?

3. In your view, what are the most important characteristics of a good teacher for your children?

4. What are the most important requirements for a good home-school relationship? What are some of the barriers?

5. What would you like for your child to learn about her (or his) culture and language in school? Do you think that the school should teach your native language to help your child maintain it?

6. Are you actively involved in your children's school? If not, what prevents your participation? How can the school help you to participate?

7. What are you most satisfied with in your child's present schooling? Least satisfied?

SPECIAL BOX 11–1 *Mrs. Escala*

Recently, a parent, Mrs. Escala, was interviewed concerning ways to improve parent-teacher cooperation among culturally and linguistically diverse families. She came here two-and-a-half years ago from Chile with her husband and five-year-old daughter, Annie. When they arrived in the United States, Mrs. Escala spoke English and Spanish, her husband spoke Spanish and very limited English, and her daughter spoke only Spanish. The family spoke only Spanish at home.

When she took her daughter to enroll her in the public elementary school, Mrs. Escala offered to help in any way that she could since Annie spoke no English. However, the teacher did not respond to Mrs. Escala's offer, but suggested that Annie probably needed special education since she had a language problem. No English as a second language (ESL) classes were available.

The teacher asked Mrs. Escala to speak only English at home, but that was not possible. Mr. Escala did not speak English well and they had always used Spanish at home. Mrs. Escala also pointed out to the teacher that

Annie needed to maintain Spanish at home while learning English at school. The teacher continued to remind Mrs. Escala that Annie had a problem with language and probably needed special education; however, her mother believed that Annie was a bright child for whom special education was inappropriate. Mrs. Escala described the situation as "taking a happy child to school the first day who became increasingly unhappy."

In order to end the school's pressure to evaluate Annie for special education, Mrs. Escala located a bilingual psychologist who was able to test Annie in Spanish. The results of the complete evaluation confirmed that Annie was a bright child who did not need a referral for special education.

Based upon her experience, Mrs. Escala made several recommendations for other schools. She believes that the school should recognize a second language as an asset for the child rather than a disadvantage. She believes that teachers and staff should learn about the culture and language of children and consider that children from other cultures have advantages. In addition, a school district must prepare for the diverse children that it receives and answer the question, "Who are these children and what is their culture?" For example, there may be conflict between the teacher's expectations for Annie and the family's cultural values and beliefs. The teacher wants Annie to be more independent and individualistic, but this is not a part of her culture. In the family, cooperation and interdependence are valued. "Teachers need inservice and preservice courses in multicultural education to help them become more culturally sensitive," according to Mrs. Escala.

Mrs. Escala thinks that support groups for parents are also needed. She mentioned that parents who have recently emigrated to this country need assistance in understanding the school system, how it works, how to get help for their child, and how to participate as a parent.

She does not believe that schools should be required to provide instruction in a diversity of languages. However, other languages should be valued and reflected in the school, perhaps on bulletin boards and posters. Foreign language instruction should be available to children only in those languages spoken by large numbers of the school population.

At this time, after two-and-a half-years in this country, Mrs. Escala is most pleased with the school's academic strengths and least satisfied with the school's lack of attention to the social/emotional growth of children. She remains unhappy about the ignorance of other cultures and lack of sensitivity among the teachers and staff of the school.

The Escala case is an example of how easy it is to mislabel a child as having a language disability when the reality is a language difference. It also illustrates the importance of cultural sensitivity in the school staff and support for parents who are recent immigrants to this country.

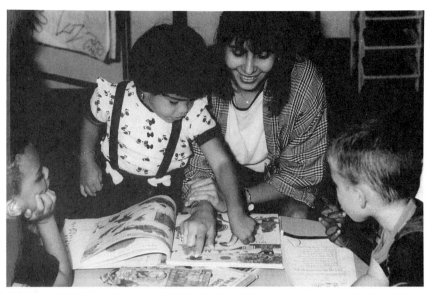

Educators must be sensitive to the cultural and language background of a child.

SPECIAL BOX 11–2   *Mrs. DuBois*

Mrs. DuBois came from Haiti twenty-sever years ago when she was eleven-years-old. She speaks French, Creole, and English. Mrs. DuBois lives with her husband and four children, ages eleven to eighteen. Her youngest son, eleven years old, is in grade five at a local public school. Although all of the children were born in the United States, they attended school in Jamaica several years ago and, as a result, according to Mrs. DuBois, "They have an accent."

In response to the question, "What are the most important cultural and linguistic needs of your school-aged children?" Mrs. DuBois spoke about recognition of cultural values and beliefs and respect for different languages.

She would like the school to know important aspects of her culture and language and the important beliefs that her culture and family hold. For example, they are Christians who do not believe in mythology. In school, her son's teacher was using a textbook to teach about mythology. In Mrs. DuBois' words,

> I teach my children that there is only one God and I insisted that my son could not read the book about mythology. He is at a very impressionable age. I told the teacher to 'either give him an F or a different book.'

Another of her cultural values involves the way in which people are addressed. She pointed out that "When a child calls the teacher by her first name, it does not show respect." Mrs. DuBois does not want her children to address the teacher in that manner. Fighting is also against her values and she has taught her children not to fight. In her words, "They are not allowed to fight."

Mrs. DuBois pointed out that "Teachers need to understand that there are different ways of doing things in different cultures. Messages from the teacher may be received differently by different children."

They do not take into account that his (her son) second language is very relevant. The world is not made up of only English-speaking, or French-speaking, or Spanish-speaking (people). We are a diversity of languages. The first thing that anyone experiences here from any country is forget your language, forget your culture. Somehow this negates the person. It is as if the person does not exist.

Mrs. DuBois said that the first problem that they met in the school was that the psychologist wanted to retrain her children through placing them in remedial English classes so that they could become "Americanized." She considered this an insult and pointed out that "Schools must recognize that children who come to this country from a different background have an advantage; they are enriched." Mrs. DuBois believes that there should be a mutual sharing of cultures.

Mrs. DuBois expressed strong feelings about the way that a child who speaks a different language may be received by the school. The value placed on the child's language and culture are very important to her. The comments underscore the importance and value of cultural pluralism and the need for cultural sensitivity and competence in educators.

SPECIAL BOX 11–3 *Mrs. Lee*

Mrs. Lee came to the United States from Taiwan twenty-two years ago. Her native language is Chinese. Although both she and her husband are bilingual, they have not taught their children the Chinese language. In fact, Mrs. Lee described the dilemma faced by parents when they are uncertain about which language to teach their children first. The Lees have two daughters who were born in the United States. The older girl is a college student who has recently expressed anger and frustration about her lack of knowledge of the Chinese language and culture. The younger daughter is a high school student.

When asked what she would like the schools to provide for her children, Mrs. Lee responded that she would like the school to "Prepare them to be totally bilingual. This will help them with their identity crisis in adolescence."

She would also like the school to recognize the parent's dilemma concerning which language to teach first and to encourage parents to teach their children the native language.

Mrs. Lee wants the school to understand the importance of good mental health in children and give increased attention to this. She said "Teachers should be alert to socialization problems, for example, children's feelings of being less attractive and male domination in the schools." She pointed out that "Some parents may not think that it's a problem; others may lack time to be concerned about it. Teachers should also be aware of stereotypes and encourage children to excel in diverse areas." For example, the stereotype for Asians includes interest and motivation limited to the science and technology fields. "Asian children need to be encouraged in creativity and other areas of study that do not fit the stereotypes," according to Mrs. Lee.

Finally, Mrs. Lee noted that children must be taught about their culture. "Teachers can use appropriate children's literature and teach about holidays, customs, Confucianism, and the moral code. Children also need to be taught tolerance for difference," she pointed out.

SPECIAL BOX 11–4 *The Krishnas*

Mr. and Mrs. Krishna are from India. They have been in the United States since 1965 (husband) and 1971 (wife). They described their native language as Kannada, a spoken language; however, reading and writing were conducted in English.

The Krishnas have three children, two girls, nineteen and eighteen years old and a boy, age eleven, who is currently attending grade six in a public middle school.

The Krishnas would like the school to recognize and respect their festivals and holidays. They believe that teachers should be sensitive to cultural and linguistic differences that a child may bring to school. Their concern is that children can be humiliated by their cultural differences at school when teachers do not understand them. Teachers should also know basic facts about religion and philosophy in the child's culture. The most important characteristics of a teacher for their son are: "to make the child feel comfortable in the classroom, to go beyond textbooks and learn about the culture, and to demonstrate politeness and caring." Finally, "The schools need to show interest in the cultures and languages of the children," according to the Krishnas.

SPECIAL BOX 11–5 *Mrs. Yendu*

The Yendu family came to the United States from Nigeria in 1984. Mr. and Mrs. Yendu are from different states in Nigeria with different languages. They have always spoken English at home. Of their four children, two were born in Nigeria and two in the United States. The two youngest children, ages eight and seventeen, are in grades three and twelve.

Mrs. Yendu commented that "Language is not a problem since we all speak English." In response to the first question, she would like the teacher to know about "Our food patterns, family relations, and child-rearing methods." With respect to child-rearing, she also pointed out that America "is an extravagant culture and restraint is needed for children. They cannot have everything they ask for." She described family relations in their culture thusly: "Families spend a lot of time together, regardless of age. There is no age segregation."

When asked what type of training teachers need in multicultural education, Mrs. Yendu noted that "Teachers need a course on how to infuse cultural information into the curriculum, and a good teacher shows kindness, openness, and respect for children." Mrs. Yendu would also like to see lots of well-written books on Africa in the school library.

To foster good parent-teacher relations, Mrs. Yendu likes the idea of using "home books." These are books in which parents and teachers can write notes to each other. Teachers can inform parents of important concerns and events or can describe a special accomplishment of their child; parents can raise questions, make suggestions, or share important information. Home books can facilitate continuous communication between parent and teacher.

Mrs. Yendu believes that teaching the child about her culture and language is the family's own responsibility. She pointed out that:

It is urgent for the child to fit into the mainstream as long as she can negotiate it; the cultural part has been the family's responsibility. However, since most of the time the children are to 'fit in,' they can get mixed messages. They don't want to give notice to wrongs and the system may get away with a lot. This keeps parents in a dilemma. They want children to learn and to fit in. When something outrageous happens, parents react. If teachers were more sensitive it would help.

Although the Yendu family participates in the school and has not experienced barriers, Mrs. Yendu believes that class differences might cause barriers for some parents.

All of the parents interviewed expressed the wish for teachers to know about the cultural backgrounds of their children. This knowledge included foods, festivals, holidays, family relationships, religion, philosophy/values, and child-rearing methods. However, parents varied in their concern about language differences. Where differences exist, they expressed strong feelings about the need for positive recognition of the home language and respect for its value in a child's life. Parents want their children to remain bilingual and bicultural; however, those interviewed believed that the school could not be expected, realistically, to provide instruction for maintenance of a diversity of languages. Suggestions such as Saturday schools and home instruction were recommended for maintenance of children's primary languages.

All parents were equally concerned about teachers' awareness of stereotypes and the need to eliminate their influence in teachers' expectations, instructional planning, and guidance for children.

Parental involvement in the educational process has been recognized as an important component of effective school programs. Studies have shown that parental participation can enhance the achievement of low-income students (Kroth, 1987). Programs that promote the involvement of parents in at-home teaching, for example, have improved the achievement for these children (Kroth, 1987). Specific types of involvement have been identified as most conducive to children's achievement in the elementary grades. These include community support and fund raising attendance at school meetings and school functions that involve the community.

Barth (1979) reviewed twenty-four behavior modification studies that used at-home parental reinforcement for in-school academic and behavior change activities. He found that parental involvement in the home learning activities made a significant difference. Furthermore, Becker (1984) and Cotton and Savard (1982) found that the gains made for children as result of at-home teaching were sustained at least a year and in some cases for three to five years. Epstein (1984) also studied parental influence on growth in reading and found that parents who are trained to help their children can make a difference.

Most strategies and programs to solicit parental involvement have primarily attracted white, middle-class, English-speaking parents who have sufficient economic resources and possess cultural perspectives that allow them to feel comfortable with the school authorities and the typical school environment and organization. Families who are recent immigrants may be intimidated by the strangeness of our schools and educational system. Some cultures place teachers on pedestals as esteemed authority figures and this increases the hesitation of immigrant families to approach the school to raise important questions and become fully involved.

Demographic data indicate that schools are and will continue to serve a growing number of students and families from diverse cultural and linguistic backgrounds who may not respond to traditional methods for establishing family/school partnerships (Taylor-Gibbs & Nahme-Huang, 1989). As noted earlier, students from culturally and linguistically diverse backgrounds make up the majority of students in many of our nation's urban school districts and the State of California. Teachers therefore need to be sensitive to potential barriers to the full participation of these families in the schools. Hoover and Collier (1988) have noted the following barriers to effective parent-teacher interactions (Table 11–2).

Families from different cultures vary in:

1. family structure;
2. behavioral and developmental expectations for their children;
3. disciplinary styles;
4. communication patterns;
5. linguistic differences;
6. socioeconomic level; and
7. the need for training in the skills and understanding needed to work effectively with the schools.

Each of these important areas will be discussed in the following sections. In addition, families with biracial children and the school-community relationship are included.

TABLE 11–2 Factors Inhibiting Effective Parent-Teacher Interaction

Inhibitors	Considerations
Minority parents are viewed as helpless or uneducated individuals.	Teachers need parents and what they have to offer to schools.
Minority parents are viewed as requiring special therapy, counseling, or assistance.	Many minority parents of special learners are well-adjusted and capable of making sound educational decisions and judgments.
Purposely remaining distant from minority parents to ensure one's objectivity and credibility or out of fear due to lack of understanding of their culture.	Knowledge about the student's family and sociocultural background can contribute greatly to a teacher's objective and credible decision-making.
Continually questioning the minority parents' perceptions about their children and learning needs.	Minority parents often know what is best for their children, including culturally appropriate solutions to educational concerns.
Insensitivity to cultural customs and heritages.	Minority parents must believe that teachers are genuinely concerned about them, their children, and cultural customs.

TABLE 11–2 continued

Inhibitors	Considerations
Lack of teacher's knowledge about various special needs and the interaction among culture, language, and special needs.	Lack of cultural information and knowledge may limit severely one's awareness of educational options available to these special learners.
Continually expecting problems when interacting with parents of minority students.	Although prior encounters with difficult parents may exist, each new encounter must be entered into with an open mind and positive feelings toward a successful meeting.
Limiting interactions with minority parents due to language or cultural differences.	A language or cultural difference is an unacceptable reason for lack of parent-teacher communication. Training in cross-cultural communication may be useful in this process.

Family Structure

Family structure differs among cultures and among members of the group. In addition, our society is showing an increase in single-parent families. Thus, many factors interact to determine the organization and structure of a family. While the traditional model for involving parents in the school has successfully accommodated the white, middle-class nuclear family, many cultures emphasize the extended family and the community. For example, many Native American families live within a framework of collective interdependence with family members also accountable to the clan and the tribe (LaFromboise & Graff-Low, 1989). Similarly, many African-American and Mexican-American families rely on kinship interactions to share resources and services such as child care and parenting arrangements, and provide emotional and social support (Taylor-Gibbs, 1989; Ramirez, 1989). As a result of the importance of the extended family, many families may seek assistance in solving educationally related problems from family and community members and organizations rather than from educators or public institutions such as schools. Therefore, schools and educators can attempt to reach families by exchanging information with parents through local community organizations, enlisting the support of local community groups and other significant individuals in the family's life, holding school events in neighborhood centers such as religious establishments, social clubs, or community centers, and asking community members to escort parents to school events (Coballes-Vega & Salend, 1988; Lynch & Stein, 1987; Nicolau & Ramos, 1990).

In many extended families, elders are highly respected and play a particularly important role in decisions-making and childcare. For example, elders in many Native American families spend considerable amounts of time with children and share oral traditions and wisdom (LaFromboise & Graff-Low, 1989). Since families and children are encouraged to develop loyalties to elders and other extended family members, these members can be instrumental in designing and implementing appropriate educational services. Therefore, when working with families that value and depend upon the roles of extended family members, educators can attempt to involve these family members in the decision-making and intervention processes. For example, correspondence to parents could include a statement noting that extended family members are also welcome to attend and participate in educational meetings (Nicolau & Ramos, 1990). For many African-American families, the church is an important aspect of family life and the major provider of community resources. The minister and other church representatives may function as extended family and can be helpful in seeking solutions to children's school problems. For example, African-American churches across the country are building low-cost housing, providing day care and after-school programs, organizing parent support groups, and working closely with local schools to improve education for the children (Freedman, 1993).

Another important variable for educators to understand when interacting with families is the roles of family members. Whereas there is a wide range of variation, in some traditional Asian-American and Latin-

SPECIAL BOX 11–6

In a study by O'Reilly, Tokino, and Ebata (1986) (cited by Nagata in Taylor-Gibbs & Nahme-Huang), Japanese-American families ranked important competencies for their children differently from Caucasian parents. While Japanese-Americans gave the highest importance to "behaves well," Caucasian-American parents ranked "self-directed" as the highest in importance.

In American Indian families, developmental milestones in early childhood are often celebrated. The first smile, laugh, steps, and language are honored, but not pressured. The child's own pattern of readiness is observed. Early independence is valued and children are allowed to make choices and experience the consequences (La Fromboise & Graff-Low, 1989). Emphasis is also placed on the effect of the child's behavior on others. Children and adolescents are expected to participate in various ceremonies (LaFromboise & Graff-Low, 1989).

American families, the roles of family members may be defined in adherence to a hierarchy that is based on age and gender. Fathers are responsible for the family's economic welfare and take a leadership role in making decisions, while mothers perform the main roles with respect to child care. However, in acculturated families, joint decision-making is more prevalent (Ramirez, 1989). When dealing with public institutions (e.g., schools), mothers may covertly assume the role of decisionmaker (Nahme-Huang & Ying, 1989).

Behavioral and Developmental Expectations

An important goal for students from linguistically and culturally diverse backgrounds is the development of bicultural competence. Bicultural competence refers to an individual's ability to function in two distinct cultures (deAnda, 1984). Bicultural individuals are able to adjust their behaviors to the norms of each culture. Therefore, in designing educational programs to help students from culturally and linguistically diverse backgrounds develop bicultural competence, teachers should enlist the support of parents. These were special concerns of Mrs. Lee, the parent from Taiwan (Special Box 11–3).

Since cultural groups emphasize the development of different norm-related behaviors, parents can be a valuable resource in helping teachers understand and identify important norm-related behaviors that are valued in the family's culture. For example, while many African-American families may encourage their children to respect the extended family, and be independent and assertive (Anderson & Fenichel, 1989), many of their Asian-American counterparts may encourage their children to conform, be obedient, repress their emotions, defer to authority, and subjugate their behavior to the needs of the family (Nahme-Huang & Ying, 1989; Nagata, 1989) (Special Box 11–6).

Cultures also differ on the importance of developmental milestones and rites of passage. Whereas many Anglo-American families may be concerned about developmental milestones, Mexican-American and Native American families tend to downplay the importance of prescribed developmental milestones (LaFromboise & Graff-Low, 1989; Ramirez, 1989). For many groups, the developmental and behavioral demands on their children are a function of age and sex. Ramirez (1989) studied Mexican-American families and noted that while young children are nurtured, as they reach adolescence, they are expected to demonstrate appropriate behavior and perform a variety of age and ability related tasks (e.g., cooking, child care, and errands). Since the behavioral expectations of the schools and the families may conflict, teachers must be willing to collaborate with parents to develop a culturally sensitive and relevant educational program that includes mutually agreed upon bicultural behaviors, appropriate cultural settings for displaying these behaviors, and a cross-cultural criteria for measuring progress. For example, for families that encourage their children to respect and interact appropriately with others and control their aggression, these values can be supported in the classroom (Inclan & Herron, 1989).

Disciplinary Styles

The area of discipline is complex and fraught with potential school-home conflict. In a recent article, McIntyre and Silva (1993) discussed cultural differences and the teacher's need to determine abusive versus different disciplinary practices, since teachers in most states are required to report child abuse. The authors were concerned with the teacher's misjudgment of parental practices concerning discipline. Among the examples presented by McIntyre and Silva (1993) was that of a student coming to school with welts over his body. When the teacher contacted the parents to inquire about the cause of the welts, the parents presented a religious defense based upon the Book of Proverbs in the bible. In another example, a student arrived at school beaten about the head and chest by parents who promised the teacher that the child's school attendance would improve. When confronted by the teacher, the parents became angry since they had kept their promise. Physical punishment has been associated with low-income families and may be used in response to a teacher's request for parental intervention. The teacher may find it difficult to determine child abuse in these situations.

Other examples cited by McIntyre and Silva (1993) include a Vietnamese student who tells his teacher that a classmate has a pierced ear because traditional Vietnamese families punish a misbehaving child by tying the ear to the doorknob. In another instance, a student reported to the teacher that she was made to kneel on uncooked rice when she misbehaved, a common practice in low-income Latino families from the Caribbean.

In response to the McIntyre and Silva article, a teacher of students with emotional disturbance wrote to the editor about the danger in viewing abusive practices as acceptable simply because they are culturally approved. That teacher was concerned about the confusion faced by a teacher trying to make a decision about child abuse when considering cultural practices and the possibility that abuse might be ignored.

A very recent example of a culturally based practice that has received worldwide attention is that of genital mutilation of girls that is practiced in some cultures. While some female activists have protested loudly and one notable book has been written, others have noted that critics outside the cultures may lack the cultural knowledge and understanding required to evaluate such practices.

However, teachers can be aware of the strategies with which parents may feel most comfortable when working with their children and try to make appropriate decisions. For example, in Asian cultures where it is important not to bring shame on the family, children may be strictly disciplined by the use of shame and ostracism and limited verbal feedback (Nagata, 1989).

While many Native American families also believe that the behavior of each individual member reflects on the community, misbehavior may result in the individual apologizing to group members, being ignored, or being briefly the target words of disapproval (LaFromboise & Graff-Low, 1989). Other groups may employ disciplinary methods that use physical punishment (Anderson & Fenichel, 1989). Important dilemmas for teachers may arise from a conflict in school-home methods for discipline.

Examples of school-home conflicts may include such situations as: the level of activity permitted at school versus the level allowed at home; the level of noise permitted in the classroom and the teacher's expectation that students will work quietly and independently in the classroom while on going conversation and movement are practiced when working in the home—this pattern often exists among African-American students; assertiveness, individualism, and competition expected by the teacher in contrast with the emphasis on the group, cooperation, and compliance at home—in fact, this characteristic of Native American students frustrates many teachers who expect students to be verbally assertive and competitive. Teachers may disagree with methods used by the parents. However, educators can interact with parents in a non-judgmental manner to identify and adapt appropriate interventions and strategies that both groups can employ (McIntyre & Silva, 1993).

Communication Patterns

Communication is the most critical component of an effective school-home-community relationship. Winton and Bailey (1993) define communication as messages sent to a family in face-to-face interactions and in written policies and procedures of the school. They point out that the school must make a commitment to effective communication practices and conduct a needs assessment to determine when change is needed. Communication is effective when teachers and staff of the school are able to accomplish specific communication goals or outcomes, according to Winton and Bailey. While communication goals will vary for different school programs, Winton and Bailey (1993) identify the following important message to be communicated to families:

1. respect for their opinions and priorities;
2. respect for their competence in advocacy and decision-making for their child;
3. acknowledgement and respect for families' communications;
4. the availability of teachers and staff willing to serve as resources; and
5. provision of an educational program consistent with parent/family values and priorities.

When planning meetings, the school should respect family preferences for times and places. Some meetings should be scheduled evenings, weekends, or at lunch time in order to accommodate families' schedules.

While schools may be successful in encouraging parents to attend meetings, cross-cultural communication patterns may create misunderstandings that can hinder the development of trusting relationships between families and educators. Failure to understand differences in communication styles can also limit information sharing. To facilitate communication with families, educators need to interpret parental verbal and nonverbal behaviors within their social and cultural context (Salend, 1990).

Anderson and Fenichel (1989) noted that such forms of communication as personal space, eye contact, wait time, voice quality, words, facial expressions, and touching have cross-cultural meanings. For example, in some cultures, a "yes" answer may indicate "I heard you" rather than agreement, which would be indicated by "Yes, I agree" (Anderson & Fenichel, 1989). Similarly, some cultural beliefs may limit communication or the discussion of certain topics. Nagata (1989) posited that some Japanese-American family members may refrain from talking about problems and concerns because this behavior may be viewed as being self-centered, losing control, or losing face. Locust (1990) noted that some Native American families that believe in a concept known as "holding

---

SPECIAL BOX 11–7

Educators can help parents become involved in the information sharing process by:

- showing respect for the culture and language of the parents;
- showing respect for all family members;
- asking parents questions that encourage them to respond rather than waiting for them to ask questions or spontaneously speak their minds;
- explaining to parents the problems associated with test results and specific recommendations;
- informing parents that there may be several solutions to a situation;
- encouraging parents to bring to school family or community members who have experience interacting with schools;
- employing an interpreter who is culturally sensitive;
- involving parents in informal school activities; and
- viewing interactions with families as a long-term process.

(Fradd & Wilen, 1990; LaFromboise & Graff-Low, 1989; Nagata, 1989; Nicolau & Ramos, 1990).

the future," may avoid discussing an individual's future because they believe that negative or limiting comments about an individual's future can cause it to happen. Culturally sensitive interpreters and cultural informants (community individuals who understand the family's needs and culture) can help minimize these potential barriers to communication by assisting educators in understanding and interpreting cross-cultural communication behaviors (Brandenburg-Ayres, 1990; Fradd & Wilen, 1990). Brandenburg-Ayres (1990) suggests that schools employ cultural informants to serve as liaisons between schools, families, and the communities; inform school personnel about relevant cultural variables; help orient new families to the school; and prepare culturally relevant and sensitive written documents.

Many families may view the educational system as a bureaucracy that is controlled by educated, monocultural, and monolingual individuals whom they have little right to question (Nicolau & Ramos, 1989). Therefore, out of respect for the authority of educators, families may be reluctant to disagree with professionals (Ramirez, 1989), discuss controversial ideas and share their emotions (Nahme-Huang & Ying, 1989), ask questions and seek clarification (Anderson & Fenichel, 1989), question test results and the recommendations of professionals (Nagata, 1989), and make eye contact (Salend, 1990).

Educators may also have to adjust the structure of their meetings to address the family's preferences. For families that emphasize the importance of the establishment of personal relationships, educators can attempt to create a trusting and open environment that is warm, friendly, non-judgmental, and personal (Allen & Majidi-Ahi, 1989). Effective communication with these families may involve being patient; providing enough time for family members to express themselves; demonstrating concern for and showing respect to family members; and employing self-disclosure, humor, and casual conversation to establish trust and personal relationships (Anderson & Fenichel, 1989; LaFromboise & Graff-Low, 1989). Ramirez (1989) recommends that professionals minimize the anxiety that Mexican-American families may initially experience when interacting with educators by greeting family members with a handshake and setting up the environment so that all participants are in close proximity to each other.

Other families may initially respond to educators they view as competent (Nagata, 1989). These individuals may look to professionals to establish an environment that helps participants accomplish their goals. Professionals can help these families by providing a structure for the meeting, explaining the agenda, setting goals, defining roles, and asking questions (Nagata, 1989). Conversely, families that employ communication patterns that are based on interdependence may prefer a meeting that employs a collaborative, problem-solving approach (Allen & Majidi-Ahi, 1989).

Linguistic Differences

In addition to variations in communication styles, linguistic differences may hinder communication between schools and families (Lucas, Henze, & Donato, 1990; Nicolau & Ramos, 1990). Marion (1980) noted that parents from non-English language backgrounds may be reluctant to interact with school personnel because they lack the requisite skills to communicate in English. Similarly, most schools do not have professionals who are bilingual and can communicate with parents in their native language (Fradd & Wilen, 1990; Lynch & Stein, 1987).

It is interesting to note that when parents interviewed were asked, "Should the school provide instruction in your native language to help your child maintain it?" they responded that schools should not be expected to provide instruction in the child's native language. They believed that, as parents, they should arrange that instruction outside the school. One suggestion was Saturday classes or after-school classes privately conducted. This was especially emphasized when there was a great diversity of languages in the school.

Interpreters/translators, preferably from the community, can serve as liaisons to facilitate oral and written communication between English- speaking professionals and families who speak other languages. Interpreters assist with oral communication, while translators aid in written communication (i.e., notes to parents, due process procedures). Interpreters are especially important when dealing with families from cultures that do not have written language systems (Fradd & Wilen, 1990).

In some school districts, there are many languages represented and it will be difficult to provide interpreters in every case. At times, it is even difficult to find an interpreter for a particular language. The use of parent and community volunteers should be explored. In some churches, for example, the ministry is preparing for the diversity of languages spoken among the congregation, and individuals are available who can serve as interpreters. In addition, there are agencies beginning to compile regional directories of interpreters available for the schools. This may be accomplished through a regional survey of the population. This is an important service that should be developed for all school districts (Table 11-3).

Socioeconomic Factors

Since most school-based programs for communicating and collaborating with families have been designed to accommodate the needs of middle- and upper-income families, economic factors can limit the involvement of families in their children's education. Lynch and Stein (1987) noted that long working hours, time conflicts, transportation difficulties, and child-care needs were major economic barriers that prevented parents from being able to attend school meetings.

TABLE 11–3 Individuals Who Serve as Interpreters/Translators Should Possess a Variety of Skills

---

These skills include:

▎ a knowledge of the mainstream culture
▎ an ability to speak, read, and write English
▎ an understanding of the culture of the family
▎ an ability to speak, read, and write the language of the family
▎ an understanding of the interpretation/translation process and roles and expectations of the interpreter/translator (Salend & Wilen, 1990).

The parent's child or another child should not serve as an interpreter/translator as it could be demeaning to the parents. When interpreting, interpreters should:

▎ speak the dialect that the family employs
▎ maintain confidentiality
▎ remain neutral and impartial
▎ refrain from expressing personal opinions
▎ avoid omissions, modifications, and additions in communication
▎ meet with school personnel before the meeting to ascertain the proper translation of the various terms that will be used during the meeting
▎ consult professionals or parents for clarification when they encounter difficulties communicating specific information, such as professional jargon
▎ employ reverse translation when precise translations are not feasible
▎ treat parents and professionals with respect
▎ encourage professionals to speak to parents rather than directing their comments to the interpreter (Fradd & Wilen, 1990).

Communication barriers associated with time conflicts, transportation, and child-care needs also can be minimized by use of home visits. However, since some families may view a home visit as threatening or intrusive, educators should obtain the family's consent before making the visit (Brandenburg-Ayres, 1990).

Parent Training

Parents can be valuable resources in helping their children gain the skills necessary for success in school (Lally, Mangione, & Honig, 1987; Sharma, 1988). Like all parents, many parents from linguistically and culturally diverse backgrounds may need training to help their children at home and assist teachers in the classroom.

Schools and agencies have developed successful model programs for training parents from linguistically and culturally diverse backgrounds that have been successful in teaching parents various techniques and strategies for promoting their children's academic and social development (Cotton & Savard, 1982; Lally, Mangione, & Honig, 1987; Sharma, 1988).

SPECIAL BOX 11–8 *Strategies to Alleviate Problems for Parents*

- providing transportation and establishing carpools for family members
- conducting activities and meetings at locations within the community
- enlisting the assistance of individuals and groups from the community
- offering child-care alternatives
- designing activities so that children are not separated from their parents
- meeting with parents at times that are convenient for parents: evenings, weekends, or mornings
- exchanging information with families through local community organizations
- making telephone contacts with parents (Lucas, Henze, & Donato, 1990; Nicolau & Ramos, 1990)

SPECIAL BOX 11–9

Effective elements of these programs that have been important in working with diverse groups of parents include:

1. The availability of materials in the native language of parents (Garate, Sen, Thien, & Chaleunrath, 1987)
2. Opportunities for informal meetings and contact with school staff (Peterson & Cooper, 1989); a school staff that seeks to support rather than substitute for parents (Lally, Mangione, & Honig, 1987)
3. Home visits by school staff (Lally, Mangione, & Honig, 1987)
4. Teachers who develop and lead extracurricular activities in the community (Sealey & Riffel, 1985)
5. The involvement of teachers and other professionals in the community (Garate et al., 1987; Sealey & Riffel, 1985)
6. School personnel who can communicate with parents in their native language (Davies, 1991)
7. Orientation sessions to establish the foundation for a working relationship
8. Written communications in the language that parents understand best

Successful parent training programs for linguistically and culturally diverse families offer training not only to parents, but also to extended family members. For example, grandparents and other relatives are important members of many African-American families and should be invited to participate in training sessions. Religious organizations, social agencies, grass roots community organizations, libraries, and community leaders can help schools advertise training in community-based after-school programs. Davies (1991) and Nicolau and Ramos (1990) recommend that training sessions be held in non-intimidating locations that are available to families such as religious establishments, community centers, restaurants, and shopping malls. Nicolau and Ramos (1989) suggest that making the focus of the first meeting with parents a "fun activity" rather than a formal meeting or conference can induce reluctant parents to attend school-related meetings.

In selecting the content of training programs, educators also need to consider the family's needs and language abilities (Lucas, Henze, & Donato, 1990). Therefore, when planning and designing training sessions, educators should consult parents concerning their training needs. Nicolau and Ramos (1990) reported that parents initially want to receive training in such issues as AIDS, teen pregnancy, spouse and child abuse, and drugs. Parents who speak language(s) other than English, may benefit from family-based ESL classes and instruction in the policies and practices used by the school system (Garate et al., 1987).

Training sessions and methods of sharing information with family members should also reflect the specific needs of parents. Many parents

Parents can be trained to successfully teach their children.

may feel more comfortable in sessions that employ an informal and participatory format for information sharing. For these parents, interactive formats such as small group discussions, role-plays, simulations, demonstrations, and cooperative learning groups may be more suitable thanlarge group lectures (Nicolau & Ramos, 1990). In sharing information with parents, educators can:

- Conduct sessions in the primary language of the families.
- Use terminology that parents understand.
- Share personal experiences with their own families.
- Refrain from embarrassing families.
- Recognize the contributions and efforts of parents.
- Offer opportunities for parents to showcase their skills and talents.
- Provide written materials to parents in their native language.
- Prepare materials that parents can share with others.
- Offer families refreshments (Lucas, Henze, & Donato, 1990; Nicolau & Ramos, 1990; Salend, 1990).

Experienced, skilled, and respected parents and community members also can be used to present information to others. Reciprocity in training is an important aspect of school-home partnerships.

Another format for sharing information with parents is videocassette recorder (VCR) technology. In addition to commercially produced videocassettes, teachers can use teacher-made videos to demonstrate various teaching techniques and communicate to parents the important dimensions of the classroom program. VCR technology has several advantages that make it an appropriate instructional format for presenting information to parents (Salend, 1994). These advantages include: (a) offering a visual image and model; (b) facilitating the discussion and review of content through pausing and/or replaying the segments of the video; (c) being adaptable to group and individual use; (d) minimizing the reading, writing, and language requirements; and (e) allowing parents to view programs in school or at home.

Empowerment of parents is one of the major goals of parent training programs. In a productive school-home partnership, parents will be able to participate in decision-making in addition to other school functions. One of the most important factors in this participation is the recognition by school personnel that parents, too, have expertise that they can share. The training program needs to involve parents as trainers/teachers as well as learners. One example of an excellent program is the Mirror Model for Parent Involvement (Kroth & Otteni, 1983) developed at the Parent Involvement Center, Albuquerque, New Mexico.

This model is described as a "strength as well as a needs model" (Kroth & Otteni, 1983). It is based on the belief that parents have information, knowledge, and skills that can help professionals and other parents in their work with children. In that model, workshops are planned and implemented by both parents and teachers. Parents might also become advocates for other parents. The developers of this model believe that a deficit model of parent training, in which only the parents are deficient in needed skills, can quickly reduce the confidence and self-esteem of parents.

As its name implies, the Mirror Model conceptualizes parents' involvement with professionals and professonals' involvement with parents. This consists of the information, knowledge, and skills that parents and professionals can exchange. The strengths of parents are clearly recognized. The model provides a guide for parent and professional involvement in public school settings (Figure 11–1).

In view of the growing number of students from linguistically and culturally diverse backgrounds, teachers can attempt to understand the various cultural perspectives, and the linguistic and economic factors, that affect families. They should see behaviors of individuals and families in a cultural context and not seek to label these behaviors as deviant, deficient, or dysfunctional. Rather, educators can attempt to adjust the services they provide and the strategies they employ to meet the unique cultural, linguistic, and economic needs of families.

SPECIAL BOX 11–10

Hoover and Collier (1988) have identified guidelines for working with parents of exceptional minority students.

1. Ensuring that parents are fully cognizant of their rights and responsibilities.
2. Ensuring that teachers are fully knowledgeable about the student's specific learning or behavior problems and associated sociocultural needs and abilities.
3. Respecting parental cultural customs and communication needs.
4. Being sufficiently prepared prior to each parent-teacher interaction.
5. Allowing parents to freely exercise their rights and encouraging them to become involved in their child's education by providing appropriate opportunities and avenues for this involvement.
6. Understanding the interaction among special needs and cultural and language differences.
7. Taking appropriate steps to minimize potential problems associated with language and cultural differences.
8. Creating a climate of mutual trust and respect during each parent-teacher interaction.
9. Listening to parental concerns and responding to them in a manner perceived by the parents to be positive.

FIGURE 11–1 Mirror Model of Parental Involvement

		WHAT	HOW
Few	4	Therapy–Intensive Education and Support	Counseling: Group Therapy
Some	3	Skill Training in Management Interaction with System, Child-Rearing	Parent Education Groups; Bibliotherapy; Parent Support Groups
Most	2	Knowledge of Child's Progress, Environment, Friends; Assistance in Parent-Home Programs	Notes Home; Daily/Weekly Reporting Systems; Conferences; Phone Calls; Home Visits
All	1	Parents and Children's Rights; Consent to Test and Place; School Policies and Procedures; School and Class Events	Newsletters; Handbooks; Conferences

NEEDS

		WHAT	HOW
All	1	Special Knowledge of Child's Strengths and Needs, Family Characteristics and Aspirations	Intake Interviews, Conferences, Questionnaires
Most	2	Short-term Assistance with Projects at School, Projects at Home; Special Knowledge of World of Work	Telephoning for PTAs or Parent Meetings; Assistance with Meeting Arrangements; Reinforcing At-home or School Work; Talking to Classes at School
Some	3	Leadership Skills, with Time, Energy, and Special Knowledge for _____	Serving on Parent Advisory Groups, Task Forces; Classroom Volunteers; Tutoring; Writing Newsletters; Fund Raising
Few	4	Special Skills, Knowledge, Time Energy, and Commitment for Leadership Training to _____	Lead Parent Groups; Work on Curriculum Committees; Develop Parent-to-Parent Programs

STRENGTHS

SOURCE: Kroth, R. & Otteni, H. (1983). Parent education programs that work: A model. *Focus on Exceptional Children, 15*(8), 6. Reprinted with permission from Love Publishing, Denver, Colorado.

It is important to remember that some parents will have children with disabilities. Cultural beliefs and practices will result in diverse views on disabilities and approaches to treatment. In some families, religion will strongly influence these views. In other families, experience with prejudice and discrimination will create barriers not only to involvement in the school, but also to approaching health-care agencies and personnel. Educators' sensitivity to and understanding of these conditions is important.

❖ Biracial Children

The number of biracial children is increasing as interracial marriages increase in our society (Taylor-Gibbs in Taylor-Gibbs & Nahme-Huang, 1989, pp. 322–350). Biracial children and their families face difficult issues; teachers' sensitivity and understanding can be helpful in working with the children. These are children who do not belong to a single racial/cultural group. Belonging to two different racial groups is particularly difficult for adolescents as they struggle to establish an identity (Taylor-Gibbs in Taylor-Gibbs & Nahme-Huang, 1989). The parents also face a challenge in their efforts to transmit a cultural heritage and ethnic identity to their children since biracial parents do not share the same cultural heritage.

Children of these families face ambivalence toward the two cultures to which they belong, family disapproval, community and peer rejection, social isolation, and job discrimination (Taylor-Gibbs in Taylor-Gibbs & Nahme-Huang, 1989). Although teachers cannot provide the counseling intervention that some of these students may require, it is helpful for teachers to understand the issues, be sensitive to the special needs of the students and the challenges faced by their families, and make referrals when needed.

❖ Community-School Relationship

Strong community support and involvement are required in order for multicultural education to be successful. It is essential for the school to reach out and establish an alliance with the community. In most communities, there are important organizations, agencies, and individuals who have a key role in the lives of the residents. These organizations and individuals are valuable resources that can support the school's multicultural education program, assist the school in attaining its goals and objectives, serve as liaisons in the school-home relationship, and help to identify interventions for families.

Such organizations as local branches of national civil rights organizations, the NAACP and Urban League, churches, community centers, fraternal groups, tenant groups, and other neighborhood organizations can provide volunteers for the school's liaisons with the community, mentors for the school career and vocational programs, role models and mentors for students, visitors who can present a lesson, activity, or lecture on a specific cultural group, interpreters for families of different language groups, and referral sources for newly arrived immigrants. Most importantly, these community groups can give support to the school's efforts to reform or restructure the curriculum.

It is important to hold meetings in the community. When teachers meet with families in the community setting, meetings may often be more relaxed, comfortable, and open. In addition to meetings, teachers can become involved in the community to the extent possible. Attendance at special events, a church or Sunday service, after-school programs, street fairs, and block parties are possible sources of community participation for teachers. The teacher will often, through these activities, enjoy the status of a "community friend" and receive such benefits as support, trust, and encouragement when faced with difficult problems in the classroom. In addition, teachers will learn about other cultural groups in natural settings where behaviors and customs may be easily observed.

Forty-one parents on the Jackhead Indian Reserve in Manitoba were asked what they liked best about the schools (Sealey & Riffel, 1985). Children's enjoyment in the school, art, music, physical education, and organized sports events, along with involvement of Indian people in the schools, and the new school building were cited as the aspects most liked. The least liked aspects of the school were teachers and their discipline methods, curriculum and standards, educational materials, and extracurricular activities. A few parents noted that one teacher actually disliked or even hated Indian people. Two general problems cited by parents were excessive discipline and some teachers' lack of acceptance of the community. The teachers' behavior in the community was an important factor in the community's acceptance and respect of them. Parents generally liked teachers who made an effort to participate in or lead community activities, and the majority of parents thought that teachers should be expected to conduct extracurricular activities in the evening and on weekends (Sealey & Riffel, 1985).

❖ Summary

Parent involvement in the schools is important in establishing a school-home-community partnership that ensures student achievement and progress. However, special consideration is necessary to facilitate the involvement of parents and families of color. Educators' knowledge and understanding of family structure, communication patterns, parents' behavioral and developmental expectations for their children, disciplinary styles, and the need for parent training will enable school personnel to relate to parents with respect and appreciation for their diverse strengths. The organization and structure of parent-teacher meetings can also be successful based upon this knowledge.

Family structure varies among and within cultures. African-Americans, Mexican-Americans and American Indian cultures, for example, emphasize extended families and community. Members of the extended family can be welcomed to participate in meetings and activities and may also assist the family in solving problems for the children. Family roles may also differ from those expected in a traditional structure and teachers can be sensitive to these variations.

Parents may have expectations for their children that differ or conflict with those held by the school. Consultation and collaboration can enable parents and teachers to be partners in deciding what is best for the child. Disciplinary practices may also differ and will require careful consultation and collaboration to arrive at mutually acceptable methods or to provide training for parents in such approaches as behavior modification when needed. The issue of child abuse is a complex matter that requires sensitivity and understanding by educators. There are not easy answers and children must be protected from abuse. However, knowledge of disciplinary practices among the cultures represented in the classroom can help the teacher make informed decisions concerning reports of abuse and choice of interventions in the classroom.

Communication is the most essential element in the development of effective school-home partnerships. Communication styles vary among cultures and include gestures, facial expressions, personal space, wait time, and touching. Cultural informants and interpreters can help the school and family to communicate successfully. Interpreters and translators will also be required when parents speak a different language. There are important guidelines to follow when selecting an individual to serve as interpreter or translator.

When working with families and communities in lower income areas, strategies may be needed to remove the barriers that may be encountered in participating in the school. Transportation, child care, community liaisons, Saturday meetings, and other special considerations may be needed. The school can also provide training, education, support groups, and leadership opportunities for parents. In turn, parents can offer essential information and assistance to educators and other parents and valuable support to their children. Models of parent training such as the Mirror Model can empower parents, their children, and communities.

Note: Some of the material in this chapter has been taken from: *Working with Families: A Cross-Cultural Perspective*. L.S. Taylor, & S.J. Salend (1993). *Remedial and Special Education*, 14(5), 25–32. Copyright (1993) by Pro-Ed, Inc. Reprinted with permission.

❖ CHAPTER 11 **Questions**

1. What are the most important principles for establishing productive relationships with parents from diverse cultural and linguistic groups?
2. Describe some ways in which teachers can recognize and affirm different languages of children in the classroom.
3. What is the significance of different communication styles among families of color?
4. Some educators believe that teaching children about their culture and that of others is the responsibility of the home. What are some specific benefits of this instruction at school?
5. Discuss some of the important barriers to effective school-home partnerships and identify ways to prevent them.
6. What are the benefits of community-school partnerships?
7. How can teachers manage a conflict between school-home disciplinary methods?
8. What are some approaches to use when teachers are faced with a conference involving parents from an unfamiliar culture and language? How can the teacher prepare in order to have a mutually satisfactory meeting?
9. How would you determine the type of parent training programs needed in your school community?
10. Describe some approaches for empowering parents and families in your school district. As a new teacher in your district, how would you begin to work with parents from this perspective?

❖ References

Allen, I., & Majidi-Ahi, S. (1989). Black American children. In J. Taylor Gibbs & L. Nahme-Huang (Eds.), *Children of color: Psychological interventions with minority youth.* San Francisco: Jossey-Bass.

Anderson, P. P., & Fenichel, E. S. (1989). *Serving culturally diverse families of infants and toddlers with disabilities.* Washington, DC: National Center for Clinical Infant Programs.

Barth, J. (1979). Home-based reinforcement of school behavior: A review and analysis. *Review of Educational Research, 49*(3) 436-458.

Becker, R. (1984). *Parent involvement: A review of research and principles of successful practice.* ERIC Clearinghouse on Elementary and Early Childhood Education. (ERIC Document Reproduction Service No. ED 247-032).

Bradenburg-Ayres, S. (1990). *Working with parents.* Bilingual/ESOL Special Education Collaboration and Reform Project. Gainesville, FL: University of Florida.

Clark, R. (1983). *Family life and school achievement: Why poor black children succeed or fail.* Chicago: University of Chicago Press.

Coballes-Vega, C., & Salend, S. (1988). Guidelines for assessing migrant handicapped students. *Diagnostique, 13,* 64-75.

Cotton, K., & Savard, W. (1982). *Parent involvement in instruction K-12: Research synthesis*. St. Ann, MO: Cemrel, Inc. (ERIC document reproduction service no. ED 235 397).

Davies, D. (1991). Restructuring schools: Increasing parent involvement. In K. Kershner & J. Connolly (Eds.), *At-risk students and school restructuring*. Philadelphia: Research for Better Schools.

de Anda, D. (1984). Bicultural socialization: Factors affecting the minority experience. *Social Work, 29*, 101-107.

Epstein, J. L. (1984, April). *Effects of teacher practices on parental involvement on change in student achievement in reading and math*. Paper Presented at aAnnual meeting, American Educational Research Association.

Fradd, S. H., & Wilen, D. K. (1990). *Using interpreters and translators to meet the needs of handicapped language minority students and their families*. Washington, D.C.: National Clearinghouse for Bilingual Education.

Freedman, S.G. (1993). *Upon this rock: The miracles of a black church*. New York: HarperCollins Publisher.

Garate, D., Sen, P., Thien, H.T., & Chaleunrath, V. (1987). *Involving LEP parents*. Washington, DC: Trinity College. (ERIC Document Reproduction Service No. ED 275 313).

Hoover, J. J., & Collier, C. (1988). *Educating students with learning and behavior problems: Stategies for assessment and teaching*. Lindale, TX: Hamilton Publications.

Inclan, J. E., & Herron, G. (1989). Puerto Rican adolescents. In J. Taylor Gibbs & L. Nahme-Huang (Eds.), *Children of color: Psychological interventions with minority youth*. San Francisco: Jossey-Bass.

Kroth, R. L. (1987). Mixed or missed messages between parents and professionals. *Volta Review, 89*(5), 1-10.

Kroth, R., & Otteni, H. (1983). Parent education programs that work: A model. *Focus on Exceptional Children, 15*(8), 1-16.

LaFromboise, T. D., & Graff-Low, K. (1989). American Indian children and adolescents. In J. Taylor Gibbs & L. Nahme-Huang (Eds.), *Children of color: Interventions with minority youth*. San Francisco: Jossey-Bass.

Lally, J. R., Mangione, P., & Honig, A. (1987). *The Syracuse University family development research program: Long range impact of early intervention with low-income children and their families*. San Francisco: Center for Child and Family Studies, Far West Lab for Education Research and Development.

Locust, C. (1990, October). *Handicapped American Indians: Beliefs and behaviors*. Paper presented at the Council for Exceptional Children Symposium on Culturally Diverse Exceptional Children. Albuquerque, NM.

Lucas, T., Henze, R., & Donato, R. (1990). Promoting the success of Latino language-minority students: An explanatory study of six high schools. *Harvard Educational Review, 60*, 315-340.

Lynch, E. W., & Stein, R. C. (1987). Parent participation by ethnicity: A comparison of Hispanic, black, and Anglo families. *Exceptional Children, 54*, 105-111.

Marion, R. L. (1980). Communicating with parents of culturally diverse exceptional children. *Exceptional Children, 46*, 616-623.

McIntyre, T., & Silva, P. (1993). Culturally diverse child-rearing practices: Abusive or just different? *Beyond Behavior, 4*(1), 8-11.

Nagata, D. K. (1989). Japanese American children and adolescents. In J. Taylor Gibbs & L. Nahme-Huang (Eds.), *Children of color: Psychological interventions with minority youth*. San Francisco: Jossey-Bass.

Nahme-Huang, L., & Ying, Y. (1989). Chinese American children and adolescents. In J. Taylor Gibbs & L. Nahme-Huang (Eds.), *Children of color: Psychological interventions with minority youth.* San Francisco: Jossey-Bass.

Nicolau, S., & Ramos, C. L. (1990). *Together is better: Building strong partnerships between schools and Hispanic parents.* New York: Hispanic Policy Development Project.

O'Reilly, Tokino, & Ebata (1986). Cited by Nagata in J. Taylor-Gibbs & L. Nahme-Huang (Eds.), *Children of color: Psychological interventions with minority youth.* San Francisco: Jossey-Bass.

Peterson, N. L., & Cooper, C. S. (1989). Parent education and involvement in early intervention programs for handicapped children: A different perspective on parent needs and the parent-professional relationship. In M. J. Fine (Ed.), *The second handbook in parent education: Contemporary perspectives.* New York: Academic Press.

Ramirez, O. (1989). Mexican American children and adolescents. In J. Taylor Gibbs & L. Nahme-Huang (Eds.), *Children of color: Psychological interventions with minority youth.* San Francisco: Jossey-Bass.

Salend, S. J. (1990). Effective mainstreaming. New York: Macmillan.

Salend, S. J. (1994). Effective mainstreaming (2nd ed.). New York: Macmillan.

Sealey, D. B., & Riffel, J. A. (1985). *Jackhead education review.* Dallas, Manitoba, Canada: Jackheaf Indian Reserve. (ERIC Document Reproduction Service No. ED 264 0074).

Sharma, V. (1988). *A transitional services model for preschool children preparing to enter kindergarten involving parents, teachers, and public schools.* Miami: Nova University. (ERIC Document Reproduction Service No. ED 303 248).

Taylor-Gibbs, J. (1989a). Assessing and treating minority youth. In J. Taylor-Gibbs & L. Nahme-Huang (Eds.), *Children of color: Psychological interventions with minority youth.* San Francisco: Jossey-Bass.

Taylor-Gibbs, J., (1989b). Black American adolescents. In J. Taylor Gibbs & Huang-Nahme (Eds.). *Children of color: Psychological interventions with minority youth.* San Francisco: Jossey-Bass.

Taylor Gibbs, J., & Nahme-Huang, L. (1989). *Children of color: Psychological interventions with minority youth.* San Francisco: Jossey-Bass.

Winton, P. J., & Bailey, D. B. (1993). Communicating with families: Examining practices and facilitating change. In James L. Paul & Rune J. Simeonsson, (Eds.), *Children with special needs: Family, culture, and society.* Fort Worth, TX: Harcourt, Brace, Jovanovich.

CHAPTER 12

Conclusion

This book has explored one of the greatest challenges facing elementary and secondary teachers today—how to educate an increasingly diverse student population so that all children, regardless of their racial, ethnic, or cultural background, can succeed in school and can develop the skills to live and work together in the complex and diverse America of the twenty-first century. Several issues are at stake here.

❖ Ending Alienation in the School Environment

The first of these is the sense of alienation from the school environment that children of color—particularly African-Americans, American Indians, Asian-Americans, and Latinos—as well as poor children from all racial and ethnic groups often feel. This alienation may be academic, social, or both. Teachers must become more aware of the role culture plays in education and must build upon the cultural strengths of all students. Some of those strengths include a historical commitment to individual betterment through education, cooperative and collaborative values that contribute to the achievement of the entire group, a bilingual/bicultural literacy that has become increasingly crucial in an interdependent world, respect for the wisdom of elders, and strong family and community bonds. Teachers must appreciate the fact that most children of color have had to adjust early on to the dominant cultural values traditionally transmitted by the school. The existence of these dominant values in the school need not be a source of alienation if the values and contributions of other cultures are acknowledged and shared.

The teaching strategies explored in this textbook can be a means of presenting and sharing alternative perspectives. Through cooperative learning, children from a wide variety of backgrounds and skills can work together, contributing their part toward a common goal. By using a pure or modified whole language approach, teachers can incorporate print and nonprint materials from a variety of perspectives into the curriculum and can build upon the cultural knowledge of students, parents, and community members through writing, storytelling, and other language-related activities. Culturally sensitive teachers can offer a "second chance" to parents whose own experiences with school may have been one of failure, humiliation, or alienation, but who nonetheless play a crucial role in the academic achievement of their children. Teachers must bridge the cultural gap to make parents their partners in the process of education.

❖ Teaching Children About Each Other's Culture

A second issue is the need to teach children about each other's culture. Many have pointed out the lack of awareness that European-American children often have about their own or any other American culture. This lack of awareness frequently translates into a sense of being *cultureless*, a fear of "foreign" cultures, or an inability to understand that events or questions can be seen from more than one perspective. Similar problems exist among children of color. Violence in and out of school has often been motivated by racial or ethnic hatreds, and not all of the violence has involved European-American students. It is a sad fact that long-oppressed groups, such as African-Americans and Mexican-Americans, have sometimes attacked each other. Thus, teachers must help students understand not only the importance of their own culture, but also the value and contributions of all cultures that have made the United States the first, the largest, and the most successful multicultural nation. Children must learn respect for all cultures and respect for the democratic values at the core of our shared society. In teaching about what is unique about each of our cultures, we should never lose sight of what we have in common—our shared humanity and our shared experience as Americans.

In allowing children to share their experiences and to see what they have in common, cooperative learning is a proven strategy for reducing potential conflict between children of different racial and ethnic backgrounds. Many school districts have built upon cooperative learning strategies to train students in conflict resolution and mediation, with a resulting decrease in school violence. In terms of a whole language approach, students can be exposed to a wide variety of materials that show how groups are similar, different, diverse, and constantly changing with the passage of time. School-community partnerships are also a means of exploring a number of cultures and helping to reduce conflict among them.

❖ Avoiding Stereotyping

A third issue is the need to avoid stereotyping. Even positive stereotypes, such as the model minority stereotype often applied to Asian-Americans, can be damaging. Those who stereotype assume that all members of a given cultural group will think, speak, look, and act alike; their group identification becomes their individual identity. In reality, children and adults may be members of a racial, ethnic, or cultural group, but they are, above all, individuals, with unique personal characteristics, needs, and learning styles. Through cooperative learning, all of these individual characteristics, abilities, and styles come into play as children work together. In using trade books and other materials, teachers must be aware of stereotyping and must not allow one book to carry the weight of the entire culture. In approaching parents, teachers must be sensitive to the personality of the individual and not simply assume a parent will behave in a certain way because he or she belongs to a certain group. This was strikingly demonstrated in the interview with the Haitian-American mother who objected to the teaching of mythology in her daughter's class.

❖ Educational Equity

A fourth issue is that of educational equity. In many cases, children of color remain overrepresented in classes for the learning disabled and emotionally disturbed and underrepresented in classes for the talented and gifted. Poor children of all groups, but especially poor African-American and Latino children, attend schools that are underfunded and lacking in essential resources. As many educators have pointed out, multiculturalism without a corresponding focus upon broader issues of equity and social justice is incomplete. For example, we are a better and stronger multicultural nation because of the efforts of the abolitionists and those who participated in the Civil Rights movement, both African-Americans and European-Americans. These heroic Americans should inspire us and our students to continue pursuing the dream of equal opportunity for all, regardless of race, ethnicity, gender, or culture.

❖ Keep Your Hopes High

Finally, as teachers and prospective teachers, we should keep our hopes high. Despite the problems and obstacles, children of color are succeeding in school, and the recent signs point to continued improvement. Hundreds of schools across the country are showing that culturally diverse populations can be taught successfully, that high expectations can be maintained and fulfilled, and that children of all backgrounds can learn to respect and work productively with one another. These gains are being made as a result of parents and communities becoming involved, state Education Departments putting their resources and expertise behind new programs, universities helping school personnel to develop their cultural awareness and sensitivity, districts making a commitment to multicultural education, principals taking a leadership role, and, above all, teachers like you who, on a day-to-day basis, are making school a culturally affirming, culturally broadening, and positive experience for all children.

Index

Page numbers in italics indicate figures and page numbers followed by a "t" indicate tables.

Author/Title Index for Children's Literature

Aardema, Verna, 311, 332
Abbott, Jack Henry, 17
Abdul and the Designer Tennis Shoes, 324
Adams, Hunter Havelin, 129
Addam, Jane, 3
Aeson: Tales of Aethiop the African, 324
Afolayan, Michael, 332
African Origin of Civilization: Myth or Reality? (Diop), 130
African-American Baseline Essays, 127–131
Against Borders: Promoting Books for a Multicultural World, 294
Airmail to the Moon, 258
Ajeemah and his Son (Berry), 317
Amazing Grace (Hoffman), 291
American Indian Holocaust and Survival (Thornton), 294
Ancona, George, 335
Angelou, Maya, 325
Arctic Explorer: The Story of Matthew Henson (Ferris), 312
Asante, Molefi Kete, 130
Ashabranner, Brent, 334–335
Audience, concept of, 317–318
Aunt Flossie's Hats (and Crab Cakes Later) (Howard), 317
Austin, Mary, 307
Autogiography of Malcolm X, 294

Back in the Beforetime: Tales of the California Indians (Curry), 261
Baker, Jeannie, 335
Becerra de Jenkins, Lyll, 316–317
Ben's Trumpet (Isadora), 291
Berry, James, 317
Bierhorst, John, 342
Biko, Stephen, 130
Binch, Caroline, 291
Bishop, Claire, 291
Black Indians: A Hidden Heritage (Katz), 287
Black Scientists and Inventors, 324
Bloom, Benjamin, 24
Blue Tights (Williams-Garcia), 311, 318, 325
Boateng, Felix, 135
Booklist, 294
Breaking the Chains (Katz), 286, 320
Brooks, Bruce, 309
Brown, D., 253–254
Bruchac, Joseph, 287, 335
Bryan, Ashley, 344
Bryant, Michael, 287
Bulletin of the Center for Children's Books, 294
Bury My Heart at Wounded Knee (Brown), 253–254
Buss, Fran Leeper, 320

Caduto, Michael, 335
Call for Cooperative Pluralism: From Me to We (Nakagawa), 14–15
Carmen Sandiego software, 279
Carter, Forrest, 315
Cay, The, 324
Changes in Latitudes (Hobbs), 313
Changing Conceptions of Education (Krug), 2–3
Children of the Rainbow: First Grade, 15
Children of the River (Crew), 313
Choi, Sook Nyul, 316
Circle of Gold, 324, 325
Clifford, the Big Red Dog, 292
Cohen, Caron Lee, 334
Cohen, Robert, 245
Color of Man (Cohen), 245
Conger, David, 261
Corey, 325
Council on Interracial Books for Children, 306
Courlander, Harold, 261
Cowtail Switch and Other West African Stories (Courlander), 261
Crävecoeur, St. John de, 3
Crew, Linda, 313
Cultural Pluralism and the American Idea (Kallen), 3–4
Curry, Jane L., 261

Daly, Niki, 344
Dancing Teepees: Poems of American Indian Youth (Sneve), 142
DeFelice, Cynthia, 287
DeLoria, Vine, 335
Different Mirror (Takaki), 293
Diop, Cheikh Anta, 130
Discover the World (software), 311
Doctor Coyote: A Native American Aesop's Fables (Bierhorst), 342
Dorris, Michael, 316
Dove, The, 344
DuBois, W.E.B., 79
Duvalier, Jean-Claude, 58

Education of Little Tree (Carter), 315
El Norte (film), 288
Eyes on the Prize (video), 295–296

Fanon, Frantz, 130
Fast Sam, Cool Clyde, and Stuff, 324
Fernandez, Joseph, 134
Ferris, Jeri, 312
Finding Out, 199
Five Chinese Brothers (Bishop), 291, 310
Frederick Douglass: The Black Lion (McKissack), 316
Freedom Crossing, 325
Freedom Songs (Moore), 317
Friendship (Taylor), 309, 320

Gates, Henry Louis, 293
Gathering of Flowers: Stories about Being Young in America (Thomas), 258, 303–304
George Washington Carver, 324
Giant Devil-Dingo (Roughsey), 334
Gilchrist, Jan Spivey, 287
Global Voices, Global Visions: A Core Collection of Multicultural Adult Books (Miller-Lachmann), 294
Goble, Paul, 334
Golden Pasture, 324
Goldstein, A.P., 192
Gordimer, Nadine, 313–314
Grab Hands and Run (Temple), 320
Greenfield, Eloise, 287, 288, 302
Guidelines for Selecting Bias-Free Textbooks and Storybooks, 306
Guthrie, Donna, 316
Guy, Rosa, 287, 334

Hamilton, Virginia, 311, 320, 334
Harding, Vincent, 286
Heather Has Two Mommies, 133
Her Seven Brothers (Goble), 334

Herzog, George, 261
High-Low Handbook, 295
Hispanic Heritage (Schon), 294, 308
Historic Black Pioneers, 324
Historic Black Women, 324
Hobbs, Will, 313
Hoffman, Mary, 291
Honorable Prison (Becerra de Jenkins), 316–317
Hoops (Myers), 287
Horn Book, 294–295
Howard, Elizabeth Fitzgerald, 317
Hughes, Langston, 82, 236

I Know Why the Caged Bird Sings (Angelou), 325
In the Beginning: Creation Stories from Around the World (Hamilton), 334
In the Belly of the Beast (Abbott), 17
Interracial Books for Children Bulletin, 295
Invisible Hunters (Rohmer), 334
Isadora, Rachel, 291
Island of the Blue Dolphins, 324

Jenkins, Esther C., 307
Joseph, Chief of the Nez Perces, 254
Journey of the Sparrows (Buss), 320
Kallen, H. M., 3–4
Katz, William L., 286, 287, 320
Keats, Ezra Jack, 291
Keepers of the Animals (Caduto), 335
Keepers of the Earth (Caduto), 335
King, Martin Luther, 285
Knutson, Barbara, 344
Kohl, Herbert, 82
Kozol, Jonathan, 82, 93–94, 96, 135
Kraus, J., 258
Krug, M., 2–3

Latinos (Shorris), 294
Let the Circle Be Unbroken (Taylor), 309
Lewis, Oscar, 73
Literature for Children about Asians and Asian-Americans (Jenkins), 307–308
Magical Adventures of Pretty Pearl, 325
Malcolm X, 81
Malcolm X, Autogiography of, 294
Malinowski, Bronislow, 3
Many Lands, Many Stories: Asian Folktales for Children (Conger), 261
Many Thousand Gone: African-Americans from Slavery to Freedom (Hamilton), 320
Martel, Erich, 129
McGinnis, E., 191
McKissack, Patricia, 311, 316
Medearis, Angela Shelf, 287, 318

Miller-Lachmann, L., 294, 308, 315
Mirandy and Brother Wind (McKissack), 311
Mississippi Bridge (Taylor), 309, 320
Mohr, Nicholasa, 287, 339
Mollel, Tololwa, 334
Momaday, N. Scott, 335
Moore, Yvette, 317, 339
Morning Girl (Dorris), 316
Morning Star, Black Sun: The Northen Cheyenne Indians and America's Energy Crisis (Ashabranner), 334–335
Mother Crocodile (Guy), 334
Moves Make the Man (Brooks), 309, 325
Mud Pony: A Traditional Skidi Pawnee Tale (Cohen), 334
Mufaro's Beautiful Daughters (Steptoe), 332, 344
Multicolored Mirror: Cultural Substance in Literature for Children and Young Adults, 294
Multicultural Review, 294–296
My Side of the Mountain, 324
Myers, Walter Dean, 287, 339

Nakagawa, M., 14–15
Nathaniel Talking (Greenfield), 288
Nation at Risk, 120
Nelson, Rachel West, 317
New York Times Book Review, 294, 296
Night Journey, 325
Nobiah's Well (Guthrie), 316, 342
Not Separate, Not Equal (Wilkerson), 320
Not So Fast, Songololo (Daly), 344

Oregon Trail software, 279, 325
Orphan Boy (Mollel), 334
Ortiz, Simon, 320
Our Family, Our Friends, Our World (Miller-Lachmann), 294, 308, 315
Our People (Medearis), 287, 318
Ox of the Wonderful Horns and Other African Folktales (Ashley), 344

Pearl, The, 325
People Could Fly: American Black Folktales (Hamilton), 311, 325
People Shall Continue (Ortiz), 320
Phillip Hall Likes Me, I Reckon, Maybe, 325
Pilgrim Quest (software), 323
Pinocchio (film), 322
Politi, Leo, 291

Ravitch, Diane, 138–139
Reader's Adviser, 294
Red Ribbons for Emma, 334
Ringgold, Faith, 316
Road to Memphis (Taylor), 309

Rohmer, Harriet, 334
Roll of Thunder, Hear My Cry (Taylor), 309
Rosie the Cool Cat, 258
Roughsey, Dick, 334

Savage Inequalities (Kozol), 93–94, 96, 135
Schlesinger, Arthur, 131, 138–139
Schon, Isabel, 294, 308
School Library Journal, 294, 296
Seale, Doris, 307
Sebgugugu the Glutton (Aardema), 311, 332
Secret of Gumbo Grove, 325
Selma, Lord, Selma (Webb), 317
Shabanu: Daughter of the Wind (Staples), 313
Shadow and Substance: Afro-American Experience in Contemporary
      Children's Fiction, 307
Shimmershine Queen, 324
Shorris, Earl, 294
SimCity software, 279
Sims, Rudine, 307
Sister, 324
Six Hour Retarded Child, 4
Skillstreaming the Adolescent (Goldstein), 192
Skillstreaming the Elementary School Child (McGinnis), 191
Slake's Limbo, 324
Slapin, Beverly, 307
Sneve, Virginia Driving Hawk, 142
So Far from the Bamboo Grove (Watkins), 316, 320
Song of the Trees (Taylor), 309, 324
Soto, Gary, 287
Sounder, 324
Sour Land, 325
Soyinka, Wole, 130
Staples, Suzanne Fisher, 313
Steptoe, John, 332, 344
Stewart, Dianne, 344
Stock, Catherine, 344
Strangers from a Different Shore (Takaki), 293
Sungura and Leopard (Knutson), 344

Takaki, Ronald, 293
Tales of an Ashanti Father, 325
Tales Out of School (Fernandez), 134
Talk About a Family, 324
Tall Bosy's Journey (Kraus), 258
Tar Beach (Ringgold), 316
Taste of Salt (Temple), 319
Taylor, Mildred D., 309, 317, 320, 324
Temple, Frances, 319, 320
There Is a River (Harding), 286

Thiong'o, Ngugi, 130
Thomas, J.C., 258
Thomas, Joyce Carol, 303–304
Thornton, Russell, 294
Through Indian Eyes: The Native Experience in Books for Children, 307
Tooyalaket, Helinmot, 254
Turtle Watch (Ancona), 335

Upstairs Room, 324

Voice of Youth Advocates, 295

Washington, Booker T., 79
Watkins, Yoko Kawashima, 316, 320
We Live in Chile, 313
Weasel (DeFelice), 287
Webb, Sheyman, 317
Where Are You Going, Manyoni? (Stock), 344
Where the Forest Meets the Sea (Baker), 335
Where the Red Fern Grows, 324
Who Am I?/My People, 324
Wilkerson, Brenda, 320
Williams, Chancellor, 130
Williams-Garcia, Rita, 311, 318, 339
Willis Hudson, Wade and Cheryl, 287
Wilson, William Julius, 73
Without Bias: Through Indian Eyes (Slapin), 307
Won't Know 'Til I Get There, 325
Woodson, Jacqueline, 339
Wretched of the Earth (Fanon), 130

Year of Impossible Goodbyes (Choi), 316, 320

Subject Index

Academic skills, activities for, 235-273
"Achievement gap," 135
Acquired immunodeficiency syndrome (AIDS), 178
"Additive" approach, to multicultural materials, 345
Adoption, transracial, 110
Africa Access, Silver Springs (Md.), 297
African-Americans, Black English and, 167–170, 169t
    Civil Rights movement and, 5, 82–84
    current needs of, 97–103, 98t 101t, *102*
    early history of, 34–35
    educational inequality among, 79–82
    immersion schools for, 128, 134–141
    population of, 35–36, 36f, *37*

Afrocentric perspectives, 130
AIDS. See Acquired immunodeficiency syndrome (AIDS).
Alaska Natives, 108
Alienation, in schools, 381
American Indians, current needs of, 108–109
    early contacts with, 30–31
    education coalition for, 297
    population of, 31–34, 33
    schools for, 141–142
Americans with Disabilities Act, 157
"Ancestors' Day" activity, 238
Annexation, immigration by, 38
Anthropology, 20–21
Apologizing skills, 191t, 192
Aregullin, Dr. Manuel, 243
Aristide, Jean-Bertrand, 319
Aronson, Eliot, 200
Art classes, "Commemorative Postage Stamps" for, 260
    multicultural materials for, 336
Asian Indians, 54
Asian-Americans, 39, 51–56. See also Chinese immigrants.
    current needs of, 106–108
    stereotype of, 57, 291
Attention deficit, 164–165
Author background, 312–315
Autism, 179–180
Aztecs, 32

Balance, multidimensionality and, 319–320
Baldwin School, Bryn Mawr (Pa.), 297
Banks and Banks' approach, to multicultural education, 10–11, 12t
Barrera, Rosalinda, 289–290, 293
Basal readers. See Readers.
Base Group meetings, 210
Baseline essays, 127
Behavior, disorders of, 171–174
    expectations of, 362–363
Bilingual education, 11–13, 13t, 20, 84–87
    misclassification with, 167
    multicultural materials for, 292
    Navajo, 141–142
    segregation and, 90
Bilingual Education Act, 85
Biracial children, 374
Black English, 167–170, 169t
Black Pride movement, 5, 84, 119
Black Seminoles, 33–34
Blind students, 178–179
Bradley, Milliken v., 87
Brain injured students, 180

Brown v. Board of Education, 3, 6, 59, 81, 83, 135
Busing, 83–84

Cajuns, 38
California, multicultural programs in, 121–124
California Gold Rush, 39
California State University, Center for the Study of Books in Spanish at, 297
Cambodian immigrants, 55, 61
Caribbean immigrants, 56–58
Carter, Forrest, 315
"Cartoons and Comics: Stereotypes and Caricatures" activity, 264
Carver, George Washington, 285
CD-ROM software, 279
Center for the Study of Books in Spanish, 297
Chall, Jeanne, 280–282
"Chemicals from Nature" activity, 241–244
Children. *See also* Students.
    biracial, 374
    blind, 178–179
    exceptional, 152–182
    hearing-impaired, 176–177
    interracial, 109–110
    of color, 69–113, 97–110, 98t 101t, *102*
    poor, *71*
Chinese Exclusion Act, 39
Chinese immigrants, 39, 51–52, 54. *See also* Asian-Americans.
Civil Rights movement, 5, 296. *See also* Desegregation.
Coalition for Indian Education, 297
Columbus, Ohio, multicultural program in, 126–127
"Coming to Consensus" activity, 232–234
"Commemorative Postage Stamps" activity, 260
Communication, disorders of, 165–170, 166t, 169t
    patterns of, 364–366
Community-school relationship, 84, 374–375
Consensus, building of, 232–234
"Controversy is Constructive" activity, 230–231
Co-op co-op activities, 217–220
Cooperative Children's Book Center, 297
Cooperative learning, 24–25, 186–212
    activities for, 216–273
    approaches to, 199–207, 201t
    college classes and, 207, 207t
    competitive versus, 189t
    components of, 188–192, 189t, 191t
    curriculum for, 199, 201t
    effectiveness of, 192–197
    examples of, 208–212
    principles of, 188
    problems with, 208
Cooperative/collaborative skills, 221–234

Council on Interracial Books for Children, 286, 295, 306
Cuban-Americans, 48–49
Cultural deprivation, 72–76, 75t
Cultural diversity, approach to, 11, 13t
   community programs for, 338–341
   group names for, 9
   information on, 318–319, 346–347
   sensitivity to, 16–20, *19*
   stereotypes of, 57, 105–106, 291
   writing about, 288–289
"Cultural gap," bridging of, 293–297
Cultural identity, education and, 20–23
   elements of, *19*
Curriculum, Eurocentric, 5
   multiculturalism across, 333–338
   Rainbow, 7, 133–134
   standardized, 344–347

Davidman, P.T., 146–147
Deaf students, 174–177
"Deficit" model, 72–76, 75t
Desegregation, 87–88
   busing and, 83–84
   housing, 6, 60
   school, 3–4
Dialects, in books, 292
Diana v. State Board of Education, 154
Dick and Jane readers, 284–285
Disability(ies). *See also* Exceptional Children and Special education classes.
   concentration ratio for, 91t
   labeling of, 157–158, 158t
   learning, 163–165
   legislation on, 155, 156t, 157
   prevalence of, 155
   referral process for, 160–163
   types of, 163–182
Disciplinary styles, 363–364
Discrimination, overt, 79–81
Diversity, among Latinos, 50–51
   among teachers, 110–113, 113t
   cooperative learning for, 186–212
Dominican-Americans, 49
"Dr. Eloy Rodriguez" activity, 241–244
Drop-out rates, *102*
DuSable High School, Chicago, 76–79, 77t
Dyslexia, 164

Educational equity, 383
   culture and, 20–23

history of, 79–81

Emotional disorders, 171–174

Empowerment, of parents, 371–372
   of schools, 138

English as a second language (ESL), 86
   immersion program for, 143–145
   Whole Language approach and, 289

English classes, 273. *See also* Language Arts classes and Writing.
   Norton model for, 341–344
   poetry for, 236–237

English immigrants, 36–37

ESL. *See* English as a second language (ESL).

"Esteem through Silhouettes" activity, 219–220

"Ethnic Music" activity, 256

"Ethnic Origin of Words" activity, 257

Ethnocentrism, 302

Eurocentric curriculum, 5

European immigrants, 30–31, 36–38, 40–44, *41*, *42*

Exceptional children, 152–182. *See also* Special education classes.
   referral process for, 160–163
   teachers for, 159

Families. *See also* Parents.
   communication patterns with, 364–366
   interracial, 109–110
   multicultural education and, 25
   structure of, 360–362

Ferguson, Plessy v., 59, 79, 164

Fernandez, Joseph, 133–134

Filipino immigrants, 52–53

Folklore, 12t, 14, 279, 286, 309, 322
   illustrations of, 344
   problems with, 332–333

Follow Through program, 83

Friendship-making skills, 191t, 192, 217

Funding limitations, 344–347

Garcia, Jesus, 147

Genocide, 34

German immigrants, 37–38

Gibson's approach, to multicultural education, 11–13, 13t

Gifted classes, legislation on, 155–156
   race and, 91–92

Goodman, Kenneth, 227

Group meeting procedures, 210

Group skills, 190–192, 191t

Guadalupe-Hidalgo, Treaty of, 44

Guam, 54

Guatemalan immigrants, 61

Guidance counselors, 92–94

Haitians, 57–58
  bilingual education for, 86, 292–293
Handicaps. *See* Disability(ies).
Hawaiians, 108
Head Start programs, 83, 87
Hearing impairment, 174–177
Hicks, Louise Day, 84
Hilliard, Asa, 127
History activities, "Commemorative Postage Stamps," 260
  multicultural, 272
HIV. *See* Human immunodeficiency virus (HIV).
Hmong immigrants, 55, 61
Holocaust, 44
Homosexuality, in Rainbow curriculum, 7, 133–134
Hong Kong immigrants, 54
Huguenots, 36
Hull House, Chicago, 3
Human immunodeficiency virus (HIV), 178
Hyperactivity, 164–165
Hypersegregation, 88

IDEA. *See* Individuals with Disabilities Education Act (IDEA).
IEP. *See* Individual Educational Program (IEP).
"Illustration of a Story" activity, 258–259
Illustrations, criteria for, 321
  folklore, 344
Immigrant Exclusion Act, 51
Immigration, Asian, 51–56
  by annexation, 38
  from 1980–to 1990, 52
  from Central America, 49–50
  from South America, 49–50
  future trends in, 61–62
  illegal, 46
  nineteenth century, 36–44, 41, 42
  twentieth century, 44–59
Incas, 32
"Indian Children" activity, 239–240
Indian Removal Act, 33
Indians, American. *See* American Indians.
  Asian. *See* Asian Indians.
Indigenous Peoples, 9
Individual Educational Program (IEP), 161–163, 162
Individuals with Disabilities Education Act (IDEA), 155, 156t
Internal migration, 59–61
International High School, New York City, 143–145
Interpreter skills, 367, 368t
Irish Catholic immigrants, 36–38

Jackhead Indian Reserve, 375
Jackson, David, 132

Japanese-Americans, 39, 51–52
   during World War II, 39
   self-esteem among, 22
Jefferson, Thomas, 308
Jemison (Mae) Academy, 138
Jews, Sephardic, 36–37
Jigsaw approach, to cooperative learning, 200
Jim Crow laws, 56, 59, 124

King (Martin Luther) Elementary School, 136–138
Kiswahili, 311
Korean immigrants, 53–54, 62
Kruse, Ginny Moore, 315

Labeling disabilities, 157–158, 158t
Language Arts classes, 273. *See also* English classes and Writing.
   "Book Report" for, 261–263
   "Cartoons and Comics: Stereotypes and Caricatures" for, 264
   "Coming to Consensus" for, 232–234
   "Commemorative Postage Stamps" for, 260
   "Controversy is Constructive" for, 230–231
   "Esteem through Silhouettes" for, 219–220
   "Ethnic Origin of Words" for, 257
   "Illustration of a Story" for, 258–259
   Norton model for, 341–344
   "Put-Downs Don't Really Make it Better" for, 226–229
   "Roles to Make or Break a Group" for, 221–225
   "Show and Tell" for, 271
Language disorders, 167
Laotian immigrants, 55
Larrick, Nancy, 286
Larry P. v. Riles, 154
Latinos, bilingual education for, 84–86
   current needs of, 98t 101t, *102*, 103–106
   diversity of, 50–51
   ethnic origins of, *47*
   immigration of, 44–51, *47*
   Indian heritage of, 32
   stereotypes of, 105–106, 291
Leap, William, 291–292
Learning disabilities, 163–165. *See also* Disabilities.
Learning together approach, 202–207
Least restrictive environment (LRE), 156, 158
Lee, Spike, 296
Legislation, for disabilities, 155, 156t, 157
   for gifted classes, 155–156
   for special education, 155–159, 156t, 158t
Linguistic groups, 9, 367
Literature, Norton model for, 341–344
Louisiana Cajuns, 38
LRE. *See* Least restrictive environment (LRE).

Lynch's approach, to multicultural education, 12t 13t, 13–14

Mae Jemison Academy, 138
Malcolm X Academy, 136–138, 283, 324
Manumission, 35
Mariel boatlift, 48
Martin Luther King Elementary School, 136–138
Mastery learning, 24
Mathematics classes, "A Class Quilt" for, 267–268
    "Measurement: Our Size" for, 269–270
    multicultural materials for, 272, 336
    proficiency in, 99t
    "Solving Word/Story Problems" for, 265–266
"Measurement: Our Size" activity, 269–270
Melting pot philosophy, 3, 7, 43
Mental retardation, 170–171
    President's Committee on, 4
Mestizos, 50
Mexican-Americans, 38
    population of, 44–46, 47
    prejudice against, 43
Migration, internal, 59–61
Milliken v. Bradley, 87
Mirror Model, of parental involvement, 371–372, *373*
Mitchell, Bruce, 121, 145
Multicultural education, approaches to, 9–16, 12t 13t, 23–25
    bilingual materials for, 292–293
    defined, 9–10
    development of, 2–7
    elements of, *16*
    family involvement in, 25, 360–362
    funding of, 344–347
    goals of, 7
    issues in, 7–8
    materials for, 301–327, 330–347
    programs in, 120–134
    purposes of, 6–7
    teaching of, 381–382
Multicultural Resource Center, 297
Multidimensionality, balance and, 319–320
Multihandicapped students, 177
Music classes, ethnic, 256, 322
    multicultural materials for, 336
"My County Tis of Thy People You're Dying," 252

Native Americans. See American Indians.
Navajos, original name for, 9
    schools of, 141–142
New Literacy. See Whole Language movement.
"New South," 60

New York, multicultural program in, 121–124
New Zealand, literacy in, 280, 281
Nichols, Lau v., 5, 85
Nonprint materials, advantages of, 286–288
   selection of, 321–326
     Whole Language, 279
Norton model, for teaching literature, 341–344

Orthopedic impairment, 177–178

Pacific Islanders, 54–55
Parents. *See also* Families.
   conference with, 350–357, 351t 352t
   empowerment of, 371–372
   handicapped children and, 176–177, 181–182
   interaction with, 359t 360t
   Mirror Model for, 371–372, 373
   socioeconomic factors of, 367–368
   training of, 368–374, *373*
Perspective, 314–317
Philippine immigrants, 52–53
Plessy v. Ferguson, 59, 79, 164
Pluralism, 11, 13t, 195
Pocahontas, 285
Population, African-American, 35–36, *36, 37*
   American Indian, 31–34, *33*
   by national origin, *42*
   Cuban-American, *47,* 48–49
   Dominican-American, 49
   foreign-born, *41*
   future trends in, 61–62
   Mexican-American, 44–46, *47*
   Puerto Rican, 46–47, *47*
Portland, Oregon, multicultural program in, 127–131
"Postage Stamps" activity, 260
Potato famine, Irish, 38
Poverty, children in, *71*
   culture of, 72–76, 75t
   war on, 83
Preparation programs, for teachers, 145–148
President's Committee on Mental Retardation, 4
Prophet, Matthew, 127–128
Prospect Middle School, Pittsburgh, 15
Public Law 94-142, 155
Puerto Ricans, citizenship of, 51
   immigration of, 46–47
   population of, 46–47, 47
Pugh, Sharon L., 147
Pupil expenditures, 73–74
"Put-Downs Don't Really Make it Better" activity, 226–229

"Quilt" activity, 267–268

Racism, 302
    reverse, 95
Rainbow curriculum, 7, 133–134
Readers, advantages of, 286–288
    basal, 283–284, 345–346
    Dick and Jane, 284–285
    problems with, 283–284
Reading proficiency, 98t
Reagan, Ronald, 87, 119
Resegregation, 88–90
Reverse racism, 95
Reyhner, Jon, 283, 284
Riles, Larry P. v., 154
Rock Point Community School, 141–142
Rodiguez, *San Antonio Independent School District v.*, 96
Rodriguez, Demetrio, 96
"Roles to Make or Break a Group" activity, 221–225
Rough Rock Demonstration School, 141
Roundrobin activities, 218
Roundtable activities, 218
"Rust Belt," 60

Sacajawea, 285
Samoa, 54
San Antonio Independent School District v. Rodriguez, 96
Saturday classes, 358, 367
Schizophrenia, 172
Schniedewind, Nancy, 132
Scholarship standards, 308–309
Schools, alienation in, 381
    American Indian, 141–142
    community relations and, 84, 374–375
    empowered, 138
    funding of, 95–97
    governance of, 95
    immersion, 134–141
    multicultural efforts in, 120–134
    negative climate in, 74, 75t
    policies of, 95
    pupil expenditures in, 73–74
    segregation within, 88–95, 91t
Science classes, "Chemicals from Nature" for, 241–244
    "Dr. Eloy Rodriguez" for, 241–244
    multicultural materials for, 272, 334–335
    "What Makes Different Skin Colors?" for, 245–246
Scots-Irish immigrants, 36–37
Segregation. *See also* Desegregation.
    bilingualism and, 90

gifted classes and, 91–92
school funding and, 95–97
special education and, 90–91, 91t
within schools, 88–95, 91t
Seminoles, Black, 33–34
Sephardic Jews, 36–37
"Sexual Harassment" activity, 251
Shared-Book Experience. *See* Whole Language movement.
Shoreham-Wading River School District, multicultural program at, 131–134
"Show and Tell" activity, 271
Sign language, 175–176
Silhouettes, 219–220
Slavery, 34–36
Social Studies classes, 272
    "Ancestors' Day" for, 238
    "Cartoons and Comics: Stereotypes and Caricatures" for, 264
    "Indian Children" for, 239
    "Sexual Harassment" for, 251
    "Who Is This Famous Person?" for, 247–248
Socially maladjusted students, 172
Socioeconomic factors, parental, 367–368
"Solving Word/Story Problems" activity, 265–266
Southeast Asian immigrants, 55–56
Spain, Louise, 144–145
Spanish, books in, 297
Special education classes, 90–91, 91t. *See also* Disability and Exceptional children.
Speech disorders, 165–170, 166t, 169t
Standardized tests, 120
Stereotyping, 57, 105–106, 291
    avoidance of, 302–305, 309–311, 382
    caricatures and, 264
Students. *See also* Children.
    hearing-impaired, 174–177
    learning teams of, 195–196, 201
    multihandicapped, 177
    socially maladjusted, 172
    visually impaired, 178–179
Suina, Joseph H., 284–285
Swahili, 311

Taiwanese immigrants, 54
Teachers, characteristics of, 113t
    cooperative learning and, 197–199, 198t
    cultural sensitivity among, 16–20, *19*
    diversity among, 110–113, 113t
    ESL. *See* English as a second language (ESL).
    preparation programs for, 145–148
Team-building activities, 217–220
Team-Games-Tournaments approach, 201–202
Texas annexation, 38

Textbooks. *See also* Readers.
   problems with, 285–286
Thai immigrants, 55
Thomas, Clarence, 251
Tokenism, 306
Translators, skills of, 367, 368t
Traumatic brain injury, 180
Treaty of Guadalupe-Hidalgo, 44

Underachievement, risk factors for, 76–79, 77t
University of Wisconsin, Children's Book Center at, 297
Ute Indians, 291–292

Videocassettes, for family training, 371
Vietnamese immigrants, 55
Visually impaired students, 178–179

Wallace, George, 315
War on Poverty, 82–84
Washington, George, 308
"What Makes Different Skin Colors?" activity, 245–246
"White flight," 135
"Who Is This Famous Person?" activity, 247–248
Whole Language, 24, 275–297
   critiques of, 280–284
   nonprint materials for, 279
   synonyms for, 227
Writing. *See also* English classes and Language Arts classes.
   cultural studies and, 288–289
   proficiency with, 100t
   Whole Language movement and, 278
Writing Across the Curriculum. *See* Whole Language movement.